T0332037

Financial Fragility and Instability in Indonesia

This book examines the underlying causes of the financial crisis that struck Indonesia during the second half of 1997 and 1998. It argues that the roots of the crisis lay in the financial activities undertaken by the Indonesian corporate sector during the boom years from 1994 to 1997, which encouraged the development of fragile and unstable financial structures, involving increased corporate leverage, reliance on external debt and the introduction of riskier and more complicated financial instruments and transactions. It goes on to consider four detailed conglomerate-level case studies that illuminate the microeconomic foundations of the crisis, showing how Indonesian capitalists sought to liquidate their Indonesian assets without losing control of their corporate empires, by taking advantage of increased access to foreign loans and complex financial re-engineering actions which ultimately precipitated instability and crisis throughout the entire financial system. Finally, it reflects upon the policy implications of this episode, putting forward the case for comprehensive capital controls for open and developing economies until they establish appropriate financial institutions to monitor and manage the level of indebtedness and the volatility of capitalists' behaviour. Overall, this book provides incisive analysis of a critical phase in recent East Asian financial history.

Yasuyuki Matsumoto is Senior Manager of Asian Investments, The Norinchukin Bank. He was Vice President and Head of Corporate Finance team at PT Bank LTCB Central Asia in Indonesia from 1993 to 1997. He received his PhD in economics from SOAS, University of London, MA from Cornell University and BA from Keio University and also holds a certificate of the USCPA.

Routledge Contemporary Southeast Asia Series

Financial Fragility and Instability in Indonesia

Yasuyuki Matsumoto

LONDON AND NEW YORK

First published 2007
by Routledge
2 Park Square, Milton Park, Abingdon, Oxon OX14 4RN

Simultaneously published in the USA and Canada
by Routledge
270 Madison Ave, New York, NY 10016

*Routledge is an imprint of the Taylor & Francis Group,
an informa business*

© 2007 Yasuyuki Matsumoto

Typeset in Times New Roman by
Newgen Imaging Systems (P) Ltd, Chennai, India
Printed and bound in Great Britain by
Biddles Ltd, King's Lynn

British Library Cataloguing in Publication Data
A catalogue record for this book is available
from the British Library

Library of Congress Cataloging in Publication Data
Matsumoto, Yasuyuki, 1963–
       Financial fragility and instability in Indonesia / Yasuyuki Matsumoto.
          p. cm. – (Routledge contemporary Southeast Asia series)
       Includes bibliographical references and index.
       1. Financial crises – Indonesia. 2. Indonesia – Economic
    conditions – 1997– I. Title. II. Series.

    HB3815.M38 2006
    330.9598–dc22   2006012732

ISBN10: 0–415–39904–1 (hbk)
ISBN10: 0–203–96668–6 (ebk)

ISBN13: 978–0–415–39904–3 (hbk)
ISBN13: 978–0–203–96668–6 (ebk)

To Kanako and Marina
and
To the Memory of
Katsu Yanaihara and Takashi Uehara

Contents

Figures

Tables

Preface

This book applies Hyman P. Minsky's financial instability hypothesis, with necessary modifications, to the Indonesian case. Indonesia experienced an extreme boom-bust cycle within ten years of liberalization. The book argues that the fragile and unstable financial structures, which ultimately led to the financial crisis, emerged during the finance boom from 1994 to the first half of 1997. The increase in corporate leverage, the increasing reliance on external debt and the introduction of riskier and more complicated financial transactions and structures were all characteristic of the boom.

Indonesia in the 1990s experienced an era of private capital mobilization. The corporate sector, that is, private non-financial companies, played an important role in mobilizing private capital. During the finance boom, the sector drove up leverage through the use of offshore syndicated debt. The sector rapidly increased its reliance on foreign currency debt, and at the same time, offshore mobile capital occupied a dominant position in the financial structure. As a result, the sector became in Minsky's terms a highly leveraged 'speculative financing unit'.

The process was driven by business groups' aggressive financial activities and offshore financiers' enthusiasm for Indonesian assets. The business groups initiated complex financial activities during the boom. The finance boom enabled business group owners not only to make new investments without the need for additional capital contributions, but also to liquidate their Indonesian investments. Four case studies of Indonesian business groups (Salim, Lippo, Sinar Mas and Gajah Tunggal) provide detailed accounts of the endogenous evolution of fragile and unstable financial structures at the microeconomic level.

Finally this book reviews the collapse of Indonesia's fragile and unstable financial structures during the financial crisis.

Acknowledgements

This book is based on my PhD thesis, 'The Political Economy of Financial Fragility and Instability in Indonesia during the 1990s Finance Boom', which was submitted to the University of London. Both this book and the PhD thesis would never been completed without the generous assistance of numerous individuals and institutions.

First of all, I would like to express my profound gratitude to the supervisor of my PhD thesis, Jonathon Pincus. The constructive and critical comments he provided on my research studies posed intellectual challenges and provided me with ideas for my work. His advice and support has helped me to further develop my ability to form and express theoretical arguments. His dedication to my thesis went beyond his duty as supervisor. Dr Pincus also gave me a great deal of precious advice for writing this book. To him I owe my most sincere thanks. Both the thesis and this book could not have been completed without his encouragement, support, guidance and supervision.

I am very grateful to Anne Booth and Costas Lapavitsas for their time and patience in guiding me through my theoretical arguments and also to Ben Fine for providing me with a fresh angle on my research in his PhD research seminars. Furthermore, I am grateful to The School of Oriental and African Studies (SOAS), University of London, which provided excellent PhD programmes and stimulating intellectual circumstances for my research. My sincere thanks go to the School.

My thanks also go to the examiners of my PhD thesis, Ajit Sing (University of Cambridge) and Machiko Nissanke (SOAS, University of London). Both examiners asked me many valuable questions and passed comments on the thesis during and after the *viva voce* examination. I was really excited to argue with both examiners and introduced the arguments into this book. The examination at Professor Sing's room at Cambridge will be my life-time memory.

I would like to express my thanks to Takashi Shiraishi, Vice-President of The National Graduate Institute for Policy Studies (Japan), who had supervised my master thesis at Cornell University (USA) and encouraged me to continue with my research. He offered me many opportunities to present my preliminary arguments, which ultimately developed into my PhD research studies. Without his generosity, I would not have been able to commence work on my PhD thesis. In addition, I benefited from the excellent research programmes at Cornell

University and obtained advanced analytical skills and knowledge of political economy and South East Asia, which were exploited for my PhD research. My sincere thanks also go to Cornell.

Also, I would like to express my sincere thanks to the late Katsu Yanaihara who had taught me methods of analysing international economy at Keio University, and guided me towards looking at economies in developing countries. Here, I beg his pardon for being unable to attend his funeral in Japan from London. I am deeply appreciative of the late Takashi Uehara who played an important role in my career and academic developments whilst I was working at The Long-Term Credit Bank of Japan, Ltd. This book is dedicated to both of them. I believe that they will read this book in heaven. I am looking forward to having their comments and criticisms on the book after completing my life.

I benefited enormously from the many valuable insights provided by Takeshi Hamashita (Kyoto University), Toshihiko Kinoshita (Waseda University), Masaaki Komatsu (Hiroshima University), Yuri Sato (JETRO), Nobuto Yamamoto (Keio University), Yukiko Fukagawa (Waseda University), Peter Nolan (University of Cambridge), Lim Hua Sing (Waseda University) and Yasushi Suzuki (Ritsumeikan Asia Pacific University). Furthermore, I wish to thank the following institutes and research groups for allowing me a variety of opportunities to present my research: Keio University (Japan), Columbia University (USA), University of Cambridge, Judge Business School (UK), Institute for Economic and Financial Research (Japan), Nomura Research Institute (Japan), Kobe Association of Corporate Executives (Japan), Institute for Social Affairs in Asia (Japan) and Shizuoka Research Institute (Japan).

My field research was fully indebted to numerous Indonesian businessmen. They spared their precious time for my interviews and provided useful information and opinions for my fieldwork. They all deserve my thanks. Nevertheless, I would like to express my thanks particularly to the following persons: Anthony Salim, Andree Halim, Benny S. Santoso, Eva Riyanti Hutapea, Cesar M. dela Cruz, Sri Dewi Subijanto, Andi Zahiri, Jahja Setiaatmadja, Teddy P. Rachmat, Rini M. S. Soewandi, Benni Subianto, Budi Setiadharma, Michael D. Ruslim, Danny Walla, Indra R. Aziz, Tossin Himawan, Mochtar Riady, James T. Riady, Jeffrey Koes Wonsono, Charles L. De Queljoe, Markus Parmadi, Eddy Handoko, Roy E. Tirtadji and Sjamsul Nursalim.

My thanks go to my past and present colleagues at The Long-Term Credit Bank of Japan, Ltd, PT Bank LTCB Central Asia (Jakarta) and The Norinchukin Bank. In particular, I extend my best thanks to Chen Huan Fong and Masaaki Sakaguchi. They were respected bankers at LTCB Merchant Bank (Singapore). Together with them, I could enjoy my banker's life in Jakarta and was able to achieve an excellent performance there. Some time in the future, I would be happy if we could work together again. I also extend my sincere thanks to The Norinchukin Bank for providing me with the opportunity to work in London. Without this, I would not have submitted my PhD thesis to the University of London nor have published my book in the United Kingdom.

A number of individuals aided the production of this book in other ways. I highly appreciate Peter Sowden, Editor of Routledge, for editing this book, Paul Vermes for revising the manuscripts of both the PhD thesis and this book and N. Nuranto for supporting my data collection. Also, a number of my friends encouraged me to complete my research and publication. Many thanks go to them.

Finally, my family played a very significant role in supporting me through these four years of work. My special thanks and great love go to my wife and best friend, Kanako and also to my daughter, Marina. With their understanding and encouragement, I was able to overcome the most stressful moments and managed to accomplish this thesis. My thanks and love also go to my parents, Yoshiaki and Akiko, and my in-laws, Shojiro and Michiko.

Abbreviations

ABS	Asset-Backed Securities
ADB	Asian Development Bank
AFP	Asia Food and Properties Ltd.
AMC	Asset Management Company (Thailand)
APIC	Additional Paid-In Capital
APP	Asia Pulp and Paper Co. Ltd.
Bank EXIM	Bank Expor-Impor Indonesia
BAPEPAM	Badan Pelaksana/Pengawas Pasar Modal (Capital Market Executive/Supervisory Agency)
Bapindo	Bank Pembagunan Indonesia
BBA	British Bankers' Association
BBD	Bank Bumi Daya
BBKU	Bank Beku Kegiatan Usaha (Frozen Banks in 1999)
BBO	Bank Beku Operasi (Frozen Banks in 1998)
BCA	Bank Central Asia
BDL	Bank Dalam Likuidas (Closed Banks)
BDN	Bank Dagang Negara
BDNI	Bank Dagang Nasional Indonesia
BI	Bank Indonesia
BII	Bank International Indonesia
BILA	Bank Indonesia Liquidity Assistance
BKPM	Badan Koordinasi Penan Man Modal
BLBI	Bantuan Likuiditas Bank Indonesia (Bank Indonesia Liquidity Assistance)
BNI	Bank Negara Indonesia
BPS	Biro Pusat Statistik (Central Bureau of Statistics)
Bps.	Basis Points
BRI	Bank Rakyat Indonesia
BTN	Bank Tabungan Negara
BTO	Bank Taken Over
BULOG	Badan Urusan Logistik (National Logistic Agency)
BUN	Bank Umum Nasional
CAR	Capital Adequacy Ratio (Kewajiban Penyertaan Modal Minimum)

CD	Certificate of Deposit
CDRAC	Corporate Debt Restructuring Advisory Committee (Thailand)
CDRC	Corporate Debt Restructuring Committee (Malaysia)
CEO	Chief Executive Officer
CFO	Chief Financial Officer
CGI	Consultative Group on Indonesia
CPI	Consumer Price Index
CS	Common Stock
EBIT	Earning before Interest and Tax
EBITDA	Earning before Interest and Tax, plus Depreciation and Amortization
ECA	Export Credit Agency
FRA	Financial Sector Restructuring Authority (Thailand)
FRCD	Floating Rate Certificate of Deposit
FRN	Floating Rate Note
FSPC	Financial Sector Policy Committee (Komite Kebijakan Sektor Keuangan)
GAAP	Generally Accepted Accounting Principles
GDP	Gross Domestic Products
IBRA	Indonesian Bank Restructuring Agency (Badan Penyehatan Perbankan Nasional)
IFC	International Finance Corporation
IFR	International Financing Review
IGGI	Inter-Governmental Group on Indonesia
IMF	International Monetary Fund
INDRA	Indonesian Debt Restructuring Agency
IPO	Initial Public Offering
IRC	Independent Review Committee
JITF	Jakarta Initiative Task Force
JSX	Jakarta Stock Exchange
KAMCO	Korea Asset Management Corporation
KEPPRES	Keputusan Presiden (Presidential Decree)
KKN	Korupsi, Kolusi dan Nepotisme (Corruption, Collusion and Nepotism)
LIBOR	London Interbank Offered Rate
MLA	Marga Lestari Abadi
MOBNAS	Mobil Nasional (National Car)
MRA	Master Restructuring Agreement
MRNIA	Master Refinancing and Notes Issuance Agreement
MSAA	Master Settlement and Acquisition Agreement
NBFI	Non-Bank Financial Institution
NIES	Newly Industrialized Economies
OSC	Oversight Committee
PAKDES I	Paket 23 Desember 1987 (Capital Market Policy Package I)
PAKDES II	Paket 20 Desember 1988 (Capital Market Policy Package II)

PAKMAR	Paket 25 Maret 1989 (Financial, Monetary and Banking Policy Reform Package)
PAKTO	Paket 27 Oktober 1988 (Financial, Monetary and Banking Policy Reform Package)
Pertamina	Perusahaan Tambang Minyak dan Gas Bumi Negara (State Oil Company)
PDI	Partai Demokrasi Indonesia (Indonesian Democratic Party)
PKLN	Pinjaman Komersian Luar Negeri (Offshore Commercial Loan)
PKPS	Penyelesaian Kewajiban Pemegang Saham (Shareholders Settlement Program)
PLN	Perusahaan Listrik Negara (State Electricity Company)
PMA	Penanaman Modal Asing (Foreign Capital/Investment)
PMDN	Penanaman Modal Dalam Negeri (Domestic Capital/Investment)
PTP	Perseroan Terbatas Perkebunan (State Farm)
REPELITA	Rencana Pembangunan Lima Tahun (Five-Year Development Plan)
Rp.	Indonesian Rupiah
SBI	Sertifikat Bank Indonesia (Bank Indonesia Certificate)
SBPU	Surat Berharga Pasar Uang (Money Market Security)
SIBOR	Singapore Interbank Offered Rate
SMART Corp.	Sinar Mas Agro Resources and Technology Corporation
UIC	Unggul Indah Cahaya
US$	United States Dollars
WTO	World Trade Organization

Short profile of author

Dr Yasuyuki Matsumoto received his PhD (economics) from SOAS, University of London, MA from Cornell University (USA) and BA from Keio University (Japan). He is now a Senior Manager of Asian Investments, The Norinchukin Bank. He has engaged in international finance, mainly in Asia, for more than 20 years, including his 4-year corporate finance business for Indonesian companies as a Vice President of PT Bank LTCB Central Asia (Jakarta). Dr Matsumoto's academic objectives are financial economics and political economy of Asian business, and he is actively writing academic and business articles on the subjects. He is also a certificate holder of Certified Public Accountant in the United States.

Introduction

The economy is an aggregate of economic entities' balance sheets and balance sheets are connected to each other by cash flows. In a capitalist economy, capitalists develop chains of cash flows through their economic activities driven by their various motivations, and financial structures evolve as they do so. Balance sheets have an asymmetric nature. Asset values in balance sheets represent capitalists' expectations reflecting market prospects and may fluctuate. On the other hand, liabilities are payment commitments and are not flexible. This asymmetry between expectations and commitments creates volatility in a capitalist economy. Furthermore, realizable cash flows through the use or liquidation of assets determine the sustainable level of leverage in the economy. The downgrading of cash flows can lead to difficulties in meeting debt service and can cause shrinkage of asset values in balance sheets. As liabilities do not change, leverage increases. The higher the leverage the more vulnerable the economy. If leverage reaches an unsustainable level, cash-flow chains unwind and/or breakdown and crises may occur. A capitalist economy cannot operate without liabilities and is therefore fragile and unstable by nature. This book is based of an understanding of capitalist economies as fragile because of the ever-present risk of the breakdown of cash-flow chains.

Hyman P. Minsky developed this view of the capitalist economy in his 'financial instability hypothesis'. However, Minsky's theory departs from a closed and advanced economy (Minsky 1986). This work reinterprets Minsky's theory in the context of corporate finance and has modified it for an open and developing economy. The work, furthermore, applies the modified financial instability hypothesis to Indonesia using a political economy approach. Indonesia experienced an extreme boom–bust cycle between 1994 and 1999, and this experience provides the empirical basis for the elaboration of the modified theory. The work argues that fragile and unstable financial structures ultimately led to the financial crisis and that these structures evolved during the finance boom from 1994 to the first half of 1997. Sharply increased leverage, heavy reliance on external debt and the introduction of riskier and more complex financial transactions in the corporate sector were the characteristics of the finance boom in Indonesia.

Indonesia experienced an era of rapid private capital mobilization in the 1990s. The corporate sector, that is, private non-financial companies, played an important role in mobilizing private capital. During the finance boom, the sector drove up leverage through the use of offshore syndicated debt. The sector rapidly increased its reliance on foreign currency debt. As a result, offshore mobile capital occupied a substantial proportion of the corporate sector's debt. In Minsky's terms, the corporate sector became a highly-leveraged 'speculative financing unit' financed by offshore mobile capital (Minsky 1986).

The evolution of the earlier-mentioned financial structure was driven by Indonesian business groups' aggressive financial activities and offshore financiers' enthusiasm for Indonesian corporate borrowers. During the finance boom, Indonesian business groups initiated complex financial transactions with international financial institutions on a large scale. These resources enabled business group owners not only to carry out new investments without additional investment capital but also to liquidate their existing investments in Indonesia. The case studies of four business groups' financial activities presented in this book (Salim, Lippo, Sinar Mas and Gajah Tunggal) during the finance boom provide a detailed account of the endogenous evolution of fragile and unstable financial structures at the microeconomic level. This work also analyses in detail the collapse of cash-flow chains that occurred in 1997 and 1998, that is to say, the outcome of the financial crisis. The collapse of these business groups is shown to be a consequence of the financial structures created during the finance boom.

A number of researchers have discussed the causes of the East Asian financial crisis in academic journals, books and magazine articles. However, no one has yet properly analysed the microeconomic processes that create crisis-prone financial structures leading to the crisis. Empirical studies of business groups have focused too much on the asset side of the balance sheet, in other words their investment activities. Few studies have considered in detail the liability side of the balance sheet and the development of unstable financial structures. This is because analysis of liabilities requires intensive field research to collect detailed transaction data in the corporate sector, a large part of which is not easily available. Furthermore, the analysis of liabilities demands a familiarity with the practice of financial economics, accounting and management. This work is the first microeconomic study of the liability side of the financial activities of the Indonesian corporate sector.

The book is structured as follows. Chapter 1 reviews the impact of the East Asian financial crisis on the Indonesian economy and analyses the transformation of Indonesian debt in the 1990s. Chapter 2 reinterprets Minsky's financial instability hypothesis by focusing on liability structures and the cash-flow mechanism, and modifies and applies his theory to the Indonesian case. Chapter 3 sets out the methodology of the study and describes the database used in the macroeconomic analysis and case studies. Chapter 4 explains how the financial structures of the Indonesian economy evolved in the 1990s by analysing leverage positions in the corporate sector. Chapter 5 argues that offshore capitalists aggressively promoted offshore debt finance to the Indonesian corporations and that over time structural power shifted from offshore capitalists to Indonesian borrowers. This is demonstrated through a detailed analysis of debt transactions during the period. These chapters (4–5) demonstrate how highly leveraged speculative financing units were created in the corporate sector, thus generating a fragile and unstable financial system during the finance boom of 1994–7 in Indonesia.

Nevertheless, the aggregated statistics presented in these chapters cannot fully explain the endogenous emergence of financial fragility and instability. This is because the causes of fragility and instability must ultimately be traced to individual financial transactions driven by capitalists' motivations, which Keynes describes as 'capitalists' animal spirits' and Minsky as 'the profit-seeking and forward-looking nature of capitalists' (Keynes 1936; Minsky 1986). Subsequent chapters therefore adopt the case method to demonstrate these mechanisms. I have selected four Indonesian business groups, Salim, Lippo, Sinar Mas and Gajah Tunggal, as these conglomerates represent the full range of financial activities pursued by Indonesian business groups during the finance boom.[1]

Chapters 6 to 9 elucidate the incentives and motivations that drove Indonesian capitalists to adopt destabilizing financial structures. The conglomerate-level analysis in these chapters illustrates that Indonesian capitalists – perhaps wary of imminent political instability – sought to liquidate their Indonesian assets without losing control over their corporate empires. Access to foreign loans, in combination with financial re-engineering, provided the means to do so. Thus, the result of individual, rational decisions was systemwide instability, as Minsky predicts. Chapter 10 reviews debt restructuring and the institutional arrangements in Indonesia, analysing the four business groups' struggles to manage their debt. The discussion enables us to check consistency with these group's financial activities during the finance boom. Chapter 11 concludes and briefly considers the policy implications of the empirical and theoretical findings of the book.

1 Indonesia's external debt problem in the 1990s

The East Asian crisis and Indonesia

The devaluation of the Thai baht on 2 July 1997 set in motion a large-scale reversal of capital flows that developed into the East Asian financial crisis.[1] This was a capital-account crisis rather than a conventional current-account crisis caused by large budget deficits, high rates of inflation and real currency appreciation (Furman and Stiglitz 1998; Krugman 1998a, 1999a; Yoshitomi and Staff of ADB Institute 2003). The aggregate capital account surplus of the five countries that were most affected (Indonesia, Korea, Malaysia, the Philippines and Thailand) fell sharply by US$90.9 billion from US$100.6 billion (9.27 per cent of Gross Domestic Product (GDP)) in 1996 to US$28.8 billion (4.52 per cent of GDP) in 1997. Furthermore, the capital account recorded a deficit of US$0.5 billion (0.07 per cent of GDP) in 1998.

This sudden and huge reversal was mainly due to the withdrawal of offshore commercial bank lending. Until the crisis, offshore commercial banks had made the largest contribution to the capital account surplus. Their contribution to net capital inflows into the five countries was US$53.2 billion (5.27 per cent of GDP) in 1995 and US$65.3 billion (6.02 per cent of GDP) in 1996. Once the crisis began, the banks led the reversal of capital flows by withdrawing US$25.6 billion (4.01 per cent of GDP) in 1997 and US$35.0 billion (4.61 per cent of GDP) in 1998 (Yoshitomi and Staff of ADB Institute 2003, p.69). This sudden and large-scale reversal of capital flows pushed the corporate sectors of the affected countries towards insolvency and brought an end to nearly three decades of uninterrupted growth.

The East Asian crisis not only set back economic development in Indonesia but also forced the country to restructure the social and political systems established by the Suharto regime. The crisis had a huge political impact throughout East Asia (Haggard 2000). However, Indonesia's political crisis was the most severe, and this commingling of political and economic crises was a defining feature of the Indonesian collapse. The contraction of the economy in 1998, the inability of the government to intervene effectively, stalled negotiations with international financial authorities and evidence of massive corruption increased public frustration with the Suharto regime. The increasingly visible and lucrative business dealings of

Suharto's children had alienated former supporters of the regime during the 1990s. The economic crisis brought these concerns to a head, eventually leading to nationwide popular movements calling for an end to corruption, collusion, and nepotism (KKN). In March 1998, despite calls for Suharto to resign and the risk of anti-Chinese and antiregime violence across the archipelago, Suharto was reappointed as President of the Republic of Indonesia for a seventh term. Suharto appointed B. J. Habibie as Vice-President and provided ministerial positions to his eldest daughter and his long-time business associates. These appointments accelerated the collapse of the regime. Finally, the shooting of student protesters by the army led to an escalation of the student movement and eventually to the fall of the regime on 21 May 1998.

The Indonesian corporate sector was seriously damaged by the economic and political chaos of 1997–8. In 1997, 47.5 per cent of leading Indonesian non-financial companies suffered a net loss, and the average net loss per company was Rp. 27.3 billion (US$9.4 million). In 1998, these figures were even worse. Around 58.0 per cent of companies booked a net loss, and the average net losses increased in rupiah terms to Rp. 92.8 billion (US$9.1 million).[2] This marked an unprecedented collapse of the corporate sector.[3] The main cause of the reversal was the depreciation of the rupiah against major currencies which increased debt-service payments and the cost of imported inputs. Financial distress rapidly spread through the sector as demand contracted. The growth of real GDP fell from 7.8 per cent in 1996 to 4.7 per cent in 1997 (Table 4.9 in Chapter 4). The Indonesian economy contracted by 13.1 per cent in 1998.

These events came as a shock to long-term observers of the Indonesian economy. Average growth of real GDP was 7.2 per cent from 1990 to 1996 and output in the manufacturing sector grew by 9.8 per cent on average. Demand was driven by investment and private consumption. Investment grew by an average of 10.7 per cent per annum and private consumption by 7.8 per cent.[4] Focusing on the investment boom of 1994–6, the average growth of real GDP was 7.8 per cent, in line with other rapidly growing Asian countries (e.g. 7.6 per cent in Thailand, 9.1 per cent in Malaysia and 8.2 per cent in South Korea). Although price inflation was higher than in most other East Asian countries, consumer prices still rose by less than 10 per cent (9.2 per cent in 1994, 8.6 per cent in 1995 and 6.5 per cent in 1996) (Table 4.9 in Chapter 4).

Balance-of-payments data for the 'finance boom' in Indonesia (between 1994 and the first half of 1997) reveal a gradual increase in the current account deficit from US$3.0 billion in 1994 to US$7.8 billion in 1996. However, this size of deficit was still controllable and was financed by a widening capital account surplus. This increased sharply from US$4.0 billion in 1994 to US$11.0 billion in 1996. The most important feature of this huge surplus is that it was created mainly by private-to-private capital inflows. Net private capital inflows were US$3.7 billion in 1994, US$10.3 billion in 1995, and US$11.5 billion in 1996. Official foreign exchange reserves increased sharply from US$13.2 billion in 1994 to US$19.1 billion in 1996 (Table 4.9 in Chapter 4). The growth of official reserves bolstered confidence among investors wary of Latin American-type current-account crises.

From the viewpoint of balance-of-payments management, the increase in private-to-private capital inflows could be seen as a response to fundamentals. However, the acceleration of private capital flows could also be interpreted as the introduction of more risk–return sensitive mobile capital into the financial structure. Official mobile capital, such as International Monetary Fund (IMF), World Bank and other CGI (Consultative Group on Indonesia) lending, is coordinated and cannot withdraw unexpectedly or suddenly given the purpose of their institutions.[5] Private capital, on the other hand, is neither coordinated nor organized. Most individual investors do not possess structural power, yet, once they move in the same direction, private lenders acting as a group can exercise enormous structural power. Private capital movements are often volatile and subject to booms owing to investors' 'irrational exuberance' (Shiller 2000; Yoshitomi and Staff of ADB Institute 2003).[6] Reversals occur quickly, and policy makers do not have time to react. Furthermore, Indonesia is only one among many emerging market economies and investments in Indonesia account for only a small percentage of the total investment portfolio. Fund managers can easily move money to other countries to realize gains from remaining holdings or simply to cut losses. The decision-making process is also very rapid and cannot wait for policy makers' responses.

By way of contrast, investments in equities and foreign direct investment do not create pressures for cash outflows. This is simply because equities do not entail scheduled payment commitments. On the contrary, if capital inflows consist of debt with payment commitments, such as offshore loans and bonds, trade account payables and offshore leases, the economy can experience a reversal of capital flows. In addition, if this offshore private debt finance is deeply integrated into the financial structure of the economy it results in it becoming fragile and unstable. During the finance boom, the Indonesian corporate sector accumulated offshore private debt and transformed the economy from robust to fragile and unstable while economic fundamentals remained essentially sound.

A number of studies link debt accumulation by the private sector to the liberalization policies that were actively pursued in East Asia's crisis-affected countries in the 1980s and 1990s. In particular, the private sector's external debt problem is viewed as a result of capital account liberalization. Indonesia undertook a dramatic deregulation of its financial sector in the 1980s and by the 1990s had one of the most liberalized financial markets in the world (Cole and Slade 1996; Pangestu 1996; Pincus and Ramli 2003). Deregulation policies were introduced between 1983 and 1989. In June 1983, bank credit ceilings and most interest rate controls were eliminated. In Desember 1987, a deregulation package for the investment and capital markets Paket 23 Desember 1987 (PAKDES I) was introduced, in which daily price controls on the Jakarta Stock Exchange were eliminated. In October 1988, the government introduced a major banking reform and deregulation package Paket 27 Oktober 1988 (PAKTO) that eliminated restrictions on the opening of new banks, branches and foreign joint-venture banks. In December 1988, the amendment and supplemental package Paket 20 Desember 1988 (PAKDES II) was introduced allowing foreign ownership of securities companies. The government refined PAKTO in March 1989 Paket 25 Maret 1989 (PAKMAR) and changed foreign borrowing restrictions on bank and non-bank financial institutions (NBFI) to controls on net open positions. It is not surprising that the monitoring system and regulatory framework was not put in place as quickly as the new financial products, services and institutions. In addition, Indonesia had already abolished practically all controls on foreign capital movements between 1966 and 1970 and has maintained the policy since then. In other words, Indonesia had already opened the capital account for financial flows out of the country and for most inflows from 1970 (Cole and Slade 1996, pp.3–4).

Balance-of-payments management has instead concentrated on restraining offshore borrowing by state companies and banks. In September 1991, the Coordinating Team for the Management of Offshore Commercial Loans (Tim Koordinasi Pengelolaan Pinjaman Komersian Luar Negeri) was established in order to control and monitor all offshore commercial loans for state companies, banks and projects (Presidential Decree No.39 (Keputusan Presiden 39)).[7] In addition, both state and private banks were under strict control by Bank Indonesia, the central bank, for annual offshore borrowing quotas and timing to access offshore markets. However, although reporting to the team was required, private non-financial companies were able to obtain offshore loans to the extent that offshore banks were willing to lend to them. Therefore, the deregulation policies in the 1980s were not a direct reason for the sharp increase of external debt by the private non-financial companies in Indonesia.

What is most remarkable about the build up of private debt in the 1990s was the fact that cautious investors would have found many reasons for concern in Indonesia's recent credit history. In August 1990, Bank Duta, one of the leading private banks owned by three of Suharto's charitable foundations, violated net open position rules that had been imposed by Bank Indonesia in 1989 and took risky foreign exchange positions. The bank booked a US$420 million loss and was ultimately bailed out by Sudono Salim (Liem Sioe Liong) of the Salim Group and Prajogo Pangestu of the Barito Group, two close associates of Suharto. In 1992, Bank Summa, the flagship bank of the Summa Group (a sister business group of the Astra Group) and run as a purely family business by the Soeryadjaya family, failed due to excessive finance to its affiliated speculative and unprofitable businesses. As a result, the Soeryadjaya family lost ownership of the Astra Group.[8] This was handed over to a consortium of mainly Indonesian Chinese business groups. Furthermore, in 1992 and 1993, other large business groups, such as the Bentoel Group and the Mantrust Group, went bankrupt due to excessive borrowing and failure of investments. In 1993, a controversial list of 26 major business groups that had accumulated more than Rp. 100 billion (US$48 million) in unpaid debt to the six state banks was leaked to the local press. This list confirmed widespread rumours that close associates of Suharto, including the Suharto family, had amassed huge fortunes at the expense of the state banks (Schwarz 1999). In 1994, the Golden Key Scandal erupted at Bapindo, one of the state banks, resulting in the loss of US$449 million to the state.[9] In 1995, the Sinar Mas Group also booked a huge loss from derivatives transactions and the owner injected new funds in order to compensate for the loss. These events could have changed investors' views of the Indonesian credit market in the 1990s. Yet, offshore investors enthusiastically brought their funds into Indonesia as if credit conditions had in fact improved during this period. As will be seen, the sudden rush of foreign loans into Indonesia during the period of the finance boom from 1994 to 1997 gave rise to important changes in financial structure, which would ultimately lead to the Indonesian economic crisis.

Review of Indonesian external debt data in the 1990s

All East Asian governments affected by the crisis had maintained macroeconomic stability and had prudently controlled external debt levels. In the case of Indonesia, since oil prices and state revenues began to decline in 1981, and state and quasi-state expenditures were put under pressure, the government had minimized the increase of its external debt by responding to the demands of international institutions, such as IMF, World Bank and CGI. Instead, the government expected the private sector to directly access offshore funds for investment. This work focuses on the private sector and, in particular, the corporate sector. The work defines the corporate sector as the private non-financial sector (or the private non-bank sector, depending on the availability of data) and focuses on the period from 1994 to the first half of 1997, a period that will be referred to as the *finance boom*. During this boom, the corporate sector obtained various types of finance on a huge scale from offshore as well as from domestic markets.

As shown in Tables 1.1, 1.2 and 1.3, during the 1990s and before the crisis in Indonesia, the state sector had limited the increase in external debt to an average of 5.3 per cent per annum from US$49.4 billion to US$62.0 billion. During the finance boom in Indonesia, the increase in the state sector's external debt was only 2.7 per cent per annum, and that government, state companies (mainly the state oil company Pertamina and the national airline Garuda) and state banks

Table 1.1 Indonesian external debt 1989–98 (billion US dollars)

Sector	1989	1990	1991	1992	1993	1994	1995	1996	1997	1998
State	43.2	49.4	50.5	55.8	60.6	66.4	68.3	62.0	63.8	76.2
Government	39.6	45.1	45.7	48.8	52.5	58.6	59.6	55.3	53.9	67.3
Non-banks	3.2	3.1	3.4	4.5	5.1	5.1	4.8	3.7	4.0	4.2
Banks	0.4	1.1	1.4	2.5	3.1	2.8	3.9	3.0	5.9	4.8
Private	8.8	13.5	15.2	17.5	19.9	30.1	39.6	48.1	62.0	69.4
Financial	0.9	2.2	2.8	4.0	5.5	6.8	8.1	8.5	11.9	8.1
Banks	0.4	1.5	2.0	3.2	4.6	5.4	6.2	6.1	8.5	6.0
Finance companies	0.5	0.7	0.8	0.8	0.9	1.4	1.9	2.4	3.4	2.1
Corporate	7.9	11.3	12.4	13.5	14.4	23.2	31.4	39.7	50.2	61.3
Total	52.0	62.8	65.7	73.4	80.6	96.5	107.8	110.2	125.8	145.6

Sources: Memorandum (by financial advisors) and Bank Indonesia.

Table 1.2 Annual growth of Indonesian external debt (% per annum)

Sector	1990	1991	1992	1993	1994	1995	1996	1990–3 average[a]	1993–6 average[a]	1990–6 average[a]
State	14.2	2.3	10.6	8.7	9.6	2.7	−9.1	8.8	2.7	5.3
Government	14.0	1.4	6.7	7.6	11.7	1.7	−7.2	7.3	3.2	4.9
Non-banks	−3.1	7.5	34.4	12.1	0.2	−4.9	−22.4	11.9	−4.6	2.2
Banks	169.0	23.3	81.2	23.5	−11.7	39.8	−22.7	65.0	4.2	32.3
Private	53.9	13.2	15.1	13.7	50.7	31.6	21.7	22.9	28.7	27.6
Financial	154.8	28.3	44.2	36.4	24.4	18.7	4.2	59.3	20.4	38.7
Banks	300.2	36.9	58.1	43.7	17.5	14.3	−2.5	87.8	17.1	49.0
Finance companies	42.9	9.8	6.9	7.5	60.9	35.4	26.2	15.9	31.1	25.7
Corporate	42.9	10.2	8.5	7.0	60.7	35.5	26.2	16.3	30.9	25.9
Total	20.9	4.6	11.6	9.9	19.7	11.7	2.2	11.6	10.7	11.3

Sources: Memorandum (by financial advisors) and Bank Indonesia.

Notes
The figures in Table 1.2 are based on the original data (not figures in Table 1.1).
a Average: geometric mean.

Table 1.3 Share of Indonesian external debt (by sector) (%)

Sector	1989	1990	1991	1992	1993	1994	1995	1996	1997	1998
State	83.2	78.6	76.8	76.1	75.3	68.9	63.3	56.3	50.7	52.4
Government	76.1	71.8	69.6	66.5	65.1	60.7	55.3	50.2	42.8	46.2
Non-banks	6.2	5.0	5.1	6.2	6.3	5.3	4.5	3.4	3.2	2.9
Banks	0.8	1.8	2.1	3.5	3.9	2.9	3.6	2.7	4.7	3.3
Private	16.8	21.4	23.2	23.9	24.7	31.1	36.7	43.7	49.3	47.6
Financial	1.6	3.5	4.3	5.5	6.8	7.1	7.5	7.7	9.4	5.6
Banks	0.7	2.4	3.1	4.4	5.7	5.6	5.8	5.5	6.7	4.1
Finance companies	0.9	1.1	1.2	1.1	1.1	1.5	1.8	2.2	2.7	1.4
Corporate	15.2	18.0	18.9	18.4	17.9	24.1	29.2	36.0	39.9	42.1
Total	100.0	100.0	100.0	100.0	100.0	100.0	100.0	100.0	100.0	100.0

Sources: Memorandum (by financial advisors) and Bank Indonesia.

Note
The figures of Table 1.3 are based on the original data (not figures in Table 1.1).

managed to minimize the rate of increase in their external debt. However, even though total external debt expanded by an average of 11.3 per cent per annum from 1990 to 1996, the state sector's share decreased from 78.6 per cent to 56.3 per cent.

During the 1990s, external debt was driven by the private sector. During the 3 years of the finance boom, private sector offshore debt rose from US$19.9 billion to US$48.1 billion and its share of total external debt jumped from 24.7 per cent to 43.7 per cent.[10] These figures indicate that Indonesia's debt problem shifted from the state to the private sector in the 1990s.

Furthermore, it is clear that the external debt of the corporate sector was the most critical issue throughout the period and drove the growth of Indonesia's external debt. The corporate sector's external debt increased by an average of 25.9 per cent per annum from US$11.3 billion to US$39.7 billion. The share of this sector in total external debt also doubled from 18.0 per cent to 36.0 per cent. Dividing this period (1990 to 1996) into the first half (1990 to 1993) and the second half (1993 to 1996), the annual average growth of the private non-financial sector's external debt for each half was 16.3 per cent and 30.9 per cent respectively. This second half constitutes the investment and finance boom in Indonesia.

Although the external debt of the financial sector increased from US$3.3 billion to US$11.5 billion from 1990 to 1996, most of this took place before the finance boom. Financial deregulation spurred foreign borrowing in the sector after 1988. However, by 1991, Bank Indonesia had moved to restrict new borrowing by banks.[11] This form of capital controls proved to be reasonably successful. Ironically, it was the absence of controls on corporate external borrowing that ultimately destroyed the banking system rather than over-borrowing within the financial sector itself.

In sum, during the 1990s, the state restricted foreign debt while the private sector expanded overseas borrowing at an increasing rate. The distinctive characteristic of the Indonesian external debt problem during this period was the rapid debt build-up of the corporate debt. This contrasts with the situation in Thailand, for example, where debt was concentrated in the financial sector. As explained above, the corporate sector accumulated massive offshore debt after 1994. This work examines the reasons for the accumulation of corporate debt and the implications of debt build-up for the Indonesian economy.

External versus domestic private debt

Liberalization of the capital account was completed in 1970, long before the liberalization of the domestic financial sector began in the 1980s. The Indonesian private sector, therefore, in principle enjoyed unrestricted access to international financial markets for offshore fund raising. However, few private Indonesian companies were considered an acceptable risk in offshore markets in the 1970s and 1980s. Even leading international banks familiar with Indonesian risk since the beginning of New Order, financed only state companies and banks, such as Pertamina and BNI (Bank Negara Indonesia), and top private companies also needed foreign partners or governmental support to obtain offshore finance. In short, the private sector did not qualify for international credits prior to the 1990s. It needed Bank Indonesia or state banks to serve as intermediaries to access offshore funds.

Until the early 1980s, the state banks functioned as a funnel for pouring oil money into the corporate sector. They were provided with Bank Indonesia liquidity credits at subsidized interest rates and told to which sectors they must lend and under what terms and conditions (Pangestu 1996). However, the end of the oil boom in 1981–3 forced this system to come to a halt. In the absence of public sector accumulation in the oil sector, the technocrats turned to the private sector and in particular to private banks.[12] A further sharp drop in oil prices in 1986 accelerated this shift of power, and the Indonesian financial sector rushed in the direction of liberalization (Winters 1996).

As is shown in Tables 1.4 and 1.5, rapid liberalization of the financial sector in the 1980s led to an expansion of domestic credit during the 1990s before the Indonesian crisis.[13] In order to prevent overheating, the technocrats introduced a series of market-based policies and new governance procedures to control banks. These included liquidity management through control over interest rates on SBI (Sertifikat Bank Indonesia) and discontinuing purchases of SBPU (Surat Berharga Pasar Uang), and 'new risk weighted capital adequacy measures (such as Capital Adequacy Ratio CAR)'.[14] These measures, combined with other contractionary policies, slowed the growth of domestic credit in 1992, but beginning the following year domestic debt again accelerated.

Table 1.4 External and domestic debts by Indonesian private sector (billion US dollars)

	1990	1991	1992	1993	1994	1995	1996	1997
External debt	13.5	15.2	17.5	19.9	30.1	39.6	48.1	62.0
Bank sector	1.5	2.0	3.2	4.6	5.4	6.2	6.1	8.5
Non-bank sector[a]	12.0	13.2	14.3	15.3	24.6	33.3	42.1	53.6
Domestic debt[a]	29.9	35.0	38.0	47.9	58.8	69.7	84.8	58.4
Rupiah	24.2	27.4	29.6	35.6	43.7	51.1	61.8	35.0
Foreign currency	5.7	7.5	8.4	12.3	15.1	18.6	23.0	23.4
Total	43.4	50.2	55.5	67.8	88.9	109.2	133.0	120.4

Sources: Memorandum (by financial advisors) and Bank Indonesia.

Note
a Including non-bank finance companies.

Table 1.5 Annual growth of Indonesian private sector's external and domestic debts (% per annum)

	1991	1992	1993	1994	1995	1996	1997	1991–3 average	1993–6 average
External debt	13.2	15.1	13.7	50.7	31.6	21.7	28.9	14.0	34.1
Bank sector	36.9	58.1	43.7	17.5	14.3	-2.5	39.4	46.0	9.4
Non-bank sector[a]	10.2	8.4	7.0	60.7	35.5	26.2	27.4	8.5	40.1
Domestic debt[a]	16.8	8.5	26.1	22.9	18.4	21.8	-31.2	16.9	21.0
Rupiah	13.1	7.8	20.3	23.0	16.9	21.0	-43.4	13.6	20.3
Foreign currency	32.6	11.2	46.5	22.9	23.0	23.9	1.5	29.3	23.2
Total	15.7	10.5	22.2	31.1	22.9	21.8	-9.4	16.0	25.2

Sources: Memorandum (by financial advisors) and Bank Indonesia.

Note
a Including non-bank finance companies.

Dividing the period 1990–6 into two sub-periods, the figures indicate that domestic debt had begun to expand in the first sub-period (1990–3) even under the newly introduced banking sector controls. The corporate sector's demand for debt was also rapidly directed to the offshore market during the latter half of the period (1993–6). As summarized in Table 1.5, the average annual growth rates of domestic and external indebtedness in the first sub-period were respectively 16.9 per cent and 14.0 per cent per annum. However, the corresponding rates in the second half were 21.0 per cent and 34.1 per cent per annum.

It is therefore incorrect to conclude that funding activities by the Indonesian private sector shifted from the domestic to the offshore market after 1993–4. Borrowing expanded in both markets throughout the 1990s under the finance boom. The important point is that the offshore market was rapidly becoming open and accessible to the Indonesian corporate sector after 1993–4, and that Indonesian companies' demand for foreign exchange loans also increased sharply under the relatively stable rupiah exchange rate against the US dollar under the crawling peg policy. The larger gap of funding costs between rupiah and US dollar loans, greater availability of rupiah–US dollar cross-currency swaps and forward transactions also spurred the growth of overseas borrowing.

Table 1.6 indicates that the Indonesian corporate sector's reliance on external and foreign exchange denominated debt increased during the 1990s. The reliance on external debt had hovered at around 30 per cent until 1993, but suddenly jumped from 29.4 per cent in 1993 to 36.2 per cent in 1996. Focusing on just the non-bank sector, mainly consisting of the industrial sector and non-deposit taking finance companies, reliance on external debt had decreased from 28.6 per cent in 1990 to 24.2 per cent in 1993, but suddenly turned upwards to 33.2 per cent in 1996. Taking onshore foreign exchange debt into consideration, the private sector's reliance on total foreign exchange debt increased constantly throughout the 1990s until the Indonesian crisis from 44.1 per cent in 1990 to 53.5 per cent in 1996. The corresponding figure for the non-bank sector also reached 51.3 per cent in 1996. Even before the heavy depreciation of the rupiah, the largest share of the funding requirements of the corporate sector was given over to foreign exchange

Table 1.6 Indonesian corporate sector's reliance on external and foreign currency debts (%)

		1990	1991	1992	1993	1994	1995	1996	1997
External debt[a]	Total	31.0	30.3	31.6	29.4	33.8	36.2	36.2	51.5
	Non-bank sector[c]	28.6	27.4	27.4	24.2	29.5	32.4	33.2	47.9
Foreign	Total	44.1	45.4	46.7	47.6	50.8	53.2	53.5	70.9
currency debt[b]	Non-bank sector[c]	42.1	43.1	43.4	43.7	47.6	50.4	51.3	68.7

Source: Bank Indonesia.

Notes
a External debt reliance = external debt/total debt.
b Foreign currency debt reliance = foreign currency debt/total debt.
c Corporate sector + non-bank finance company.

debt. In short, these ratios prove that the accumulation of the corporate sector's foreign exchange debt accelerated during the period.

This heavy reliance on offshore markets and foreign exchange debt left the Indonesian economy extremely vulnerable to external shocks, such as Latin American-type crises involving a sudden shift in the direction of capital flows. Whether the Indonesian government recognized the situation or not, such a heavy reliance on external and foreign exchange debt by the private sector left the Indonesian financial structure fragile and unstable and placed limits on the country's financial autonomy. That is to say, Indonesian policy makers were forced to respond to the requests of offshore private financiers who controlled mobile capital and had the power to inflict a major financial crisis on the country.

Furthermore, these two reliance indicators (offshore markets and foreign exchange debt) suggest that Indonesia faced increasing risk of crisis during the 1990s.[15] In the case of Indonesia, most external finance was obtained from bank loans rather than portfolio investment. However, offshore bank loans differ from domestic bank loans provided under heavily relationship-oriented bank-based financial systems. Offshore bank loans are money from the market-based financial world, and offshore financiers do not hesitate to make simple judgements based on risk–return calculations. In addition, technically, even long-term bank loans can be easily converted into short-term claims under currency crises through breach of covenant provisions triggering an acceleration of debt repayment.[16] Such technical provisions put unmanageable repayment pressure on Indonesian borrowers and caused a sudden reversal of offshore bank money during the Indonesian crisis. The emphasis that some observers place on the distinction between short- and long-term credits is therefore not warranted.

If this risk potential increases to a certain level, mobile capital investors (including offshore banks) become extremely sensitive to any negative information regarding their investments and how other investors judge the information.[17] The expectation and perception of other investors' opinions start to play an important role. Therefore, their actions tend to go into one direction and this causes a sudden reversal of capital flows and contagion to other countries.

Instruments, markets and players

As discussed earlier, the Indonesian corporate sector played a critical role in external debt accumulation in the 1990s. The most important period for offshore fund raising activities was the 3 years from 1994 to the first half of 1997, and funds were mostly obtained through loans. Loans outstanding in 1994 totalled US$20.6 billion or 84 per cent of private sector debt. The corresponding figures for 1995 and 1996 were US$28.1 billion and 84 per cent, and US$34.7 billion and 82 per cent.[18] This period corresponds to the investment boom in Indonesia. A range of investors rushed in to take advantage of a variety of investment opportunities. However, emerging market portfolio investors generally prefer equity over debt instruments, such as bonds, because they put more priority on upside gain from the investments rather than downside hedge. Therefore, except for a few top business groups, such as the Salim Group, the Sinar Mas Group and the Astra Group, most companies could not access the bond market and therefore relied on offshore bank loans for debt finance.[19]

Offshore commercial banks generally understood that it would be impossible to execute their interests in pledged collateral in Indonesia such as land, buildings and machinery because of the poor quality of the legal system. They therefore concentrated on so-called *blue chip companies* belonging to leading business groups and provided them with essentially unsecured loans.[20] Moreover, during the finance boom that began in 1994, the amount of funding required increased, reflecting borrowers' investment needs and other uses, such as divesting owners' family holdings. Therefore, offshore syndicated loans involving a consortium of international banks were actively used to respond to the need for larger loans. Leading offshore banks competed fiercely to obtain mandates to arrange syndicated loans. This competition created further opportunities to obtain offshore finance for lower quality Indonesian borrowers.

A variety of Indonesian borrowers actively used syndicated loans to raise funds from 1994 to the first half of 1997. The core syndication market for the Indonesian corporate sector was Singapore, but the financial sector, particularly, banks, tended to go to the Hong Kong market.[21] This is because the majority of leading international commercial banks had their South-East Asia offices in Singapore. Investment banks that arranged FRCD issuance for banks were mainly located in Hong Kong.

Offshore private bankers also directed their lending to high net worth individuals and their family businesses through loans secured by offshore deposits and/or securities. These loans were called 'back-to-back finance'.[22] Facing the fading of the Suharto regime and anticipating an unstable political situation in the post-Suharto era, politically vulnerable Chinese businessmen and politico-bureaucrats had been actively using finance and offshore deposits to evacuate money from Indonesia. The country most committed to South-East Asia, including Indonesia, was Japan. The top lenders to Indonesia's private sector were the leading Japanese commercial banks. European and American banks followed them. However, until the beginning of the 1990s, Japanese banks had mostly directed finance to Indonesian sovereign borrowers (Bank Indonesia for the Republic of Indonesia), top state companies, such as Pertamina and the state banks, and Japanese joint-venture companies. From 1994, Japanese banks aggressively shifted to the private sector, mainly non-financial borrowers. This change in Japanese banks' lending behaviour is one of the key factors that drove the supply side of the Indonesian external debt problem.

The development of Indonesia's speculative financing position during the 1990s

The Indonesian external debt problem was transformed drastically from a public to a private sector issue during the 1990s before the Indonesian crisis. In particular, offshore syndicated loans to non-financial firms between 1994 and the first half of 1997 were the driving force behind this dramatic change. Moreover, the accumulation of external debt by the corporate sector made the Indonesian economy more vulnerable to external shocks as the government placed few restrictions on movements of capital into and out of the country. In sum, the most important characteristic of Indonesia's financial structure during the 1990s, which led to the Indonesian crisis, was the heavily leveraged speculative financing position driven by the corporate sector's external debts.

This situation was in part caused by the liberalization of the financial sector in the 1980s. However, the capital account had already been liberalized in the early 1970s for the Indonesian corporate sector, so in principle they did not need to wait until the 1990s and could have accessed the offshore market before that time. In addition, reliance on the liberalized domestic rupiah market decreased relative to the offshore foreign currency market in the 1990s. Therefore, the rapid accumulation of offshore corporate debt was made possible by changes on the supply as well as on the demand side. On the supply side, overseas banks began to offer larger loans under easier terms to a wider array of Indonesian corporate borrowers.

Concerning the demand side, it is necessary to study changes in Indonesian borrowers' behaviour in order to understand the origins of the external debt problem in the 1990s. Domestic capitalists used their improved access to foreign credits to liquidate their Indonesian assets, and in doing so, they created increasingly unstable and fragile financial conditions in that country. Indonesian capital thus became ever more 'mobile' in response to the policy environment and the needs of specific capitalists.

The primary purpose of this work is to examine the factors that drove the financial structure from hedge to speculative and, thus, the Indonesian capitalist economy from robust to fragile and unstable. The work identifies the factors underlying the boom-to-crisis cycle and emphasizes the endogenous processes within the capitalist economy that generate instability. As a macroeconomic framework, the work builds on Minsky's financial instability hypothesis, which argues that the capitalist economy is inherently unstable. However, this author has modified his essentially Keynesian closed economy model and adapted it to an open and developing economy context. The microeconomic case is supported by evidence from Indonesia's leading business groups and the evolution of their financial activities during the finance boom. Conglomerate-level analysis provides appropriate case material through which the motivations driving the evolution of financial structure from stable to unstable and fragile can be explored, an aspect of Minsky's theory that he himself was not able to explain sufficiently.

2 Minsky's financial instability hypothesis

Interpretation and critical adjustments for the Asian context

This work applies Hyman P. Minsky's financial instability hypothesis, with necessary modifications, to the Indonesian case, the country most affected by the East Asian crisis. The work posits the following basic characteristics of the capitalist economy:

1 The capitalist economy does not rest at equilibrium, but becomes more fragile and unstable;
2 Fragility and instability are endogenously created in economies through the evolution of the financial structure;
3 The fragility and instability of the financial structure originates in the existence of debt, that is, payment commitments;
4 The endogenous process of financial fragility and instability is driven by capitalists' complex motivations and behaviour;
5 Crises occur when the system collapses, that is, when chains of debts can no longer be maintained.

In sum, the work adheres to Minsky's financial instability hypothesis. However, Minsky's theory was developed with the assumption of a closed and advanced economy. The theoretical contribution of this work is to offer critical adjustments, corrections and clarifications to augment Minsky's theory in order to apply it to open and developing economies, such as in the case of Indonesia.

Moreover, the evolution of financial instability in developing countries is further complicated by political factors. Capitalists' motivations and behaviour in these countries are influenced by complex political considerations that often produce decisions that appear irrational to economists. Mainstream economics assumes that capitalists behave rationally. Minsky characterized capitalists as 'profit-seeking' and 'forward-looking', while Keynes used the term 'animal spirits' to describe capitalists' motivations (Keynes 1936; Minsky 1986). While both authors recognize the inadequacy of simple descriptions of capitalists' motivations, they were unable to introduce the role of political factors into the general theoretical argument. This work contributes to the literature on financial instability through an explication of the role of political factors in the specific case of Indonesia's crisis of the 1990s.

This chapter has three objectives. First, existing explanations of the East Asian financial crisis are reviewed and the shortcomings of these approaches are discussed. Second, the chapter sets out the main points of Minsky's financial instability hypothesis. Finally, this work is adapted to the open developing economy context and the implications of the proposed changes to the theory are focused on.

Theorizing the East Asian financial crisis

Prior to surveying Minsky's financial instability hypothesis and applying the theory to Indonesia in the 1990s, this section reviews mainstream explanations of the East Asian financial crisis and analyses their applicability to the crisis in Indonesia. Since the outbreak of the East Asian crisis in 1997, economists have debated various aspects of the crisis and proposed policies to prevent future crises. The literatures address both the nature of the crisis and policy implications.

With regards to the former, most economists agree that the East Asian crisis was not a conventional balance-of-payments crisis. That is to say, the East Asian crisis was a capital rather than current-account crisis. This view is strongly critical of the approach pursued by the IMF at the time, which generally interpreted the crisis as a standard adjustment problem and therefore demanded a sharp increase in interest rates and fiscal contraction during the early stages. These policies had a sharply negative impact on corporate profitability, and thus intensified the crisis (Stiglitz 2002; Wade and Veneroso 1998). In Indonesia, the IMF-endorsed tight monetary policy through high interest rates was unable to defend the value of the rupiah, and instead resulted in an uncontrolled depreciation of the currency. High interest rates sharply increased the funding costs of the corporate sector and created a negative margin problem in the banking sector. Indonesia's case was evidence that the exchange rate could not be an effective policy target for interest rates and base money management during a crisis (Cole and Slade 1998a; Grenville 2000a). Moreover, in Indonesia the IMF demanded the immediate closure of insolvent banks and political concessions from a weakened Suharto regime, both of which increased rather than decreased financial instability in the short period. Supporters of IMF policies stress the necessity of strong medication to stabilize the rapidly deteriorating currency and to control the expanding monetary base in the context of a weak financial sector and external imbalance (Fane 2000b; Goldstein 1998). They explain the ineffectiveness of the IMF policies in terms of the lack of confidence of market participants in the affected countries' structural reforms, political stability, short-term debt work-outs, and therefore future prospects (Goldstein 1998).

Over time, most economists have come to accept the capital account approach. According to this view, improving economic fundamentals in East Asia in the early 1990s and rapidly liberalizing international financial markets encouraged offshore capital to move into the region. This led to huge capital account surpluses and thus to an increase in foreign exchange reserves, stimulating domestic absorption in the form of consumption and investment. The region entered an investment and finance boom. However, accelerated absorption led to inflationary pressure in the domestic economy, and large current account deficits. As long as the capital account remained in surplus, these current account deficits could be sustained. However, a sudden change in offshore capitals' perceptions of the prospects for these economies caused a sharp reversal of capital flows. In addition, a combination of open foreign exchange positions and short-dated maturities on external debt, both products of rapid liberalization in the 1990s, left debtors unable to meet their obligations once the reversal in capital movements had begun. This model generally matches the case of Indonesia. During the 1990s until the crisis occurred, current-account deficits were financed by capital-account surpluses, mainly by private capital inflows. As a result, foreign exchange reserves increased every year. In particular, the current-accounts deficits increased sharply in 1995 and 1996 but were financed by enthusiastic private lenders, with the result that reserve increased to around US$20 billion.

Another key characteristic of the crisis was that it was a private-to-private debt crisis (Kenward 1999; Winters 1999). In the 1990s, the most affected Asian countries had pursued prudent fiscal policies and had maintained public debt at sustainable levels. At the same time, rapid liberalization of financial markets and the Asian economic boom led to the integration of domestic and international financial markets and facilitated huge capital flows between offshore private capital providers and onshore private capital recipients. This situation was totally different from traditional patterns of capital flows in emerging Asia, which were mainly sovereign-to-sovereign and private-to-sovereign. In Indonesia, observers tracking the normal set of macroeconomic indicators failed to predict the crisis (Kenward 1999, pp.73–9). The government maintained a balanced-budget policy and prudently controlled state-related external debt. In 1996, the government actually reduced its external debt. However, rapidly accumulating external private debt was generating instability in the domestic economy.

In terms of problem sectors in East Asia, most economists focus on the banking sector, which had accumulated short-term foreign currency debt prior to the crisis. This sector is generally viewed as suffering from a double mismatch, that is, a mismatch of both currency positions and maturity profiles between investments and debts (Yoshitomi and Staff of ADB Institute 2003). From this perspective, the East Asian crisis was a banking sector crisis, and in some cases this view is linked to financial liberalization and the absence of adequate regulation and supervision (Furman and Stiglitz 1998). From the perspective of bank governance, this model is relevant to Indonesia. Bad debt, which was accumulated due to the poor and politically distorted enforcement and supervision, deepened the financial crisis in Indonesia (Cole and Slade 1998a,b; Enoch *et al.* 2003). However, from the perspective of the accumulation of external debt, the arguments to a large extent apply to Thailand and Korea, but do not fully explain the case of Indonesia. Here the non-bank sector was the locus of the external debt problem, as explained in Chapter 1.

If these can be considered the proximate causes of the crisis, economists have also debated the ultimate causes. Four approaches have been put forward in this context. The East Asian crisis has been alternately viewed as:

1   A short-term foreign currency debt problem;
2   A result of fixed or pegged exchange rate systems;
3   A result of financial liberalization;
4   A problem of moral hazard and crony capitalism.

The first set of arguments focus on: (i) short-term external debt; (ii) unhedged foreign currency debt and (iii) the double mismatch (i.e. both short-term and unhedged foreign currency debt). One group of economists focuses on the short-term debt accumulated in the affected countries' banking sectors, which was then used for domestic long-term finance (Furman and Stiglitz 1998). As Fisher argues in his debt-deflation theory, this mismatch of maturity profiles between investments and debt, the urgent need for cash to fulfil payment commitments and the liquidation of investments pushes down asset prices and forces debtors into insolvency (Fisher 1933). This group also considers the sharp depreciation of the affected countries' currencies to be a by-product of the reversal of short-term capital flows. Compared to the Mexican crisis in 1993, the ratio of short-term debt to foreign exchange reserves at the onset of the Indonesian crisis was much higher (Kenward 1999). In addition, around 40 per cent of the Indonesia's private sector's external debt was short-term (INDRA 1998a). As Minsky also explains, the mismatch of cash flows, due to large short-term payment commitments, created a fragile financial structure and finally led to the inevitable breakdown of cash-flow chains, that is, to a crisis.

Other economists stress the accumulation of unhedged foreign currency debt as the primary cause of the crisis, and argue that corporate insolvency resulting from unhedged foreign currency liabilities brought down the banking system. In this version, the behaviour of debtors is often seen as part of a larger moral hazard problem, in which borrowers intentionally maintained open foreign exchange positions assuming that the exchange rate would be kept stable (Yoshitomi and Staff of ADB Institute 2003). One of the empirical studies in Chapter 5 shows that during the finance boom in Indonesia, the difference between funding costs for unhedged foreign currency debts and those for rupiah debts (i.e. cost savings) gave Indonesian borrowers strong incentives to take foreign currency loans without hedging their positions. This also provided opportunities to enthusiastic offshore lenders to pump funds into Indonesia. As a result, a vulnerable financial structure resulting from speculatively unhedged foreign exchange positions emerged during the finance boom in Indonesia.

Arguments focusing on fixed or pegged exchange rate systems as the primary cause of the crisis appear in two versions. In the first, fixed or pegged exchange rate systems grant offshore fund providers and recipients an implicit exchange rate guarantee allowing them to socialize the risks of overseas borrowing.

These systems accelerated the accumulation of unhedged external debt in the context of an open capital account. This view is typically supplemented by the assumption of moral hazard among fund users, who failed to manage their foreign exchange risks. However, these writers pay less attention to the problem of moral hazard among fund providers who made foreign currency loans available to local borrowers on increasingly attractive terms. The other version is that fixed or pegged exchange rate systems and limited foreign exchange reserves induced speculative attacks against the affected countries' currencies according to the conventional currency crisis model based on the familiar trilemma theorem (Furman and Stiglitz 1998, pp.23–32; Krugman and Obstfeld 2000, pp.712–14).

In Indonesia, the crawling peg system was fundamental to the rise of unhedged foreign currency borrowing. Assuming that the government was committed to the currency system, Indonesian borrowers and offshore lenders aggressively assumed foreign exchange risks. Both Indonesian borrowers and offshore lenders shared the benefits of the implicit exchange rate guarantee through unhedged foreign currency loans (as analysed in Chapter 5), and thus socialized foreign exchange risks. Nevertheless, in reality in Indonesia the availability of foreign exchange hedging tools, such as BI (Bank Indonesia) swaps, was limited. Moreover, Indonesian business groups had huge funding needs for that could not be met by domestic lenders at costs comparable to overseas debt. The business groups had no option but to acquire unhedged foreign currency debt, which were from this perspective both evidence of moral hazard and a necessary evil. In the event, the government's decision to allow the rupiah to float on 14 August 1997 derailed domestic borrowers, leading to panic among both Indonesian borrowers and their offshore creditors.

A third group regards financial liberalization as the ultimate cause of the crisis. Liberalization of financial markets, which started with the end of the Bretton Woods system in 1971, created a new international financial system characterized by highly liquid capital being traded in huge volumes in an ever-expanding complex of markets for an evolving portfolio of instruments (Eatwell and Taylor 2000, p.5). Liberalization resulted in the global integration of financial markets and rendered legal jurisdictions irrelevant. Under the liberalized system, national economies cannot help but take on financial risks outside of their jurisdictions, and the huge scale and high speed of capital flows have caused financial turmoil and repeated crises all over the world. In other words, the new system is highly volatile, subject to short-term fluctuations, long-term swings and is susceptible to contagion (Eatwell and Taylor 2000, pp.5–6).

Mainstream economists counter that as long as the benefits of liberalization are greater than the costs, liberalization should be pursued. Furthermore, they argue that liberalization cannot be reversed and is now a basic condition of current and future financial arrangements (Eichengreen 1999). Yet the view of financial liberalization as a force of nature and therefore inevitable contributed to the poorly planned and implemented liberalization policies of the 1990s. These policies in turn created the crisis-prone financial conditions in the Asian high-debt economy (Wade and Veneroso 1998).[1] In the 1980s and 1990s, based on the mainstream view and with the support of multilateral organizations (e.g. the IMF, World Bank and World Trade Organization (WTO)), Asian countries radically liberalized not only the real sector of their economies but also their financial sectors. However, since the occurrence of the East Asian crisis, a number of economists and political economists have contended that liberalization was the main cause of the crisis. They identify four problems associated with liberalization, namely:

1   The sequence of liberalization was incorrect;
2   It was too rapid;
3   It was not accompanied by the development of appropriate financial institutions;
4   It was distorted by undesirable political interference.

Incorrect sequencing refers to the opening of the capital account prior to the establishment of monitoring systems for cross-border capital flows and policies to limit disruption of the capital account. The recommended order is real sector liberalization, followed by the removal of interest rate ceilings and credit allocation targets, the establishment of capital flow monitoring systems and finally capital account liberalization (Eichengreen 2000b; McKinnon and Pill 1997; Yoshitomi and Staff of ADB Institute 2003).[2]

The core concept is that liberalization expands income opportunities and increases expected profits. If the capital account is opened prematurely, consumption will be fuelled by overseas borrowing. In this model, banks play a central role in accumulating offshore borrowing and in speculation. Furthermore, this model is combined with moral hazard among investors whose expectations are biased upwards. Banks tend to take on excess risk and over-lend, and thus send falsely optimistic signals to the non-bank sector, that is, borrowers, leading to 'manias', and ultimately to 'panics' and 'crashes' (Kindleberger 1978; McKinnon and Pill 1997).

From this perspective, Indonesia liberalized its financial market in the wrong sequence. The country opened its capital accounts in 1971 and introduced radical liberalization policies, including banking deregulation, in the 1980s. Indonesia had the most liberalized financial market in East Asia at the beginning of the 1990s. On the other hand, as explained in Chapter 1, the core problem for Indonesia's financial crisis was the accumulation of external debt in the corporate sector rather than corporate sector domestic debt or external debt in the banking sector. The problem was therefore directly related to capital-account liberalization but not to banking deregulation. Furthermore, during the more than 25 years during which Indonesia maintained an open capital account before the East Asian crisis, Indonesia had experienced a large number of serious financial disturbances but never a full-blown crisis.[3] Therefore, sequencing was probably not a major cause of the financial crisis in Indonesia.

Sequencing also relates to the speed of financial liberalization. Even in advanced countries, the development of bona fide financial institutions, such as market rules and regulations and monitoring and supervisory systems, tends to lag behind new financial practices made possible by financial liberalization. This was certainly the case in many East Asian countries in the 1980s and 1990s. In particular, the opening of capital accounts encouraged offshore banks to provide short-term foreign currency loans to the region. The financial authorities often lacked the authority, political will, or both to monitor, supervise and control such activities (Eatwell and Taylor 2000; Furman and Stiglitz 1998; Stiglitz 2002).

In liberalized developing financial markets such as Indonesia, the government had to play an important role in establishing and exercising market governance. In the 1990s, the Indonesian financial authority introduced various market-based controls on banks' financial positions, such as CAR and net open positions, and even direct controls on banks' exposure, such as Legal Lending Limit. However, the authorities struggled to exercise control for both economic and political reasons and a number of violations occurred in the market. In addition, the authority was unable to exercise effective financial control on the corporate sector, which required huge capital for growth, and in particular external debt. Under liberalized and globalized financial markets lacking appropriate governance structures, rapid financial development occurred during the finance boom in Indonesia, responding to offshore and onshore capitalists' needs, creating the preconditions of the financial crisis (Cole and Slade 1998b).

Political economists have in turn argued that liberalization must be viewed within the specific political context in which it is carried out. They assume that liberalization is good for growth. Political actors with strong vested interests in the pre-liberalized regime often affect the process of liberalization to obtain outcomes more favourable to themselves. As a result, liberalization would fail to improve national welfare and could even increase the risk of a crisis. Political parties in countries like Indonesia took advantage of liberalization to maximize access to rents for political purposes (Haggard 2000; Rosser 2002). In Indonesia in the 1980s, the technocrats aggressively introduced deregulation policies in both the real and financial sectors. Liberalization under the Suharto's patron–client system increased the level of rents to politically connected parties, while the technocrats surrendered existing tools to intervene to maintain stability. In other words, liberalization was an erroneous policy that did not take adequate account of the nature of Indonesia's political system and use and was therefore a 'high-risk strategy that relied heavily on the confidence of domestic and foreign investors' (Pincus and Ramli 1998). As a result, it created an economic structure that was vulnerable to external shocks and increased the intensity of the crisis in Indonesia.

A final group of explanations relates to moral hazard and crony capitalism. These arguments appeal to critics of Asian economic systems, for example, triangular relations among government, industries and banks, industrial policies, family-based business groups and bank-based financial systems. The centrepiece of the arguments is that the accumulation of external debt was made possible by moral hazard and crony capitalism (Krugman 1998a; McKinnon and Pill 1997). Crony capitalism is a negative reinterpretation of the triangular relations among government, industries and banks entailing personal and political connections and favouritism, rather than support for entrepreneurial development. Special business opportunities, monopolistic licences, profit guarantees, subsidies and tax exemptions and easy access to bank credits gave rise to crony or 'ersatz' capitalism (Yoshihara 1999). In addition, industrial policies, directed lending, family-owned business groups, bank-based financial systems and relationship banking provided implicit guarantees and/or safety nets for crony capitalists. The ultimate cause of the East Asian crisis for these authors was the moral hazard and aggressive risk taking by local bank owners with political connections. Banks, bank owners, depositors and political leaders enjoyed a variety of explicit (e.g. deposit insurance) and implicit guarantees (e.g. government bailouts) from government.

In Indonesia, financial activities have always been politicized. The state banks were forced to direct loans to political and well-connected business groups, such as the Suharto family businesses. The loans were used for speculative investments and were often not repaid. Once the financial crisis occurred, it was revealed that the state banks' portfolios were totally laden with non-collectible direct lending to the groups (IBRA 1999). The ineffectiveness of financial governance structures, such as Bank Indonesia regulations and monitoring activities, was also due to politics. Continuing violations of Legal Lending Limits (the exposure ceiling on banks' owners, management members and their businesses) by banks controlled by the leading conglomerates were typical examples. Moral hazard was unchecked in both the corporate and banking sectors and created the precondi-tions for the financial crisis. The failure of initial actions to and the severity of the crisis can be explained as a consequence of politicized financial activities in Indonesia (Cole and Slade 1998a).

Chang, for one, questions the usefulness of such arguments. He makes the important historical point that moral hazard and crony capitalism are not special features of East Asian economies but have been an integral part of the develop-ment of capitalism across the globe (Chang 2000). As Kindleberger has shown the scope for corrupt behaviour increases during periods of economic euphoria (Kindleberger 1978, pp.66–82). Both authors have situated moral hazard and crony capitalism within the historical context of capitalist development across regions and historical periods.

Another problem associated with moral hazard explanations of the East Asian financial crisis is that they tend to focus exclusively on borrowers rather than on lenders. Krugman criticizes bank owners for accepting implicit state guarantees and thereby lending to excessively risky borrowers and projects (Krugman 1998a, p.3, 1998b, p.3). Nevertheless, his criticisms and analysis of moral hazard are mainly directed at bank owners rather than depositors and offshore lenders. In theory, depositors monitor their banks and put pressure on them through the market. However, implicit guarantees by states resulted in a weakening of moni-toring and incentives to shift deposits to safer institutions. In times of crisis, the government cannot help but assume responsibility for guaranteeing deposits in order to maintain the payments system. Post-crisis state policies in Indonesia (as explained in Chapter 10) were typical examples of state imperatives to recover financial stability. The same logic applies to offshore lenders, who accepted the premise that some debtors were 'too big to fail'. In their enthusiasm they failed to incorporate default risks into the returns they required to lend to the region. Empirical studies in Chapter 5 demonstrate offshore lenders' enthusiasm towards Indonesian credit risks during the finance boom.

As subsequent chapters show, these explanations of the East Asian financial crisis are partial, particularly to the extent that they focus on characteristics that are assumed to be specific to East Asian economies. Too much emphasis on the peculiarity of the East Asian crisis led to considerable confusion within economics. In addition, while some explanations are appropriate to Indonesia, many are not. This book maintains that the East Asian crisis, including the financial crisis in Indonesia, was not Asia specific, but rather an episode of boom to bust that has been a common feature of global capitalism. The crisis was not an Asian anomaly in the smooth development of capitalism, but instead an expression of the financial instability that Minsky argues is endemic to capitalism. Based on firm-level data from Indonesia, the book will demonstrate that financial instability emerged endogenously during the finance boom of the 1990s.

Minsky's financial instability hypothesis

The position of Minsky's financial instability hypothesis in economics

Hyman P. Minsky devoted most of his life as an economist to the development of his financial instability hypothesis. The most comprehensive statement of his views can be found in his book: *Stabilizing an unstable economy* (Minsky 1986). His hypothesis seeks to explain the endogenously fragile and unstable nature of capitalist economies by focusing on the financial structure of the economy.

Minsky focuses on the following characteristics of the capitalist economy: capital asset investment by debt finance, chains of payment commitments (i.e. indebtedness), and the profit-seeking and forward-looking nature of capitalists. As is clear from his reinterpretation of Keynes in his book *John Maynard Keynes*, Minsky's point of departure is Keynesian (Minsky 1975). This largely explains his lack of popularity among neoclassical economists, for whom the notions of endogenous instability and the absence of equilibrium are an anathema. Like Keynes, Minsky rejects the theoretical assumption of neoclassical economics that natural forces propel the economy towards equilibrium and that government intervention is therefore unwarranted. On the contrary, he assigns an important role to big government and the lender of last resort to stabilize asset values and profitability in an environment characterized by inherent instability (Minsky 1986, pp.13–67).

Another reason for the general ignorance concerning Minsky among contemporary economists is timing. Minsky put forward his financial instability hypothesis in the 1970s and 1980s as the post-war financial structures, in part designed by

Keynes, collapsed. In 1974, the United States abolished capital controls, and worldwide free capital flows began (Eatwell and Taylor 2000). Ironically, subsequent events have demonstrated the importance of Minsky's financial instability hypothesis, that is to say, the increasingly fragile and unstable nature of financial structures. Governments not only socialized risks, but also introduced expectations and uncertainty into financial systems. The wealth of capitalist economies became merely expectations among capitalists. That is to say, the assets of the balance sheet are a creation of capitalists' imagination, so net worth is merely a hope.[4] Wealth could disappear at any time. Nevertheless, when Minsky was writing, neoclassical economics was in the ascendancy and little attention was paid to the original Keynesian position.[5]

Minsky's financial instability hypothesis, although essentially Keynesian, incorporates Irving Fisher's debt-deflation theory. Fisher is also sceptical regarding equilibrium and sensitive to endogenous disequilibrating forces. For Fisher, 'free cycle (or cyclical tendency)' is 'not forced from outside, but [is] self-generating, operating analogously to a pendulum or wave motion'. He also assumed that once economies move beyond certain limits, they cannot return to equilibrium and could descend into panic and crash (Fisher 1933, pp.338–9).[6]

Furthermore, Fisher considers both over-indebtedness (the 'debt diseases') and deflation (the 'price-level diseases' or 'dollar diseases') as the dominant factors among related variables in booms and depressions. He concludes that in the absence of over-indebtedness and deflation, other disturbances are powerless to cause severe crises.[7] For Fisher, it is the combination and sequencing of debt disease and the subsequent price-level disease that causes crises (Fisher 1933, pp.341–4).

In particular, the 'great paradox' and 'chief secret' of great depressions is that if over-indebtedness is great enough at the beginning of deflation, 'the liquidation of debts cannot keep up with the fall of prices', and 'the liquidation defeats itself'. In other words, 'the very effort of individuals to lessen their burden of debts increases it, because of the mass effect of the stampede to liquidate in swelling each dollar owed'. Thus, 'the more the debtors pay, the more they owe' (Fisher 1933, p.344). Finally, the process of extensive financial disintermediation and disappearance of assets is accelerated. This is the most important phase of panics and crashes after booms in Fisher's debt-deflation theory.[8]

By way of contrast, mainstream economists do not consider the devastating power of debt. Modern finance theory argues that, in the absence of bankruptcy costs, corporate income taxation and/or other market imperfections (e.g. under-developed financial markets, insufficient information disclosure systems and inefficient legal systems) the value of the firm is independent of its financial structure (Modigliani and Miller 1958, 1961, 1963; Stiglitz 1969), that is to say, the value of the firm is determined by real assets (debit side of the balance sheet) and cannot be changed by financial transactions (credit side of the balance sheet). However, the history of crises shows that the realized value of real assets through emergency liquidation falls far below the rationally expected value listed in balance sheets. Debt has the power to determine the value of the firm's and the economy's assets through changes in capitalists' views of future cash flows. This work supports Fisher and Minsky's views on debt.

The definition of the capitalist economy and the margin of safety in the financial instability hypothesis

Hyman P. Minsky described the capitalist economy as a 'set of interrelated balance sheets and income statements'. Profit-seeking and forward-looking capitalists invest in long-life and expensive capital assets through financing by future payment commitments, that is, exchanging present money for future money.[9] As a result, the balance sheets and income statements of economic units that comprise the economy are intricately connected through cash flows, and thereby a sophisticated financial structure is formed consisting of complex chains of payment commitments and financial assets. In short, Minsky viewed the capitalist economy as a system of complicated aggregates of cash-flow chains (Minsky 1991, p.11, 1992a, pp.12–13, 1993, p.14).

Therefore, the capitalist economy is characterized by its financial structure, which is determined by debt and cash-flow positions. Stability or coherence is required to validate the debt liabilities of the financial structure, that is, fulfilling payment commitments. The validity of debt liability ensures the maintenance of a system of borrowing and lending, and validity is measured by a variety of 'margins of safety'. Minsky used two of these and defined them as follows: (i) the excess of anticipated cash flows from asset ownership or participation in income production over the cash flows committed by the liability structure and (ii) the excess of the market or the pledge value of assets over the value of liabilities, which can require the payment of some principle amount (Minsky 1991, p.12, 1992a, p.13, 1993, p.15).[10]

The first margin of safety is a current cash-flow measurement at any point of payments in the future. This tests whether or not the future cash flow from capital and financial assets is sufficient to meet payment commitments. These are determined by the financial structure, that is, past payment commitments (and subject to future interest fluctuations in the case of floating rate debt). Therefore, movements in this margin of safety stem from changes in forecasted future cash flows, which investors and financiers imagine as market valuation. Furthermore, this continuously and significantly fluctuates due to the interplay between outcomes (i.e. realized financial performance, such as cash flows), reconciliation with previous valuations and changing market valuations.[11]

The second margin of safety is the net of the disposal value of capital and financial assets and total payment commitments. This tests whether or not debtors can fulfil their payment commitments by disposing of assets or obtaining finance through pledging them when creditors require immediate payment. In Minsky's framework, this margin of safety is the same as the net present value of future cash flows from capital and financial assets and total payment commitments by the discounted cash-flow method.[12] However, this also reflects capitalists' expectations of forecasted future cash flows from capital and financial assets, that is, the numerator of the discounted cash-flow formula and future interest movements, meaning the denominator as a discount factor of the formula and a part of the numerator as a cash-flow component.

In this way, the margin of safety is an indicator imagined by profit-seeking and forward-looking capitalists of market valuations of future prospects. In general terms, the margin of safety is imagined by capitalists in the context of specific institutional frameworks.[13] Capitalists' imagination is also shaped by their views about what everyone in the market believes what everyone else believes, that is, Keynes' metaphor of financial markets as a 'beauty contest' (Eatwell and Taylor 2000, pp.12–15; Keynes 1936, p.156). Unavoidable changes in forecasts of income and interest rates in a positive or negative direction affect the margin of safety and create instability in the financial structure. Positive signs in the margin of safety stimulate the spirits of profit seekers and accelerate their investments in capital and financial assets through speculative financing. The financial structure thereby evolves from robust to speculative. On the other hand, negative movements in the margin of safety awaken the risk-averse nature of capitalists and prompt them to evacuate their investments and financial assets. Fulfilment of payment commitments occurs and the chain of payment commitments starts to unwind. If the unwinding of these occurs at the same time and on a huge scale, the economy is pushed into crisis as Fisher explained in his debt-deflation theory (Fisher 1933). A sharp drop in asset prices results from fire sales to fulfill payment commitments and insolvency spreads throughout the economy. The capitalist economy is thus always governed by uncertainty.

As Minsky stressed, 'A capitalist economy is inherently flawed because its investment and financial processes introduce endogenous destabilizing forces' (Minsky 1986, p.288). He inherited the traditional view of the business cycle and economic stability as the natural, inherent and endogenous consequence of profit-motivated activities in complex economies with sophisticated financial structures as developed by Marx, Schumpeter, Kalecki and Keynes. That is to say, Minsky's capitalist economy is fragile and unstable with internal disequilibrating forces and an endogenously developed, complex financial structure. The economy does not always return to equilibrium as in classical, neoclassical and monetarist theories and stability (or periods of tranquillity) is merely transitory in the modern capitalist economy. The dynamics of the capitalist economy alternate between two ultimate forms: booms and crises.

The methodology of the financial instability hypothesis – the cash-flow approach

The lack of synchronization between cash inflows and outflows due to the mismatch between income from debt-financed capital assets and debt-service payments plays a central role in Minsky's financial instability hypothesis. Minsky states, 'To analyse how financial commitments affect the economy, it is necessary to look at economic units in terms of their cash flows. The cash-flow approach looks at all units – be they households, corporations, state and municipal governments, or even government – as if they were banks' (Minsky 1986, p.198). He considers the potential for a break in the chain of cash flows as a source of the fragility and instability in the economy and the most critical factor in depression or crisis.[14] He therefore focused on financial intermediaries, represented by banks, as the economic unit possessing the most leveraged balance sheets and most mismatched cash-flows. Thus, banks have the potential to disrupt the cash-flow chains of the economy.

In order to 'look at economic units in terms of cash flows', Minsky introduced the following three steps. First, he categorizes cash flows into three types, 'income cash flows', 'balance sheet cash flows' and 'portfolio cash flows' (Minsky 1986, pp.200–1). Second, he describes three types of economic unit: 'hedge-financing units', 'speculative financing units' and 'Ponzi financing units' (Minsky 1986, pp.206–8). Finally, he characterizes the economy in two ways: an 'economy with a robust financial structure' and an 'economy with a fragile and unstable financial structure' (Minsky 1986, pp.203–4). Stability depends on which type of financing unit is more significant. In this cash-flow approach, Minsky applies a corporate accounting methodology to economics and thereby bridges micro- and macroeconomic analyses.[15]

With regards to the first step, Minsky's three types of cash flows are similar to those of corporate accounting: 'cash flows from operating activities', 'cash flows from financing activities', and 'cash flows from investment activities', respectively.[16] According to Minsky's definitions, income cash flows are 'results from the process of production, such as wages and salaries'; 'the payments from one stage of production, and trade to another'; and, 'gross profits after taxes of business' (Minsky 1986, p.200). That is to say, Minsky adopted the Kalecki-Levy view of profits as the most important component of income cash flows.[17] He therefore often uses 'income' and/or 'gross income' for income cash flows.[18] Balance sheet cash flows are 'mandated by existing and inherited liabilities' and 'determined by debt contracts'. Moreover, he broke down balance sheet cash flows into the following types: 'dated cash flows' (e.g. scheduled payments such as instalments and bonds), 'demand cash flows' (e.g. deposits) and 'contingent cash flows' (e.g. guarantees) (Minsky 1986, p.200). Portfolio cash flows are 'results of transactions in which capital and financial assets change hands' and 'the outcome of decisions to acquire or to sell assets or to put new liabilities into circulation' (Minsky 1986, pp.200–4). A significant difference between Minsky's cash flows and those in standard corporate accounting is that he included new financial debts in portfolio cash flows, while standard corporate accounting categorizes new financial debts in cash flows from financing activities.[19]

With regards to the second step, Minsky grouped economic units into three types: 'hedge-financing units', 'speculative financing units' and 'Ponzi financing units' (Minsky 1986, pp.200–8, 335–41, 1991, p.14, 1992c, pp.7–8). By his categorization of cash flows, he defined hedge-financing units as 'units whose realized and expected income cash flows are sufficient to meet all payment commitments on the outstanding liability of it' (Minsky 1986, p.203). Thus, in hedge-financing units, cash inflows from returns on capital assets and/or sales of capital assets (not disposals through portfolio liquidation but in the ordinary course of business) are more than cash outflows for debt servicing (interest and principal payments) over a certain short period. This unit does not need to rollover or refinance any part of payment commitments to make a position. On the other hand, in speculative financing units, 'balance sheet cash flows from the units will be larger than expected income receipts, so that the only way they can be met is by rolling over (or even increasing) debt' (Minsky 1986, p.203). In other words, this unit has enough cash inflows to meet interest payment commitments but not principal repayments (but may be able to pay down part of these commitments) (Minsky 1991, p.14). Speculative financing units carry a refinancing risk at the payment date of debt obligations and need time to pay down the entire debt through income cash flows. If these units are required to fulfil payment commitments on contracts falling due, they have to use portfolio cash flows, that is, dispose of capital and financial assets. Ponzi financing units are speculative financing units but their financial positions are even more precarious than standard speculative financing units.[20] These units have to increase debt in order to pay debt service, as they do not have sufficient cash inflows to meet even interest payment commitments and cannot help but capitalize interest payments. They can never pay down principal whatever the payment period granted to them. The increase of debt is accelerated because they have to pay interest on capitalized interest. These units generally expect capital gains on invested capital assets before entering into finance. However, during the East Asian crisis, for example, the depreciation of home currencies drastically increased unhedged foreign currency (mainly US$) denominated offshore loans in terms of the home currencies, and, thereby, a number of Asian companies, which did not have sufficient foreign currency cash inflows, unintentionally emerged as Ponzi financing units. This is a case of Ponzi financing units emerging from speculative financing units due to externally driven events.

Minsky's third step is to characterize the capitalist economy in terms of two types of financial structure, an 'economy with a robust financial structure' and an 'economy with a fragile/unstable financial structure'. The characteristics of these are defined by the relative significance of the earlier mentioned three types of economic units in the economy. In an economy with a robust financial structure, hedge-financing units are dominant. The typical example is a merchant economy, that is, an economy in which trading represents a dominant share of economic activity, and income cash flows (or operating cash flows) from merchant sales immediately match repayments of working capital used for inventory purchases. In an economy with a fragile/unstable financial structure, speculative and Ponzi financing units are dominant. The economies always face the necessity of refinancing and/or new financing as was typical throughout Asia during the 1990s economic and finance boom.

In addition to these three steps, as Fisher argues in his debt-deflation theory, the relative increase of payment commitments against equity in the financial structure (leveraging), also changes an economy from a robust one to a speculative and Ponzi structure. Minsky does not analyse the relationship between the degree of leverage and the instability of the economy. However, he agrees that leveraging is also a critical factor for economic and financial instability, together with the mismatch of cash inflows and outflows (Minsky 1992a, p.16).[21] Furthermore, Minsky clearly treats equity, which reduces leverage, as a factor that improves the margin of safety of economic units (Minsky 1991, p.12).[22]

Based on the cash-flow approach, Minsky developed his closed market model following Keynes (Figure 2.1). His model simply assumes that 'financial institutions stand between firms and households' (Minsky 1993, p.13). Banks, speculative financing units, collect (short-term) deposits from households and provide long-term finance to non-financial companies (hedge-financing units), which invest in capital assets (Minsky 1993, p.13). Minsky expected banks to play a key role in the evolving financial structure of the economy from robust to fragile and unstable. Furthermore, this model requires normal credit curbs and term structure of yield curbs. Higher risks require higher interest (or margin) payables, and long-term interest rates are higher than short-term interest rates in order to allow the economy to function smoothly (Minsky 1986, pp.210–11). On the other hand, as Minsky focused on the United States in his empirical work, he did not develop an open market model.[23] However, several scholars have applied Minsky's closed market model to the open economy in order to analyse financial crises in developing countries (Arestis and Glickman 2002; Kregel 1998).

Finally, Minsky asserts the following fundamental problem of the financial instability hypothesis: the evolution of an economy from robust financial structures to fragile and unstable ones is an internal dynamic of the capitalist economy. In other words, financial instability is linked to 'the relative importance of the income, balance sheet and portfolio cash flows in an economy' and debts and cash-flow positions of the economy (Minsky 1986, p.203). Furthermore, when chains of cash flows in an economy with fragile and unstable financial structures are broken, the pressure of payment commitments forces the economy to dispose of assets by deep discounting, thereby reducing overall asset prices as in Fisher's debt-deflation theory (Fisher 1933). Minsky also shared this view in his financial instability hypothesis (Minsky 1993, p.16).

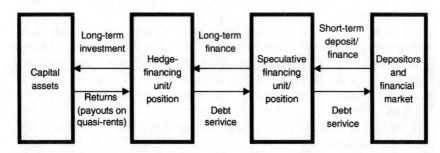

Figure 2.1 Minsky's closed market model.

The internal dynamics of the economy – evolving financial structure

Minsky's financial instability hypothesis was built upon long-standing arguments regarding business cycles and economic dynamics. He considered his work to be an elaboration of Keynes's *General Theory*, including his view of the economy as a complex, time-dependent system which is endogenously unstable, and the necessity of institutions to achieve stability.[24] In addition, Minsky maintains the necessity of preserving asset values in depression and crisis as Fisher argues in his debt-deflation theory. Minsky is strongly opposed to business cycle arguments that emphasize the endogenous stability of the economy and exogenous distur-bances to stability as developed by equilibrium theorists. He stresses that equilibrium theory fails to explain how financial crises emerge out of the normal functioning of the economy.

Minsky's financial instability hypothesis asserts that unstable financial and economic conditions are the ordinary course of capitalist economies, and that the roots of instability are internal to capitalism. Endogenous disequilibrating forces and evolving financial structures are inseparable from capitalism. The following statement clearly summarizes the essence of his financial instability hypothesis and indicates the policy implications of his approach:

> The major flaw of our type of economy is that it is unstable. This instability is not due to external stocks or to the incompetence or ignorance of policy makers. Instability is due to the internal processes of our type of economy. The dynamics of a capitalist economy which has complex, sophisticated, and evolving financial structures leads to the development of conditions conducive to incoherence – to runaway inflations or deep depressions. But incoherence need not be fully realized because institutions and policy can contain the thrust to instability. We can, so to speak, stabilize instability.
>
> (Minsky 1986, pp.9–10)

Minsky seeks endogenous disequilibrating forces in capitalists' profit-seeking or self-interested behaviour. Capitalists maximize profits by investing in long-life capital and financial assets through short-term finance. In sum, Minsky finds endogenous disequilibrating forces in the exchange between short-term and long-term money for profit maximization, that is, making on the carry. Naturally, he focuses on financial intermediaries, particularly banks, as model economic units that are most leveraged and speculative among all economic units and therefore a driving force in the change of the financial structure of the economy.

These endogenous disequilibrating forces drive through the evolution of the financial structure under capitalism and the creation of fragility and instability in the economy. In Minsky's cash-flow approach, financial evolution or evolving financial structures consists of the shift from a robust structure, where hedge financing is dominant, to a fragile/unstable structure, where speculative and Ponzi financing are dominant. This shift is not driven by exogenous forces but is the result of the internal dynamics of the capitalist economy.

Protracted periods of 'good times', during which the margin of safety constantly improves, induce capitalists to increase debt-financed investments and the proportion of short-term finance. If the margin of safety sharply improves over a short period, such *good times* can be called 'booms'. During these periods, capitalists are unconcerned about rolling over outstanding debts or even borrowing for interest payables, and speculative financing units take on riskier finance. Thus, according to the financial instability hypothesis, the financial structure evolves from robust to fragile over a period in which the economy does well.

If outcomes, in other words, if the realized margin of safety is worse than prospects or the projected margin of safety, capitalists put a halt to the evolution of the financial structure. Furthermore, if the liability structure cannot be serviced by the cash flows that capital assets can generate, the rejection of debt rollover, the unwinding of chains of cash flows, the collapse of asset prices and other downward pressures emerge. Debtors of speculative and Ponzi financing units are forced to 'make positions by selling their positions'. The result can be a sharp fall in asset values and large-scale insolvency, as Fisher argues in his debt-deflation theory. These situations are typical 'crises', which Minsky characterized as the 'inability of units to refinance their positions through normal channels' (Minsky 1986).

Minsky further developed his theory of evolving financial structures by reflecting on the institutional development of financial markets in the 1990s. In particular, with regards to the development of interrelations between finance and firms, he characterized the capitalist economy as consisting of the following four stages: (i) commercial capitalism; (ii) finance capitalism; (iii) managerial capitalism and (iv) money manager capitalism (Minsky 1992a, pp.30–2). Under commercial capitalism, trading activities have a dominant position in the economy. Financing activities are mainly the provision of short-term working capital by commercial banks, and borrowers are not always required to be corporate entities. This short-term finance is easily repaid by cash inflow from sales of inventories. The financial structure is robust with hedge financing. Under finance capitalism, capital-intensive production and investment finance for capital assets dominate, and finance requires borrowers to be corporations. Founder shareholders and/or financial institutions occupy a dominant position in the ownership (both equity and debt, that is, financial structure) of the corporate sector. In the 1990s, non-Japan Asian countries, including Indonesia, were still at this stage. Under managerial capitalism, the ownership of companies is widely dispersed to individuals due to the increase in household income and wealth. Management of companies is increasingly independent of shareholders, so management and ownership are separated. Under money manager capitalism, the ownership of companies and even underlying capital assets are more widely distributed than in the earlier-mentioned third stage, managerial capitalism. Furthermore, ownership changes into more sophisticated forms, such as mutual funds, pension funds and securitized products. Throughout the above development process, the financial structure of the economy, including relations between finance and firms, becomes extremely complex.

Finally, Minsky proposes two main 'thwarting systems' for stabilizing the instability of the economy as the financial structure evolves: big government and the lender-of-last-resort. He expects big government to 'put a high floor under the economy's potential downward spiral', that is, to maintain profits through its 'income and employment effect', 'budget effect' and 'portfolio effect' (Minsky 1986, pp.13–37). He also expects central banks, as lenders-of-last-resort, to sustain asset values through purchasing assets on a large scale and by simultaneously liquidating assets to fulfil payment commitments (Minsky 1986, pp.38–67). From the utilization of these two basic policies, Minsky intended to control economic fluctuations.

In this way, profit-seeking and forward-looking private sectors transform an initially robust financial structure into a fragile and unstable one. In the process of financial evolution, the margin of safety, which is imagined by capitalists through their economic calculations based on their uncertain future prospects, gives signals that lead to the development of financial relations to instability and to its realization. The financial evolution of the economy leads to the serious threats of financial and economic instability, which are deep-seated characteristics of capitalist economies with sophisticated financial systems. Therefore, Minsky asserts that the economy needs institutional solutions to reduce instability.

Adjustments, corrections and clarifications of Minsky's model in the context of Asian economies in the 1990s

Minsky's financial instability hypothesis is built on a closed economy model and sought empirical support from large developed economies with advanced financial systems, mainly the United States. To apply Minsky's financial instability hypothesis to the Asian economies of the 1990s, in particular to the East Asian crisis, it is necessary to adapt the model to open economies with less advanced financial systems. Furthermore, several of his assumptions must be corrected and clarified in order to apply the model to the dynamic Asian economies during the finance and economic boom. The main adjustments, corrections and clarifications are:

1 The importance of leveraging of financial positions as well as the mismatch between cash inflows and outflows;
2 Foreign exchange risk related to unhedged liability positions as a potential negative cash-flow factor;
3 Liberalization policies, that is, openness, as an institutional driving factor in financial evolution;
4 Offshore financiers as mobile capital suppliers to domestic economic units and as drivers of financial evolution;
5 The non-bank corporate sector, which invests in capital assets through debt finance, as speculative and Ponzi financing units; and,
6 Liquidity preference and other complex motivations as well as profit-maximizing and forward-looking behaviour patterns as disequilibrating forces.

The dominance of speculative financing units and the problem of leverage

As discussed earlier, Minsky does not examine the relationships between the degree of leverage and the instability of the economy. However, it is clear that he considers the inducement to increase indebtedness as an important driver in creating financial fragility, together with the mismatch between cash inflows and outflows. The leverage, which is defined as the relative size of indebtedness against equity or cash inflows, determines the magnitude of financial fragility.[25] In the debt-deflation theory, Fisher also argues that the relative increase of payment commitments against equity in the financial structure, that is, leveraging, also changes an economy from robust to unstable. It is necessary to introduce explicitly the concept of leverage in Minsky's model.

In addition to that, in the modern capitalist economy, hedge-financing units are of very limited importance, while speculative financing units are dominant. Ponzi financing units often emerge as *manias* during booms, such as heavily debt-financed real estate and stock investments, and/or the deteriorated form of speculative financing units in crises. These units are more common than hedge-financing units but less so than speculative financing units (Kindleberger 1978). Indonesia, a developing capitalist economy, aggressively accumulated debt capital for growth in the 1990s and speculative financing units assumed a dominant position in the economy. The East Asian crisis and the ensuing collapse of the Suharto regime changed these units into Ponzi financing units. The focus must be on speculative financing units as the dominant, standard economic units in the modern capitalist economy.

Realistically, the deepening of the dominant position of speculative financing units, that is, the acceleration from moderately to heavily leveraged speculative financing units, also drives the process of evolution from a robust to a fragile financial structure. Aside from the mismatch between cash inflows and outflows, which Minsky used to characterize speculative financing units, the leverage also plays a critical role in this process. As a model explicitly introducing the concept of leverage, we can split Minsky's speculative financing units into two: moderately and highly leveraged speculative financing units. The latter can be interpreted as the real speculative financing unit that Minsky intends to define.

When speculative financing units have to fulfil their payment commitments by liquidating assets during crises, the pre-crisis leverage decides the solvency of the units. As Fisher's debt-deflation theory and Kindleberger's empirical studies indicate, panics in crises lead to crashes of asset prices (Fisher 1933; Kindleberger 1978). On the other hand, the payment commitments remain as they are contracted despite the crash.[26] As a result, crashes of asset prices squeeze the net worth of economic units and increase the post-crisis leverage. Crises thus have immense power to drive up the leverage of economic units by squeezing net worth. The post-crisis leverage must be sharply higher than the pre-crisis leverage and may reach uncontrollable levels.[27] However, if the pre-crisis leverage is low, the post-crisis leverage may remain at controllable levels. Therefore, the pre-crisis leverage is the determining factor concerning the solvency of speculative financing units. Even in cases in which speculative financing units are dominant in the economy, if the pre-crisis leverage is low the fragility of the economy can be minimized.

As Minsky and Fisher stress, the irrational liquidation of assets at deep discounts to fulfil payment commitments in crises can be induced by the mismatch problem between cash inflows and outflows. However, the leverage of the units also determines the fragility of the pre-crisis economy and the severity of the crash. In view of the relationship between debt and asset deflation, the leverage may have a larger impact on the fragility of the economy than the mismatch. Moderately leveraged speculative financing units, for which cash inflows and outflows are mismatched, can be successfully restructured after minor adjustments (such as debt rescheduling). The economy dominated by such speculative financing units may not fall into systemic in so far as an irrational asset liquidation process can be avoided.

In sum, the combination of the leverage and the mismatch between cash inflows and outflows of speculative financing units determines the degree of fragility and instability of the economy. Following this line of argument, speculative financing units can be grouped into the following three categories: (i) speculative financing units with moderate leverage and small mismatch; (ii) speculative financing units with high leverage and large mismatch and (iii) speculative financing units between (i) and (ii). An economy with the large type (i) units generally requires well-organized, equity-based financial systems in which advanced capital markets and appropriate institutions for monitoring exist and whose members prudently control the leverage and the maturity profile. Even if such systems are in place, the underlying driving forces of the capitalist economy move the units towards types (iii) and (ii). The speculative financing units of the countries affected by the East Asian crisis, in particular Indonesia, quickly moved to type (ii) in the 1990s.

As has been noted earlier, a number of economists have concentrated on the mismatch problem in their studies of the East Asian crisis in the form of an offshore short-term debt problem. The rapid accumulation of offshore short-term debt followed by the sudden reversal of capital flows led to a self-fulfilling balance-of-payments crisis. As an empirical analysis, this argument mainly refers to two indicators, the ratio of short-term debt to reserves and the ratio of short-term debt to total debt. Both ratios are liquidity measures and their increase signals imprudent macroeconomic and regulatory policies. The analysis suggests that the mismatch problem is an indicator of economic vulnerability and that an increase in the mismatch is a good predictor of instability and fragility, including the self-fulfilling withdrawal of capital. Indeed, at the onset of the crisis these indicators did reach alarmingly high levels (Eichengreen 1999, pp.143–69; Furman and Stiglitz 1998, pp.51–6).[28]

However, the argument as typically presented is static in that short-term indebtedness suddenly emerged *deus ex machina*. Minsky's argument is more dynamic as it tries to explain why and how such short-term indebtedness tends to accumulate in the capitalist economy. He asserts that the process is endogenous and shifts the economy from stable to unstable through the creation of a fragile financial structure. Moreover, he identifies the driving forces behind the process as speculative financial units whose available cash runs short of cash payments required during a certain period. This occurs as firms make long-term investments in capital assets on the basis of short-term funding, thus creating a fragile financial structure. Under this financial structure the fragility of the speculative financial unit depends on the availability of finance at the time payment falls due, which is contingent upon creditors' forecasts of the unit's future performance under given economic conditions (Minsky 1986). If finance is not available, the unit is forced to dispose of its investments (capital assets) in order to fulfil payment commitments and clear the position. Furthermore, if forced disinvestments proceed on a large scale and at the same time, the result is following asset prices collapse, that is, the situation described by Fisher in his debt-deflation theory (Fisher 1933).

In the 1990s, East Asian capitalists accumulated offshore short-term debt and changed their financial structure from robust/hedged to fragile/speculative, especially in Thailand and Korea. The currency crisis, beginning in Thailand in July 1997, recast offshore lenders' forecasts of prospects in the private sector, which led to a sudden and massive rejection of offshore short-term debt rollovers. The impracticability of asset liquidation on a mammoth scale for debt repayments over such a short period led to widespread insolvency, that is, the East Asian crisis. To a certain extent, therefore, the standard emphasis on offshore, short-term debt is consistent with the Fisher–Minsky hypothesis.

Yet, to argue that the East Asian crisis was caused by the irresponsible accumulation of unhedged short-term debt is too simplistic. To begin with, during the finance boom, the Indonesian private sector actually improved its debt-term structure by obtaining offshore long-term, syndicated loans. Although Indonesian capitalists could increase profits through long-term investments using short-term funding under the normal yield curb structure at the time, this author's empirical studies show that they in fact tried to improve the tenor of borrowings.[29] However, due to the sharp depreciation of the rupiah during the crisis, Indonesian borrowers breached financial covenants in loan contracts, and therefore offshore banks accelerated their repayment schedules.[30] Long-term loans were suddenly converted into immediate payment requirements. Thus, once the crises had started, the distinction between long-term and short-term loans became irrelevant. The leverage was a more critical factor in the 1990s crisis in East Asia than loan tenor, including Indonesia.

This work redirects attention to the debt level against cash flow as a measurement of leverage. This is an equal treatment of leverage and cash flow. With regards to financial ratios used in the empirical studies, the work focuses on the ratio of debt to EBITDA (earnings before interest and tax plus depreciation and amortization) as a cash-flow proxy.

Foreign exchange risk considerations in the model

Foreign exchange risk related to unhedged liability positions is undeniably one of the most important negative cash-flow factors, and this was certainly the case during the East Asian crisis. One of the necessary adjustments to Minsky's model is to introduce vulnerability to foreign exchange movements, and therefore 'super speculative financing units', that borrow short-term money in foreign currency to finance long-term assets generating only local currency denominated cash flows. The combination of foreign exchange risk and the mismatched maturity profile (long-term investments funded by short-term finance) is known as the 'double mismatch', and the economic unit with both risks is a *super speculative financing unit* (Arestis and Glickman 2002, p.242; Yoshitomi and Staff of ADB Institute 2003, pp.12–15, 50–4).

A number of scholars have examined the problem of the double mismatch, and it is widely recognized that the realization of double mismatch risks, that is, a sudden reversal of offshore short-term finance and the sharp depreciation of the Asian currencies, had a sharply negative impact on the balance sheets of Asian corporations, pushing them into insolvency (Yoshitomi and Staff of ADB Institute 2003). Stiglitz, for one, links the double mismatch problem to the process of financial liberalization in East Asia. According to this view, liberalization in the absence of adequate mechanisms of monitoring and supervision created conditions conducive to over-borrowing of short-term, foreign currency loans (Furman and Stiglitz 1998; Stiglitz 2002).

However, subtle differences exist among the arguments concerning the double mismatch risk. One group of scholars stresses the term structure mismatch between cash inflows and outflows, that is, long-term investments by short-term funding, and explains the East Asian crisis in terms of the simultaneous and gigantic reversal of short-term capital flows (Furman and Stiglitz 1998, pp.51–6). As discussed earlier, this argument shares common ground with the Minsky's financial instability hypothesis. Moreover, this group argues that the reversal of short-term capital was the cause of the sharp depreciation of the Asian currencies, which resulted in a significant increase in unhedged foreign currency debts in local currency terms.

Another group stresses fixed or quasi-fixed exchange rate systems as an implicit guarantee of currency risks by Asian governments. This group concludes that government policy benefited both investors and fund recipients in the midst of financial euphoria and thus created moral hazard on both sides. In addition, this group cited arguments regarding implicit exchange rate guarantees within a broader analysis of so-called crony capitalism.

These arguments are built on the assumption that most local borrowers intentionally and speculatively opened foreign currency positions to maximize their margins between returns on investment and funding costs.[31] Many local capitalists did in fact respond to this motivation. On the other hand, others tried to hedge their open currency positions. In particular, Indonesia experienced two severe devaluations in the 1980s, and therefore companies earning in rupiah were generally wary of currency depreciation and prices of imported raw materials. During the 1990s, BI swaps and forward contracts were widely used to hedge currency positions between the rupiah and US dollar for both financial and trade debt. The problem was that the market was still small, and that long-term hedging was very difficult in the 1990s. BI swaps of more than 6 months in duration were not liquid, thus it was impossible to hedge sizable long-term offshore borrowings. In Singapore, emerging currency markets became apparent in the latter half of 1990s, and rupiah derivatives were also traded there. However, the market was still in its trial stages.

Therefore, foreign exchange risk is always coupled with offshore borrowing under less-developed hedging markets. In order to modify Minsky's closed and advanced economy model to adapt to conditions in open and developing (emerging) economies, one cannot help but assume *super speculative financing units*.

Institutional drivers – liberalization of financial markets

In the 1990s, Asian governments aggressively pushed forward liberalization policies in line with advice from multilateral financial institutions, such as the IMF and the World Bank. The policies were designed to change bank-based Asian financial systems into market (equity)-based Anglo-American ones. These policies can be grouped into liberalization of the domestic financial sectors and the capital account. Moreover, the former policy can be broken down into:

1   Liberalization of interest rates;
2   Openness of domestic financial markets to foreign financial institutions;
3   Deregulation to allow participation in other financial business fields (e.g. investment banking activities by commercial banks).

Market-based financial systems generally have lower leverage than those that are bank based. However, the introduction of market-based financial systems increased the leverage in Asian economies by rapidly expanding the domestic banking sector and aggressively absorbing offshore debt finance (Claessens, Djankov and Lang 1998; Pomerleano 1998; Wade 1998). In addition, the development of equity markets, which was one of the pillars of financial liberalization, did not result in substitution effects between equity and debt finance, but rather is strongly correlated to the increase in leverage (Kunt and Maksimovic 1995a,b). That is to say, the development of equity markets encouraged the corporate sector to increase debt finance. Liberalization policies leading towards market-based financial systems opened more debt finance opportunities and accelerated the leverage of the economy. Furthermore, the openness of domestic markets and the freedom of access to offshore markets internationalized domestic economic units' activities to make on the carry and rapidly intensified the drive towards financial evolution. By using Minsky's definition of the capitalist economy, the globalization of financial activities built the Asian economies into 'chains of global payment commitments and cash flows' (Minsky 1986, pp.197–220).

Another important problem associated with the double liberalizations (i.e. of the domestic financial sector and capital account) is the introduction of advanced financial products and practices, originally developed under more advanced institutional conditions. During the 1990s, these products and practices were suddenly and rapidly brought into the Asian markets. The growing Asian markets immediately became replicas of American and European markets. However, these products and practices require strong institutions to govern and monitor them. The Asian institutions lacked the capacity to handle these advanced products and practices, and as a result, their use favoured certain parties, such as owner shareholders/ borrowers. The encashment of owner shareholders' investments by restructuring group holdings using third party investors' capital and/or loans is a typical example of the misuse of newly introduced financial practices into underdeveloped markets.

In Indonesia, the combination of the open capital account since 1970, and the enthusiasm of offshore lenders in the 1990s, dramatically increased the use of international syndicated loans by a wide range of Indonesian corporate borrowers. This led to the sharp increase in the corporate sector's external debt. In addition, the liberalization of the securities market in the context of poor supervisory systems, coupled with international investment banks' aggressive approach to these markets, led to the rapid importation of hybrid capital market transactions. These transactions, such as structured bonds and corporate reorganization methods, accelerated the encashment of investments and capital flight. In just three years between 1994 and 1996, the time of the investment and finance boom, Indonesia introduced advanced and complicated financial products and practices into its infant financial structure with disastrous results.

On the other hand, political economy arguments were also put forward in favour of the liberalization of the financial sector. These assumed that liberalization is ideal for Asian countries but tried to explain why this caused so many problems in Asia. In addition to the discussion on institutional circumstances, such as poor governance, they focus on the process of introducing the liberalization into the Asian economies and the power politics between policy makers and vested-interest groups. They conclude that vested-interest groups heavily influenced the formulation of liberalization policies and that the outcomes were twisted to suit these powerful actors (Haggard 2000; Rosser 2002).

Both mainstream economists and political economists share the view that liberalization without well-organized institutions was the most important cause of the East Asian crisis. However, the mainstream economists' arguments do not address the issue of why policy makers could not build the necessary institutional framework. They also failed to ask how such cherry-picking liberalization policies, which benefited vested-interest groups, were created.[32] The fact must be considered that liberalization policies in Asia were exogenously inspired but endogenously developed, and it is necessary to attempt to identify which groups' interests drove the endogenous development of liberalization.

Supply side of debt finance as a disequilibrating force in the economy

Minsky's model mainly expects intermediaries (speculative financing units), which sit between capital asset investors (hedge-financing units) and ultimate fund providers (depositors), to evolve the financial structure of economy through their profit-seeking and forward-looking behaviour. In order to adapt Minsky's closed economy model to an open economy, it is necessary to introduce offshore banks and investors as another set of ultimate fund providers. Furthermore, these offshore banks and investors are not passive fund providers such as domestic depositors but play an active role in the evolving financial structure. During the 1990s, fund providers, particularly offshore commercial banks, had strong lending imperatives in the Asian private sector as a part of the emerging market boom. This enthusiasm on the supply side drastically increased debt levels in the Asian private sector and led to the evolution of the financial structure despite attempts by governments to control sovereign debt levels.

Furthermore, this enthusiasm drove creditors towards more risky borrowers. In Indonesia, access to offshore markets before the 1990s was limited to the state, top state banks and companies, and a very limited number of elite private banks and companies. However, during the finance boom of the 1990s, Indonesian borrowers with access to offshore markets expanded from top to second-tier business groups, from flagship companies of business groups to their subsidiaries and affiliates, established manufacturing companies to non-bank finance and real estate companies, elite banks to middle-ranking banks, and so forth. Enthusiasm on the supply side thus dramatically increased the points of contact between domestic economic units and offshore financial markets.

Moreover, in order to adjust Minsky's advanced and closed economy model to apply to developing (or emerging) and open economies, one must consider differences in financial technologies between domestic (developing) and offshore (advanced) financial markets. As is discussed in the previous section, offshore banks and investors introduced new financial products and practices as they extended the range of borrowers. As these financial products and practices are already in common use in advanced financial markets, the speed of introduction into developing markets was very fast. During the finance boom of the 1990s, offshore bankers aggressively introduced syndicated loans into Indonesia. Domestic private banks followed the trend, and syndicated loans even spread into local rupiah debt markets. With regards to financial technology, offshore fund providers made a major contribution to financial evolution in open developing financial markets and economies.

On the other hand, offshore banks' aggressive stance towards non-bank, blue chip borrowers drove down the credit quality of local banks' portfolios. Local banks, which had lost their high-quality clients to overseas competitors, took on lower quality and riskier borrowers and projects due to limited alternative investment opportunities. In developing (emerging) and open economies, offshore fund providers may in this way weaken domestic financial intermediaries' asset quality and lead to fragility in domestic financial markets.

The crisis in Indonesia, which began as a private debt problem, was thus intensified as offshore fund providers (as mobile capital) exercised their structural power by withdrawing their funds over a short period and on a large scale. Minsky's financial instability hypothesis must be supplemented by the supply-side considerations. More specifically, the theory must address the motivations of creditors, including the pressures driving lenders to even riskier borrowers and projects, even in the cases where these actions weaken their structural power.

The non-intermediary sector as a driving force in the evolution of the financial structure

A number of scholars aside from Minsky place too much emphasis on the financial sector, particularly banks, in developing their theories of the economic cycle and crises. The financial sector is indeed the most leveraged and mismatched among all economic units, and arguments regarding boom–bust scenarios that are centred on the role of banks may fit the Thai and Korean cases. In both countries, the financial systems acted as conduits to pump short-term offshore debt funds into the non-bank sector during the boom, and the banking sectors rapidly deepened the speculative features of the economy. On the contrary, in Indonesia, domestic banks' access to offshore funds was strictly controlled during the boom, and their external debt actually remained at sustainable levels.[33] The Coordinating Team for the Management of Offshore Commercial Loans and BI controlled and monitored all offshore commercial loans for both state and private banks. In particular, BI tightly restricted offshore borrowings by state banks, which were highly prized by offshore banks and could raise large amounts of funds through annual quota and queuing rules on offshore markets. Therefore, any arguments based on the role of the banking sector cannot fully explain Indonesia's boom–bust scenarios in the 1990s.

According to the theory of asymmetric information, offshore banks attempt to mitigate credit risks from directly lending to non-bank borrowers by lending to onshore banks, which are assumed to possess better information on local companies. When official disclosure and the accuracy of corporate information are very poor, as in most Asian counties, unpublished information obtained from person-to-person relations is critical for judging the creditworthiness of borrowers. Therefore, offshore banks naturally began lending to onshore banks to reduce risk. As a result, offshore banks were highly exposed to leading banks in these countries. In Indonesia, seven state and top private banks were primary targets of the offshore banks.[34] In the 1990s before the East Asian crisis, syndicated loans and notes were always oversubscribed despite the increasingly generous terms of these loans.

Nevertheless, three drivers encouraged offshore banks to shift their lending targets from bank to non-bank borrowers: (i) the saturation of exposure to bank borrowers; (ii) the search for higher-margin transactions and (iii) factors mitigating the asymmetric information problem.

First, the local (onshore) banks' monitoring capacity of borrowers and corporate governance was poor, and lending decisions were often subject to political pressures. Thus, instead of scrutinizing local banks' management, offshore banks tended to finance major banks that had a significant impact on the economy. As a result, offshore banks had a high concentration of exposure to specific top banks. In order to diversify their exposure, offshore banks attempted to finance large non-bank companies that also held important positions in the economy. In the case of Indonesia, after increasing exposure to top state and private banks, offshore banks did not approach the lower-ranked banks, but instead financed major industrial companies, such as Indocement, Indofood and Indah Kiat.

Second, a high concentration of exposure on specific borrowers meant that borrowing terms drastically improved and that the profitability of transactions sharply dropped for offshore lenders. Profit-seeking behaviour patterns naturally encouraged offshore banks to actively work on high margin and good quality non-bank borrowers, particularly during the boom. Between 1994 and 1996, the time of the investment and finance boom in Indonesia, a number of non-bank borrowers were introduced into offshore syndication markets by virtue of offshore arranger banks' enthusiastic marketing activities.

Third, qualitative information can compensate for lack of quantity. For example, the fact that borrowers are members of established local business groups may implicitly assure lenders that the borrowers have access to the groups' financial power. As a further example, the fact that business groups were involved with joint ventures with leading foreign partners may have implicitly assured them that the business groups' management and financial capacities were appreciated by their partners. In the case of Indonesia, offshore banks actively expanded their lending to non-bank borrowers based on group membership and joint venture participation.

In the 1990s, the non-financial sector of crisis-affected Asian countries, particularly Indonesia, accessed offshore debt markets aggressively and steeply leveraged their balance sheets. This sector is modelled as a hedge-financing unit by Minsky but was typically a speculative financing unit in Asia. Furthermore, direct and aggressive fund raising by the non-financial sectors led to the diversification of points of contact between the domestic market and offshore markets. This diversification created a complex and difficult financial structure for financial authorities to monitor. The structure changed from bank-based systems to market-based systems during the process, and the financial authorities were unable to control the debt levels of the non-financial sector through the banks under their supervision. In addition, poorly managed financial institutions could not govern such complex financial structures. Therefore, the non-financial sector needs to be viewed as consisting of potential speculative and Ponzi financing units.

Complex motivations driving financial evolution

With regards to motivations on the demand side, the profit-seeking and forward-looking character of capitalists, which Minsky considered a disequilibrating force in his financial instability hypothesis, is just one explanation of the modern capitalist economy. The core objectives of capitalists are maximizing profits, protecting property rights and minimizing risk. In other words, capitalists intend to maximize risk-adjusted returns with liquidity considerations. In particular, applying Minsky's theory to the Asian economies, the preference for liquidity of underlying investments is also one of the most critical characteristics of capitalists' behaviour.

Indonesian business group owners (inside shareholders in the case of public companies) created liquidity through equity transactions (e.g. initial public offerings and rights issues), debt-financed corporate restructuring, leveraging firms to create liquidity for their investments as well as increasing returns on their equity. Inside shareholders' strategies further complicated the situation. In a way, this was a power struggle among capital controllers, and in particular, inside equity holders and outside equity holders (the minority shareholders' problem) and inside equity holders and offshore debt financiers (offshore debt problem). Another vital point is that the Indonesian crisis had political dimensions, such as growing anti-Chinese and anti-*cukong* (crony) sentiment that encouraged capitalists to cash out of their investments.

Minsky's model was designed for advanced economies such as the United States. Within these economies, publicly listed companies are widely owned by a large number of shareholders. Power struggles involve shareholders and management and occur between shareholders and debt holders. On the other hand, in the case of Asia, publicly listed companies retain pre-IPO (Initial Public Offering) company owners as the majority or single largest shareholders. In addition, these shareholders directly manage companies as if they were still family-owned businesses. Therefore, power struggles naturally occur between inside (majority or single largest) and minority shareholders and between inside shareholders and debt holders. In order to apply Minsky's model to developing (emerging) economies, such as Indonesia, it is necessary to study what lies behind inside shareholders' motivations as a driving force in the evolution of the structure of the economy.

Finally, in addition to the earlier mentioned adjustments, corrections and clarifications of the model, Minsky's financial instability hypothesis requires a microeconomic approach in order to understand how such a sophisticated financial structure with its complicated chains of payment commitments is created and how such crisis-prone fragile and unstable economies develop. A microeconomic perspective can elucidate the firm-level decisions underlying the large-scale, macroeconomic changes. A focus on corporate finance activities is essential, not only at the firm level but also at the business group level through the analysis of (aggregate) financial statements, financial transactions, corporate events and so forth. Therefore, the case-study method is appropriate for the examination of the evolution of the financial structure.

The Indonesian corporate sector between 1994 and the first half of 1997 (under the finance and economic boom) is an excellent case for studying the process of the creation of a sophisticated and crisis-prone financial structure in Asia. During this short period, the financial structure of the private sector evolved from robust to fragile and unstable by aggressively utilizing offshore banks' funds. A number of business groups leveraged their financial positions to maximize profits and liquidity, and as a result, the Indonesian corporate sector became one of the most speculative financing units in Asia. Finally, the East Asian crisis transformed these firms into Ponzi financing units. This sector has been selected for this author's case studies.

3 Methods and databases for empirical studies

As argued in Chapter 2, Minsky views the capitalist economy as a set of interrelated balance sheets and income statements as well as a complicated assemblage of cash-flow chains. In other words, he describes it as an aggregate of financial statements that are created by profit-seeking and forward-looking capitalists' investments in long-life and expensive capital assets through debt-financing activities. He also examines the relationship between debt and cash flow at the macro-level from the perspective of corporate finance and applies corporate accounting methods to economics in his cash-flow approach. Furthermore, he studies the underlying financial transactions that are driven by capitalists' activities and that create a fragile and unstable financial structure.[1] In sum, Minsky applies the corporate finance approach to the empirical studies of his financial instability hypothesis at both the macro- and micro-levels.

It has been observed that the nature of Indonesia's external debt problem changed during the finance boom of the 1990s (the period from 1994 to the first half of 1997). The rapid accumulation of external debt by the Indonesian corporate sector during this period was more important than debt build-up in the state and/or banking sectors, historically the locus of Indonesia's external debt problems. This work argues that this newly emerging external debt problem created a fragile, unstable, and crisis-prone financial structure which led to the crisis in 1997 and 1998. Furthermore, this author argues that the process developed endogenously as a result of Indonesian and overseas capitalists' natural motivations and their aggressive financial activities. The empirical studies undertaken demonstrate the endogenous nature of financial instability in the Indonesian economy through an analysis of the financial positions and underlying activities associated with Indonesian private non-financial firms during the finance boom.

The empirical studies in this work examine the following three issues: (i) the financial positions of Indonesian private non-financial firms (Chapter 4); (ii) the offshore debt transactions of Indonesian borrowers (Chapter 5) and (iii) the financial activities of selected major Indonesian business groups (Chapters 6–9). The first two issues involve the analysis of aggregated firm-level data from the macroeconomic perspective. These chapters explain how Indonesian financial structures were dramatically leveraged and complicated by offshore syndicated debt during the finance boom. Case studies of business groups provide detailed illustrations of the underlying forces contributing to financial fragility and instability during the period.

Methods and database for the analysis of the financial positions of the Indonesian corporate sector

Methods – the corporate finance approach to the liability side of the financial structure

Chapter 4 analyses the liability side of the corporate sector's financial structure during the 1990s. As Minsky points out, the coherence of corporate liability is a key issue in the maintenance of the network of payment commitments underlying the capitalist economy. Leveraging, that is, increasing liabilities relative to equity and internal cash flow, increases the fragility and instability of the financial structure. Technically speaking, the leverage of the balance sheet determines the potential for insolvency.

On the other hand, leveraging is one of the most important financial methods of maximizing returns to shareholders' equity, under the post-leveraged condition that the return on assets is higher than the cost of debt. Under capitalism, endogenous profit-seeking motivations drive the leveraging of the balance sheet and may endanger the sound maintenance of the network of payment commitments. Leveraging increases default risks, which could lead to large-scale default contagion in the economy. As Fisher argued in his debt-deflation theory, once default occurs, the asset value of companies tends to be deeply discounted, in particular, for liquidation purposes (Fisher 1933). Due to the subordinated position of equity to debt, it is unavoidable that the residual value to shareholders is reduced. Therefore, the leveraging strategy to achieve maximum returns to equity may conflict with the interests of shareholders as well as debt investors.

Management generally has strong incentives to report undervalued liability figures to demonstrate the soundness of the company and to attract debt and equity investors. In particular, leveraging is the most critical factor in lenders' credit decisions. The company's leverage position and debt investors' lending appetite therefore jointly determine the company's capacity to obtain additional debt finance. From the audit point of view, liabilities, mainly debt, are a common source of fraudulent financial reporting. So-called financial engineering helps management to move booked debt off the balance sheet as contingent liabilities. Debt can also be completely erased from the balance sheet and contingent liabilities through securitization.

Therefore, it would appear to be a reasonable assumption that the figures reported as liabilities may be undervalued in Indonesia, where inside shareholders, that is, companies' founder-owners and management have a voracious appetite for debt and outside shareholders' new capital (i.e. public and third party shareholders). The use of these liability statistics would therefore present a conservative estimate of the leverage position of the Indonesian corporate sector.

In reality, these firms were much more leveraged. Although these figures are therefore not accurate, it is extremely unlikely that they underestimate the extent of leveraging.

The empirical analysis presented in this work mainly examines the liability position of the private non-bank sector. The work follows Minsky in measuring liabilities against cash flow and Fisher in the comparison of liabilities to net worth. Other indicators for measuring profitability and debt-service capacity are also used to follow Minsky's arguments on margins of safety. The financial ratio analysis of corporate finance methods is applied to the aggregate financial statement of Indonesian private non-financial firms from the beginning of the 1990s until the outbreak of the crisis.[2] The aim of this aggregation was to create a proxy Indonesian corporate sector that actively used offshore syndicated debt and thus drove the evolution of the financial structure of the Indonesian economy. In addition to the test of leverage, arguments linking the crisis-prone financial structure to heavy short-term debt reliance as put forward by Stiglitz and other mainstream economists are tested by the financial ratio analysis. The financial ratios in Tables 3.1, 3.2 and 3.3 are employed for these purposes.

Leverage and equity ratios

The 'leverage ratio' is calculated by dividing total liability by shareholders' equity, including minority interests (by convention). Prior to the 1990s, the Indonesian corporate sector had limited access to the offshore debt market. Supplier's and buyer's credits from foreign trading counter parties, in particular,

Table 3.1 Financial ratios for leverage

Ratios	Calculation
Leverage	Total liability/total equity
Equity	Total equity/total assets
Gross debt to equity	Total debt/equity
Net debt to equity	(Total debt − cash and cash equivalent)/equity
Gross debt to EBITDA	Total debt/ (operating profit + depreciation and amortization)
Net debt to EBITDA	(Total debt − cash and cash equivalent)/ (operating profit + depreciation and amortization)
Gross debt to CS + APIC	Total debt/(common stock + additional paid-in capital)
Net debt to CS + APIC	(Total debt − cash and cash equivalent)/ (common stock + additional paid-in capital)

Notes
APIC – Additional paid-in capital.
CS – Common stock.

Table 3.2 Financial ratios for liquidity

Ratios	Calculation
Long-term to short-term debt	Long-term debt/short-term debt (including short-term portion of long-term debt)
Current	Current assets/current liability
Net short-term debt to EBITDA	(Total short-term debt − cash and cash equivalent)/ (operating profit + depreciation and amortization)

Table 3.3 Financial ratios for profitability and debt-service capacity

Ratios	Calculation
Operating profit margin	Operating profit/gross revenue
Net profit margin	Net profit/gross revenue
EBITDA margin	(Operating profit + depreciation and amortization)/gross revenue
Return on assets	Operating profit/total assets
Return on equity	Net profit/equity
EBIT interest coverage	Operating profit/interest payable
EBIT funding cost coverage	Operating profit/(interest payable + foreign exchange loss)
EBITDA interest coverage	(Operating profit + depreciation and amortization)/interest payable
EBITDA funding cost coverage	(Operating profit + depreciation and amortization)/ (interest payable + foreign exchange loss)

leading Japanese trading companies (*sogo-shosha*), were the critical funding sources together with domestic bank borrowing. This type of lending was an important part of Japanese trading companies' business methods (*shosha-kinyu*) in developing countries such as Indonesia. These trade credits are not generally booked as 'borrowing' but as 'accounts payable' and 'other liabilities'. Therefore, the leverage ratio is a comprehensive indicator because it includes not only bank debt but also the earlier-mentioned quasi-borrowings in the form of trade credits.

The 'equity ratio' is in some sense the opposite of the *leverage ratio* but can be used as a check on the *leverage ratio*. This ratio is simply obtained by dividing shareholders' equity by total assets. A decrease in this ratio indicates that the company is leveraged to a greater extent and may signal the deterioration of the financial structure. It is generally argued that equity ratios in Asia, where bank-based financial systems historically operate, are smaller than those in the United States and the United Kingdom, where equity-based financial systems exist.[3]

Gross/net debt to equity ratios

The 'gross debt to equity ratio' is calculated by dividing gross debt (i.e. the total of short- and long-term debt) by shareholders' equity. The 'net debt to equity ratio' uses net debt (i.e. gross debt minus cash and cash equivalents) instead of gross debt for the same calculation. These ratios also measure the company's leverage position but focus on the relative scale of pure debt from bank borrowing and bond issuance against shareholders' funds and internally accumulated earnings (retained earnings). They also indicate the relative significance of the companies' funding attached to contractual payment commitments against funding free from payment commitments as a result of funding activities in the financial markets. Thus, the larger these ratios become, the more fragile the company's and the economy's financial position becomes.

Gross/net debt to EBITDA ratios

The 'gross/net debt to EBITDA ratio' is calculated by dividing gross/net debt by EBITDA (i.e. earnings before interest and tax plus depreciation and amortization). The simplified calculation for EBITDA is operating income plus depreciation and amortization. EBITDA is a standard proxy for companies' operating cash flows during a single fiscal year and which can be used to meet payment commitments.[4] The ratios of gross/net debt to EBITDA indicate the significance of the companies' debts to their capacity to generate cash flow. The larger these ratios become, the more the companies have to rely on cash inflows through external finance (debt and/or equity), that is, financial cash flows, to fulfil payment commitments.

Gross/net debt to CS + APIC ratios

The 'gross/net debt to CS + APIC ratio' is obtained by dividing gross/net debt by the total of CS (common stock) and APIC (additional paid-in capital). The general accounting treatment requires stock-issuing companies to book obtained shareholders' equity contributions to common stock (for par value portion) and additional paid-in capital accounts (for the excess portion over par value). Considering the fact that share buy-back/treasury stock is not yet common but that retained earnings are often withdrawn as 'uncovered dividends', 'CS + APIC' can be regarded as virtually identical to the shareholders' contribution. These ratios therefore measure the relative financial contributions of debt investors (banks and bond investors) and shareholders. Higher ratios indicate that companies have obtained more money from the debt market and face increased payment commitments in the future. Assuming that the companies have maintained a certain level of retained earnings, their funding policies and activities behind the increase of these ratios has driven their leveraged financial positions.

Long-term to short-term debt ratio

The long-term to short-term debt ratio is a simplified indicator of the debt maturity diversification profile and indicates one aspect of the companies' hedged positions against financial pressures from payment commitments. The definition of short-term debt follows the standard accounting categorization as: debt with a maturity shorter than but including 1 year. A number of scholars and researchers have focused on this ratio for part of the explanation for the East Asian crisis, arguing that long-term investments had been financed by short-term funding (Claessens *et al.* 1998, pp.11–13; Pomerleano 1998, pp.12–13).

This ratio is a relevant measure of hedged financial positions if borrower companies can maintain the right to long-term payment commitments under any conditions. However, financing terms usually contain a variety of covenants, and the breach of these triggers default resulting in an acceleration of payment obligations. Considering this technical aspect this and the following two ratios may be irrelevant in explaining the economy's and company's hedged financial positions. The East Asian crisis is a good example of this, as during the crisis, the sharp depreciation of local currencies led to breaches of financial covenants, such as leverage and EBITDA interest coverage ratios.

Current ratio

The current ratio is a standard corporate accounting method also known as the working capital ratio. This indicates the number of times current assets will payoff payment commitments within 1 year and also the liquidity of the corporate entity.

Net short-term debt to EBITDA ratio

The net short-term debt to EBITDA ratio indicates how difficult it would be for the corporate sector to payoff its financial commitments within 1 year on the basis of single-year operating cash flows and cash in hand. It also indicates the necessity of refinancing and/or disposing of fixed assets. The larger the ratio, the more likely it is that the companies will face difficulties due to a failure to refinance. Minsky also views the increase of this ratio as a 'speculative financial position', and its decrease as a 'hedged financial position'. Stiglitz and other mainstream economists use the ratio of foreign exchange reserves against short-term external debt in order to explain the vulnerability of the East Asia crisis-affected counties (Eichengreen 1999, pp.145–8; Furman and Stiglitz 1998, pp.50–3). This is similar to the net short-term debt to EBITDA ratio.

Operating, net profit and EBITDA margins

These three ratios indicate profitability at the levels of earnings before funding costs, earnings after funding costs and tax payment and operating cash flows, respectively. Current and future profits are the most important component of cash flows that determine the value of the enterprise. Therefore, the profitability of borrowers is the most relied on indicator for judging investments and loans, and this determines Minsky's margin of safety.

Returns on assets and equity

Return on assets indicates the profitability of investments at the corporate level, while return on equity measures profitability of investments for equity holders. These indicators are related to each other through the level of leverage and funding cost yield. In theory, if the return on assets is higher than the funding cost yield, shareholders prefer to leverage in order to maximize the return on equity and vice versa.

EBIT/EBITDA interest/funding cost coverage ratios

EBIT/EBITDA interest/funding cost coverage ratios indicate the debt-service capacity and debt sustainability of borrowers. Strictly speaking, these ratios signify the number of times current earnings before funding costs (EBIT) and operating cash flows (EBITDA) can pay-off single-year funding costs (interest/funding cost). In the case of Indonesia, to a large extent, the corporate sector took on foreign currency debt without hedging the currency positions. Therefore, foreign exchange losses were a substantial part of funding costs. Changes in these ratios also strongly affected investors' and lenders' views of the creditworthiness of borrowers and the value of their exposure.

The disruption of financial markets pushes leveraged companies into difficulty and ultimately they may default on their debt. Simultaneous and large-scale defaults break down the 'network of cash-flow commitments' of the capitalist economy and lead to financial crisis. The emergence of a leveraged corporate sector indicates the fragility of the economy and the extent to which it has already entered potentially risky phases prior to crisis. Therefore, the aggregation of firm-level ratios is an appropriate method to gauge to what extent the corporate sector entered into speculative financial positions.

Database – financial positions of the Indonesian private non-bank sector

Most commentators agree with the view that Indonesian companies' accounting practices lack accuracy and reliability in terms of disclosure. However, as long as intentions underlying financial reporting are carefully and logically considered, the figures reported in financial statements are still useful for analysing the overall financial character of a variety of economic units, such as the private/public sectors, industrial sectors and business groups.

The database compiled by the author covers 357 Indonesian companies listed on the Jakarta Stock Exchange and other overseas stock markets, such as

Singapore, Hong Kong, the Philippines and the United States. However, in the case of some companies, financial data are not available throughout the entire period surveyed. Data availability is reported in Table 3.4.

It is apparent that non-bank/insurance corporates, in particular, manufacturing and service sector companies, make up the large majority of listed companies. Since 1993, the share of both non-bank/insurance corporate and manufacturing companies among those listed has consistently been higher than 80 per cent. This reflects the fact that private capital has played a critical role in manufacturing and services, rather than in the historically government-dominated banking and insurance sectors. Only a limited number of private banks had qualified to list their shares on the stock exchange before the early 1990s. State banks dominated the banking sector prior to PAKTO in 1988.[5] The government had already initiated a discussion on the privatization of state banks through IPO in the stock exchange, but it had needed more time to carry it out and was unable to implement the policy before the onset of the financial crisis.[6]

Due to the nature of the banking and insurance businesses, these companies have extremely high leverage ratios. Therefore, aggregating across sectors is misleading. In addition, the external debt of the banking sector had been strictly controlled by the Indonesian financial authorities.[7] Liability-side factors, such as growth of deposits and insurance contracts, liquidity and capital adequacy ratio, had also been monitored and regulated. Moreover, the bank/insurance corporate sector had not been active in the domestic debt market. It is, therefore, logical to conclude that banks and insurance companies did not drive changes in the degree of leveraging of the Indonesian corporate sector, and for that reason, the following analyses will focus on non-bank/insurance corporate data. A central argument of this work is that leading business groups in the Indonesian corporate and financial sector became heavily leveraged speculative financing units by aggressively accessing offshore syndicated debt markets as well as liberalized domestic financial markets.

A final issue relates to the treatment of non-bank finance companies included in the 'non-bank/insurance corporate' category, such as those involved with

Table 3.4 Database of Indonesian corporate and financial sector (companies)

	1990	1991	1992	1993	1994	1995	1996	1997
All corporate and financial	78	131	171	232	274	293	312	328
Corporate[a]	57	103	142	197	233	249	267	282
Manufacturing and services	50	94	133	187	219	231	247	260
Finance companies	7	9	9	10	14	18	20	22
Bank and insurance	21	28	29	35	41	44	45	46

Source: Annual reports.

Note
a Non-bank/insurance corporate.

investment, security and leasing. Some databases include the non-bank finance companies in the corporate sector, and it is technically difficult to separate these from the dataset.[8] Investment and leasing companies are typically highly leveraged, but not as much as banks. Non-bank finance companies were historically controlled by the financial authorities, but the controls were less strict than those for banks.[9] On the other hand, non-bank finance companies were debt-financed, including onshore and offshore loans. They thus affected the debt-using leveraging of the Indonesian corporate sector to some extent. However, their impact is very limited, as can be seen in Table 3.4. This work therefore will treat non-bank finance companies as a part of the corporate sector depending on the availability of data. This treatment does not affect the conclusions.

With regards to inside equity holders, in other words, owners and major shareholders of Indonesian listed companies, Indonesian–Chinese capital occupied a dominant position. This capital used the stock markets very actively. Table 3.5 presents a list of Indonesian–Chinese business groups with more than five listed companies per group. It illustrates how leading business groups, such as Lippo, Salim and Sinar Mas, vigorously accessed stock markets to finance their corporate strategies. Furthermore, this aggressive use of stock markets had come to include medium-sized Indonesian–Chinese business groups. In addition to the most bullish groups listed in Table 3.5, five Indonesian–Chinese business groups listed four companies per group on the stock markets; four listed three companies per group; and twenty-five listed two companies per group.[10] Even though there are leading business groups that were not so active or strategic in the stock markets (such as the Gudang Garam Group), the majority of Indonesian–Chinese listed companies were active stock market players, and this contributed to the leveraging of their balance sheet.[11]

The use of the stock market by other business categories was not so active. The majority of *pribumi* listed companies belonged to the Suharto family or the

Table 3.5 Indonesian–Chinese active stock market users (1997) (companies)

Group	Listed companies (total)	Onshore listed companies		Bank and insurance	Offshore listed companies
		Non-bank/insurance			
		Non-financial	Financial		
Lippo	21	9	2	3	7
Salim	11	8	0	1	2
Sinar Mas	9	4	1	1	3
Dharmala	9	5	2	2	0
Astra	8	7	0	1	0
Gajah Tunggal	7	4	1	2	0
Panin	7	1	3	3	0
Ometraco	6	5	0	1	0
Kalbe	5	0	0	0	0

Source: Annual reports.

Bakrie Group.[12] The Texmaco Group held the most listed companies in the Indonesian–Indian category.[13] The privatization of state companies was still at the early stages. Foreign capital did not have a strong incentive to offer their shares to the public because their investments in Indonesia had functioned as a part of their parent companies' operations, and funding had originated from parent companies through direct lending and/or parent guarantees.

In this way, the character of this database appears to be oriented towards Indonesian–Chinese groups. This reflects the ethnic characteristics of Indonesia's private sector. In particular, Indonesian–Chinese business groups accounted for a significant share of large private companies. They were also offshore investors' major targets during the finance boom in the 1990s. Therefore, in terms of active users of markets, the characteristics of this database are similar to the database of offshore syndicated debt.

Methods and database for the analysis of offshore syndicated debt for Indonesian borrowers

Methods – the analysis of average tenor and all-in margin

The empirical studies of offshore syndicated debt for Indonesian borrowers aim to show that:

1   Offshore syndicated debt was the most critical driving force in the leveraging of the Indonesian private non-bank sector's financial structure;
2   The range of borrowers was expanded in a downwards direction with regards to credit risk;
3   The aggressive introduction of offshore syndicated debt was not only driven by Indonesian borrowers' funding needs but also by offshore lenders' enthusiastic approach to borrowers.

The original database is appropriately modified in order to gather evidence in support of these conclusions.

With regards to the first aim above, the work analyses the change in the shares of offshore syndicated debt for private non-bank borrowers in terms of both number and volume (dollar amount) of transactions during the finance boom. The study demonstrates a dramatic shift from the state and/or banking sector to the private non-bank sector. Concerning the second aim, the work analyses the change in the concentration of top offshore syndicated borrowers. The macro-analysis illustrates that the concentration sharply decreased during the finance boom and that there was a diversification of offshore syndicated debt users. The microanalysis examines the diversification of offshore syndicated debt users in terms of the nature of firms, for example, small and medium business groups, *pribumi* business groups and Suharto-related parties.

Referring to the third aim given earlier, the work focuses on the following two sensitive items among collected borrowing terms: average tenor and all-in margin. Average tenor is the adjusted tenor assuming bullet repayment at final maturity even though the debt has scheduled instalments.[14] Therefore, average tenor cannot be longer than absolute tenor, that is, tenor from the beginning to the end of the debt agreement. All-in margin is fee-adjusted annual return on the benchmark funding cost, such as, the London Interbank Offered Rate (LIBOR) and Singapore Interbank Offered Rate (SIBOR). The calculation of all-in margin is as follows: contractual annual margin + (upfront fee/average life) + other annual fees. During the finance boom, Indonesian borrowers and offshore lenders carefully negotiated these two most risk-return sensitive items in their offshore syndicated debt agreements. Changes in these indicate the direction of bargaining power between borrowers and lenders.

In theory, assuming all other conditions remain unchanged, there exists a positive correlation between credit risk and funding costs, between tenor and funding costs and between funding amount (particularly funding amount per transaction) and costs. That is to say, higher-risk borrowers are required to pay higher all-in margins, and longer average tenor is related to this. Larger fund sizes are associated with higher all-in margins. A negative correlation exists among credit risk, average tenor and funding amount, that is to say, higher-risk borrowers can neither easily stretch average tenor nor enlarge funding amounts. The longer the tenor borrowers need the smaller funding amount the market will offer and the larger the funding amount required the shorter tenor the market will offer them.

During the finance boom in the 1990s, Indonesian borrowers' demand for offshore foreign currency debt significantly increased, and new and lower-credit Indonesian borrowers aggressively entered the offshore debt market. Thus, Indonesian borrower markets requested larger funding from offshore lender markets. Considering this situation and the above relationships, it must have been extremely difficult for Indonesian borrowers, as a whole, to improve average tenor and all-in margin. If they were able to simultaneously improve both average tenor and all-in margin under such circumstances, this would constitute strong evidence that offshore lenders were enthusiastic about increasing exposure to Indonesia during the period and that bargaining power had shifted from offshore lenders to Indonesian borrowers. The empirical studies carefully analyse not only the change in average tenor and all-in margin, but also the relationships between the changes of average tenor and all-in margin.

Database – borrowing terms in the Indonesian offshore syndicated debt market

The empirical studies on offshore syndicated debts for Indonesian borrowers during the finance boom in the 1990s are based on the fact that at the time external debt was for the most part accumulated through offshore syndicated debt, which consisted of syndicated loans, FRCDs, and floating rate notes (FRNs). Offshore syndicated loans mainly originated in the Singapore market and were distributed to offshore commercial banks, while FRCDs and FRNs mainly originated in the

Hong Kong market and were sold to offshore commercial banks and institutional investors. Fixed income bonds, which were the most popular products for offshore institutional investors, were not common among Indonesian borrowers.[15] This is simply because the main offshore institutional investors in American and European markets remained cautious about Indonesian risk at that time. On the other hand, at the latter stages of the finance boom, leading Indonesian banks also arranged onshore syndicated loans to sell to offshore markets. These have been categorized as offshore syndicated debt in this author's empirical studies. Therefore, offshore syndicated debt in these studies is defined as syndicated loans, FRCDs and FRNs that were arranged for offshore lenders/investors.

Among the earlier-defined forms of offshore syndicated debt, FRCDs and FRNs are publicly traded securities; thus the transactions data are available through public sources. However, offshore syndicated loans, which accounted for most of the offshore syndicated debt, are not public transactions and the transactions data are not publicly available. Although all Indonesian companies' offshore finance was reported to Bank Indonesia the data were not disclosed to the public. This is perhaps the main reason that there have been no studies of Indonesian borrowers' offshore funding activities.

The present database of offshore syndicated debt was constructed from term sheets for offshore syndicated loans, which were collected by the author and checked with articles in *IFR* (*International Financing Review*).[16] This database consists of the identification of the borrowers and basic borrowing terms of syndicated debt covering 1,041 transactions from 1993 to 1997 (Table 3.6). The identification of borrowers consists of: name of borrower; state or private; name of business group (if private borrower) and business (bank or non-bank). The basic borrowing terms are: transaction date; type of facility (e.g. term loan, revolver, project finance and bridging); size of facility; tenor of facility; average tenor of facility; all-in margin (annualized actual funding cost); commitment fee; repayment method (bullet or amortization); security and guarantee and name of arranger. However, all data are not necessarily utilized to achieve the purpose of this author's empirical studies.[17]

Table 3.6 Database of offshore syndicated loans for Indonesian borrowers (transactions)

	State			Private			Total		
	Banks	*Non-banks*	*Total*	*Banks*	*Non-banks*	*Total*	*Banks*	*Non-banks*	*Total*
1993	18	5	23	44	22	66	62	27	89
1994	14	3	17	43	83	126	57	86	143
1995	17	10	27	55	136	191	72	146	218
1996	25	13	38	62	238	300	87	251	338
1997	15	9	24	45	184	229	60	193	253
Total	89	40	129	249	663	912	338	703	1,041

Source: Privately collected data (checked with IFR).

Average tenor and all-in margins of offshore syndicated debt for Indonesian borrowers, on which this empirical study focuses, are analysed on the basis of the following three datasets: (i) all Indonesian borrowers; (ii) bank borrowers and (iii) non-bank borrowers. With reference to the first dataset, transactions in the original database are not always complete, and some data lack average tenor and all-in margin. Data on incomplete transactions have been deleted. Concerning the second data set, two sub-data sets have been prepared in order to analyse average tenor and all-in margin at the same credit level: a data set for eight state banks and for the top ten private banks.

With regards to the third data set for non-bank borrowers, the work focuses on the private sector. This is simply because direct offshore borrowing by the state non-bank sector was limited to only a few state entities and independent projects.[18] Foreign currency funding for state companies was generally conducted through BI acting for the central government. In order to analyse borrowing terms at the same level of credit risk, this author has prepared the following two sub-data sets: the top ten regular corporate users of offshore syndicated debt and top-tier credit corporate borrowers. The former sub-data set includes offshore syndicated debt for the following ten business groups: Sinar Mas, Salim, Astra, Gajah Tunggal, Bakrie, Ongko, Dharmala + PSP, Ciputra + Jaya + Metropolitan, Ometraco and Napan + Risjad.[19] The latter sub-data set includes offshore syndicated debt for the borrowers in Table 3.7.[20] These were considered top-tier credit corporate borrowers by offshore lenders. They were basically listed companies on the Jakarta Stock Exchange and members of leading business groups. Furthermore, they regularly raised funds in offshore syndicated debt markets during the finance boom.

Table 3.7 Top-tier credit corporate borrowers in Indonesia

Business group	Borrowers
Salim	Indocement, Indofood, Unggul Indah Corp., Darya-Varia Laboratoria
Astra	Astra International, Federal Motor, Astra Sedaya Finance, United Tractors, Sumalindo Lestari Jaya, Astra Graphia, Astra Dian Lestari
Sinar Mas	Asia Pulp and Paper, Indah Kiat, Tjiwi Kimia, SMART Corp., Sinar Mas Multiartha, Duta Pertiwi
Gudang Garam	Gudang Garam
Lippo	Lippo Pacific
Gajah Tunggal	Gajah Tunggal, Kabel Metal, GT Petrochem Industries, Gajah Surya Multifinance
Djarum	Djarum
Karbe	Kalbe Farma, Dankos Laboratories, Enseval
Ometraco	Japfa Comfeed, Multibreeder, Ometraco Corp.
CP (Indonesia)	Charoen Pokphand Indonesia, Central Proteinaprima, Surya Hidup Satwa

Case studies of financial activities by Indonesian business groups during the finance boom

The final empirical studies are case studies at the business group level. These analyse the underlying financial activities and motivations that accelerated the leveraging of the Indonesian private sector during the finance boom. Business groups are the basic unit of corporate activity in Indonesia. With few exceptions, Indonesian business groups were simple bundles of individual companies built as the result of group owners' acquisitions in various unrelated business fields.[21] In the 1990s, a number of these conglomerates introduced a pyramid type of group shareholding structure, based on holding and sub-holding companies. However, owners and their family members directly controlled most corporate activities throughout the group, especially financial activities. In terms of management, the structures were still primitive.

In theory, diversified business groups can internally imitate the functions of institutions that are partial or absent in developing countries, such as capital, labour and products markets (Khanna and Palepu 1997, 1999).[22] In this context, Indonesian business groups were designed to put priority on the functions of capital markets. By taking advantage of the form and structure of business groups, Indonesian conglomerates increased their credibility among offshore investors, attempted to mobilize as much capital as possible, and minimized owner shareholders' capital investments. In other words, Indonesian business groups were financial-activity-oriented as if they were large private equity funds. Therefore, the analysis of financial activities at the business group level is appropriate for an understanding of the behaviour of the Indonesian private sector during the finance boom.

Furthermore, some of the financial transactions analysed in the case studies would have been strictly prohibited in advanced financial markets as they would be disadvantageous to stakeholders. In Indonesia, however, these transactions were allowed and formed part of the aggressive financial strategies of business groups. The work does not focus on the defects of corporate governance in Indonesia, but it is necessary to review this issue in order to understand the reason why certain classes of financial transactions were widely and rapidly introduced during the finance boom. Although the work does not offer an analysis of why the government failed to respond to the governance challenge, it is important to bear in mind that capitalists took advantage of the lag time between the introduction of new types of financial transactions and the legal, regulatory and supervisory response of the state.

In theory, corporate governance can be defined as the structure of rights and responsibilities with regard to corporate management among widely defined stakeholders, such as shareholders, lenders, employees, affiliated companies, suppliers and customers (Aoki 1995, p.183; Osano 2001, pp.9–11).[23] The theory generally views corporate governance as a means to increase economic welfare and has been developed within the framework of comparative institutional analysis. The empirical study of corporate governance analyses control systems that are both internal and external to the firm.

The literature on corporate governance concentrates on the following control systems: (i) organizational control structures; (ii) the role of shareholders and (iii) debt contracts. Corporate governance through organizational control structures involves both internal and external systems. Internal systems include control over management (a group of executive officers) by board of directors, employees and the design of incentives structures within which management operates (Milgrom and Roberts 1992, pp.473–96; Osano 2001, pp.21–61). External systems include independent audits (reporting to boards of directors) and compliance with rules and regulations. The role of shareholders includes the threat of takeover (which could lead to the replacement of the management team) and pressures exerted on management by shareholder activists, such as institutional investors (Milgrom and Roberts 1992, pp.568–83; Osano 2001, pp.31–4, 70–82).[24] Corporate governance through debt contracts exists under both bank-based and market-based financial systems. The former includes the control over management by main (or house/line) banks, while the latter includes the control of management by credit ratings of bonds and notes (Osano 2001, pp.125–77).

Control systems in Indonesia were seriously defective during the finance boom. The country had inherited a Dutch counterbalancing system for corporate control. That is to say, corporate actions, which were decided by board of directors (*direksi*), had to be authorized by a board of commissioners (*komisaris*). However, the boards of directors and commissioners were, in many cases, dominated by owner family members and related persons, and so the system did not function well.[25] The quality of audit was below international standards. Local independent auditors were poorly trained and often colluded with owner families.[26] External control systems through audit procedures therefore did not function well. In the early 1990s, Indonesia introduced a market-based regulatory framework, such as lending limits to business groups and exposure limits on foreign currency positions. The banks did not comply with these rules and the regulator did not actively enforce them.[27]

In the private sector, there was little separation between management and owner shareholders. Even in publicly listed companies, owner shareholders remained the majority or the single largest shareholders and fully controlled management. Therefore, the possibility of takeover was limited. Minority shareholders could not put pressure on management by threatening to take control. In addition, activists had not emerged among minority shareholders even during the finance boom. This was because local institutional investors lacked professionalism and offshore institutional investors limited their risk exposure in Indonesia through diversification and keeping their investments relatively small. Minority shareholders effectively were faced with a choice between following owner shareholders' decisions and selling out. Owner shareholders could take major decisions without consultation or considering the interests of minority shareholders. Asymmetry of information between owner shareholders (and also management members) and minority shareholders was a key mechanism through which owner managers retained control.

Non-arm's-length transactions between owner shareholders' family businesses and their public companies simply overrode minority shareholders' interests.[28]

The financial market was liberalized in the late 1980s and a market-based regulatory framework was introduced in the early 1990s. Nevertheless, the market was still largely bank-based, and state banks were expected to monitor the corporate sector.[29] In particular, when funding sources were still limited before the finance boom, state banks had significant bargaining power vis-à-vis corporate borrowers. Nevertheless, politico-bureaucrats often directed state banks to finance firms connected to allied business groups.[30] The banks' monitoring function on borrowers did not work adequately. In addition, the rapid expansion of private banks after PAKTO (the deregulation policy package for the banking sector) suddenly opened the offshore loan market and created an abundant debt supply for the corporate sector. Major business groups were able to obtain funds from their group banks and offshore banks and were no longer dependent on state banks. Consequently, state banks lost their bargaining power and thus their ability to monitor the corporate sector. Asymmetry of information between business group owners and banks became larger, and debt finance was used for non-arm's-length transactions as banks flooded the market with credit. In addition, Indonesian companies' limited access to bond markets and heavy reliance on banks meant that pressure on management exerted through bond ratings and secondary market prices was largely absent.

First, in the case studies, the author has analysed the liability side of combined balance sheets, equity funding and offshore syndicated debt for selected business groups. The methods used in the analysis are basically the same as those that can be observed in Chapters 4 and 5. Second, the author has analysed the details of capital transactions, such as corporate reorganization (e.g. the change of group holding structures) and liquidation (encashment) of business group owners' individual investments which led to their aggressive financial transactions and leveraged financial positions. In the latter analyses, it has been observed how the groups' publicly listed companies were used to achieve their targets. These detailed studies enable the understanding of the underlying driving forces behind leveraging.

For the case studies at the business group level, the following four business groups have been selected: Salim, Lippo, Sinar Mas and Gajah Tunggal. The Salim Group achieved the most dramatic corporate reorganization by actively using offshore syndicated debt. The Lippo Group also achieved very noticeable corporate reorganization but funded this mainly through equity finance and third parties' direct capital injections. Therefore, both groups, Salim and Lippo, provide interesting contrasts with regards to the pattern of leveraging. The Sinar Mas Group acted extraordinarily aggressively in its use of third party funds, such as offshore syndicated debt, fixed income bonds and equity finance. Furthermore, it completed cross-border group holding structures, thereby, accelerating international fund raising on an unbelievably large scale and developing highly complex financial structures. The Gajah Tunggal Group was also very active in the reorganization of holding structures and the encashment of the group owners' investments. Many other major business groups carried out similar financial activities during the period. Thus, the financial activities of these four business groups are valid examples, not only due to their size and importance, but also because the methods that they used were replicated by other conglomerates during the finance boom. The case studies therefore provide essential group- and firm-level analysis of the causes and collapse of the finance boom in the 1990s.

4 The financial positions of the Indonesian corporate sector in the 1990s

Following on from the methods and database described in Chapter 3, this chapter seeks to analyse the financial position of the Indonesian private corporate sector in the 1990s (until the outbreak of the Asian crisis) by focusing on the liability side of the sector.[1] The analysis also focuses on the period between 1994 and the first half of 1997, which the author has defined as the 'finance boom' of the 1990s. As argued in Chapter 1, the corporate sector accumulated huge external debt during the period by aggressively accepting offshore financiers' enthusiastic offers, thereby totally changing the nature of Indonesia's external debt problem from public-to-public to private-to-private. It is also argued that international private capital, which is mobile capital, was deeply integrated into the corporate sector's financial structures over this short period. The author locates the source of fragility and instability of the Indonesian economy, which led to the crisis in 1997 and 1998, in the financial structures of the corporate sector that emerged under the finance boom.

Empirical studies in this chapter focus on the movements of four types of leverage indicators during the finance boom, namely:

1 the leverage ratio or liability to equity ratio (standard leverage);
2 the debt to equity ratio;
3 the debt to EBITDA ratio;
4 the debt to CS + APIC ratio.

The chapter compares the movements of the indicators prior to and in the aftermath of the boom. The studies also investigate movements in these ratios that indicate profitability and debt-service capacity in relation to the analysis of leverage.[2] As argued in Chapter 2, Minsky views the historical profitability of economic units as the most important determinant of forecasted cash flows for future debt servicing. Margins of safety of investments are thereby determined in investors' minds based on these measures.

Furthermore, the studies examine the movements of the ratios that indicate the liquidity positions of the financial structure, that is to say, the short-term debt positions against long-term debt, short-term assets (liquid assets) and cash flows (EBITDA). As argued in Chapter 2, Minsky explains the endogenous fragility and instability of the financial structure in terms of the mismatch between cash inflows and outflows as well as leveraging. Stiglitz and other mainstream economists sought the causes of the East Asian crisis in the sudden reversal of short-term debt that was rapidly accumulated by the affected countries during the boom. Both arguments relate to the liquidity position of economy. However, Minsky views the process as endogenous to the capitalist economy.

All of the above ratios are calculated from the following four data sets derived from the original data base (drawn from the Indonesian private sector as explained in Chapter 3):

1   The corporate sector (comprised of non-financial listed companies, such as manufacturing, service and mining companies);
2   The 50 private non-financial companies (including private manufacturing, service and mining companies, the financial data for which are complete for the years 1990 to 1997);
3   The 187 private non-financial companies (including private manufacturing, service and mining companies, the financial data for which are available from 1993 to 1997);
4   The private non-bank sector (including private manufacturing, service, mining and non-bank/insurance finance companies).

The analysis focuses on the results from data set (1), that is, the corporate sector. The results from data sets (2) and (3) are used to corroborate the results from dataset (1) from the viewpoint of data consistency. The results from data set (4), including private non-bank/insurance finance companies, are used to check the financial positions of the sectors placed outside the strict external debt controls of the state authorities.[3] The results of the studies are also cross-checked against those of two similar studies conducted by Claessens, Djankov and Lang, and by Pomerleano.[4]

Finally, the empirical studies aim to demonstrate how fragile and unstable financial structures became in the corporate sector during this period, and thereby to define the finance boom in the 1990s in the context of leveraging. This chapter also aims to bridge the gap between the macroeconomic arguments presented in Chapter 1 and the microeconomic arguments of Chapters 5–9.

Overview of the corporate sector's financial positions in the 1990s

In the 1980s, due to the decline in oil-related state revenues, the state was no longer able to finance economic development, as had been the case in the 1970s. Growing importance was allocated to the private sector. The government encouraged the corporate sector to promote non-oil and gas and export-oriented businesses for economic development. In other words, the government expected the private sector investment rate to increase. The liberalization of the financial markets in the late 1980s and the maintenance of free capital movements were aimed at enabling the private sector to obtain the necessary capital resources to finance expansion and diversification. REPELITA (Rencana Pembaugnan Lima Tahun) V (the fifth 5-year development plan, 1 April 1989 to 31 March 1994) expected the private sector to fund approximately 55 per cent of the plan's capital requirements, and REPELITA VI (the sixth 5-year development plan, 1 April 1994 to 31 March 1999) expected the private sector to fund 75 per cent of the plan's capital requirements. From the viewpoint of the liability side of the Indonesian economy the 1990s was the age of private capital mobilization.

The corporate sector, which consists of listed manufacturing, service and other industrial companies, dramatically increased its leverage in the 1990s.[5] From 1990 to 1996, the leverage ratio, the gross debt to equity ratio, the gross debt to EBITDA ratio, and the gross debt to CS + APIC ratio all increased precipitously (Tables 4.1 and 4.2). The four ratios for the 50 private non-financial companies also increased sharply (Tables 4.3 and 4.4). Furthermore, the ratios for the private non-bank sector, which adds listed non-bank finance companies to the data set of the corporate sector, increased (Tables 4.5 and 4.6). These results clearly indicate that during the period, the corporate sector accumulated huge debts, in particular, financial debts, much faster than the growth of earnings, cash flows from operations and cash calls from equity issuances. In terms of the average gross debt to equity ratio during the period, the Indonesian economy had the third most leveraged corporate sector among the non-Japan Asian countries, following Korea and Thailand, and the sector was the sixth most leveraged in the world (Claessens *et al.* 1998).

The profitability of the corporate sector dramatically improved until 1995, and then declined in 1996. The operating profit margin, the net profit margin and the EBITDA margin increased by 45.9, 22.8 and 55.9 per cent from 1990 to 1995 (Tables 4.1 and 4.2). The same improvements were recorded for the private non-bank sector (Tables 4.5 and 4.6). Margins in the data sets of 50 and 187 private non-financial companies, however, increased until 1994, but declined thereafter (Tables 4.3, 4.4, 4.7 and 4.8). The corporate sector was able to offer an excellent credit story to its investors and creditors by demonstrating the dramatic and constant improvement of profitability before and during the finance boom in the 1990s, although profits declined during the latter stages. In particular, the sector's operating profit margin was among the best in East and South-East Asia during this period.[6] In Minsky's terms, the margin of safety on investments in the sector significantly improved during the period. These facts generated euphoria among international mobile capitalists concerning investments in the sector, thus acting as a stimulant. Following Minsky, investors' positive forecasts on their investments in the sector, supported by the excellent performance as described earlier, led to the sector's financial instability through an increase in leverage.

Table 4.1 Financial ratios of the Indonesian corporate sector

Ratios	Unit	1990	1991	1992	1993	1994	1995	1996	1997
Leverage	Times	0.67	1.17	1.26	1.18	1.18	1.37	1.47	2.15
Equity	%	59.8	46.2	44.3	45.8	45.9	42.1	40.5	31.7
Gross debt to equity	Times	0.36	0.81	0.91	0.76	0.79	0.98	1.05	1.64
Net debt to equity	Times	0.30	0.75	0.78	0.67	0.66	0.78	0.81	1.36
Gross debt to EBITDA	Times	1.48	3.19	3.68	3.04	3.21	3.66	4.16	8.14
Net debt to EBITDA	Times	1.24	2.96	3.16	2.68	2.69	2.89	3.21	6.72
Gross debt to CS + APIC	Times	0.52	1.19	1.36	1.26	1.22	1.54	1.72	2.61
Net debt to CS + APIC	Times	0.44	1.11	1.17	1.11	1.02	1.22	1.33	2.15
Long-term to short-term debt	Times	0.49	0.75	1.15	1.01	1.53	1.75	2.05	1.77
Current	Times	1.75	1.52	1.46	1.41	1.63	1.57	1.52	1.25
Net short-term debt to EBITDA	Times	0.75	1.60	1.20	1.15	0.75	0.57	0.42	1.52
Operating profit margin	%	11.7	12.2	13.4	14.9	16.1	17.1	15.9	14.8
Net profit margin	%	8.1	7.9	8.2	8.7	9.5	9.9	9.6	−4.1
EBITDA margin	%	14.1	15.2	17.5	19.3	20.2	22.0	21.5	21.4
Return on assets	%	12.1	9.4	8.4	8.9	9.0	8.8	7.6	4.4
Return on equity	%	13.9	13.1	11.5	11.4	11.7	12.1	11.2	−3.9
EBIT interest coverage	Times	4.35	4.01	3.07	3.31	3.95	3.69	3.36	2.16
EBIT funding cost coverage	Times	3.85	2.97	2.50	2.88	3.31	2.88	2.82	0.88
EBITDA interest coverage	Times	5.24	4.99	4.00	4.29	4.95	4.75	4.53	3.14
EBITDA funding cost coverage	Times	4.64	3.71	3.26	3.73	4.14	3.71	3.80	1.27

Source: Annual reports.

Table 4.2 The changes of financial ratios of the Indonesian corporate sector (1993 = 1.00)

Ratios	1990	1991	1992	1993	1994	1995	1996	1997
Leverage	0.57	0.98	1.06	1.00	1.00	1.16	1.24	1.82
Equity	1.31	1.01	0.97	1.00	1.00	0.92	0.89	0.69
Gross debt to equity	0.47	1.05	1.18	1.00	1.03	1.28	1.37	2.15
Net debt to equity	0.45	1.11	1.16	1.00	0.98	1.15	1.20	2.02
Gross debt to EBITDA	0.49	1.05	1.21	1.00	1.06	1.20	1.37	2.68
Net debt to EBITDA	0.46	1.11	1.18	1.00	1.01	1.08	1.20	2.51
Gross debt to CS + APIC	0.41	0.95	1.08	1.00	0.97	1.23	1.37	2.07
Net debt to CS + APIC	0.39	1.00	1.06	1.00	0.92	1.10	1.20	1.94
Long-term to short-term debt	0.49	0.74	1.13	1.00	1.51	1.73	2.03	1.74
Current	1.24	1.08	1.04	1.00	1.16	1.11	1.08	0.88
Net short-term debt to EBITDA	0.65	1.39	1.04	1.00	0.65	0.49	0.36	1.32
Operating profit margin	0.79	0.82	0.90	1.00	1.08	1.15	1.07	0.99
Net profit margin	0.92	0.90	0.93	1.00	1.09	1.14	1.09	−0.47
EBITDA margin	0.73	0.79	0.91	1.00	1.05	1.14	1.11	1.11
Return on assets	1.36	1.05	0.94	1.00	1.02	0.99	0.85	0.50
Return on equity	1.22	1.15	1.01	1.00	1.02	1.06	0.98	−0.34
EBIT interest coverage	1.32	1.21	0.93	1.00	1.19	1.12	1.02	0.65
EBIT funding cost coverage	1.34	1.03	0.87	1.00	1.15	1.00	0.98	0.31
EBITDA interest coverage	1.22	1.16	0.93	1.00	1.15	1.11	1.06	0.73
EBITDA funding cost coverage	1.24	0.99	0.87	1.00	1.11	0.99	1.02	0.34

Source: Annual reports.

Furthermore, the corporate sector improved its maturity profile by stretching the tenor of debt during the 1990s. The long-term to short-term debt ratio and the net short-term debt to EBITDA ratio both improved over the period 1990 to 1996 (Table 4.1). The current ratio also remained above 1.0 throughout this period (Table 4.1). The same improvements and stability can be confirmed for the 50 private non-financial companies and the private non-bank sector (Tables 4.3 and 4.5). In addition, cross-country studies by Claessens, Djankov and Lang, and by Pomerleano also report the same results (Claessens *et al.* 1998; Pomerleano 1998).[7] These findings mean that during the period, the corporate sector mitigated the potential risk of cash-flow breakdown by increasing long-term debt, controlling short-term debt against cash inflows, and maintaining liquid asset levels against short-term payment commitments. These results challenge Stiglitz's and other mainstream economists' analysis of the causes of the East Asian crisis and Minsky's arguments regarding the carry-trade under economic euphoria (Furman and Stiglitz 1998; Minsky 1986). Both arguments basically sought the causes of financial instability in the mismatch between liquidity positions and short-term payment commitments.[8] The results reported in

Table 4.3 Financial ratios of 50 private non-financial companies

Ratios	Unit	1990	1991	1992	1993	1994	1995	1996	1997
Leverage	Times	0.67	1.15	1.29	1.33	1.57	1.76	2.00	3.48
Equity	%	59.8	46.6	43.7	42.9	38.9	36.2	33.4	22.3
Gross debt to equity	Times	0.36	0.77	0.90	0.73	0.99	1.14	1.28	2.27
Net debt to equity	Times	0.30	0.71	0.80	0.59	0.76	0.81	0.98	1.82
Gross debt to EBITDA	Times	1.48	3.00	3.56	2.66	3.67	4.17	4.37	8.54
Net debt to EBITDA	Times	1.24	2.78	3.14	2.16	2.80	2.95	3.34	6.82
Gross debt to CS + APIC	Times	0.52	1.16	1.44	1.34	1.83	2.27	2.51	5.12
Net debt to CS + APIC	Times	0.44	1.07	1.28	1.08	1.40	1.60	1.92	4.09
Long-term to short-term debt	Times	0.49	0.57	0.91	0.64	1.82	1.50	1.65	1.66
Current	Times	1.75	1.49	1.48	1.45	1.69	1.59	1.52	1.24
Net short-term debt to EBITDA	Times	0.75	1.69	1.45	1.12	0.44	0.44	0.62	1.50
Operating profit margin	%	11.7	11.4	11.3	12.2	13.3	12.7	12.4	11.7
Net profit margin	%	8.1	7.1	6.0	6.3	6.9	6.7	7.1	−1.2
EBITDA margin	%	14.1	14.0	14.5	15.5	16.5	15.8	15.9	15.5
Return on assets	%	12.1	9.7	8.7	9.2	8.5	8.0	7.6	4.5
Return on equity	%	13.9	13.0	10.6	11.1	11.3	11.6	13.1	−2.0
EBIT interest coverage	Times	4.35	4.35	3.22	3.50	3.76	3.71	3.37	2.40
EBIT funding cost coverage	Times	3.85	3.19	2.61	2.90	3.31	3.00	2.73	1.13
EBITDA interest coverage	Times	5.24	5.34	4.10	4.44	4.65	4.59	4.31	3.19
EBITDA funding cost coverage	Times	4.64	3.92	3.33	3.68	4.09	3.72	3.49	1.51

Source: Annual reports.

Table 4.4 The changes of financial ratios of 50 private non-financial companies (1993 = 1.00)

Ratios	1990	1991	1992	1993	1994	1995	1996	1997
Leverage	0.50	0.86	0.97	1.00	1.18	1.32	1.50	2.61
Equity	1.39	1.09	1.02	1.00	0.91	0.84	0.78	0.52
Gross debt to equity	0.49	1.06	1.24	1.00	1.36	1.57	1.76	3.13
Net debt to equity	0.51	1.21	1.35	1.00	1.29	1.37	1.66	3.09
Gross debt to EBITDA	0.56	1.12	1.34	1.00	1.38	1.57	1.64	3.20
Net debt to EBITDA	0.58	1.29	1.46	1.00	1.30	1.37	1.55	3.16
Gross debt to CS + APIC	0.39	0.86	1.08	1.00	1.37	1.69	1.87	3.83
Net debt to CS + APIC	0.40	0.99	1.18	1.00	1.29	1.48	1.77	3.78
Long-term to short-term debt	0.77	0.89	1.42	1.00	2.83	2.34	2.57	2.59
Current	1.20	1.02	1.02	1.00	1.17	1.09	1.04	0.85
Net short-term debt to EBITDA	0.67	1.51	1.30	1.00	0.39	0.40	0.56	1.34
Operating profit margin	0.96	0.93	0.93	1.00	1.09	1.04	1.02	0.95
Net profit margin	1.27	1.12	0.95	1.00	1.09	1.05	1.12	−0.19
EBITDA margin	0.91	0.90	0.93	1.00	1.06	1.01	1.02	1.00
Return on assets	1.31	1.05	0.94	1.00	0.92	0.87	0.83	0.48
Return on equity	1.25	1.17	0.95	1.00	1.01	1.04	1.18	−0.18
EBIT interest coverage	1.24	1.24	0.92	1.00	1.07	1.06	0.96	0.68
EBIT funding cost coverage	1.33	1.10	0.90	1.00	1.14	1.04	0.94	0.39
EBITDA interest coverage	1.18	1.20	0.92	1.00	1.05	1.03	0.97	0.72
EBITDA funding cost coverage	1.26	1.07	0.91	1.00	1.11	1.01	0.95	0.41

Source: Annual reports.

this study clearly indicate that the liquidity positions of the corporate sector improved in the 1990s.

As a whole, during the 1990s until the East Asian crisis, the profitability of the corporate sector improved and the result was that it was therefore able not only to leverage its financial positions, but also to improve its liquidity positions. In other words, the sector strongly pushed for accumulating long-term debt by displaying an improving credit story to investors and lenders. However, the increase in leverage led to the deterioration of the sector's debt-service capacity. The EBIT interest coverage ratio, the EBIT funding cost coverage ratio, the EBITDA interest coverage ratio and the EBITDA funding cost coverage ratio all deteriorated in 1996 (Tables 4.1 and 4.2). Until the outbreak of the East Asian crisis, investors and lenders failed to respond quickly enough to the leverage-induced deterioration of the sector's debt-service capacity.

In order to accurately trace the shifts in the financial positions of the corporate sector during the 1990s, it is necessary to understand its funding circumstances

Table 4.5 Financial ratios of the Indonesian private non-bank sector

Ratios	Unit	1990	1991	1992	1993	1994	1995	1996	1997
Leverage	Times	0.78	1.21	1.28	1.23	1.21	1.52	1.84	2.37
Equity	%	56.1	45.2	43.8	44.9	45.3	39.7	35.2	29.7
Gross debt to equity	Times	0.43	0.83	0.92	0.80	0.82	1.02	1.11	1.71
Net debt to equity	Times	0.37	0.77	0.79	0.71	0.69	0.82	0.87	1.42
Gross debt to EBITDA	Times	1.78	3.31	3.75	3.18	3.35	3.80	4.35	8.78
Net debt to EBITDA	Times	1.54	3.09	3.23	2.82	2.83	3.04	3.39	7.29
Gross debt to CS + APIC	Times	0.62	1.22	1.38	1.31	1.25	1.60	1.83	2.67
Net debt to CS + APIC	Times	0.53	1.13	1.19	1.16	1.06	1.28	1.42	2.22
Long-term to short-term debt	Times	0.43	0.70	1.13	0.99	1.43	1.72	2.12	1.86
Current[a]	Times	NA	NA	NA	NA	NA	NA	NA	NA
Net short-term debt to EBITDA	Times	1.01	1.71	1.24	1.24	0.87	0.64	0.43	1.58
Operating profit margin	%	11.8	12.3	13.5	15.0	16.3	17.3	16.4	13.8
Net profit margin	%	8.2	8.0	8.3	8.8	9.7	10.0	9.6	−4.5
EBITDA margin	%	14.2	15.3	17.6	19.3	20.3	22.3	21.8	20.5
Return on assets	%	11.2	9.1	8.2	8.7	8.9	8.3	6.8	3.9
Return on equity	%	13.9	13.1	11.5	11.5	11.7	12.1	11.2	−4.3
EBIT interest coverage	Times	3.32	3.25	2.76	2.97	3.63	2.86	2.00	1.30
EBIT funding cost coverage	Times	3.02	2.55	2.30	2.62	3.08	2.36	1.81	0.69
EBITDA interest coverage	Times	3.98	4.04	3.59	3.84	4.52	3.69	2.67	1.93
EBITDA funding cost coverage	Times	3.63	3.17	2.99	3.39	3.85	3.04	2.41	1.02

Source: Annual reports.

Note
a Not available.

Table 4.6 The changes of financial ratios of the Indonesian private non-bank sector (1993 = 1.00)

Ratios	1990	1991	1992	1993	1994	1995	1996	1997
Leverage	0.64	0.99	1.05	1.00	0.98	1.24	1.50	1.93
Equity	1.25	1.01	0.97	1.00	1.01	0.88	0.78	0.66
Gross debt to equity	0.54	1.04	1.15	1.00	1.03	1.28	1.39	2.15
Net debt to equity	0.52	1.09	1.12	1.00	0.98	1.15	1.23	2.01
Gross debt to EBITDA	0.56	1.04	1.18	1.00	1.05	1.19	1.37	2.76
Net debt to EBITDA	0.55	1.10	1.15	1.00	1.01	1.08	1.20	2.59
Gross debt to CS + APIC	0.47	0.93	1.05	1.00	0.96	1.22	1.40	2.04
Net debt to CS + APIC	0.46	0.98	1.03	1.00	0.91	1.10	1.23	1.91
Long-term to short-term debt	0.43	0.71	1.14	1.00	1.44	1.74	2.15	1.88
Current[a]	NA	NA	NA	NA	NA	NA	NA	NA
Net short-term debt to EBITDA	0.82	1.39	1.01	1.00	0.70	0.52	0.35	1.28
Operating profit margin	0.79	0.82	0.90	1.00	1.09	1.16	1.10	0.92
Net profit margin	0.93	0.91	0.94	1.00	1.10	1.14	1.09	−0.51
EBITDA margin	0.73	0.79	0.91	1.00	1.05	1.15	1.13	1.06
Return on assets	1.28	1.04	0.95	1.00	1.02	0.95	0.78	0.45
Return on equity	1.21	1.14	1.00	1.00	1.02	1.05	0.98	−0.37
EBIT interest coverage	1.12	1.10	0.93	1.00	1.22	0.96	0.68	0.44
EBIT funding cost coverage	1.15	0.97	0.88	1.00	1.18	0.90	0.69	0.26
EBITDA interest coverage	1.04	1.05	0.94	1.00	1.18	0.96	0.70	0.50
EBITDA funding cost coverage	1.07	0.93	0.88	1.00	1.13	0.90	0.71	0.30

Source: Annual reports.

Note
a Not available.

and financial positions at the beginning of the period, and thereafter analyse subsequent changes by dividing the period into the following three stages: 1990–2; 1993–4 and 1994–6. The first period was marked by the initial leveraging process of the sector, which was mainly caused by the deregulation of the Indonesian financial sector in the late 1980s. The second period saw a temporary de-leveraging process in the sector mainly due to the stock market boom and the turning point of its financial positions in the 1990s. In particular, financial ratios in 1994 do not indicate a clear shift in the sector's financial position. That is to say, the ratios indicate both de-leveraging and re-leveraging. Finally, the third period was characterized by a re-leveraging process coincident with the finance boom of the 1990s, as argued in Chapter 1. The corporate sector steeply increased its leverage by acquiring debt, in particular, offshore syndicated debt, and thereby absorbed mobile capital and created a fragile and unstable financial structure.

Table 4.7 Financial ratios of 187 private non-financial companies

Ratios	Unit	1993	1994	1995	1996	1997
Leverage	Times	1.18	1.16	1.36	1.51	2.57
Equity	%	45.8	46.3	42.3	39.9	28.0
Gross debt to equity	Times	0.76	0.78	0.97	1.09	1.91
Net debt to equity	Times	0.67	0.65	0.75	0.85	1.58
Gross debt to EBITDA	Times	3.04	3.18	3.81	4.38	8.51
Net debt to EBITDA	Times	2.68	2.65	2.96	3.43	7.04
Gross debt to CS + APIC	Times	1.26	1.21	1.60	1.80	2.97
Net debt to CS + APIC	Times	1.11	1.00	1.24	1.41	2.46
Long-term to short-term debt	Times	1.01	1.59	1.62	1.82	1.61
Current	Times	1.41	1.67	1.59	1.54	1.17
Net short-term debt to EBITDA	Times	1.15	0.69	0.60	0.60	1.79
Operating profit margin	%	14.9	16.3	15.8	14.7	13.3
Net profit margin	%	8.7	9.6	9.5	8.7	−6.0
EBITDA margin	%	19.3	20.3	19.9	19.2	18.8
Return on assets	%	8.9	9.0	8.6	7.6	4.5
Return on equity	%	11.4	11.6	12.2	11.3	−7.2
EBIT interest coverage	Times	3.31	4.00	3.78	3.19	1.97
EBIT funding cost coverage	Times	2.88	3.35	2.91	2.58	0.77
EBITDA interest coverage	Times	4.29	4.99	4.75	4.18	2.79
EBITDA funding cost coverage	Times	3.73	4.19	3.66	3.38	1.10

Source: Annual reports.

Table 4.8 The changes of financial ratios of 187 private non-financial companies (1993 = 1.00)

Ratios	1993	1994	1995	1996	1997
Leverage	1.00	0.98	1.15	1.28	2.17
Equity	1.00	1.01	0.92	0.87	0.61
Gross debt to equity	1.00	1.02	1.27	1.43	2.50
Net debt to equity	1.00	0.96	1.12	1.27	2.35
Gross debt to EBITDA	1.00	1.05	1.25	1.44	2.80
Net debt to EBITDA	1.00	0.99	1.10	1.28	2.63
Gross debt to CS + APIC	1.00	0.96	1.27	1.44	2.36
Net debt to CS + APIC	1.00	0.91	1.12	1.28	2.22
Long-term to short-term debt	1.00	1.57	1.59	1.80	1.59
Current	1.00	1.18	1.13	1.09	0.83
Net short-term debt to EBITDA	1.00	0.60	0.53	0.53	1.56
Operating profit margin	1.00	1.09	1.07	0.99	0.89
Net profit margin	1.00	1.10	1.09	1.00	−0.69
EBITDA margin	1.00	1.05	1.03	1.00	0.97
Return on assets	1.00	1.02	0.97	0.85	0.50
Return on equity	1.00	1.01	1.07	0.99	−0.63
EBIT interest coverage	1.00	1.21	1.14	0.96	0.59
EBIT funding cost coverage	1.00	1.16	1.01	0.89	0.27
EBITDA interest coverage	1.00	1.17	1.11	0.98	0.65
EBITDA funding cost coverage	1.00	1.12	0.98	0.91	0.29

Source: Annual reports.

Shifts in the corporate sector's financial positions during the 1990s

The starting point of the 1990s

As is argued earlier, the 1990s was the age of private capital mobilization in Indonesia. To the extent that macroeconomic conditions were sustainable, government policies were in line with the underlying strong expectations of private-to-private capital mobilization during the period. The basic Indonesian financial architecture, which was designed to facilitate private sector capital mobilization in the 1990s, had already been installed before the 1990s. The system was put in place through three waves of financial deregulation: (i) the removal of capital account controls between 1966 and 1970; (ii) the relaxation of equity market regulations in 1987 and 1988 and (iii) the relaxation of banking regulations between 1983 and 1990.

The equity market deregulation policy was introduced in December 1987 (PAKDES I) and December 1988 (PAKDES II). In these packages, two important changes were to instantly drive the stock market. First, foreign investors were allowed to purchase up to 49 per cent of listed shares (excluding bank shares).[9] After 1988, overseas funds played a major role in pushing up the stock market.[10] Second, the 4 per cent limit on daily price fluctuations was abandoned and the stock market was freed from direct price controls. The second policy created a great upside potential in investors' minds. The equity finance boom followed in 1989 and 1990. Listed companies of the Jakarta Stock Exchange increased by 99 from 24 to a total of 123 within only a two period. In April 1990, the Jakarta Stock Price Index reached 638.80, historically, the highest point ever at that time.[11] Market capitalization soared from Rp.449.2 billion at the beginning of 1989 to Rp.14.2 trillion by the end of 1990.[12] Although both overseas and domestic investors were aware of the very poor governance of the market, for example, insider trading, manipulation and speculation among brokers, poor auditing and superficial disclosure and the overriding of listing rules, they were intoxicated by the stock market boom.[13] By fully taking advantage of the situation, leading private non-financial companies obtained cheap funds through the market.

Focusing on the results from the dataset of 50 private non-financial companies, the level of leverage in 1990 was almost half of that in 1991. The leverage ratio, the gross debt to equity ratio, the gross debt to EBITDA ratio, and the gross debt to CS + APIC ratio were still relatively low in 1990 (Table 4.3). The non-financial companies that had access to the equity market were not leveraged. Furthermore, the low leverage of financial positions naturally led to high debt-service capacity. The EBIT interest coverage, EBIT funding cost coverage EBITDA interest coverage and the EBITDA funding cost-coverage ratios of 1990 indicated very sound levels (Table 4.3). Equity finance opportunities improved the leverage of the Indonesian corporate sector.

During the same period, a series of major banking reforms were also put into place through a combination of deregulation policies and market-based controls.

The most important deregulation package was introduced in October 1988 (PAKTO), which abolished restrictions on the opening of new banks and branches, allowed foreign banks to establish joint venture banks and reduced the reserve requirements from 15 per cent to 2 per cent. As a result, the number of new banks mushroomed, and branch networks suddenly expanded.[14] This situation fuelled the banking boom in Indonesia. As the government expected, the sharply expanding banking sector mobilized private funds as a result of increased real interest rates and the diversification of the financial products in the market. The process of financial deepening accelerated during the period. The M2 to GDP ratio increased from 29.6 per cent in 1988, 35.1 per cent in 1989 and to 43 per cent in 1990.[15] In addition, competition among banks both for deposits and lending dramatically reduced margins.

The rapid expansion of the banking sector also led to aggressive lending attitudes to high-risk and speculative businesses. While bank loans were mainly directed towards productive purposes in the manufacturing and service sectors as well as to consumer credit, they were also used for speculative purchases of stock shares and real estate. The shortage of qualified and experienced staff worsened this situation (Pangestu 1992; Pangestu and Habir 2002). Private non-financial firms, regardless of whether they could or could not access the equity market, sharply increased their leverage by rigorously absorbing domestic private debt.

On the other hand, as explained in Chapter 1, Indonesia has maintained an open capital account since 1970. The government encouraged the corporate sector to access the offshore debt market, and external debt sharply increased by 43 per cent from US$7.9 billion in 1989 to US$11.3 in 1990. Nevertheless, the sector's external debt still accounted for merely 18.0 per cent of Indonesia's total external debt. Offshore lenders were still sceptical and cautious of the corporate sector at that time. Offshore loans were largely limited to joint venture companies, which were supported by their world-leading parent companies, and the leading private companies.[16] In short, offshore debt finance had not made a significant contribution to the leveraging process of the corporate sector at the beginning of the 1990s.

In this way, at the start of the 1990s, the corporate sector was presented with two dynamic funding opportunities. One was competitive equity finance resulting from the stock market boom and the other was rapidly expanding debt finance from the domestic banking boom. These opportunities pushed financial structures in opposite directions, that is, de-leveraging through equity finance or leveraging through domestic debt. Both methods afforded the sector an excellent chance to access capital and expand the balance sheet.

The period from 1990 to 1992

The main economic issue facing Indonesian policy makers during the first period was macroeconomic management of rapid growth, and in particular, rapidly rising inflation rates and private capital mobilization.[17] Speculative activities, which were induced by the stock and banking market booms, accelerated price inflation. This was further fuelled by foreign exchange transactions by leading business groups' overseas investments.[18] At the beginning of 1990, BI initiated a tight monetary policy by reducing liquidity credits and increasing the interest rate on Bank Indonesia Certificates (SBI) in order to slow economic growth and foreign exchange speculation.[19] However, the government discovered that the policies were ineffective for the purpose.[20]

On 27 February 1991, Sumarlin, the Minister of Finance, announced a dramatic policy to shift eight trillion rupiah of deposits of state-owned enterprises to Bank Indonesia Certificates (the Second Sumarlin Shock).[21] Simultaneously, the following four regulations were introduced or strengthened: (i) net open position; (ii) capital adequacy ratio; (iii) loan to deposit ratio and (iv) legal lending limits.[22] After this, banks sharply increased interest rates resulting in reduced speculation. However, the ineffectiveness of market-based controls under Indonesia's socio-politico circumstances was made evident by a number of high-profile violations of the regulations.[23]

Bank Indonesia was concerned about inflation and foreign exchange speculation, and therefore maintained its tight monetary policy until signs of a slowdown in the growth of money supply became evident. The policy was finally reversed in 1992. However, it had already severely damaged the stock market. The average Jakarta Stock Price Index dropped to 335 in 1991 and to 293 in 1992 (Table 4.9). The corporate sector lost the incentive to raise funds through equity finance and was unable to decrease its leverage. It had to rely on bank loans during the period. However, tight monetary policies forced banks to slow down their rate of expansion, although they continued lending to the corporate sector.[24]

As a result, during the period from 1990 to 1992, the corporate sector slowed down the rate of accumulation through equity finance and leveraged its financial positions. The ratios of leverage, gross debt to equity, gross debt to EBITDA and gross debt to CS + APIC of the sector sharply increased (Tables 4.1 and 4.2). The four ratios in the data sets of 50 private non-financial companies also increased (Tables 4.3 and 4.4), as well as the four ratios for the private non-bank sector also increased (Tables 4.5 and 4.6). All three results are identical and illustrate that non-finance companies, such as those involved in manufacturing, service and mining, as well as non-bank finance companies leveraged their financial positions during the period. In particular, the gross debt to CS + APIC ratio deteriorated more than the other three ratios. This reflected the slowdown of equity funding, which is indicated by the increase in CS + APIC.

However, the results indicate that the increase of leverage in the corporate sector was larger than that in the private non-bank sector. The difference between the two data sets is non-bank finance companies. It can be concluded that non-finance companies increased their leverage much faster than non-bank finance companies during the period. This is because banks maintained active lending levels to non-finance companies even under the tight monetary policy and thus the corporate sector was still able to increase its access to debt financing.

With regards to profitability during the period, the corporate sector improved its operating margin and EBITDA margin by 14.7 and 24.2 per cent. However, the

Table 4.9 Major economic indicators for Indonesia

		1990	1991	1992	1993	1994	1995	1996	1997
GDP growth (real)	% p.a.	7.2	6.9	6.5	6.5	7.5	8.2	7.8	4.7
Nominal GDP	Rp. trillion	214	248	284	330	382	452	533	624
Inflation (CPI)	% p.a.	9.5	9.5	4.9	9.8	9.2	8.6	6.5	11.1
Balance of payment									
Current account balance	US$ billion	-3.2	-4.4	-3.1	-2.3	-3.0	-6.8	-7.8	-5.0
Capital account balance	US$ billion	4.7	5.8	6.5	6.0	4.0	10.6	11.0	2.5
Official	US$ billion	0.6	1.4	1.1	0.7	0.3	0.3	-0.5	2.9
Private	US$ billion	4.1	4.4	5.4	5.2	3.7	10.3	11.5	-0.3
Official reserves	US$ billion	8.7	9.9	11.6	12.4	13.2	14.7	19.1	17.4
Rupiah exchange rate									
Average	Rp. per US$	1,901	1,982	2,030	2,086	2,159	2,243	2,327	2,890
Year end	Rp. per US$	1,901	1,995	2,067	2,102	2,199	2,287	2,363	5,402
State banks reference rate									
Working capital	% p.a.	19.22	23.51	22.17	19.36	16.77	16.86	17.02	18.49
Investment finance	% p.a.	19.01	20.86	18.83	16.48	14.25	14.51	15.08	15.37
Time deposit (6 M)	% p.a.	16.75	23.03	20.03	14.48	11.57	14.71	16.29	15.33
Offshore reference rate									
US$		8.28							
3-month LIBOR	% p.a.		5.96	3.82	3.31	4.75	6.04	5.51	5.74
3-month SIBOR	% p.a.	NA	6.01	3.87	3.34	4.76	6.05	5.51	5.73

Japanese yen									
3-month LIBOR	% p.a.	7.77	7.37	4.45	3.00	2.29	1.22	0.57	0.57
Short-term prime	% p.a.	7.18	7.66	5.22	3.86	3.00	2.27	1.63	1.63
Long-term prime	% p.a.	8.04	7.50	5.96	4.86	4.43	3.49	3.06	2.58
Approved investment									
PMDN (domestic capital)	US$ billion	31.5	20.7	14.5	18.9	24.7	31.1	43.3	41.5
PMA (foreign capital)	US$ billion	8.8	8.8	10.3	8.1	23.7	39.9	29.9	33.8
Stock market									
JSX index (average)	1982 = 100	526	335	293	383	502	474	585	607
JSX index (closing)	1982 = 100	418	247	274	589	470	514	637	402
Number of listed companies	Companies	123	139	153	172	217	238	253	282
Value of transactions	Rp. trillion	3.8	5.5	8.0	19.1	25.5	32.5	75.7	121.4
Market capitalization	Rp. trillion	14.2	16.4	24.8	69.3	103.8	152.2	215.0	159.9
Bank sector									
Number of banks	Banks	171	192	208	234	240	240	239	222
Private bank	Banks	106	126	141	158	166	165	164	144
Number of offices	Offices	3,563	4,247	4,407	4,613	4,888	5,288	5,919	6,308
Private bank	Offices	2,052	2,639	2,747	2,926	3,203	3,458	3,964	4,150
Loan to GDP	%	46.3	45.4	43.8	45.6	59.3	51.6	55.0	60.2

Sources: Bank Indonesia, BPS, Sato (2001, 2002), Bloomberg.

net profit margin remained flat (Tables 4.1 and 4.2). The ratios for the private non-bank sector were almost identical (Tables 4.5 and 4.6). However, for the 50 private non-financial companies, operating margin and EBITDA margin remained virtually flat, and net profit margin fell by 25.2 per cent (Tables 4.3 and 4.4). The deterioration of net profits was clearly caused by increased funding costs under the tight monetary policy during the period. The ratios that indicate the debt-service capacity of the corporate sector, that is, EBIT interest coverage, EBIT funding cost coverage, EBITDA interest coverage and EBITDA funding cost coverage reveal the negative impact of the tight monetary policy on the sector (Tables 4.1 and 4.2). During the period, the exchange rate of the rupiah against US dollar was relatively stable and depreciated by only 4.9 per cent in 1991 and 3.6 per cent in 1992 (Table 4.9). However, domestic lending rates sharply increased reflecting the effects of the tight monetary policy. The state banks' working capital and investment lending rates increased from 19.22 and 19.01 per cent in 1990 to 23.51 and 20.86 per cent in 1991 respectively (Table 4.9). Although the tight monetary policy was relaxed in 1992, the rates remained at 22.17 and 18.83 per cent during the year (Table 4.9). Furthermore, as explained earlier, the leverage of the sector continued to increase during the period. The increases of both leverage and funding rates negatively affected the profitability and internal cash flow of the sector.

Moreover, return on assets and return on equity also eroded by 30.7 and 17.6 per cent from 12.1 and 13.9 per cent to 8.4 and 11.5 per cent (Tables 4.1 and 4.2). The deterioration of these two ratios is confirmed among the 50 private non-financial companies and the private non-bank sector (Tables 4.3, 4.4, 4.5 and 4.6). The cross-country study by Claessens, Djankov and Lang also achieves the same result (Claessens, Djankov and Lang 1998).[25] During the period, the sector's return on assets was the second highest among non-Japan Asian countries, following Thailand. However, the tight monetary policies pushed up the sector's funding costs to much higher levels than the return on assets. In this situation, the increase in leveraging led to a deterioration in returns on equity.[26] Nevertheless, the sector continued to invest in new projects by utilizing debt finance, and therefore its balance sheet was stretched and leveraged. Due to the fact that new projects were unable to contribute to the sector's profit and cash flow instantly, both ratios deteriorated sharply.

The government was also concerned about the increase in offshore borrowing.[27] In September 1991, the Coordinating Team for the Management of Offshore Commercial Loans (Tim Koordinasi Pengelolaan Pinjaman Komersian Luar Negeri) was established in order to manage all foreign commercial borrowing undertaken by the government (outside foreign aid), state enterprises and banks and government related projects (including private sponsored projects).[28] In addition, BI introduced controls on private banks' offshore borrowing, such as the quota and queuing system.[29] However, private borrowing purely undertaken by the corporate sector was placed outside the controls. The government simply requested that firms report offshore borrowing to BI and finding itself free to borrow without limits the sector increased total debt by 42.9 per cent in 1990.[30]

The rate of the increase in the sector's external debt slowed down in 1991 and 1992, and the volume in these years was still small (Tables 1.1, 1.2 and 1.3 in Chapter 1). The share of overseas in total debt declined from 28.6 per cent in 1990 to 24.2 per cent in 1993 (Table 1.6 in Chapter 1). This was simply because off-shore lenders continued to be very cautious about increasing their exposure to Indonesian private, non-financial borrowers. In addition, offshore lenders were concerned about the sector's performance under the tight monetary policy. As a result, the contribution of external debt towards the sector's leverage was still limited. The massive increase in its leveraging during the period was mainly due to the expansion of credits from domestic banks.

In this way, during the first period, the tight monetary policy reduced the corporate sector's profitability and damaged its debt-service capacity. In addition, it damaged the equity market and limited the capacity of the sector to raise funds on the equity markets. Offshore lenders became more cautious about increasing their exposure to the sector. Nevertheless, the booming domestic banking sector continued to finance new investments. As a result, the corporate sector dramatically increased its leverage and the increase in leverage reduced profitability and debt-service capacity.

The period from 1993 to 1994

The tight monetary policy was basically revoked in 1992. However, the government had to struggle with high inflation in 1993 and 1994. The inflation rate sharply increased from 5 to 10 per cent from 1992 to 1993 and remained high in 1994. The government saw no alternative but to revive the tight monetary policy occasionally to reduce inflationary pressures.[31] In particular, the inflationary pressures originated from the financial expansion of the private sector, which the government expected in REPELITA VI. Domestic banks continued to mobilize private capital and simultaneously to expand lending to the non-bank sector. Credit expansion steeply accelerated by 20.3 per cent in 1993 and 23 per cent in 1994. The loan to GDP ratio also increased to 43.8 per cent in 1992, 45.6 per cent in 1993 and 59.3 per cent in 1994 (Table 4.9). In particular, low domestic interest rates fuelled consumer finance and induced speculation in the property and stock markets. For example, loans to the property sector jumped in both volume and as a share of the total as follows: Rp.21.7 trillion (US$10.3 billion) and 14.5 per cent in 1993 to Rp.33.2 trillion (US$15.1 billion) and 17.6 per cent in 1994 (Pangestu and Habir 2002, p.12).

Moreover, global portfolio money was actively entering non-Japan Asian markets at this time. This returned to the Indonesian stock market and created an equity finance boom after 1993. The privatization of state companies (e.g. Indosat) also stimulated the market. Foreign direct investment also sharply increased. Approved foreign investment jumped from US$8.1 billion in 1993 to US$23.7 billion in 1994 (Table 4.9). In particular, the relaxation of foreign ownership restrictions, which allowed 100 per cent foreign ownership, and the shift of Japanese capital from China to South-East Asia (mainly, Thailand and Indonesia) made a major contribution to the increase in foreign direct investment. Furthermore, offshore debt capital also entered the Indonesian private sector mainly through offshore syndicated loans. In 1993 and 1994, the Indonesian private non-financial sector faced an extremely favourable funding environment.

In 1993, the leverage, gross debt to equity, gross debt to EBITDA and the gross debt to CS + APIC ratios all decreased (Tables 4.1 and 4.2). Identical movements in the four ratios can be confirmed in the data sets of 50 private non-financial companies and the private non-bank sector, except for the leverage ratio of 50 private non-financial companies (Tables 4.3, 4.4, 4.5 and 4.6). In 1994, the leverage ratio and the gross debt to CS + APIC ratio remained flat or slightly decreased, but others started increasing. These movements were almost identical in the data sets of 187 non-financial companies and the private non-bank sector (Tables 4.7, 4.8, 4.5 and 4.6). However, the four ratios in the dataset of 50 non-financial companies sharply increased (Tables 4.3 and 4.4). The cross-country studies by Claessens, Djankov and Lang, and by Pomerleano also support the above results (Claessens, Djankov and Lang 1998; Pomerleano 1998).[32]

This situation was created by the stock market boom in 1993 and 1994. The average Jakarta Stock Price Index recovered to 383 in 1993 and to 502 in 1994 (Table 4.9).[33] The number of listed companies increased by 64 within 2 years. This was the second highest in history, following the first stock market boom in 1989 and 1990 shortly after financial deregulation was introduced (PAKDES I in 1987, PAKTO and PAKDES II in 1988 and PAKMAR in 1989).[34] Market capitalization also jumped by 179 per cent in 1993 and 50 per cent in 1994 (Table 4.9). Within the 2 years, Indonesian companies obtained Rp.15.8 trillion (US$7.4 billion) in new liquidity through the equity markets.[35] In particular, they obtained Rp.11.2 trillion (US$5.2 billion) in 1994 alone. In the data sets of 50 and 187 private non-financial companies, CS + APIC increased by 40.7 and 59.2 per cent, respectively. These were the sharpest increases in the 1990s (Tables 4.3, 4.4, 4.7 and 4.8). New liquidity contributed to the decrease in the corporate sector's leverage in 1993 and 1994. In other words, a de-leveraging of the sector's financial positions occurred during this period. Furthermore, a more important issue is that the de-leveraged financial position created a new euphoria that led to the finance boom from 1994 to the first half of 1997 and the re-leveraging of the sector's financial positions.

Within the 2 years, the sector's fundamental profitability had improved markedly. The operating margin, the EBITDA margin and the return on assets increased by 20, 15 and 8 per cent respectively (Tables 4.1 and 4.2). In 1993, the same three ratios increased by 11, 10 and 6 per cent respectively (Tables 4.1 and 4.2). In addition to the improvements in fundamental profitability, the de-leveraged financial position, the drop in rupiah interest rates and stable exchange rates all improved profitability after funding cost payments as well as debt-service capacity.[36] The net profit margin, EBIT interest coverage, EBIT funding cost coverage, EBITDA interest coverage and the EBITDA funding cost coverage ratios all improved sharply (Tables 4.1 and 4.2). The data sets of 50 private non-financial companies and the private non-bank sector confirm the same improvements (Tables 4.3, 4.4, 4.5 and 4.6). These improvements also encouraged positive forecasts in the minds of investors and lenders.

Furthermore, the corporate sector improved its liquidity position during the period. Long-term to short-term debt, current, and the net short-term debt to EBITDA ratios all improved (Tables 4.1 and 4.2). The data sets of 50 private non-financial companies and the private non-bank sector also support these results (Tables 4.3, 4.4, 4.5 and 4.6). In particular, focusing on the data set of 50 private non-financial companies, short-term debt grew by only 28.2 per cent during the period, while the long-term debt grew by 156.0 per cent and equity increased by 71.9 per cent. In terms of the maturity profile, the sector's financial structure was clearly strengthened. Moreover, the results are supported by cross-country studies carried out by Claessens, Djankov and Lang and by Pomerleano (Claessens *et al.* 1998; Pomerleano 1998).[37] Investors' and lenders' positive forecasts were supported by liquidity positions.

The period from 1993 to 1994 was thus the turning point during the 1990s. Euphoria concerning the sector gathered momentum in the minds of investors and lenders. The most dramatic change during the period was that, as argued in Chapter 1, offshore debt began to enter into the corporate sector. In 1994, the external debt of the private non-financial sector suddenly jumped by US\$8.6 billion or 60.7 per cent (Tables 1.1, 1.2 and 1.3 in Chapter 1). As argued in Chapter 5, the increase in the sector's external debt was mainly financed through offshore syndicated loans. In sum, during the period, offshore banks' mobile capital started entering into the financial structures of the corporate sector on a large scale. The period was the turning point not only of the leverage but also of the nature of financial structures in the corporate sector.

The period from 1994 to 1996

The period from 1994 to 1996 is identical to the finance boom as defined in Chapter 1. Domestic capital was actively mobilized through both the equity and lending markets. International mobile capital also flooded into Indonesia through both equity investments and debt finance. At the end of 1994, the Mexican peso crisis affected the Indonesian stock market. Bad debt problems in the banking sector, and in particular, state banks, were widely repeated, and the mood shifted among offshore financiers.[38] However, offshore investors' euphoric views of the corporate sector remained basically unchanged. Offshore investors quickly returned to the stock market and contributed to its stable growth. Offshore lenders accelerated their lending to the sector despite the earlier-mentioned problems and encouraged the rapid accumulation of external debt within the sector. Domestic credit exposure was also growing continuously. However, due to competition from offshore bankers' cheap foreign currency debt, domestic banks began to look to more risky borrowers (Pangestu and Habir 2002). As a result, although BI pushed forward market-based controls, the central bank could not help but revert to direct intervention to slow domestic credit growth. The expansion of balance sheets and the increase in leverage of the corporate sector were obvious during this period.

The leverage, gross debt to equity, gross debt to EBITDA and the gross debt to CS + APIC ratios sharply increased from 1994 to 1996 (Tables 4.1 and 4.2). The four ratios in the data sets of 50 private non-financial companies also dramatically increased (Tables 4.3 and 4.4), as did the four ratios in the data sets of 187 private non-financial companies (Tables 4.7 and 4.8). Moreover, the four ratios in the data set of the private non-bank sector increased sharply (Tables 4.5 and 4.6). The studies by Claessens, Djankov and Lang and by Pomerleano also reveal an increase in the sector's leverage during this period (Claessens *et al.* 1998; Pomerleano 1998).[39] All these figures clearly indicate that the sector dramatically increased its leverage and thereby created a fragile and unstable financial structure during the finance boom.

The profitability of the corporate sector improved until 1995. Operating, net profit and EBITDA margins rose steadily until 1995 (Tables 4.1 and 4.2). However, all of these indicators dropped in 1996. On the other hand, debt-service capacity began deteriorating in 1995. The EBIT interest coverage, EBIT funding cost coverage, EBITDA interest coverage and the EBITDA funding cost-coverage ratios all dropped (Tables 4.1 and 4.2). During this period, domestic and offshore interest rates rose slightly, but borrowing margins dramatically improved.[40] Therefore, interest rates on loans did not rise. In addition, the rupiah exchange rate against the US dollar was stable.[41] Therefore, the deterioration in debt-service capacity was mainly due to the increasing leverage of the sector. Debt-financed investment also led to erosion in returns on assets by 14.8 per cent (Tables 4.1 and 4.2). Furthermore, the erosion of returns on assets, which was combined with the increase in leverage, led to the erosion of the return on equity (Tables 4.1 and 4.2).[42] In this way, the profitability and debt-service capacity of the private non-financial sector showed a downtrend during the period.

However, the sector dramatically improved the long-term to short-term debt and the net short-term debt to EBITDA ratios by 102.7 and 63.8 per cent from 1994 to 1996, respectively (Tables 4.1 and 4.2). The current ratio also remained above 1.5. This situation does not contradict the earlier-mentioned increase in leverage in the sector. As argued in Chapter 5, the sector introduced long-term offshore syndicated debt and thereby improved its maturity profile during the period. The shift in bargaining power from offshore lenders to Indonesian borrowers enabled the latter to stretch the maturity profile of their financial debt. The studies by Claessens, Djankov and Lang and by Pomerleano also support this contention (Claessens *et al.* 1998; Pomerleano 1998).[43] Based on these results, it can be concluded that the sector's liquidity positions were relatively sound at the onset of the East Asian crisis. This conclusion is the opposite of that put forward by Stiglitz and other mainstream economists with regards to the short-term debt problem as the main cause of the East Asian crisis.

The period 1994 to 1996 differed from the period from 1990 to 1992 in a variety of ways. First, the stock market was booming throughout the period. The net increase in listed companies was 81, and the closing figure of the Jakarta Stock Price Index increased from 470 in 1994 to 514 in 1995 and 637 in 1996 (Table 4.9).[44] Listed companies obtained Rp.33.6 trillion (US$14.9 billion) through equity finance.[45] Including the cash call in 1997, they obtained Rp.55.2 trillion (US$22.4 billion).[46] Second, the growth of debt was dramatically quicker than that of equity. Focusing on the non-bank sector, domestic debt increased by 77.0 per cent from US$47.9 billion at the beginning of 1994 to US$84.8 billion at the end of 1996.[47] External debt increased by 175.2 per cent from US$15.3 billion to US$42.1 billion. In particular, the sudden growth of external debt was a major contribution to the leveraging of the corporate sector. Third, the exposure of the corporate sector to foreign exchange risk increased. During the period, its foreign currency exposure, that is, the total of external debt and foreign currency domestic debt, increased by 120.8 per cent from US$32.2 billion to US$71.1 billion.[48] Its reliance on foreign currency debt increased from 43.7 per cent to 51.3 per cent. In sum, external-debt-driven leveraged financial structures emerged in the corporate sector with a dramatic expansion of the balance sheet.

Furthermore, during the period, the corporate sector aggressively absorbed enthusiastic offshore mobile capital into its financial structure. As a result, this accounted for large parts of both debt and equity and the sector was strongly connected to volatile global financial markets. In particular, offshore commercial banks became dominant in its leading companies' debt structures through off-shore syndicated loans. Although its profitability and debt-service capacity started to decline from the peak year of the finance boom, offshore commercial banks' enthusiastic attitude towards it did not change, but rather intensified, until the Indonesian crisis. Then, the sector also aggressively absorbed funds. It dramatically increased its fragility and instability not only by increasing its leverage but also by increasing its exposure to unstable mobile capital. The period from 1994 to 1996 can be defined as the process of re-leveraging financial positions and the emergence of market-based unstable financial structures in the corporate sector.

In addition, the increase in external debt in the corporate sector meant that off-shore lenders attracted prime borrowers away from domestic banks and increased competition in the domestic market. Domestic banks could not help but shift their lending to lower-quality borrowers and speculative projects (Pangestu and Habir 2002, pp.12–14). Actually, during the period, loans to the property sector steadily increased in both volume and share from Rp.33.2 trillion (US$15.1 billion) and 17.6 per cent in 1994 to Rp.58.9 trillion (US$24.9 billion) and 20.1 per cent in 1996. Finally, BI carried out non-market based interventions in the credit market, such as controlling commercial banks' lending to the property sector and slowing down the growth of non-bank finance companies' lending.[49] The accumulation of external debt in the corporate sector weakened the asset quality of the financial sector.

In this way, during the period from 1994 to 1996, the corporate sector dramatically expanded and leveraged its financial structure using external debt. At the same time, offshore mobile capital began to occupy a substantial share of the financial structure. A fragile and unstable financial structure emerged in the corporate sector and also created fragility and instability in the financial sector.

Conclusions

On the liability side of the Indonesian economy, the 1990s was the age of private capital mobilization. The government officially expected the private sector to mobilize capital for economic development. The basic financial architecture to achieve this purpose had already been installed before the beginning of the 1990s, although it had a number of defects. The corporate sector, which was expected to serve as a new agent to diversify the Indonesian economy to non-oil and gas industries, fully utilized the architecture and mobilized both equity and debt capital from both domestic and offshore markets. In particular, the corporate sector directly and aggressively accessed offshore markets. The basic stance of the government towards external debts was: to control the growth of external debt; to reduce public debt and to create room for the private sector (The World Bank 1996, pp.xxii–xxv). As a result, Indonesian financial structures were connected to global markets at a variety of contact points.

At the beginning of the 1990s, the liberalized financial architecture dramatically expanded equity and domestic debt-finance opportunities for the corporate sector. The equity finance boom in 1988 and 1989 de-leveraged the corporate sector for a short period. However, the rapid and dynamic expansion of the domestic debt market easily exceeded that of the equity market. During the period from 1990 to 1992, the government introduced a tight monetary policy, including the second Sumarlin Shock, to curb inflation. The policy severely damaged the stock market and discouraged the sector from raising funds through equity finance. The tight monetary policy also squeezed the money supply and slowed down the growth of banks' overall credit creation. Nevertheless, the corporate sector continuously increased its debt. Offshore lenders were still cautious of the sector throughout the period, and the sector was able to rely on domestic debt. As a result, from 1990 to 1992, the sector significantly increased its leverage by heavily relying on domestic debt-finance.

During the period from 1993 to 1994, the corporate sector was placed in a favourable position vis-à-vis global capital flows. The stock boom in 1993 and 1994 suddenly de-leveraged its financial position and improved the after-funding-cost profitability and debt-service capacity. Foreign direct investment, mainly in non-oil and gas industries, also returned to Indonesia and expanded the income opportunities of the private non-financial sector. The domestic debt market continued to grow in a highly competitive environment. Domestic funding costs declined and the corporate sector improved its debt-service capacity. Offshore lenders began to change their assessment of the sector and suddenly began to finance it aggressively. The euphoric view of the sector, which was supported by improved financial performance and positions, generated even more euphoria.

Starting in 1994, the corporate sector steeply increased its leverage. The equity market boom continued, but the debt market expanded much faster than the equity market. In particular, offshore lenders enthusiastically provided capital to the sector in the form of offshore syndicated loans. The sector not only leveraged its financial structures but also absorbed mobile capital into these structures.

The increase in leverage had a negative impact on its after-funding-cost profitability and debt-service capacity at the later stages of the finance boom. The increase in mobile capital led to market integration of the financial structures. These double risks created fragility and instability in its financial structures. That is to say, the period from 1994 to 1996 saw a process of external-debt-driven re-leveraging and destabilization in the corporate sector.

The ratio analyses provided so far indicate the shifts in the corporate sector's financial performance and positions during the 1990s, and the manner in which fragile and unstable financial structures emerged before and during the East Asian crisis. The analyses of the underlying financial transactions and related activities in the following chapters provide further support for the interpretation of these ratios as presented in this chapter.

5   The analysis of offshore syndicated debt for Indonesian borrowers during the finance boom in the 1990s

Chapter 4 argued that Indonesia's financial structure was steeply leveraged during the finance boom in the 1990s due to the private sectors' aggressive fund raising in offshore debt markets.[1] This fund raising was supported by the enthusiastic lending behaviour of offshore lenders at the time, and in particular, that of offshore commercial banks. Using Kindleberger's terminology, offshore lenders were caught up in a 'mania' to finance Indonesian borrowers during the period. Offshore syndicated debt, such as offshore syndicated loans, FRNs and FRCDs, was the favoured tool for leveraging the Indonesian financial structure and for integrating Indonesian financial markets into global financial markets. In other words, offshore syndicated debt drove the trend towards the financial complexity of the Indonesian economy.

This chapter analyses the offshore syndicated debt transactions arranged for Indonesian borrowers from 1993 to 1997. The empirical analysis in this chapter demonstrates that offshore syndicated debt was the favoured device for leveraging Indonesia's financial structure and that the accumulation of offshore syndicated debt created the conditions for the financial crisis of the 1990s.[2] Next, this chapter explains that the range of borrowers expanded in a downwards direction with regards to credit risk. In other words, the downwards diversification of offshore syndicated debt borrowers occurred together with the increase in the use of these instruments. It is argued that the downwards diversification dramatically increased the number of contact points between the Indonesian economy and offshore financial markets and complicated Indonesia's financial structure during the finance boom. Third, the chapter introduces a supply-side analysis of external debt developments in the 1990s. The empirical studies show that the aggressive introduction of offshore syndicated debt was not only driven by Indonesian borrowers' strong funding demands, but also by offshore banks' enthusiastic approach to Indonesian borrowers. Finally, the empirical studies of this chapter illustrate how this lending mania leveraged the Indonesian financial structure during the period.

The scale of offshore syndicated debt for Indonesian borrowers during the finance boom

Tables 5.1 and 5.2 summarize offshore syndicated debt arranged for Indonesian borrowers from 1993 to 1997.[3] In 1993, just 1 year before the finance boom,

Table 5.1 Offshore syndicated debts for Indonesian borrowers (by volume) (transactions, US$ million)

	State			Private			Total		
	Banks	Non-banks	Total	Banks	Non-banks	Total	Banks	Non-banks	Total
1993	18	5	23	44	22	66	62	27	89
	1,236	820	2,056	2,172	548	2,720	3,408	1,368	4,776
1994	14	3	17	43	83	126	57	86	143
	1,827	228	2,055	2,820	3,245	6,065	4,646	3,473	8,119
1995	17	10	27	55	136	191	72	146	218
	1,820	911	2,731	2,870	10,805	13,675	4,690	11,716	16,406
1996	25	13	38	62	238	300	87	251	338
	2,081	1,352	3,433	3,410	18,034	21,444	5,491	19,386	24,877
1997	15	9	24	45	184	229	60	193	253
	1,330	1,683	3,013	2,231	18,219	20,450	3,561	19,902	23,463
Total	89	40	129	249	663	912	338	703	1,041
	8,293	4,994	13,287	13,503	50,851	64,354	21,796	55,845	77,641

Source: Privately collected data (checked with IFR).

Notes
Upper: the number of syndicated debts.
Lower: the dollar amount of syndicated debts.

Table 5.2 Offshore syndicated debts for Indonesian borrowers (by share) (%)

	State			Private			Total		
	Banks	Non-banks	Total	Banks	Non-banks	Total	Banks	Non-banks	Total
1993	20.2	5.6	25.8	49.4	24.7	74.2	69.7	30.3	100.0
	25.9	17.2	43.0	45.5	11.5	57.0	71.4	28.6	100.0
1994	9.8	2.1	11.9	30.1	58.0	88.1	39.9	60.1	100.0
	22.5	2.8	25.3	34.7	40.0	74.7	57.2	42.8	100.0
1995	7.8	4.6	12.4	25.2	62.4	87.6	33.0	67.0	100.0
	11.1	5.6	16.6	17.5	65.9	83.4	28.6	71.4	100.0
1996	7.4	3.8	11.2	18.3	70.4	88.8	25.7	74.3	100.0
	8.4	5.4	13.8	13.7	72.5	86.2	22.1	77.9	100.0
1997	5.9	3.6	9.5	17.8	72.7	90.5	23.7	76.3	100.0
	5.7	7.2	12.8	9.5	77.6	87.2	15.2	84.8	100.0
Total	8.5	3.8	12.4	23.9	63.7	87.6	32.5	67.5	100.0
	10.7	6.4	17.1	17.4	65.5	82.9	28.1	71.9	100.0

Source: Privately collected data (checked with IFR).

Notes
Upper: the number of syndicated debts.
Lower: the dollar amount of syndicated debts.

Indonesian debtors took out only 90 offshore syndicated debts, approximately 26 per cent of the peak year level during the boom. Although the private sector had more actively used offshore syndicated debt than the state sector in terms of the number of transactions, the state sector still had a significant share in terms of the volume (dollar amount) of transactions. Moreover, banks were major borrowers of offshore syndicated debt in terms of both the number and volume of transactions (69.7 per cent and 71.4 per cent shares, respectively), and this situation was the same in both the state and private sectors. Offshore lenders' financing appetite was mainly directed to state banks and leading private banks.[4] In terms of private non-bank borrowers, in 1993, only elite business groups, such as Sinar Mas, Salim and Astra, had access to the offshore syndicated debt market. Offshore lenders had not accepted mid- and small-sized business groups at this stage. Furthermore, Suharto-related borrowers and politically connected parties did not yet have access to the market. In sum, the data in Tables 5.1 and 5.2 indicate that the offshore syndicated debt market was not widely open to the private sector in 1993.

In 1994, this situation changed dramatically. Both the number and volume of offshore syndicated loans for Indonesian borrowers sharply increased to 143 transactions and US$8.1 billion in volume. The number of offshore syndicated loans for the private sector almost doubled from 66 in 1993 to 126 in 1994 and was around seven times as much as that for public sector. The volume of offshore syndicated loans for the public sector remained at the same level as in 1993, while that for the private sector steeply increased in 1994. As a result, the volume of offshore syndicated loans for the private sector increased to around three times as much as for the public sector. This situation was created by non-bank borrowers' aggressive use of offshore syndicated loans. Both the number and volume of offshore syndicated loans for the non-bank sector exceeded those for the banking sector. This indicates that in 1994, private non-bank companies began to access the offshore syndicated debt market, and that at the same time, offshore lenders also started accepting the risks associated with the sector.[5] This fact is consistent with the leveraging of Indonesia's corporate sector in the 1990s as shown in Chapter 4.

In 1995, this trend accelerated. Offshore syndicated debt for the state (both banks and non-banks) and private bank sectors did not significantly increase, while the borrowing of private non-banks dramatically increased. The number of offshore syndicated loans for private non-banks increased by 1.6 times and the volume jumped by 3.3 times. Both the number and volume of offshore syndicated loans for private non-bank borrowers accounted for 62.4 per cent and 65.9 per cent of all Indonesian borrowers respectively. The data indicates that offshore lenders enthusiastically provided liquidity to Indonesia's private non-bank sector and expanded the range of non-bank borrowers. In 1995, Indonesia's external debt problem shifted from a state sector problem to that of the private sector, and in particular, that of the private non-bank sector.

In 1996 and 1997, offshore fund raising reached its peak. The number of offshore syndicated loans for private non-bank borrowers sharply increased to

238 in 1996 and 184 in 1997, and the volume reached US$18.0 billion in 1996 and US$18.2 billion in 1997. Both the number and volume of offshore syndicated loans for private non-bank borrowers accounted for more than 70 per cent of the Indonesian total. Unbridled enthusiasm among offshore lenders created unimaginable foreign currency liquidity for a variety of Indonesian non-bank borrowers. The combination of offshore lenders' enthusiasm and Indonesian debtors' demand for offshore funds created an extremely fragile and crises-prone financial structure. In addition, new borrowers with higher credit risks, such as grandchild subsidiaries of leading business groups, medium and small business groups and real estate oriented business groups entered the offshore syndicated debt market aggressively.[6] Regarding offshore lenders, new players, such as Korean and Taiwanese banks, entered the market.[7] This situation diversified the contact points between offshore financial markets and the Indonesian economy, and thereby rendered Indonesia's financial structure more complex.

The downward diversification of Indonesian borrowers' offshore syndicated debt during the finance boom

The scale of offshore syndicated debt for Indonesian borrowers is an important indicator of offshore lenders' risk capacity and preferences regarding Indonesian debtors during the period. In addition, the range of borrowers is also important. Tables 5.3, 5.4 and 5.5 illustrate the major Indonesian private users of offshore syndicated debt from 1993 to 1997. In 1993, the top five syndicated debt users, which were also the largest Indonesian business groups, such as Sinar Mas, Salim and Astra, had significant shares in terms of both the number and volume of offshore syndicated loans. The top five borrowers accounted for 31.8 per cent of debt by number and 42.4 per cent of debt by volume. The top 15 users accounted for more than 55 per cent of debt by both number and volume. The top 30 users accounted for more than 70 per cent of debt by both number and volume. In sum, the use of offshore syndicated debt was highly concentrated among these leading Indonesian business groups. This also means that offshore lenders' risk

Table 5.3 Debtors' concentration in offshore syndicated debts for Indonesian business groups (only non-bank borrowers) (%)

	Number of transactions						Funding amount					
	1993	1994	1995	1996	1997	Average	1993	1994	1995	1996	1997	Average
Top 5	31.8	31.7	26.2	24.7	18.3	24.9	42.4	38.3	22.8	29.2	18.0	25.7
Top 10	43.9	41.3	38.7	34.3	31.0	36.1	50.5	47.4	32.6	39.5	27.7	35.5
Top 15	57.6	48.4	47.6	42.3	35.8	43.8	56.7	49.2	35.9	46.4	33.0	40.6
Top 20	63.6	54.8	53.9	47.3	41.5	49.5	63.5	54.7	41.5	49.6	34.9	44.3
Top 25	68.2	59.5	59.2	51.3	43.2	53.3	68.9	59.6	45.0	51.9	37.6	47.4
Top 30	72.7	61.9	62.3	55.0	45.4	56.4	70.6	62.0	46.3	54.0	40.9	49.7
Top 35	72.7	64.3	63.9	56.7	48.9	58.4	71.7	63.9	47.1	55.7	42.5	51.1

Source: Privately collected data (checked with IFR).

Table 5.4 Offshore syndicated debts for Indonesian business groups (by the number of transactions) (transactions)

		1993	1994	1995	1996	1997	Total
1	Sinar Mas	5	11	19	23	9	67
2	Salim	5	9	9	15	9	47
3	Astra	7	9	9	11	10	46
4	Bakrie	1	4	7	12	10	34
5	Ongko	3	7	6	13	4	33
6	Gajah Tunggal	4	5	6	7	5	27
7	Dharmala + PSP	1	2	5	6	8	22
8	Ciputra + Jaya + Metropolitan	0	1	5	5	7	18
9	Ometraco	2	3	5	4	4	18
10	Napan + Risjad	1	1	3	7	5	17
11	Bank Bali	2	4	4	5	2	17
12	Lippo	2	2	4	4	2	14
13	Modern	2	2	1	7	2	14
14	CP	3	1	3	3	3	13
15	Mulia	0	0	5	5	2	12
16	Niaga	1	2	2	4	3	12
17	Panin	2	3	3	2	2	12
18	Kalbe	0	3	2	2	3	10
19	Argo Mannungal	0	0	4	3	3	10
20	Tirtamas	1	0	1	4	2	8
21	Gunung Sewu	0	2	4	1	1	8
22	Aneka Kimia Raya	2	1	2	2	0	7
23	Danamon	0	0	2	5	0	7
24	Sierad	1	2	2	1	1	7
25	Raja Garuda Mas	0	1	0	3	2	6
26	Medco	0	0	1	4	1	6
27	Gudang Garam	1	1	2	2	0	6
28	Sungai Budi	1	1	1	1	2	6
29	Maspion	0	0	2	3	1	6
30	Sampoerna	1	1	0	1	1	4
31	Artha Graha	0	0	0	0	4	4
32	Texmaco	0	2	1	0	1	4
33	Hadtex	0	1	0	2	1	4
34	Bukaka	0	0	0	3	1	4
35	Tigaraksa	0	0	2	0	1	3
36	Ever Shine	0	0	1	2	0	3
37	Barito Pacific	0	0	1	0	1	2
—	Suharto family	0	2	5	7	7	21
—	Others	18	43	62	121	109	353
	Total	66	126	191	300	229	912

Source: Privately collected data (checked with IFR).

capacities and preferences were limited to those elite business groups and not diversified to others, such as medium and small and politically connected business groups at this stage.

After the finance boom began in 1994, the concentration of offshore syndicated debt users was reduced. That is to say, the range of offshore syndicated debt users

Table 5.5 Offshore syndicated debts for Indonesian business groups (by the funding amount) (US$ million)

		1993	1994	1995	1996	1997	Total
1	Sinar Mas	300	671	1,446	2,008	872	5,296
2	Salim	381	668	662	1,132	1,133	3,977
3	Astra	325	628	538	1,318	602	3,410
4	Gajah Tunggal	117	288	243	951	543	2,142
5	Bakrie	30	70	230	863	537	1,730
6	Ongko	45	190	174	692	121	1,222
7	Dharmala + PSP	26	50	208	488	435	1,207
8	Ciputra + Jaya + Metropolitan	0	40	261	170	710	1,181
9	Ometraco	88	80	355	315	223	1,061
10	Napan + Risjad	60	192	338	537	489	1,616
11	Mulia	0	0	333	510	180	1,023
12	Raja Garuda Mas	0	33	0	290	325	648
13	Sampoerna	96	25	0	150	300	571
14	Aneka Kimia Raya	72	50	48	370	0	540
15	Medco	0	0	75	155	280	510
16	Bank Bali	70	75	108	190	48	490
17	Lippo	31	60	156	154	88	489
18	Kalbe	0	75	125	55	215	470
19	Tirtamas	25	0	175	216	42	458
20	Gudang Garam	60	120	195	82	0	457
21	CP	65	25	120	89	146	445
22	Argo Mannungal	0	0	126	207	73	406
23	Gunung Sewu	0	86	141	57	100	384
24	Niaga	40	65	40	96	137	377
25	Panin	42	122	62	47	93	366
26	Danamon	0	0	50	273	0	323
27	Artha Graha	0	0	0	0	312	312
28	Modern	47	45	25	171	15	303
29	Texmaco	0	100	75	0	100	275
30	Barito Pacific	0	0	24	0	250	274
31	Bukaka	0	0	0	122	150	272
32	Hadtex	0	50	0	106	50	206
33	Sierad	18	46	33	50	25	172
34	Sungai Budi	12	22	25	35	65	159
35	Maspion	0	0	50	39	40	129
36	Tigaraksa	0	0	75	0	15	90
37	Ever Shine	0	0	21	31	0	52
—	Suharto family	0	36	238	831	1,270	2,375
—	Others	769	2,154	6,903	8,647	10,467	28,940
	Total	2,720	6,065	13,675	21,444	20,450	64,354

Source: Privately collected data (checked with IFR).

expanded downwards with regards to credit quality. In terms of the number of transactions, the concentration on the top five business groups dramatically decreased as follows: 31.7 per cent in 1994, 26.2 per cent in 1995, 24.7 per cent in 1996 and 18.3 per cent in 1997. In terms of volume, the share of the top five business groups fell as follows: 38.3 per cent in 1994, 22.8 per cent in 1995,

29.2 per cent in 1996 and 18.0 per cent in 1997. Thus, the diversification of borrowers occurred in parallel with the expansion of offshore syndicated debt for Indonesian borrowers. Furthermore, the details of the data point out that with regards to Indonesian credit risks, this diversification was downwards-directed and driven by the deepening of offshore lenders' risk capacities and preferences.

Analysing the details of Tables 5.4 and 5.5, it can be seen that leading Indonesian–Chinese business groups that had strong non-financial (manufacturing) operations generally had better access to offshore syndicated debt markets than others at the early stages of the finance boom. They also had strong business alliances with foreign partners and these enhanced their credibility as borrowers. The Sinar Mas Group (pulp and paper, and agribusiness), the Salim Group (cement, food, agribusiness, chemicals and automotive), the Astra Group (automotive and heavy equipment), the Ongko Group (ceramics), the Gajah Tunggal Group (tires and textiles) and the Ometraco Group (fertilizers and agribusiness) are typical examples.[8] On the other hand, at the early stages of the finance boom, offshore lenders had maintained their distance from the Suharto family, other politically related parties, finance- and real estate-oriented business groups and medium and small business groups. Even leading *pribumi* business groups, such as the Bakrie Group and the Bukaka Group, were not preferred borrowers in the early stages. This was simply because offshore lenders remained sceptical of *pribumi* business groups' management capabilities. In sum, at this stage, offshore lenders' risk capacities and preferences were still limited to a small part of the private sector in Indonesia.

However, in the latter stages of the finance boom in the 1990s (from 1995 to the first half of 1997) the situation totally changed. Offshore lenders aggressively expanded their credit boundaries and provided syndicated debt to a variety of business groups in Indonesia. During this stage, even the Suharto family obtained more than two billion US dollars in offshore syndicated debt, and other politically related business groups, such as the Tirtamas Group, had access to huge amounts of offshore funds. The Bakrie Group, a representative of *pribumi* business groups, obtained US$1.6 billion in the 3 years from 1995 to 1997. The Dharmala Group (incorporating the PSP Group) and the Ciputra Group (incorporating the Jaya Group and the Metropolitan Group), which were typical finance-and real estate-oriented business groups, also obtained US$1.0 billion and US$1.1 billion in offshore syndicate loans respectively.[9] Among medium and small business groups, the Mulia Group amazingly raised US$1.0 billion in funds through offshore syndicated debt during the period. Other medium and small-size business groups also obtained US$200–300 million in offshore syndicated debt.

As shown in Table 5.3, the top 35 users of offshore syndicated debt during the period in terms of the number of transactions decreased from 72.7 per cent in 1993 to 48.9 per cent in 1997. In terms of the face value of transactions, their share also decreased from 71.7 per cent in 1993 to 42.5 per cent in 1997. These figures indicate that the users of offshore syndicated debt became extremely diversified to include small business groups, independent project and other non-prime borrowers. This is due to the fact that offshore lenders' risk tolerance for

Indonesian private sector firms dramatically increased and that the offshore syndicated debt market opened up considerably to Indonesian borrowers during the latter stages of the 1990s finance boom.

Throughout the period, there were leading business groups that did not actively use offshore syndicated debt. The Gudang Garam Group, the Djarum Group and the Rodamas Group are typical examples. The Gudang Garam Group, the largest tobacco producer with the fourth highest revenues among Indonesian business groups, obtained only six offshore syndicated loans for a total of US$457 million (27th in terms of number and 20th in terms of volume). The Djarum Group, the second largest tobacco producer with the ninth largest revenues, obtained only two offshore syndicated loans for US$150 million. The Rodamas Group, which had the tenth highest revenues and was involved in glass production, seasoning production and real estate development, obtained few offshore syndicated loans. They had bilateral and smaller offshore loans with relationship banks but never obtained a large amount of offshore syndicated debt. They conservatively managed their investments and debt finance and relied more on rupiah funding, that is, both internal cash flow and borrowing from domestic banks. These groups survived the East Asian crisis. A strong, positive correlation exists between the use of offshore syndicated debt and distress during the crisis.

As is argued in Chapter 1, offshore debt funding was totally liberalized for Indonesian corporate borrowers. In addition, the Indonesian government encouraged the corporate sector to raise funds in offshore markets.[10] During the finance boom, this liberal regulatory stance was combined with the enthusiasm and increased risk tolerance of offshore lenders towards the Indonesian private sector. This combination naturally led to a dramatic accumulation of external debt in the private sector in only a few years.[11] Offshore syndicated debt was integrated into the financial structure of the corporate sector. In addition, the private-to-private nature of external debt means that the contact points between the Indonesian economy and offshore markets increased and that communication with global financial markets became more complex. In this way, the increased leverage of the Indonesian corporate sector created a crises-prone financial structure, while the increased exposure of the corporate sector to external debt at a variety of corporate levels created the possibility of a complex, uncontrollable and extended financial crisis.

Borrowing terms of offshore syndicated debt for Indonesian borrowers during the finance boom

The scale of the syndicated debt of Indonesian borrowers and the downwards diversification of borrowers are indicators of offshore lenders' risk capacities and preferences regarding Indonesian debtors during the finance boom in the 1990s. On the other hand, the borrowing terms of offshore syndicated loans are a more sensitive indicator reflecting offshore lenders' views of credit risk. Moreover, borrowing terms also illustrate offshore lenders' lending appetite and enthusiasm towards Indonesian borrowers. This section analyses the borrowing terms of offshore syndicated debt for Indonesian borrowers during the period and shows how these terms dramatically improved over a short period of time. Offshore lenders' tolerance for credit risks associated with Indonesian borrowers is measured and the balance of bargaining power between borrowers and lenders is analysed, and finally offshore lenders' enthusiasm towards Indonesian credit markets is demonstrated.

As explained in Chapter 3, this section focuses on the following most sensitive items among all lending/borrowing terms: (i) average tenor and (ii) all-in margins. In addition, the database of offshore syndicated loans to Indonesian borrowers is analysed in terms of the following three categories: (i) all Indonesian borrowers; (ii) bank borrowers and (iii) non-bank borrowers. Furthermore, the data set of bank borrowers is further segregated into state and private banks. The data set of non-bank borrowers focuses on the private sector because of the fact that direct offshore borrowing by the state non-bank borrowers was limited to only a few state entities and independent projects.[12] Furthermore, in order to analyse borrowing terms at the same level of credit risk, a few sub-data sets are used.

Borrowing terms of offshore syndicated debt for all Indonesian borrowers

This section analyses the borrowing terms of offshore syndicated debt for all Indonesian borrowers during the finance boom in the 1990s. In theory, assuming all other conditions do not change, there is a positive correlation between credit risk and funding cost, between tenor and funding cost and between funding amounts (particularly funding amount per transaction) and costs. That is to say, higher-risk borrowers are required to pay higher all-in margins. As to the whole of the borrowers' market, the downwards diversification of borrowers (meaning lower-quality entrants) is associated with higher all-in margins.[13] On the other hand, longer average tenor is related to higher all-in margins. Larger fund size is also tied to higher all-in margins. Therefore, this and the following sections carefully analyse not only the changes in average tenor and all-in margins but also the relationship between the changes. The change of all-in margins is also viewed in the context of the downwards diversification of borrowers.

During the finance boom of the 1990s, the average tenor of offshore syndicated debt for Indonesian borrowers dramatically improved (Table 5.6). Simple and weighted averages of average tenor were respectively stretched from 2.1 and 2.3 years in 1993 to 3.4 and 4.9 years in 1997. In particular, offshore lenders' aggressive approach to Indonesian borrowers enabled high-credit borrowers that preceded other Indonesian companies in the offshore markets, such as state banks, leading private banks and flagship companies of elite business groups, to obtain long-term finance and thereby the average tenor sharply increased in 1995. In 1996, offshore lenders' strong lending appetite led to the downwards diversification of borrowers, and second- and third-tier companies in the private sector began entering the offshore syndicated debt market. Offshore syndicated debt for these new entrants was basically short-term finance. Although high-credit and preceding borrowers stretched their average tenors, the increase of new entrants'

Table 5.6 Average tenor of offshore syndicated debts for Indonesian borrowers (years)

	Simple average			Weighted average		
	Banks	Non-banks	All	Banks	Non-banks	All
1993	2.1	2.1	2.1	2.3	2.3	2.3
1994	2.3	2.6	2.5	3.0	2.8	2.9
1995	2.8	2.9	2.9	4.6	4.1	4.2
1996	3.1	3.0	3.1	4.4	3.8	3.9
1997	2.9	3.5	3.4	4.2	5.0	4.9

Source: Privately collected data (checked with IFR).

Table 5.7 Average all-in margins of offshore syndicated debts for Indonesian borrowers (basis points per annum)

	Simple average			Weighted average		
	Banks	Non-banks	All	Banks	Non-banks	All
1993	165.14	234.27	205.54	155.40	219.86	186.48
1994	155.49	229.80	207.44	145.29	225.45	196.88
1995	127.77	205.17	188.34	100.78	195.88	177.45
1996	115.02	209.20	192.54	91.84	213.89	192.15
1997	110.44	207.65	191.13	85.74	197.30	184.68

Source: Privately collected data (checked with IFR).

short-term financing halted the stretching of average tenors for all Indonesian borrowers in 1996. However, the power to stretch tenors exceeded the increase in short-term finance for new entrants in 1997 and the average tenor for all Indonesian borrowers dramatically improved in 1997.

The same interpretation of the data can be applied to the improvement in all-in margins for offshore syndicated debt for all Indonesian borrowers during the period. Simple and weighted averages of all-in margins respectively tightened from 205.54 and 186.48 basis points in 1993 to 191.13 and 184.68 basis points in 1997. However, all-in margins in 1994 and 1996 increased from those in the previous years. The lowest all-in margins during the period were in 1995 (Table 5.7). Therefore, it is impossible to observe a stable trend of improvement of all-in margins during the period. This is mainly due to the fact that the increase in offshore debt with high all-in margins for new and low-credit borrowers exceeded the high-credit and preceding borrowers' powers to push down margins. In particular, this situation occurred in the non-bank sector. Subsidiaries and grandchild subsidiaries of leading business groups, small- and medium-size business groups, and independent projects entered the offshore syndicated debt market by offering attractive borrowing terms to enthusiastic offshore lenders.

Furthermore, high-credit and preceding borrowers attempted to obtain long-term debt that had longer than 3-year tenor in order to improve their maturity profiles.

They aggressively pushed down all-in margins for their short-term offshore debt and were willing to pay higher all-in margins for the long-term facilities. In addition to the above-mentioned downwards diversification of borrowers, the improvement of the maturity profile by high-quality borrowers thus also countered the decrease of all-in margins for all Indonesian borrowers.

Therefore, in order to accurately understand the improvement of borrowing terms for offshore syndicated debt during the period the change of borrowing terms for the transactions at the same level of credit risk and same average tenor must be analysed. All that national averages can do is only point out the general direction of improvements in borrowing terms during the period. The aggregated data do not provide a detailed picture of trends in terms of shifts in bargaining power. The following two sections clarify these trends by disaggregating the data into two categories of banks and corporate borrowers.

Borrowing terms of offshore syndicated debt for the Indonesian banking sector

As in other Asian countries, the Indonesian banking sector had a presence in offshore syndicated debt markets earlier than the non-bank sector. The central bank (BI), seven state commercial banks (BNI, Bank EXIM, BRI, BBD, BDN, Bapindo and BTN) and top private banks (BCA, BII, Lippo Bank, Bank Bali, Bank Niaga and BDNI) were welcomed by offshore lenders and regularly appeared in offshore syndicated debt markets.[14] Even after offshore lenders' interest in Indonesian credit risk had dramatically expanded (not shifted) to the private non-bank sector, they rigorously approached the banking sector at the same time. As discussed in Chapter 1, offshore debt funding to the banking sector was strictly controlled by the central bank, thus the sharp increase in offshore lenders' supply to the sector naturally led to a sharp improvement in borrowing terms. Therefore, although the work focuses on the private non-bank sector, it is relevant to analyse the borrowing terms for the banking sector in order to understand offshore creditors' enthusiasm and lending appetite towards Indonesian borrowers in general.

First, state banks dramatically improved the average tenor of their offshore syndicated debt during the finance boom of the 1990s (Table 5.8). In particular, this was sharply stretched in 1995. The simple average jumped from 3.5 years in 1994 to 5.8 years in 1995, and the weighted average jumped from 4.2 years in 1994 to 6.2 years in 1995. At that time, BI (mostly acting for the Republic of Indonesia), obtained improved borrowing terms for its offshore syndicated debt (in particular, tenor) and attempted to establish a benchmark of borrowing terms for state commercial banks' offshore funding.[15] State commercial banks, by themselves, also attempted to improve their borrowing terms by referring to each other, that is, cross benchmarking. In 1996 and 1997, their focus shifted to further improvements in their funding costs (i.e. all-in margins), thus tenor was not further stretched. As a result, during the latter stages of the finance boom, state banks maintained an average tenor of around 4 years (in terms of simple average) for their offshore syndicated debt. However, this level is significantly longer than that at the inception of the finance boom.

Table 5.8 Average tenor of offshore syndicated debts for Indonesian banks (years)

	Simple average			Weighted average		
	Eight state banks	Selected private banks	All banks	Eight state banks	Selected private banks	All banks
1993	2.8	1.5	2.1	2.8	1.5	2.3
1994	3.5	1.7	2.3	4.2	1.5	3.0
1995	5.8	2.4	2.8	6.2	2.3	4.6
1996	4.9	3.1	3.1	5.7	3.0	4.4
1997	4.0	2.9	2.9	5.3	2.8	4.2

Source: Privately collected data (checked with IFR).

Table 5.9 All-in margin of offshore syndicated debts for Indonesian banks (basis points per annum)

	Simple average			Weighted average		
	Eight state banks	Selected private banks	All banks	Eight state banks	Selected private banks	All banks
1993	151.29	171.83	165.14	151.87	163.85	155.40
1994	141.03	148.10	156.49	139.02	135.78	145.29
1995	88.75	112.30	126.77	83.80	105.09	100.78
1996	74.33	103.17	115.02	74.81	100.83	91.84
1997	59.89	97.55	110.44	64.82	93.64	85.74

Source: Privately collected data (checked with IFR).

They achieved more dramatic improvements in funding costs on offshore syndicated debt (Table 5.9). Amazingly, all-in margins suddenly dropped from three to two digits in 1995. The simple average dropped from 141.03 basis points in 1994 to 88.75 basis points in 1995 and the weighted average from 139.02 basis points in 1994 to 83.80 basis points in 1995. State commercial banks, furthermore, squeezed margins in 1996 and 1997 instead of stretching average tenor, as mentioned earlier. In 1997, the simple average dropped to 59.89 basis points and the weighted average to 64.82 basis points. As state commercial banks basically stretched average tenor during the period, in theory, all-in margins for them should have increased. However, they achieved a reduction of all-in margins at the same time. The *International Financing Review's* interviews with offshore bankers often reported that the state banks' approach to offshore markets was too aggressive and difficult.[16] However, the results of syndication were always successful during the period. Finally, offshore lenders surrendered themselves to their enthusiasm towards state bank borrowers and strongly supported their efforts to improve borrowing terms.

In observing the details of the underlying transactions, the trend becomes much clearer. In terms of average tenor, only BNI and Bank EXIM, the top two state commercial banks, were able to obtain 5-year loans in 1993 with facility amounts of US$70 million and US$75 million, respectively (Table 5.10). In spite of these small syndications, nine and ten banks underwrote the facilities, respectively. This reflected the banks' careful approach to 5-year lending. In 1994, BDN achieved a US$250 million 5-year FRN, and BNI also obtained a US$165 million 7-year FRN (Table 5.10). In 1995 and 1996, BRI, BBD, Bapindo and BTN, the other state commercial banks, also obtained sizable 5-year loans from offshore syndication markets.[17] Over a short period, the average tenor for state commercial banks was dramatically stretched.

In analysing all-in margins for longer than 5-year offshore syndicated debt for BNI and Bank EXIM, which have a longer track record than other state commercial banks, the tightening of the margins during the period is clear (Table 5.10). Moreover, the same tightening of all-in margins for other state commercial banks can be seen (Table 5.10). State commercial banks dramatically reduced their funding costs by taking full advantage of offshore lenders' enthusiasm. This sharp tightening of all-in margins also indicates that bargaining power quickly shifted from offshore lenders to state banks during the period.

Second, the analysis of borrowing terms for private banks requires careful handling. The data set includes all offshore syndicated debt for private banks at a variety of credit-risk levels. The gap in credit-risks between the higher and lower ends is very large, while that among state banks is small. Therefore, a group of private banks with similar credit-risk levels must be selected, and their borrowing terms analysed. In this section, the focus is on the following ten leading private banks, most of which were also regular users of offshore syndicated debt: Bank Central Asia (Salim), Bank Internasional Indonesia (Sinar Mas), Lippo Bank (Lippo), Bank Bali, Bank Niaga (Tahija/Sudarpo to Tirtamas), Bank Umum Nasional (Ongko), Bank Dagang Nasional Indonesia (Gajah Tunggal), Bank Danamon (Danamon), Bank Panin (Panin) and Bank Universal (Astra) ('Selected private banks' in Tables 5.8 and 5.9).

This group of private banks (the 'group') constantly improved its average tenor during the finance boom of the 1990s. However, in 1993 and 1994 during the early stages, their access to long-term offshore finance was very limited; therefore both simple and weighted averages of average tenor were less than 2 years. They did not significantly improve in 1994. Most offshore syndicated debt for the group consisted of 1-year transactions (55.3 per cent in 1993 and 61.4 per cent in 1994 in terms of funding amount). In 1995, just as for the state banks, the average tenor for the group suddenly improved. Both the simple and weighted average jumped from 1.7 years and 1.5 years in 1994 to 2.4 years and 2.3 years in 1995, respectively (Table 5.8). Furthermore, average tenor for the group improved in 1996 and almost remained at the same level in 1997. In sum, average tenor for the group doubled over the period.

All-in margins for the group also improved constantly throughout the period. Both simple and weighted averages of all-in margins tightened from 171.83 basis points and 163.85 basis points in 1993 to 97.55 basis points and 93.64 basis points in 1997, respectively (Table 5.9). In particular, all-in margins for the group dropped sharply by more than 20 per cent in 1995. Although the group stretched

Table 5.10 The borrowing terms for the leading five state commercial banks (US$ million, years, basis points per annum)

	BNI	Bank EXIM	BRI	BDN	BBD
1993	$74, 4 yr, 147 bp $70, 5 yr, 158 bp	$75, 5 yr, 165 bp	$60, 1 yr, 125 bp $19, 2 yr, 140 bp $25, 2 yr, 150 bp $120, 2 yr, 149 bp	$75, 3 yr, 162 bp $75, 2 yr, 145 bp $100, 3 yr, 158 bp	$42, 3 yr, 168 bp $80, 2 yr, 145 bp
1994	$165, 7 yr, 145 bp	$159, 5 yr, 123 bp $59, 5 yr, 134 bp	$54, 1 yr, 125 bp $87, 2 yr, 146 bp	$250, 5 yr, 130 bp	$105, 3 yr, 153 bp $28, 3 yr, 145 bp $150, 3 yr, 150 bp
1995	$170, 7 yr, 85 bp	$130, 7 yr, 86 bp	$120, 5 yr, 81 bp	$180, 5 yr, 86 bp	—
1996	$155, 5 yr, 74 bp $26, 5 yr, 68 bp $50, 3 yr, 53 bp	$45, 5 yr, 75 bp $90, 5 yr, 65 bp $100, 2 yr, 49 bp	—	—	$150, 5 yr, 84 bp $155, 5 yr, 80 bp $35, 5 yr, 85 bp $50, 5 yr, 78 bp
1997	$70, 3 yr, 50 bp	$65, 5 yr, 67 bp $120, 3 yr, 50 bp	$50, 5 yr, 65 bp $70, 5 yr, 73 bp	$25, 3 yr, 57 bp	$105, 5 yr, 76 bp

Source: Privately collected data (checked with IFR).

Notes
Facility size ($); average tenor (yr); all-in margin (bp).

average tenor for its offshore syndicated debt, it also successfully reduced funding costs. This was due to a combination of the strict control of private banks' off- shore borrowings by Bank Indonesia and offshore lenders' strong lending supply to the group of private banks. Bargaining power clearly shifted from offshore lenders to the group of the private banks.

Data on transaction levels further emphasize this fact. Table 5.11 indicates the borrowing terms of major offshore syndicated loans for the leading five private banks. These clearly improved average tenor and all-in margin for their offshore syndicated debt during the period.[18] In this table, it is reconfirmed that the group of banks sharply improved their borrowing terms, particularly all-in margins, in 1995. On the other hand, a clear improvement in terms of facility size can be observed, that is to say, the trend increase in facility size is not clear. This may be due to BI's control of offshore debt in the banking sector.

In this way, borrowing terms for offshore syndicated debt for Indonesian banks sharply and constantly improved throughout the finance boom of the 1990s. They successfully stabilized the structure of offshore funding by stretching the matu- rity and simultaneously reducing offshore funding costs by squeezing borrowing margins.[19] In particular, they dramatically improved borrowing terms in 1995. This situation is fully attributable to offshore lenders' enthusiasm and clearly indi- cates the shift in bargaining power from offshore lenders to Indonesian banks (borrowers).

Borrowing terms of offshore syndicated debt for the Indonesian private non-bank sector

The data set of offshore syndicated debt for the Indonesian private non-bank sector includes a variety of borrowing terms for a wide range of credit risks. Compared to offshore lenders' approach to the banking sector, offshore lenders more aggressively financed higher-risk non-bank borrowers during the finance boom of the 1990s.[20] In addition, offshore fund raising by private non-bank bor- rowers was mostly unregulated by the government.[21] It encouraged the private non-bank sector to obtain offshore funds by themselves rather than controlling offshore fund-raising.[22] This policy environment also encouraged the dramatic accumulation of external debt by the private non-bank sector and the downwards diversification of private non-bank borrowers. Therefore, in terms of credit risk, the range of private non-bank borrowers of offshore syndicated debt became wider than that of bank borrowers. During the period, large, private non-bank bor- rowers aggressively improved borrowing terms for their offshore loans. On the other hand, new private non-bank borrowers entered the offshore syndicated debt market by offering attractive borrowing terms to offshore lenders. In sum, there were strong opposing forces affecting borrowing terms for the private non-bank sector.

Initially, this section analyses the dataset of borrowing terms of offshore syndicated debt for the whole private non-bank sector in order to understand the direction of the changes in borrowing terms. However, in order to correctly

Table 5.11 Borrowing terms for the leading five private banks (US$ million, years, basis points per annum)

	BCA	BII	Lippo	Panin	Bali
1993	$70, 1 yr, 140 bp $100, 1 yr, 145 bp $150, 1 yr, 103 bp	$50, 2 yr, 175 bp	—	$10, 2 yr, 200 bp $32, 1 yr, 175 bp $16, 2 yr, 183 bp $16, 1 yr, 180 bp	$50, 2 yr, 182 bp $20, 1 yr, 150 bp $30, 2 yr, 145 bp
1994		$30, 2 yr, 200 bp	$30, 2 yr, 180 bp		
1995	$70, 3 yr, 83 bp	$25, 5 yr, 141 bp $100, 1 yr, 100 bp	$30, 2 yr, 100 bp $30, 2 yr, 90 bp	$25, 3 yr, 125 bp	$20, 3 yr, 120 bp $15, 1 yr, 100 bp $50, 1 yr, 80 bp
1996	$150, 3 yr, 74 bp	$22, 5 yr, 113 bp $50, 3 yr, 97 bp $22, 3 yr, 100 bp	—	$15, 3 yr, 95 bp $32, 3 yr, 95 bp	$15, 3 yr, 85 bp $50, 3 yr, 93 bp
1997	—	$35, 5 yr, 109 bp $100, 2 yr, 93 bp	$60, 2 yr, 101 bp	$65, 3 yr, 87 bp	$30, 5 yr, 90 bp

Source: Privately collected data (checked with IFR).

Notes
Facility size ($); average tenor (yr); all-in margin (bp).

Table 5.12 Average tenors of offshore syndicated debts for Indonesian non-bank borrowers (years)

	Simple average			Weighted average		
	Top ten regular borrowers	Top-tier credit borrowers	All borrowers	Top ten regular borrowers	Top-tier credit borrowers	All borrowers
1993	1.6	1.9	2.1	1.7	1.7	2.3
1994	2.4	2.7	2.6	2.7	2.8	2.8
1995	2.7	2.8	2.9	3.0	3.1	4.1
1996	2.7	3.2	3.0	2.9	3.2	3.8
1997	3.3	3.7	3.5	3.9	3.9	5.0

Source: Privately collected data (checked with IFR).

understand how borrowing terms of offshore syndicated debt for the private non-bank sector changed during the period this section further disaggregates the data into two groups with similar credit risks namely: (i) top ten private non-bank regular borrowers and (ii) top-tier credit private non-bank borrowers.[23]

Table 5.12 provides the details of the average tenor of offshore syndicated debt for Indonesian private non-bank borrowers during the finance boom. The whole non-bank sector constantly and dramatically stretched average tenor on their offshore syndicated debt throughout the period. Simple and weighted averages of average tenor respectively improved from 2.1 and 2.3 years in 1993 to 3.5 and 5 years in 1997. In particular, the introduction of project finance, which has longer than a 5-year average tenor, contributed to stretching average tenor at the latter stages of the boom. Average tenor for both top ten private non-bank regular borrowers and top-tier credit private non-bank borrowers also constantly improved during the period. Simple and weighted averages almost doubled from 1993 to 1997. As a matter of fact, Indonesia's leading private non-bank borrowers, such as Indocement (Salim), Indofood (Salim), Indah Kiat (Sinar Mas) and Tjiwi Kimia (Sinar Mas), obtained 5-year syndicated loans even during the early stages of the finance boom.

Table 5.13 shows all-in margins of offshore syndicated debt for private non-bank borrowers during the finance boom. The whole private non-bank sector improved all-in margins for their offshore syndicated debt. Both simple and weighted averages of all-in margins declined from 234.27 and 219.86 basis points in 1993 to 207.65 and 197.30 basis points in 1997. Considering offshore lenders' enthusiasm for the sector during the period, this tightening up appears to be relatively moderate. In addition, all-in margins for this sector increased in 1996. However, this year was the peak of the finance boom and a number of low credit and new private non-bank borrowers entered the offshore syndicated debt market with attractive borrowing terms to offshore lenders. In sum, the downwards diversification of borrowers with high-margin transactions pushed up average all-in margins for the sector.

Table 5.13 Average all-in margins of offshore syndicated debts for Indonesian non-bank borrowers (basis points per annum)

	Simple average			Weighted average		
	Top ten regular borrowers	Top-tier credit borrowers	All borrowers	Top ten regular borrowers	Top-tier credit borrowers	All borrowers
1993	222.94	218.33	234.27	203.42	210.32	219.86
1994	212.79	201.58	229.80	221.90	202.25	225.45
1995	202.68	187.46	205.17	199.37	190.44	195.88
1996	198.17	164.67	209.20	190.98	163.25	213.89
1997	193.15	159.93	207.65	185.30	158.96	197.30

Source: Privately collected data (checked with IFR).

On the other hand, all-in margins for both top ten private non-bank regular borrowers and top-tier credit private non-bank borrowers constantly improved. Simple and weighted averages of all-in margins for top ten private non-bank regular borrowers sharply declined from 222.94 and 203.42 basis points in 1993 to 193.15 and 185.30 basis points in 1997. Simple and weighted averages of all-in margins for top-tier credit private non-bank borrowers also sharply declined from 218.33 and 210.32 basis points in 1993 to 159.93 and 158.96 basis points in 1997. This amazingly sharp tightening of all-in margins for top-tier credit private non-bank borrowers by more than 25 per cent indicates that offshore lenders were extremely enthusiastic about so-called blue chip private non-bank borrowers in Indonesia.

In this way, despite the downwards diversification of Indonesian borrowers' risk profile during the finance boom in the 1990s, offshore lenders enthusiastically accepted worsening lending terms, that is, longer tenor and tighter margins, particularly for high-credit private non-bank borrowers. On the other hand, offshore lenders attempted to compensate declining profitability of the lending portfolio to blue chip private non-bank borrowers by aggressively financing low-credit and new private non-bank borrowers with attractive lending terms. Offshore lenders' enthusiasm diversified the contact points between the Indonesian private non-bank sector and global financial markets, and Indonesia's external debt problem became complex.

Interpretations of the improvement of borrowing terms for Indonesian borrowers during the finance boom

As argued in Chapter 1, the fundamentals of the Indonesian economy steadily improved in the 1990s until the outbreak of the East Asian crisis. Nevertheless, the 1990s began with a number of credit events that had a negative impact on offshore lenders' views on Indonesian risks. In 1990, Bank Duta violated net open-position rules, became involved in highly speculative foreign exchange transactions, and booked huge foreign exchange losses. In 1992, the Soeryadjaya family's Summa Group collapsed due to bad debt shouldered by its flagship bank as a result of aggressive and large-scale financing deals to risky businesses. In 1993, the press actively reported on the bad debt problem of the Indonesian banking sector, and in particular, focused on state commercial banks. The government also investigated the problem intensively and the results were reported to parliament.[24] However, offshore lenders were sceptical of the disclosed bad debt figures due to the fact that the figures were far below market estimations and the basis of calculation was unclear.[25] These events naturally led to offshore lenders' cautious stance against the Indonesian banking sector. Even BNI and Bank EXIM, the elite state banks, struggled to stretch the tenor of their syndicated debt and had to pay higher than 150 basis points all-in margins for 5-year funds.

Serious credit events also occurred in the non-bank sector. In 1991, the Bentoel Group suddenly disclosed fraudulent financial reporting in the past and declared itself insolvent.[26] Under opaque legal circumstances, a consortium of offshore creditors undertook a variety of efforts to recover their losses, for example, attempting to team up with state commercial banks, seeking support from ministers, and negotiating with the new owner of the group (the Rajawali Group). Finally, when these efforts did not achieve satisfactory results, offshore creditors filed lawsuits in the Indonesian courts to enforce the old shareholders' personal guarantees and to liquidate the group. However, in 1992, the courts rejected the offshore creditors' appeals. Offshore creditors lost any effective means to recover their losses. This event sent a strong message to offshore markets with regards to local accounting practices, the unpredictability of the legal system and the political nature of business dealings in Indonesia. At the same time, other large business groups, for example, the Mantrust Group, faced bankruptcy, and offshore creditors struggled to enforce their claims under extremely difficult conditions.

In 1993, 1 year before the onset of the finance boom, offshore lenders' lending attitudes towards Indonesian borrowers were basically cautious but ambivalent.[27] The private sector's access to offshore syndicated debt markets was very limited. The downwards diversification of borrowers had not yet occurred at this stage. Only flagship companies of top business groups and leading private banks were able to obtain offshore syndicated debt, and borrowing terms were still favourable to offshore lenders (e.g. around 2 year average tenors, US$20–50 million facility size, and 200–50 basis points all-in margins). However, although offshore lenders' targets were limited, paradoxically, their lending appetite in Indonesia gradually increased even under these poor business conditions.[28] This ambivalence of offshore lenders' attitudes indicated the turning point of the finance boom.

In 1994 and 1995, Indonesian fundamentals were improving, but negative credit events also continued. In 1994, the US$650 million Bapindo scandal was disclosed to the public.[29] This scandal shocked offshore lenders who were already sceptical of Indonesian banks following the bad debt problems in 1993. In 1995, BRI, the third most successful state commercial bank in terms of quality, made misrepresentations regarding in-house financial figures in the information memorandum for a US$120 million FRCD.[30] Problems also occurred in the non-bank sector. Indah Kiat and Tjiwi Kimia, two flagship companies of the Sinar Mas Group, booked US$67 million in derivatives losses. In 1995, the Dharmala group also booked US$69 million in losses and sued Bankers Trust in connection with the derivative transactions.

However, despite these circumstances, offshore lenders accelerated lending to Indonesian borrowers in 1994. Major international banks increased their exposure to Indonesia and competed for arrangers' positions in syndicated loans. In particular, leading Japanese commercial banks were the most active players.[31] At the time, the so-called Japanese bubble economy had already collapsed, and Japanese commercial banks struggled under a huge bad debt problem resulting from real estate and non-bank finance transactions in the 1980s. They sought profit-making opportunities in non-Japan Asia in order to cover their domestic bad debt. In relation to this problem, a risk premium was imposed on Japanese commercial banks above normal interbank funding costs. The increased funding costs pushed them forwards to much higher-margin finance, such as financing Indonesian private non-bank borrowers. Furthermore, Japanese banks, which had lost their leading positions in America and Europe due to their weakened funding capacities, attempted to establish their position in East and South East Asia, including Indonesia, where Japanese manufacturing companies had developed their production bases and formed business alliances with local companies. These motivations prompted Japanese commercial banks to compete in both financing and arranging syndicated debt for Indonesian borrowers. They introduced new Indonesian borrowers to the offshore syndicated debt markets.[32] Even minor Japanese regional commercial banks, which had little international banking experience, became involved in financing the Indonesian private sector. European banks, mainly German and French commercial banks, also challenged Japanese commercial banks by offering cheap funding. In the process, borrowing terms significantly improved in favour of Indonesian borrowers. As argued in the sections earlier, the average tenor for leading companies was stretched and all-in margins were significantly squeezed.

In addition to the major players, new creditors, mainly Korean, Taiwanese and Middle Eastern banks, began active financing activities for Indonesian borrowers.[33] Middle Eastern banks instigated operations in Indonesia and began financing the Indonesian private sector.[34] On the other hand, many offshore syndicated credits were designed for Korean and Taiwanese banks.[35] Due to the fact that their funding costs were obviously much higher than the major players, they mainly targeted high-margin finance for second-tier credit borrowers and relatively risky projects. Furthermore, after 1995, Korean banks started acting as arrangers for offshore syndicated loans for the second-tier credit borrowers. These new players accelerated the expansion of offshore syndicated debt markets for Indonesian borrowers and the downwards diversification of borrowers.

In late 1994, contagion effects from the Mexican crisis affected Indonesia. Portfolio investors suddenly withdrew their investments from some countries and relocated them to safe havens. The Jakarta Stock Exchange was also affected by the sudden reversal of capital flows, and a number of public listings and right issues were postponed. At the beginning of 1995 the rupiah was also devalued sharply. This could be viewed as a minor financial crisis. Nevertheless, offshore syndicated credits were actively arranged for Indonesian borrowers as if the earlier-mentioned financial turmoil had not occurred. In 1995, the downwards diversification of borrowers progressed, and terms further improved for Indonesian borrowers. Offshore lenders were clearly enthusiastic about Indonesian risks.

In 1996, crucial political incidents occurred and these revealed Indonesian political risks to foreign bankers. On 27 July 1996, Megawati Sukarnoputri and her PDI (Indonesian Democratic Party) supporters, who were growing in strength in opposition to President Suharto, were attacked by military-backed thugs and some were killed or injured.[36] In late 1996, religious intolerance and ethnic conflict between *pribumi* and the Chinese emerged.[37] In October 1996, in Situbondo, East Java, anti-Chinese rioters burned down 20 churches and several people died. Furthermore, in December 1996, in Tasikmalaya, West Java, rioters burned down churches, Chinese schools, shops and residences killing several Chinese. Concerning the unstable political situation in Indonesia and the sharply increased exposure of Korean banks, the Korean central bank requested Korean banks to report their exposure in Indonesia and implicitly cautioned them on further lending.[38]

Furthermore, in 1996, the nepotism of Suharto family reached previously unimagined levels and became a serious threat to established business circles in Indonesia. The worst case was the privileged treatment received by Tommy (Hutomo Mandala Putra), Suharto's youngest son, regarding the national car project (MOBNAS). His company (Timor Putra Nasional) was granted exclusive import- and luxury-tax exemptions. His company sold cars by taking advantage of these tax concessions and took market share from other auto companies, such as Astra and Indomobil (Salim). Offshore lenders were concerned that Suharto's nepotism might harm their borrowers' positions. Other Suharto family members also obtained privileges, exclusive business opportunities and state bank financing.[39] New business opportunities, which were emerging together with the growth and liberalization of the Indonesian economy, were granted to Suharto family members and politically connected people in visible ways. This situation frustrated not only domestic business circles and overseas investors and lenders but also ordinary Indonesian people. In 1996, the Indonesian political situation became increasingly unstable before the general elections in May 1997.

However, the fundamentals of the Indonesian economy continued to improve, and credit ratings were also upgraded to Baa3 (Moody's) and BBB (S&P), slightly below China (A3 and BBB), in 1996. International financial markets viewed Indonesia very positively. The Republic of Indonesia's US$100 million 10-year Yankee bond was issued with a 100 basis point margin, and this level was lower than the secondary trading level of the People's Republic of China's 10-year global bond (105 basis points).[40] Supported by this situation, Indonesia reached the peak of the finance boom in 1996.

Private borrowers were offered abundant liquidity from offshore markets and aggressively took offshore syndicated debt into their capital structures.

In addition, borrowing terms improved dramatically.[41] Major offshore banks, which fiercely competed for arrangers' positions, stretched tenors and cut margins for prime borrowers, brought new names into offshore syndicated debt markets and financed huge projects. Korean and Taiwanese banks accelerated their financing of middle-credit borrowers, which had relatively high exposure to the financial and real estate sector and paid much higher margins than prime credit borrowers. Furthermore, Indonesian bankers also began arranging syndicated debt for both onshore and offshore markets.[42] However, domestic banks generally surrendered their prime clients to offshore bankers, which could offer huge US$finance with better borrowing terms. Domestic banks could not help but shift their client base to the remaining lower-credit borrowers and risky projects, and thereby the quality of domestic banks' portfolio gradually deteriorated.

This situation further intensified during the first half of 1997. Offshore lenders' enthusiasm towards Indonesian borrowers exceeded their concerns on realized and potential Indonesian risks. Offshore lenders continued to provide huge liquidity, longer tenor and attractively low margins to Indonesian borrowers. Offshore lenders seemed to totally forget risk premiums on Indonesian borrowers. They aggressively took on the risks of new and lower-credit borrowers. Subsidiaries and grandchildren companies of large business groups, small- and medium-size business groups, second-class private banks, real estate and financial services-oriented business groups and real estate projects obtained offshore syndicated debt. The downwards diversification of borrowers continued. The Indonesian government was seriously concerned about the accumulation of external debt in the private non-bank sector, which was outside the control of BI.[43] Nevertheless, this situation continued for some time, even after the Thai baht crisis in July 1997 and Indonesia was seriously affected by contagion.

In this way, there were two contradictory pressures, that is, the steady improvement of economic fundamentals and the fragility of the business climate (e.g. the unstable political situation and frequent credit events), throughout the finance boom in Indonesia. Under these conditions, offshore lenders surrendered themselves to their enthusiasm towards expanding their finance activities in Indonesian credit markets. This naturally provided huge amounts of liquidity to Indonesian borrowers in the form of offshore syndicated debt, the downwards diversification of borrowers, the improvement of borrowing terms for borrowers and the quick shift of bargaining power from offshore lenders to Indonesian borrowers.

On the other hand, it is necessary to analyse offshore lenders' economic calculations that led to such an enthusiastic approach to the Indonesian credit markets. Even during the finance boom, forward and swap markets for hedging foreign currency exposure were less developed in Indonesia. Only BI swaps, cross-currency swaps between rupiah and US dollars, were available for short-tenor and limited-volume transactions. It was impossible for lenders and borrowers to hedge large rupiah exposure. Moreover, until the East-Asian crisis, the Indonesian government maintained a crawling peg against the US dollar and implicitly guaranteed the depreciation risk of the rupiah. In addition, the value of the rupiah was supported by abundant capital inflows during the finance boom. The rupiah was stable during this period. Offshore lenders and Indonesian borrowers tended to keep open their foreign currency positions and maximize benefits from them. In other words, moral hazard with regards to foreign exchange risk spread among fund providers and users.[44]

Under the earlier-mentioned situation, assuming the absence of transaction costs, default risk and capital controls, offshore lenders and Indonesian borrowers calculations were based on the following uncovered interest rate parity: $R_{onshore} = R_{offshore} + (E_{expected} - E)/E - RP$, where $R_{onshore}$ is the rupiah interest rate, $R_{offshore}$ is the US dollar interest rate, $E_{expected}$ is the expected exchange rate of the rupiah against the US dollar, E is the spot exchange rate and RP is the risk premium or extra expected returns that investors demanded in compensation for holding rupiah assets. Furthermore, assuming that the exchange rate is an independent variable and that the rupiah interest rate is a dependent variable, $R_{onshore}$ is deemed to be the expected rupiah interest rate, that is, expected returns on investment for offshore lenders and expected borrowing costs for Indonesian borrowers.

As is mentioned above, until the East-Asian crisis, Indonesia maintained a crawling peg system for the rupiah, and the target of the annual depreciation rate was less than 5 per cent. Therefore, RP should be zero and $(E_{expected} - E)/E$ was implicitly capped by the government. As a matter of fact, the annual depreciation rate of the rupiah during the finance boom was controlled far below the target (Table 5.14). The foreign exchange risk of the rupiah appeared to be predictable and mitigated for offshore lenders and Indonesian borrowers as far as they had confidence in government policy. In sum, lenders and borrowers assumed that exchange-risk-free interest rate parity conditions applied.

Furthermore, $R_{actual} - R_{offshore}$, where R_{actual} is the actual rupiah interest rate in the market, is shared between offshore lenders and Indonesian borrowers, that is, margin income for lenders, including default risk premium (for country and credit risks) and transaction costs (for due diligence and monitoring) and funding cost savings for borrowers. This could be one of the driving forces for offshore debt finance during the finance boom. As Table 5.14 shows, the rupiah interest rate ('Rp. borrowing rate' in Table 5.14) and foreign exchange losses were stable from 1994 to 1996, while the US dollar interest rate ('US$ 3-month LIBOR' in Table 5.14) increased to the level of over 5 per cent per annum. As a result, the benefits to be shared between offshore lenders and Indonesian borrowers declined during the period, and thereby funding cost savings for borrowers were pushed down. Nevertheless, both parties could still share an average of over 6.5 per cent per annum, and Indonesian borrowers could still save on funding costs by an average of over 4.5 per cent per annum.

As previous sections in this chapter have argued, during the finance boom offshore lenders could not improve all-in margins for their lending to Indonesian corporate borrowers ('margin incomes for offshore lenders' in Table 5.14) due to their enthusiasm and lending imperatives. However, as Table 5.14 indicates, they could improve the excess-margin income over Indonesian sovereign risk.[45]

Table 5.14 Direct benefits from offshore loans for offshore lenders and Indonesian borrowers (% per annum)

	1993	1994	1995	1996	1997 (– June)
Rp. borrowing rate (R_{actual})[a]	17.92	15.51	15.69	16.05	15.91
US$ base cost $(R_{onshore})$	6.07	8.29	9.93	9.24	12.39
US$ 3-month LIBOR $(R_{offshore})$	3.31	4.75	6.04	5.51	5.69
Foreign exchange loss $((E_{expected} - E)/E)$	2.77	3.54	3.89	3.72	6.70
Benefit to be shared $(R_{actual} - E_{onshore})$	11.85	7.22	5.76	6.81	3.52
Margin income for offshore lenders[b]	2.34	2.30	2.05	2.09	2.08
Excess margin income over sovereign risk[c]	0.83	0.82	1.16	1.35	1.48
Margin income for offshore lenders[d]	2.23	2.13	2.03	1.98	1.93
Excess margin income over sovereign risk[c]	0.72	0.72	1.14	1.24	1.33
Margin income for offshore lenders[e]	2.18	2.02	1.87	1.65	1.60
Excess margin income over sovereign risk[c]	0.67	0.61	0.99	0.90	1.00
Cost savings for Indonesian borrowers[b]	9.51	4.99	3.71	4.72	1.44
Cost savings for Indonesian borrowers[d]	9.62	5.09	3.73	4.83	1.59
Cost savings for Indonesian borrowers[e]	9.67	5.20	3.88	5.17	1.92

Sources: Bank Indonesia, Bloomberg, and privately collected data (checked with IFR).

Notes
a Average of state banks' lending rates for working capital and investment.
b Simple average of all-in margins for all Indonesian non-bank borrowers (Table 5.13).
c Excess of margin incomes for offshore lenders ((b), (d) and (e)) over those charged to state banks' offshore borrowings (Tables 5.7 and 5.9).
d Simple average of all-in margins for top ten regular borrowers (Table 5.13).
e Simple average of all-in margins for top-tier credit borrowers (Table 5.13).

In particular, offshore lenders improved excess all-in margins for the top ten regular borrowers ((d) in Table 5.14) and top-tier credit borrowers ((e) in Table 5.14).[46] Offshore lenders received greater compensation for taking credit risks of corporate borrowers and paying transaction costs required to finance them. Assuming that credit risks and transaction costs were unchanged, offshore lenders improved risk-adjusted returns on their lending to the Indonesian corporate sector.[47]

However, as is argued in Chapters 4 and 6–9, the financial positions of Indonesian corporate borrowers, including top-tier credit and regular borrowers of offshore syndicated loans, were heavily leveraged by aggressive debt finance during the finance boom and their credit risk increased. In addition, offshore lenders aggressively expanded their lending activities to lower-credit borrowers during the period, that is, the downwards diversification of borrowers. Therefore, it is fair to conclude that offshore lenders could partially compensate for the increase in corporate borrowers' credit risks by improving excess returns over Indonesian sovereign risk. In this sense, although offshore lenders surrendered themselves to their enthusiasm to lend to Indonesian corporate borrowers and squeezed their gross margins, they attempted to mitigate the deterioration of risk-adjusted returns. However, the improvement in excess returns on corporate lending over sovereign risk further increased offshore lenders' enthusiasm and induced new entries of different types of offshore lenders. At the macro-level more offshore private capital, mainly through offshore syndicated debt, entered into the Indonesian corporate sector.

During the period, lenders of offshore syndicated debt, that is, the supply side of external debt, drove the accumulation of external debt by the Indonesian private sector and the change in the nature of Indonesian external debt problems. Together with borrowers' demand for offshore funds, offshore lenders' enthusiasm created a complex financial structure in Indonesia during the finance boom.

6   Case study 1

The Salim Group's financial activities in the 1990s

General views on the Salim Group

The Salim Group, the largest and most diversified business conglomerate in Indonesia, officially divides its businesses into 11 divisions: agribusiness, food and consumer goods, automobile and auto parts, construction materials, chemicals, computer and telecommunication, natural resource development, trading and distribution, multi-industries, real estate development, financial services and overseas business. However, the conglomerate has not adapted a group holding structure such as the Astra Group (i.e. a shareholding structure consisting of a holding company, a sub-holding company and an operating company), so it is not clear by whom and how it is owned.

With regard to the ownership of conglomerates, the Salim Group can be separated into the following three types: (i) Salim family businesses (the 'Salim family'); (ii) co-investments by the Salim family and long-standing domestic partners (the 'Salim investors') and (iii) joint ventures with foreign capital (the 'Salim joint ventures'). Long-standing domestic partners are the Djuhar family and two people related to former president Suharto: Sudwikatmono and Ibrahim Risjad (the 'Salim partners'). Suharto and his family were also critical business partners offering patronage and political protection to the Salim investors. The Salim Group has behaved as an apparatus with a view to maximize the Salim family's and their partners' interests. This ultimate business target of the group influenced its management.

The diversification of their businesses is a result of the group's opportunistic investment style rather than a target-investment strategy. The pursuit of monopolistic or oligopolistic market share in their business fields reflects the group's strong desire to obtain excess returns on investments by utilizing market power. The aggressive acquisition strategy is a critical method for shortening the gestation period of projects and for maximizing profits and cash flow in the short term.[1] A corporate entity, that is, company, is an apparatus for realizing profits and cash flow from investments. In a way, the Salim Group is a financial institution such as a large private equity fund.

Political economists have stressed the strong political connection between the Salim Group and Suharto. The group has come under heavy criticism in the aftermath of the East Asian crisis as a symbol of crony capitalism in the region. Some scholars argue that business groups such as the Salim Group did not make a contribution to economic development in terms of technology, exports, and so forth, and they therefore define these groups as 'traders-turned capitalist', 'comprador capitalists', 'technologically dependent capitalists', 'rent-seekers and speculators' and 'ersatz capitalists' (Yoshihara 1988, pp.68–86, 107–20, 130–1).

Others do not deny the fact that the political connections with Suharto led to the success of the Salim Group but pay more attention to the dynamism of the group's management. They view political connections as a part of the process of its growth, and treat the Salim Group's opportunistic investment style, mono-polistic or oligopolistic business strategy, acquisition strategy and business partnerships as an engine for further business development. They argue that even this management style is transitory and will change in parallel with the growth (Sato 1992).

These two different views of the Salim Group naturally focus on the asset side of the group's balance sheet, which is a tangible outcome of its investment activities. However, this is only half of the story. It is necessary to look at how these investments were financed in order to understand the group's investment activities and ultimate business targets. In terms of the number of listed companies, the Salim Group is the second most active user of the stock market among Indonesian private conglomerates and currently has 11 onshore and offshore listed companies.[2] Furthermore, the Salim Group was one of the most active users of the onshore and offshore debt markets during the 1990s. After the East Asian crisis, the group's accumulated debt accounted for a large share of Indonesia's total private sector debt. As is argued later, from 1994 until the outbreak of the crisis, the Salim Group had been rapidly building up an unstable financial structure by leveraging its balance sheet and changing its financial positions, which increased its vulnerability to external economic turmoil.

First, this chapter surveys (i) the changes in the Salim Group's financial position by referring to its balance sheet; (ii) its aggressive use of the offshore debt market and the improvement of its borrowing terms and (iii) its structural changes coupled with the large size of its debt and equity transactions. In this manner, it can be explained how Salim Group's financial structure and position became unstable and fragile during the finance boom of the 1990s.

Second, this chapter attempts to ascertain an endogenously disequilibrating force of the internal unstabilizing process of economy, which Minsky argued in his financial instability hypothesis, in the combination of leading Indonesian business groups' finance activities, such as the Salim Group, and enthusiastic offshore bankers' lending activities during the 1990s. Following Minsky's defin-itions, their finance activities evolved the financial structure of the Indonesian economy from a robust/hedged to fragile/speculative one and created a dynamic of capitalism, which has a complex, sophisticated and further evolving financial structure and leads to the development of conditions conducive to downside incoherence – to deep depression or crisis, in Indonesia (Minsky 1986).

The Salim Group's financial position

The rapid expansion of the domestic private banking sector after the financial sector deregulation of 1988 (PAKTO) coupled with offshore banks' aggressive marketing in Indonesia provided the Salim Group with a great opportunity to obtain debt finance and leverage its financial position. In particular, after 1994 the Salim Group aggressively used not only standard offshore syndicated debts but also other hybrid types of finance, such as project finance, offshore CP (commercial paper) programme, bonds and share finance. The group also used equity-linked debts, such as exchangeable bonds. The change in offshore lenders' and investors' behaviour in Indonesia in the 1990s enabled the Salim Group to diversify its funding from conventional state bank borrowing and suppliers' credits to international fund raising, and to expand its funding capacity both in terms of volume and quality (i.e. terms and conditions, such as pricing and tenor).

Table 6.1 presents the combined historical financial position of the Salim Group's listed companies in Jakarta, Hong Kong and Singapore. It shows that it had consistently leveraged its balance sheet during the 1990s, and in particular accelerated leveraging from 1994 to the onset of the East Asian crisis. The leverage ratio doubled from 1.61 in 1993 (i.e. at the beginning of 1994) to 3.33 in 1996, and the equity ratio also sharply dropped from 38 per cent in 1993 to 23 per cent in 1996 (Table 4.9 in Chapter 4). During this period, the exchange rate of the Indonesian rupiah against the US dollar had moderately depreciated by 7.5 per cent from Rp.2,199 in 1994 to Rp.2,363 in 1996. Even if the group had not hedged its foreign currency denominated liability, the upwards effect on the leverage by foreign exchange rate movements would have been small. The increase in leveraging came therefore mainly from the increase in liabilities versus equity. Using a definition for corporate banking in developed countries, the Salim Group became a typical leveraged corporation during this period.

The sharp increase in gross/net debt to equity ratios from 1.11/1.04 in 1993 to 2.45/1.89 in 1996 shows that the group's leveraging had been driven mainly by

Table 6.1 The Salim Group's financial position (non-financial listed companies) (times)

Ratios	1990	1991	1992	1993	1994	1995	1996	1997
Leverage	0.92	1.07	1.70	1.61	2.38	2.26	3.33	5.31
Equity	0.52	0.48	0.37	0.38	0.30	0.31	0.23	0.16
Gross debt to equity	0.54	0.68	1.24	1.11	1.90	1.74	2.45	3.99
Net debt to equity	0.46	0.64	1.17	1.04	1.62	1.26	1.89	3.36
Gross debt to CS + APIC	0.77	1.14	2.35	2.43	3.96	3.96	4.58	7.07
Net debt to CS + APIC	0.65	1.07	2.23	2.28	3.37	2.86	3.53	5.96
Gross debt to EBITDA	1.80	2.42	3.22	2.59	5.27	5.08	5.09	10.27
Net debt to EBITDA	1.53	2.27	3.04	2.43	4.49	3.68	3.92	8.65
Current	1.49	1.55	1.10	0.94	1.45	1.74	1.46	1.28
Short to long-term debt	1.33	0.61	0.51	0.88	0.26	0.27	0.36	0.35

Source: Annual reports.

debt financing in the financial markets, rather than by other types of liabilities such as trade finance. The gross/net debt to CS + APIC ratios also jumped from 2.43/2.28 in 1993 to 4.58/3.53 in 1996. This indicates that the group had obtained new funds more rapidly and largely through debt markets rather than equity markets and that such easier access to debt markets resulted in the group's highly leveraged financial position. Furthermore, the gross/net debt to EBITDA ratios sharply increased from 2.59/2.43 in 1993 to 5.09/3.92 in 1996. This indicates that the potential risk was that the group's cash-generating capacity from their operations could not keep up with increased debt servicing and/or that the debt might not be used for cash-generating investments but for simply cashing out shareholders' interests in the group.

Focusing on individual companies in the Salim Group, group flagship companies such as Indofood, Indocement, Indomobil (including Indomulti), UIC and First Pacific can be observed as the most active debt-finance users and leverage drivers among its non-financial listed companies. The gross debt of Indofood in 1996 (Rp.2,837 billion) rose by 8.96 times from the 1993 figure (Rp.320 billion) mainly due to heavily debt-financed intra-group acquisitions, such as asset acquisition of Bogasari from Indocement. The gross debt of First Pacific also grew dramatically by 9.05 times from Rp.1,406 billion in 1993 to Rp.12,717 billion in 1996, mainly due to active debt-financed corporate acquisitions outside Indonesia. Indomobil was virtually a non-debt company with merely Rp.45 billion in borrowing in 1993. Nevertheless, the company's gross debt sharply increased to Rp.1,395 billion in 1996 mostly due to debt assumption for corporate consolidation and heavily debt-financed investments. UIC did not undertake any major corporate consolidations or acquisitions but sharply increased its gross debt by 85.3 per cent from Rp.229 billion in 1993 to Rp.424 billion in 1996 due to debt-financed capital expenditure. Only Indocement reduced its gross debt by 15.5 per cent from Rp.2,552 billion in 1993 to Rp.2,156 billion in 1996. However, considering the fact that Indocement had transferred its related Rp.450 billion debt to Indofood in the Bogasari transaction, gross debt remained at very high levels.

On the other hand, Indofood and Indocement's CS + APIC accounts stayed the same between 1994 and 1996 (Rp.872 billion and Rp.1,380 billion respectively), and UIC increased the account by only 27.8 per cent from Rp.125 billion in 1993 to Rp.159 billion in 1996. First Pacific and Indomobil increased their CS + APIC accounts by 4.70 times from Rp.242 billion in 1993 to Rp.1,138 billion in 1996 and by 6.93 times from Rp.39 billion in 1993 to Rp.269 billion in 1996 respectively. However, the increase in their CS + APIC accounts was much slower than the increases of their gross debt accounts as explained earlier. Other data indicates that the fund the Salim Group raised in the Jakarta Stock Exchange between 1994 and 1996 (i.e. cash calls) was merely Rp.479 billion. This amount was much smaller than the increase of gross debt of Indonesia-domiciled Salim Group's companies (Rp.1,367 billion).[3]

As a result, these Salim Group flagship companies heavily leveraged their financial positions during the period. Indofood de-leveraged its balance sheet by stock listing in 1994. However, the company rapidly re-leveraged itself over next 3 years as shown by the movement of key ratios. Indocement, which consolidated Indofood in its financial statement, basically followed a similar path but displayed more moderate results.

In the same way as Indofood, Indomobil augmented its capital and de-leveraged its balance sheet by equity finance in 1995 and improved the above five ratios to very sound levels. However, huge debt-financed investments weighed heavily on the company's financial position. On the other hand, the financial position of UIC did not change as much as Indofood and Indomobil but consistently deteriorated between 1993 and 1996 due to debt-financed investments without equity enhancements. First Pacific, which pushed forward aggressive debt-financed acquisitions outside Indonesia, also heavily leveraged its balance sheet as the changes of the above five ratios between 1993 and 1996 indicate.[4]

As explained earlier, the highly leveraged financial position of the Salim Group's listed companies including entities consolidated into them is explained, but the financial position of a number of non-listed companies is difficult to ascertain simply due to lack of information. However, as Holdiko (Holdiko Perkasa) was established in 1998, a part of the Salim Group's non-listed company data since 1996 became available even though accessible financial data are only sales, gross profits, operating profits, EBITDA, total assets and equity. The leverage ratio, equity ratio and liability to EBITDA ratio (a substitute of gross debt to EBITDA ratio) are used for checking the financial position of the group's non-listed companies.[5]

Based on this data, the following ratios apply to the Salim Group's non-listed companies in 1996: a leverage ratio of 3.13, an equity ratio of 0.24 and a liability to EBITDA ratio of 1.11. The leverage ratio and equity ratio are almost in line with those of the group's listed companies. However, the liability to EBITDA ratio is extremely high relative to listed companies (6.91 times). This means that the cash-generation capacity of the group's non-listed companies was below the listed companies and their consolidated subsidiaries. A number of new businesses, which were at the start-up stage and unable to contribute to the group financial performance, might be in the population of non-listed companies.

On the other hand, even though both offshore and onshore financial markets were very supportive to the Indonesian private sector during the period, how was the Salim Group able to rapidly leverage its financial position by such aggressive bank borrowing? What were lenders' views of the group's credit in terms of finance theory?

Table 6.2 lists the profitability, funding cost and debt-service capacity of the Salim Group in the 1990s. All profit margins, that is, operating profit margin, profit before tax margin, net profit margin and cash-flow margin (EBITDA margin) reached the highest level in 1994 and 1996. Moreover, the financial costs, that is, interest and foreign exchange loss, sharply dropped due to the switching from high-interest-rate rupiah finance to low-interest-rate foreign currency finance and stable rupiah exchange rate versus US dollars. Therefore, the group's debt-service capacity, which is indicated by EBIT/EBITDA interest and funding cost-coverage ratios, also improved in 1994 and 1995.

Table 6.2 The Salim Group's profitability, financial costs and debt-service capacity (non-financial listed companies) (margin and cost: %, coverage: times)

Margins, costs and coverage ratios	1990	1991	1992	1993	1994	1995	1996	1997
Operating profit margin	11.90	10.52	12.55	12.52	13.66	12.91	11.47	10.42
Profit before tax margin	7.88	7.91	7.72	7.75	9.15	8.57	7.80	−3.49
Net profit margin	6.87	6.86	6.08	5.94	6.87	7.36	5.91	−4.57
EBITDA margin	14.26	12.93	15.99	16.10	17.36	16.27	14.67	13.90
Interest cost	12.30	13.06	12.46	10.76	6.96	5.91	7.75	4.09
Funding cost (interest + forex loss)	12.88	14.21	13.29	11.87	7.78	6.81	8.57	8.59
EBIT interest coverage	4.43	3.43	2.88	3.10	3.58	3.82	2.90	3.15
EBIT funding cost coverage	4.23	3.15	2.70	2.81	3.20	3.31	2.62	1.50
EBITDA interest coverage	5.31	4.22	3.67	3.98	4.55	4.81	3.71	4.20
EBITDA funding cost coverage	5.07	3.88	3.44	3.61	4.07	4.17	3.36	2.00

Source: Annual reports.

All of these indicators deteriorated in 1996 due to the increased costs and cash outflows incurred by aggressive new investments and debt finance. However, the profitability, funding costs and debt-service capacity of the Salim Group in 1994 and 1995 achieved the best figures since offshore investors and lenders started keeping their eyes on the Indonesian private sector in the early 1990s. In addition, as shown in Table 6.1, the liquidity aspect of the balance sheet, current ratios and short-term to long-term debt ratios also improved in 1994 and 1995. These figures undoubtedly supported enthusiastic bankers' finance logic to increase loan exposure to the group. Following Minsky, the years of 1994 and 1995 were an inflationary and expansionary boom for both the Salim Group and offshore bankers (Minsky 1986). All of the results reported clearly demonstrate that the Salim Group had heavily leveraged its financial position under the finance boom between 1994 and 1996 by obtaining more funds through debt markets than equity markets and intra-group funding sources, such as internal cash flow and the Salim family's additional capital injections. As discussed later, the group's listed companies aggressively used offshore syndicated debts and evolved the borrowing terms and conditions over a period of only 3 years. After that, the Salim Group's financial structure drastically changed from robust and stable to fragile and unstable.

The Salim Group's offshore fund-raising activities

Syndicated debts arranged through offshore markets, which had been widely opened up to the Indonesian private sector after 1994 due to international banks' aggressive marketing activities, were the most important tools for the Salim Group in leveraging its financial position. In addition, the group amazingly improved terms and conditions for their syndicated loans, mainly tenor and pricing, over the 3 years between 1994 and 1996. Furthermore, they introduced advanced types of financing, such as project finance, acquisition finance, share finance and fixed income bonds. Considering the group's conventional funding style, that is, borrowing from state banks by using political and private connections with politico-bureaucrats and intra-group borrowing from BCA, the expanded use of offshore syndicated debts and the introduction of new financial products led to an evolution in the Salim Group's funding strategies.

During this period, offshore banks were generally concerned about the Salim Group's political connections to the Suharto family and the possibility that the group could suffer a substantial setback in the post-Suharto era. Nevertheless, the fact that the Salim Group included a number of leading companies that held dominant positions in their business fields (such as Indocement in cement, Indofood in instant noodles, UIC in alkyl benzene and BCA in private banking) could counter offshore bankers' fears concerning the group's position, including its future prospects. As Minsky has stressed, a monopolistic position with market power could provide lenders with confidence with regards to borrowers' future profits and cash flow for fulfilling their payment commitments (Minsky 1986). Moreover, offshore bankers' irresistible temptation towards the Indonesian corporate sector provided great funding opportunities for the Salim Group, the top private business group in Indonesia.

Table 6.3 supports the view that the Salim Group had heavily leveraged its financial position between 1994 and 1997 by using offshore syndicated debts. Both the number and the volume of these rapidly increased during the period. The group obtained a total of US$3.6 billion (Rp.8.8 trillion equivalent) through 42 offshore syndicated debts between 1994 and 1997. There is no doubt that the group obtained much more from offshore finances than those listed in Table 6.3. In particular, bilateral transactions are not included in the data. Therefore, the

Table 6.3 The Salim Group's offshore syndicated debts: 1993–7 (summary) (transactions, US$ million)

	Including BCA		Not including BCA	
	No. of deals	Amount	No. of deals	Amount
1993	5	381	3	211
1994	9	668	7	448
1995	9	662	8	592
1996	15	1,132	14	982
1997	9	1,133	9	1,133
Total	47	3,977	41	3,366

Source: Privately collected data (checked with IFR).

large part of the group's funding relied on debt finance in the offshore market, mainly in Singapore and Hong Kong.

Offshore banks preferred core non-finance and operating companies, mainly Indocement, Indofood and UIC, in order to avoid their structurally subordinated position for payback, and to obtain good cash flow supported by those companies' monopolistic positions and broad customer base. As a result, offshore bankers provided an unimaginably huge amount of finance to these companies and furthermore, gave funding opportunities to other group subsidiaries and Salim family holding companies which were unable to access the offshore market prior to this period. The group's non-bank companies obtained US$3.2 billion (Rp.7.9 trillion) through 38 offshore syndicated debts during the same period.

Another important aspect of the Salim Group's offshore financing is that these core borrowers were not exporting companies and had insufficient foreign currency cash flow to repay foreign currency debt. Indocement, Indofood and UIC had strategically targeted large domestic consumers, from which they could obtain abundant hard (rupiah) cash by fully utilizing their dominant market position and market power.

Although they were able to use forward and currency swaps between US dollars and Indonesian rupiah for hedging their foreign currency positions, the market was still small and the cost was very high. The group sharply increased its fragility against foreign exchange risk. In addition to that, the group failed to adequately disclose its foreign currency positions to bankers and equity investors. Nevertheless, offshore bankers enthusiastically supplied money to the borrowers.

The offshore bankers' aggressive approach to the Salim Group also enabled its member borrowers to drastically improve their borrowing terms. The most important terms for the group were tenor and pricing (i.e. spread over benchmarks, such as SIBOR and LIBOR). For example, in the first half of the 1990s, '1-year' was still the standard tenor for Indonesian private companies, and a '3-year' tenor was challenging. Even the so-called good quality Indonesian state banks such as Bank EXIM, BNI and BRI, the best Indonesian borrowers after the Republic of Indonesia and Pertamina, could borrow up to '4-year' money but struggled to access to '5-year' finance. Thus, *5-year* finance was generally impossible for the private sector. However, the change in offshore bankers' approach to the Indonesian private sector after 1993 and their strong interest in the Salim Group as the lending target, led to favourable borrowing terms for the group. Evidence relating to offshore syndicated debts arranged for four major borrowers, Indocement, Indofood, UIC and BCA, demonstrates this change.

First, Indocement had frequently financed its funding requirements through syndicated and club loans. Between 1994 and 1997, Indocement obtained US$89 million through 12 syndicated loans (excluding pure bridging finance) and used the funds not only for expansion but also to replace domestic rupiah borrowing. In 1994, Indocement were only able to obtain the following short- and medium-term finances and paid them in these all-in margins: 113.0 basis points for US$100 million 1-year facility, 175.0 basis points for US$20 million 2-year facility, 215.0 basis points for US$35 million 3-year facility and 205.0 basis points for

US$100 million 3-year facility. These terms remained in line with the standard terms for top-class corporate borrowers in the Indonesian private sector. However, Indocement broke this standard, and following that, a period of longer than 3-year unsecured finance became standard for the company. Moreover, the all-in margin also became increasingly tighter each year and the level was much lower than the 3-year syndicated loans arranged in 1994 (e.g. 145 basis points for 5-year facility (4-year average tenor) arranged in December 1995). Indocement dramatically improved its borrowing terms from the offshore syndication market.

The same improvement in borrowing terms is also apparent in the case of Indofood. Immediately after the IPO in 1994, the company made its debut in the offshore syndication market with the Bogasari acquisition transaction which is explained in the next section. Indofood obtained three 5-year unsecured syndicated loans with a total amount of US$675 million between 1995 and 1997. As discussed earlier, the 5-year unsecured finance was record breaking for the Indonesian private sector, and ever since then offshore banks have offered these terms to only a limited group of top Indonesian companies. The improvement of all-in margin is also clear. The company paid 157 basis points for 5-year unsecured finance arranged in July 1995, 147.5 basis points for the same in July 1996 and merely 96.8 basis points in June 1997. In addition, it should be noted that the US$300 million syndicated loan arranged in 1995 was at the time the largest 5-year unsecured syndicated facility in the history of the Indonesian private sector.

UIC was regarded as a core company for the Salim Group's chemical business but as a joint venture company with the Wings Group. Therefore, the company was not utilized for Salim investors' and/or family's financial strategies. The company obtained US$149 million from the offshore market through three syndicated loans between 1993 and 1995. The all-in margins of the last two 3-year secured syndicated loans in 1994 and 1995 show clear improvements. The average tenor and all-in margin of the US$45 million secured syndicated loan in 1994 was two and half years and 224.0 basis points and in line with other Indonesian blue chip companies' borrowing terms. However, those of the US$84 million secured syndicated loan in 1995 were improved to 3 years and 147.5 basis points. In particular, the improvement of pricing was very sharp and reflected the then offshore bankers' preference for manufacturing companies.

Between 1993 and 1997, BCA, the largest Indonesian private bank and the core group bank of the Salim Group, issued six FRCDs, including refinancing and wavering put option: US$70 million in June 1993, US$100 million in October 1993, US$70 million in May 1994, US$150 million in October 1994, US$70 million in June 1995 and US$150 million in October 1996 (Table 5.11 in Chapter 5 and Table 6.4). A drastic improvement of issue conditions emerged in 1994. The bank was able to reduce the all-in margin by around 40.0 basis points from 140.0–145.0 in 1993 to 102.5–132.0 in 1994. In addition, in 1995, the bank was able to stretch the tenor by 2 years, from 1 to 3 years, and reduce the all-in margin to 83.3 basis points. Furthermore, the bank pushed down the all-in margin to 74.0 basis points in 1996. BCA did not challenge the drastic borrowing terms as did Indocement and Indofood, but the improvement in terms clearly indicates

Table 6.4 The Salim Group's offshore syndicated debts: 1993–7 (breakdown) (US$ million, years, basis points per annum)

Date	Borrower	Amount	Type	Average tenor	All-in margin	Security	Repayment
Mar.-93	Batamindo	106	TL	3	135.0	NA	Amortized
June-93	BCA	70	FRCD	1	140.0	NA	Bullet
Aug.-93	Indocement	85	TL	2	191.0	NA	Bullet
Sep.-93	UIC	20	NA	NA	NA	NA	NA
Oct.-93	BCA	100	FRCD	1	145.0	NA	Bullet
Feb.-94	Batamindo	98	TL/Bdg	5/1	NA	NA	NA
Mar.-94	UIC	45	TL	2.5	224.0	Fix	Amortized
Apr.-94	Indocement	100	NA	1	113.0	NA	NA
May-94	BCA	70	FRCD	1	132.0	NA	Bullet
Aug.-94	Indocement	20	TL	2	175.0	NA	Bullet
Sep.-94	Indocement	35	RC	3	215.0	NA	Bullet
Oct.-94	BCA	150	FRCD	1	102.5	NA	Bullet
Oct.-94	Indocement	100	TL	3	205.0	NA	Bullet
Dec.-94	Indocement	50	CP	1	NA	NA	Bullet
May-95	Swadharma Indotama	37	TL	1.5	225.8	NA	Bullet
May-95	Darya-Varia	10	RC	2	210.0	Float + fix	Bullet
June-95	Indocement	40	TL	1	107.5	NA	Bullet
June-95	BCA	70	FRCD	3	83.3	NA	Bullet
July-95	Indofood	300	TL	4.7	157.0	NA	Balloon
Aug.-95	UIC	120	TL/RC	3/1	147.5 −120.0	Float + fix	Bullet
Dec.-95	Indocement	25	TL	4	145.0	NA	Balloon
Dec.-95	Indofood	50	TL	3	140.0	NA	Bullet
Dec.-95	Indomiwon	10	RC	1	85.0	LG	Bullet
Mar.-96	Petrocentral	20	TL/RC	3/1	190.0/ 165.0	Fix + LG	Amortized/ bullet
Apr.-96	Darya-Varia	27	Bdg	0.5	200.0	NA	Bullet
May-96	Central Sumahi Motor	10	FRN	3	200.0	Float + LG	Bullet
July-96	Indofood	125	TL	5	147.5	NA	Bullet
Aug.-96	Swadharma Indotama	52	TL	2	185.0	Float	Bullet
Aug.-96	Indocement	25	NA	5+	Tighter	NA	Bullet
Aug.-96	Sriboga Raturaya	35	NA	5	250.0	Fix + LG	NA
Aug.-96	Bringin Indotama Sejahtera	22	RC	1	220.0	CL	Bullet
Sep.-96	Indocement	25	NA	5	Tighter	NA	Bullet
Oct.-96	BCA	150	FRCD	3	74.0	NA	Bullet
Oct.-96	Turnas Int'l (Group SPV)	200	TL	3	205.8	Shares	Bullet
Oct.-96	Darya-Varia	45	TL/RC	2/2	198.8/ 198.8	NA	Amortized/ bullet
Dec.-96	Petrowida	31	NA	NA	NA	NA	NA
Dec.-96	Indolampung	20	NA	NA	NA	NA	NA
Dec.-96	Indo Kodeco Cement	345	PF	6.25	253.5 −278.5	Project	Amortized

Table 6.4 Continued

Date	Borrower	Amount	Type	Average tenor	All-in margin	Security	Repayment
Jan.-97	F. Pacific Invest. (Group SPV)	245	TL	3	209.0	Shares	Bullet
Mar.-97	NA (The Salim Group)	100	NA	3	150.0	Shares	Bullet
Mar.-97	Satomo Indovyl Monomer	94	PF	NA	200.0	Project	NA
May-97	Indocement	100	Bdg	5	99.0	NA	Bullet
May-97	Indocement	100	Bdg	5	99.0	NA	Bullet
June-97	Indofood	250	TL	4.7	96.8	NA	Balloon
June-97	Central Sumahi Motor	20	FRN	1	210	Float + LG	Bullet
Nov.-97	Indocement	124	TF	4	230c	LG	Amortized
Dec.-97	Indocement	100	NA	NA	1650c	NA	NA

Source: Privately collected data (checked with IFR).

Notes
TL: term loan; RC: revolver; PF: project finance; Bdg: bridge finance;
Float: floating asset; Fix: fixed asset; LG: guarantee.

the direction of offshore investors' ideas with regard to the Indonesian private sectors as a credit risk.

In addition to the huge size of the conglomerate's offshore finance and improved borrowing terms during the period, the group successfully introduced very risky share finances in 1996 and 1997. In October 1996, the Salim Group (through Turnas International) obtained a US$200 million 3-year syndicated facility by pledging their holding shares of Indofood, Indocement and First Pacific. In January 1997, the Salim Group (through First Pacific Investment) also obtained a US$245 million 3-year syndicated facility by pledging their First Pacific shares. The all-in margins for both transactions were 205.8 and 209 basis points respectively, which were very generous for risky share finance.

This share finance, that is, lending to equity holders against their equity shares, is one of the riskiest lending activities for bankers. The lenders' position is subordinated to corporate lenders to the companies of pledged equity shares. Therefore, if the borrowers, the Salim investors, were to become insolvent and the prices of pledged shares simultaneously collapsed lenders of share finance would face an extremely difficult situation. They could only recover their exposure to borrowers from the residual value of the companies pledged after senior lenders had fully recovered their exposure to the companies. The share finance lenders stood in the same position as the Salim investors. In other words, Salim could pass their risks on to the lenders through this form of finance.

Nevertheless, enthusiasm for the Indonesian corporate sector led bankers to accept such risks. The US$245 million share finance in January 1997 was originally launched on the market at only US$150 million. However, the facility was increased from US$150 million to US$245 million due to heavy oversubscription. A rather interesting aspect is that strong demand for this risky finance came from offshore Asian bankers, who were ahead of Indonesian borrowers in the offshore market with regards to borrowing volumes and terms. As for this share finance, only seven Western participating banks, including the arranger (UBS), retained US$74.5 million (30.4 per cent of the facility), and 33 Asian banks in Korea, Singapore, Malaysia, Thailand and so forth took the remainder.[6]

In this way, through the study of the Salim Group's financial transactions by focusing on offshore syndicated loans it can be clearly understood that offshore bankers brought financial evolution, as Minsky explained, into Indonesia with tremendous enthusiasm. Then, this financial evolution and its escalation heavily leveraged the group's financial position towards a fragile financial structure and increased potential risk to worsen the position from speculative to Ponzi finance in the case of the sharp increases in financial costs, such as margin and foreign exchange losses.

The Salim Group's corporate restructuring and asset transfers in the 1990s

The asset transfers from the Salim family and partners to Indocement in 1992

In 1992, Indocement bought: (i) Bogasari Flour Mills (flour milling business); (ii) a 51 per cent stake of food-related companies, which were merged into Indofood in 1994 and (iii) a central Jakarta office building from the Salim family and partners and paid them approximately US$850 million.[7] Through this transaction, the Salim family and partners earned around US$300 million net profit and obtained cash.

Listed companies under the group's control, such as Indocement, played a critical role for liquidation purposes. This is because a huge financing capacity through both equity and debt markets was required for purchasing the Salim family's and their partners' accumulated investments. Furthermore, strong control of the public companies (acquisition vehicles) was also very important, as they had to push forward transactions which were against the interests of minority shareholders. The above assets which were transferred to Indocement were totally unrelated businesses, and there was almost no synergy from the acquisition.[8]

Due to this debt-financed acquisition, Indocement's gross debt suddenly increased from Rp.584 billion in 1991 to Rp.2,611 billion in 1992. The company's leverage ratio, gross debt to equity ratio, gross debt to CS + APIC ratio and gross debt to EBITDA ratio jumped from 0.42, 0.38, 0.47 and 1.55 in 1991 to 1.63, 1.43, 2.09 and 3.76 in 1992. Indocement's robust financial structure suddenly deteriorated, and the company was highly leveraged. This simple and straightforward asset disposal for the Salim family and partners by the utilization of Indocement's funding capacity heralded the onset of the Salim Group's liquidation process in the 1990s. Debt financing arranged for such asset transactions led to the group's heavily leveraged financial position during the period.

Two IPOs – Indofood in 1994 and Indomulti in 1995

The strict control of conglomerate and family information was one of the characteristics of the Salim Group and an important policy to protect it from political attack. In particular, financial data concerning related companies, which could provide clues as to the group's size and profitability, was treated as confidential. As a result, this policy forced the group to very conservative access to equity markets which required adequate disclosure of corporate information, and, thereby, even the Salim joint-venture partners were unable to obtain a clear picture of the conglomerate. This policy, furthermore, created a variety of sceptical views on the reality of the group in the minds of offshore investors.

However, the Salim Group had started to use the equity market actively and strategically together with offshore debt finance since 1994, and thereby aggressively generated a tremendous amount of liquidity for the founder Salim family and partners. Listed companies' credibility to third party investors and lenders strengthened a large financing capacity which was required for the Salim Group's investment strategy in the 1990s.

In 1994, the Salim Group's food and consumer goods business was restructured through the merger of a number of various affiliated food companies into Indofood (Indofood Sukses Makmur), and the Salim Group listed the company on the Jakarta Stock Exchange. The restructuring and stock listing of Indofood did not generate any substantial cash for the Salim family and partners. However, the most important aspects of Indofood were: (i) the family and partners were able to obtain liquidity for their investments in the food and consumer goods business and (ii) the Salim Group had another vehicle for liquidating its illiquid assets.

In June 1995, the Salim Group brought together a number of medium- and small-size family businesses and turned them into Indomulti (Indomulti Inti Industri (previously Indosepamas Anggun)) and listed the company on the Jakarta Stock Exchange. This company has five business lines: (i) shoe manufacturing (Primashoes Ciptakreasi, etc.); (ii) mosquito coil production (Sinar Plataco, Waletkencana Perkasa, Obor Jaya Abadi, Persada Mostindo Utama, etc.); (iii) galvanized iron sheet processing (Kerismas Witikco Makmur, Semarang Makmur, Poli Contindo Nusa, etc.); (iv) textiles (Adilanggeng Kencanatex, etc.) and (v) printing (Indographica Ekakarsa, etc.).[9]

However, it is obvious that these business lines were not linked to each other. Even though one Salim family member managed all companies under Indomulti and its subsidiaries, this merger did not create any synergy effects. However, the family managed to create liquidity for its illiquid family businesses by amalgamating them into a sizable company and publicly offering shares. In other words, the Salim family obtained the opportunity to liquidate its investments through the stock market.

The internal asset transfer in 1995 – the sale of Bogasari from Indocement to Indofood

Bogasari was a monopoly business dealing in the flour milling of wheat imported by BULOG (Indonesia's national logistics board) and the most critical source of profit and cash for the Salim Group. This business was originally established as

Bogasari Flour Mills by Djuhar Sutanto (Liem Oen Kian), one of Salim's business partners, in May 1969. Following that the Salim family acquired a substantial share of the company and since then the Salim and Sutanto families have jointly managed the business. In July 1992, Indocement suddenly decided to acquire the flour milling business and related assets of Bogasari Flour Mills, which were totally unrelated to cement production, for a gross purchase consideration of Rp.1,179 billion (US$581 million), consisting of a net purchase consideration of Rp.829 billion (US$408 million) and the assumption of Rp.350 billion (US$172 million) of liabilities. Indocement constituted this flour milling business as the 'Bogasari division'. This was the first profit realization and cash-out for the Salim investors.

In June 1995, only 3 years after the acquisition by Indocement, the Salim Group decided to make Indofood purchase the assets of Bogasari's business and related assets from Indocement for a gross consideration of Rp.1,860 billion (US$829 million), including Rp.450 billion (US$201 million) debt assumption.[10] Within just 3 years, the gross purchase consideration became 1.6 times as expensive as it was in 1992. Following this, Indofood paid this consideration to Indocement for Rp.1,260 billion in cash and a Rp.150 billion zero coupon bond (Figure 6.1).

At the time of this transaction Indocement still held a majority (50.1 per cent) of outstanding Indofood shares, and Indofood was consolidated into the financial statements of Indocement. Thus, this transaction was merely an intra-Indocement group asset transfer from Indocement's accounting viewpoint, and Indocement's balance sheet management were not able to explain the purpose of this transaction. The revalued Bogasari assets and additional borrowing by Indofood for this transaction merely stretched Indocement's balance sheet through the process of consolidation.

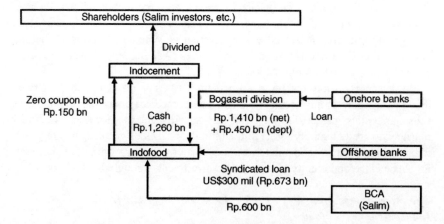

Figure 6.1 The Salim Group's internal asset transfer in 1995 (Bogasari division).

Source: Annual reports, prospectuses, circulars and various news.

On the other hand, this appeared to make sense from Indocement's operational viewpoint, as it could separate totally unrelated businesses and pass them on to Indofood, the management of the group's food and consumer products division. However, even after Bogasari had been transferred from Indocement to Indofood, the Salim family continued to manage Bogasari independently as it was a part of Indocement. That is to say, the management and operation of Bogasari remained unaltered even though the owner was internally changed.

The most important point is that Indofood was totally de-leveraged due to a huge cash inflow through the IPO in 1994. Indofood's leverage ratio, net debt to equity ratio and net debt to EBITDA ratio were reduced to 0.27, 0.11 and 0.39 respectively as of the end of 1994, and the company retained the capacity to obtain additional debt. Therefore, Indocement was able to absorb a large sum of cash from Indofood by selling Bogasari to Indofood and making Indofood pay the proceeds through bank borrowings. The Salim investors of Indocement thereby had an opportunity to absorb cash from Indocement. As a matter of fact, the cash dividends of Indocement in 1995 (Rp.193 billion) indicated a relatively high amount compared to other years (Rp.125 billion in 1994 and Rp.145 billion in 1996).

On the other hand, this internal asset transfer was financed by (i) US$300 million in offshore syndicated loans; (ii) Rp.600 billion bilateral borrowing from Salim Group's Bank Central Asia and (iii) Rp.450 billion debt assumption (including borrowings from BNI, BCA and Bogasari's suppliers). In particular, the US$300 million syndicated loan, which was jointly arranged by The Bank of America, Bankers Trust, Chase Manhattan Bank, Fuji Bank, The Long-Term Credit Bank of Japan and Mitsubishi Bank, was historically the largest unsecured facility to an Indonesian private company. In addition, the terms and conditions of the facility were also very aggressive:

Facility type:	Unsecured term loan
Amount:	US$300 million (split into six US$50 million facilities)
Tenor:	5.0 years
Average life:	4.7 years
Repayment:	Instalments with 80 per cent balloon payment
Spread:	140.0 basis points per annum for direct lenders
	100.0 basis points per annum for standby letter of credit issuers
Management fees:	35.0–80.0 basis points flat
All-in margin:	147.4–157.0 basis points per annum for direct lenders
	107.4–117.0 basis points per annum for standby letter of credit issuers.

Moreover, this entire deal was concluded in record time taking less than six weeks from mandate to signing and a total of 30 banks (6 senior arrangers, 10 arrangers, 8 co-arrangers, 3 managers and 3 participants) participated in the facility. Just by considering the fact that these offshore bankers took unsecured acquisition financing risks with challenging borrowing terms, it is possible to imagine how enthusiastic the offshore banking community was for lending to the Indonesian corporate sector. The scenario in 1995 was totally different from that prior to 1994.

The internal acquisition of palm oil businesses by Indofood in 1997

According to the Salim Group's official explanation, the palm oil business was located within the 'Agribusiness division'. Among the 12 business units of the group, this was one of the most rapidly growing and strategically important for the division. The group's palm oil plantation was already the second largest, following PTP, a state company, and larger than the Sinar Mas Group, and the division had been planning to consolidate a number of small plantation companies into one large sub-holding company.[11] However, in 1997, the Salim Group suddenly decided to sell an 80 per cent share of six palm oil-related companies (core plantations and distributors for the Agribusiness division and owned by the Salim family) to Indofood, one of the flagship public companies of the group and the core company of the Food and Consumer Goods division of the group.[12]

As illustrated by Figure 6.2, firstly, six family companies issued Rp.488 billion (US$210 million) in convertible bonds to balance the debt of each company. A Salim Group overseas acquisition vehicle underwrote these bonds and then exercised the bonds for new shares for each company. Indofood then acquired 80 per cent of the shares held by the overseas acquisition vehicle. Regarding

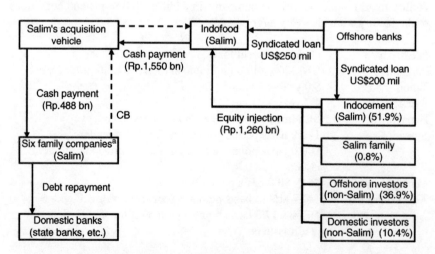

Figure 6.2 The disposal of the Salim family's palm oil businesses to Indofood in 1997.

Source: Annual reports, prospectuses, circulars and various news.

Note

a Six family companies' stock.

the funding for this acquisition, Indofood executed a rights issue that granted existing shareholders rights to purchase newly issued Indofood shares at a set price of Rp.3,300 per share, and borrowed balancing investment funds and additional working capital through offshore syndicated loans. Indocement, at that time 51.92 per cent shareholder of Indofood, also raised investment capital to exercise the rights and pay for new shares in Indofood through offshore syndicated loans.

These two offshore syndicated loans, the US$200 million 5-year facility for Indocement in May 1997 and the US$250 million 5-year facility for Indofood in June 1997, were executed just prior to the outbreak of the East Asian crisis in July 1997. However, there was no indication of the crisis at that time and the market welcomed the loans. As a matter of fact, the arrangers, Credit Lyonnais, Commerzbank, CSFB, Fuji Bank, The Bank of America and Chase Manhattan Bank, offered extremely aggressive terms and conditions for Indofood's US$250 million loan, that is, a 5-year tenor (4.7-year average life), all-in margin 96.8 basis points and unsecured for acquisition purposes. Then, more than 30 banks (6 lead arrangers, 10 co-arrangers, 4 lead managers and 12 managers), including Japanese regional, Korean and Taiwanese banks, committed to the facility, and this became finally oversubscribed to US$330 million. These excited bankers, who had committed to such a risky share-financing facility, had never envisaged that the Salim Group would enter a difficult position due to the crisis.

Finally, the Salim family gained Rp.1,550 billion (US$666 million) gross cash from selling 80 per cent of its shares of the six companies. Even in the case of Rp.488 billion (US$210 million) proceeds for convertible bonds being fully used for debt repayment, the Salim family could still retain more than US$456 million.

The most important point concerning the Salim Group is that the family converted their illiquid investment in Indonesian palm oil businesses into cash by directly and indirectly obtaining non-family and non-group money, that is, offshore syndicated loans and public equity investors' capital. In terms of financial technique, the Salim Group strategically used the high credibility of their two public companies, Indofood and Indocement, as funding vehicles for obtaining offshore debt money and by taking advantage of the aggressive stance of overseas banks vis-à-vis the Indonesian private sector. As a result, the Salim Group leveraged their financial position for debt-financed liquidation of family investments.

Another important aspect is the fact that the controllability of those two public companies enabled the Salim Group to execute the above acquisition. There is no doubt that conflicts of interest existed between Salim-related and non-related public shareholders, in particular, in terms of the valuation of the acquired six companies and the meaning of the acquisition itself (e.g. synergy effects for Indofood). This acquisition was a typical related-party transaction that had the potential to harm the interests of both Indofood and Indocement minority share-holders.[13] In addition, if the gap between the acquisition price and the real value of the six companies, a real goodwill, was lower than newly injected equity money, syndicated banks would also suffer from this transaction. Therefore, an obvious question must be asked as to why offshore bankers financed such a risky acquisition, and undoubtedly a related-party transaction, with extremely favoured terms and conditions to the borrower.

The not-finalized transfer of Indofood shares from Indonesia to Singapore

In 1997, the Salim Group spun off its indirect share of Indofood from Indocement to its direct holding and attempted to transfer the entire share from Indonesia to Singapore. Furthermore, in the process, the group tried to cash-out by both leveraging QAF, the group acquisition vehicle and listed company in Singapore, and by introducing third party investors' capital.

First, in July 1997, Indocement, a 50.1 per cent shareholder of Indofood, sold a part of Indofood shares (10.54 per cent equivalent) to the Sampoerna Group, a 5.63 per cent shareholder of Indofood and an Indonesian tobacco tycoon. At the same time, Indocement distributed the remaining Indofood shares (39.56 per cent equivalent) to Indocement shareholders as a 'special dividend-in-specie'. Following this transaction, the Salim Group became a 46.34 per cent direct shareholder of Indofood, and the Sampoerna Group (16.17 per cent), the Indonesian government (10.18 per cent) and public investors (27.31 per cent) owned the remaining shares.

As a second step, the Salim Group planned to sell its entire Indofood share to the group acquisition vehicles.[14] The group prepared the following three finances for the acquisition by the vehicles: (i) the Salim Group's S$1.54 billion cash injection into QAF out of S$2.44 billion projected cash proceeds from the disposal of Indofood share; (ii) a S$470 million new capital to QAF from its public investors and (iii) a US$470 million syndicated loan secured by Indofood share (Figure 6.3).

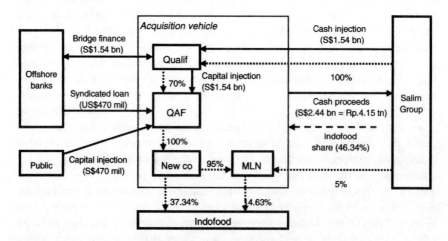

Figure 6.3 The planned ownership transfer of Indofood to offshore in 1997.

Source: Various news and memorandums.

Finally, a QAF's newly established wholly owned subsidiary ('New co') and Marga Lestari Abadi ('MLA'), a New co's Indonesian subsidiary, planned to hold Indofood shares of 37.34 per cent and 14.63 per cent respectively.[15] Moreover, after QAF increased its capital for this acquisition through right issues, the Salim Group planned to hold around 70 per cent through Qualif Pte Limited ('Qualif'), the group's 100 per cent owned subsidiary in Singapore.[16] In this way, the Salim Group attempted to transfer its majority ownership of Indofood from Indonesia to Singapore and obtain approximately S$900 million cash proceeds by leveraging QAF through offshore share finance and QAF's right issue.[17]

In terms of debt finance for this transaction, Citibank launched two syndicated loans: S$1,540 million (approximately US$1 billion) 30-day bridging loan and US$470 million 2-year secured term loan facility. The short-term bridging loan facility was to finance this transaction between the timing of the acquisition vehicles' purchase of a 52 per cent Indofood share and the timing of new capital injection into the vehicles.[18] The facility was secured by acquired Indofood shares and guaranteed by Sudono Salim, Anthony Salim and KMP Private Limited ('KMP'), the Salim family's strategic investment company in Singapore. The funding cost was an interest of SIBOR plus 75.0 basis points per annum and a participation fee of 12.5 basis points flat.

On the other hand, the secured term loan facility was arranged for financing a part of the cost of QAF's acquisition of the Indofood share. This was secured by approximately 40 per cent of the issued capital of Indofood (732.5 million shares) with a 200 per cent security coverage condition. The all-in funding cost was SIBOR plus 147.5 basis points per annum. This means of finance was typical of risky share finance.

Due to the collapse of the stock market due to the East Asian crisis and the withdrawal of offshore bankers' aggressive financing attitude to Indonesia, this transfer of Indofood shares to Singapore with leveraging was not finalized. (However, the Salim Group's share of Indofood was finally sold to First Pacific in 1999.[19]) Nevertheless, the fact that this action was undertaken by not only the Salim Group but also offshore investors and bankers is also an example to illustrate the group's management direction and the offshore investors' and lenders' enthusiasm during the finance boom.

Conclusions

During the 1990s, the Salim Group aggressively liquidated their investments and created cash flow for the Salim family and partners in mainly two ways: (i) transferring assets from family members and partners to the group's public companies, such as Indocement and Indofood and (ii) selling family members' and partners' interests through IPO. This liquidation process was strongly supported by rapidly expanding and widening financial markets for the Indonesian private sector, that is, the stock market boom, the liberalized domestic banking sector and offshore bankers' aggressive lending behaviour. In particular, offshore bankers' aggressive marketing from 1994 onwards brought about a financial evolution, as Minsky argued, in Indonesia, and the Salim Group were able to take full advantage of this.

The Salim family and partners managed to obtain abundant cash flow through these liquidation activities, while the Salim Group heavily leveraged its financial position by aggressively utilizing debt finance for these activities. Since 1994, offshore bankers' enthusiastic approach to the Indonesian corporate sector accelerated the group's offshore fund raising through syndicated loans, and drastically leveraged the group's balance sheet. As a result, the financial structure of the Salim Group became very unstable and extremely fragile in the face of external economic factors, such as the depreciation of the rupiah against foreign currencies, increased interest rates and offshore investors' negative views on Indonesian credit.

During the late Suharto period, given the uncertainty about conditions in the post-Suharto era the Salim family's and investors' liquidity preference led to the liquidation of their investments – in particular, the apprehension that the rise of new politico-business groups' aspiring interests in both new and existing business fields (e.g. Suharto's sons and daughters and their cronies) might threaten the Salim Group's established businesses through the opening of monopolistic and oligopolistic positions to those groups and/or transfer existing interest directly to them.

Within this political economy's context, the IPO was an effective method for realizing returns on investment before the political forces discussed earlier decreased the Salim Group's investment value. This method also protected the group's remaining interests from political interference and pressure by using the status of 'public company'. The boom in the offshore financial market during the 1990s strongly supported the group's efforts to maximize its investment value, more than protecting its value. Furthermore, the increased credibility of the group through the IPO and due to offshore bankers' enthusiasm enabled the Salim Group to leverage its financial position to be prepared for liquidating its investments. In addition, the enlarged presence of foreign shareholders and offshore bankers in the group's debt and equity structure became a strong counter-power against political forces.

On the other hand, a foreign direct investment boom in Indonesia in existence since 1993 provided the Salim Group with a great opportunity to enlarge its business fields and markets through the formation of joint ventures with international blue chip companies. Foreign investment law still required foreign investors to have local partners in most investment fields before the Indonesian crisis, and they actually needed capable local partners to handle complex and unclear regulatory and political issues, to access complicated and invisible local distribution networks and to deal with culturally challenging labour administration. The Salim Group became indispensable as a partner for the foreign direct investments that was the driving force behind economic development in Indonesia. This fact also became a political hedge for the group's investments and also enhanced its credibility with offshore investors and lenders, and as a result, this enabled the group to borrow more money from offshore markets.

In this way, the risk-hedging behaviour derived from these political economic factors led the group to leveraging its financial position. Together with the Salim Group's aggressive profit-seeking behaviour leveraging created endogenously destabilizing forces, as noted by Minsky. Nevertheless, facing a suddenly opened market and increased liquidity, it was very logical and natural for the group to leverage its financial position to minimize any future risk and maximize the owner family's interests. The creation of the Salim Group's fragile financial structure in the 1990s was a typical outcome of an endogenous process under capitalist principles during an economic and financial boom.

7 Case study 2

The Lippo Group's financial activities in the 1990s

General views on the Lippo Group

The Lippo Group, which was founded on Mochtar Riady's financial expertise, is a relatively young business group based in Indonesia, and at the outset, the Riady and the Salim families held equal shares.[1] However, in the early 1990s, the Riady family obtained full control of the Lippo Group by exchanging its BCA shares with the Salim Group for its shares in the Lippo Group. Mochtar Riady resigned from his management positions of BCA and concentrated the family's capacity, that is, capital and reputations earned by virtue of Mochtar's financial expertise, into the Lippo Group.[2] Since then, it has grown rapidly into one of the leading Indonesian business groups. Furthermore, Mochtar gradually handed over management of the group to his two sons: James Riady and Stephen Riady. J. Riady has managed the Indonesia operation and S. Riady the overseas affairs. Mochtar has supervised both sons, and when problems emerged he took direct control of the management.

The Lippo Group officially organizes its Indonesia businesses into four divisions: (i) financial services (commercial banking, investment banking, insurance and non-bank finance); (ii) urban development (real estate development); (iii) strategic investment services (retailing and health care) and (iv) strategic investment industries (auto parts, home appliances, electronics products and other industrial or service types of business). The group has focused on financial services, real estate development and retail business. It has maintained a high profile in overseas investment, mainly in Hong Kong and China, and also focused on real estate and financial services. However, the group has been more opportunistic with its investments in China, for example, infrastructure development and manufacturing.[3]

The Lippo Group's management strategy was to maximize cash flow from the businesses, that is, realized profit in the cash-flow statement, rather than recognized profit in the income statement. In other words, as the core businesses the group chose sectors that could generate abundant hard cash flow and collect invested capital over a short period. Commercial banking, insurance and retail businesses provided a huge amount of hard cash flow into the group. The real estate business is generally considered capital intensive. However, the

Lippo Group focuses on real estate development and sales which requires relatively short-term development finance compared to real estate investment which fixes the capital over a long period. The Lippo Group intends to maximize the profit and liquidity and minimize the risk of investment by following the chain of cash flow.[4]

Even though the Lippo Group had possessed a clear and logical business model and an excellent management track record over a long period it had been confronted with various difficulties in its ability to access offshore loans, in particular, from Japanese banks. This was simply because the core businesses of the group were finance and real estate. At the end of the 1980s, Japanese banks experienced a crash in the real estate market and a collapse in the non-bank finance sector at home, and furthermore, a failure of real estate finance in the United States in the early 1990s. In the mid-1990s, Japanese banks accelerated lending to non-Japan Asian corporate sectors, which paid relatively high margins, in compensation for losses from their failed financing in Japan and the United States. They remained extremely cautious about real estate and finance sectors as a reaction to their bad experiences within Japan, and thus, they naturally distanced themselves from the group.[5] A few Japanese banks, which had long-established relations with Mochtar Riady since he was at BCA and understood his management style, financed the Lippo Group. Therefore, Lippo could not help but rely on domestic bank borrowing rather than on offshore loans.

Furthermore, a speculative rumour concerning the Lippo Group in November 1995 made it more difficult for it to access the cheap offshore bank finance that flooded into the Indonesian corporate sector in 1994. The rumour was that Lippo Bank had failed to clear its accounts with BI due to the introduction of a huge amount of promissory notes issued by Lippo Land in the clearing at the beginning of November, and that the bank was facing trouble from the financing of Lippo Land, which was unable to sell its huge inventory of property and obtain tenants for its offices and shopping malls in the time of a sluggish real estate market.[6] After a number of media reports on this, overseas investors and banks, lacking in sufficient information, rushed to sell the Lippo Group's shares and square their positions.[7]

In mid-November, an unofficial statement that four Indonesian–Chinese banks (Bank Danamon, Bank Bali, Bank International Indonesia (Sinar Mas) and Bank Central Asia (Salim)) had agreed to help Lippo Bank with the approval of BI was also reported.[8] The Lippo Group announced that Lippo Bank did not need the support and all of the Lippo Group's high-ranking officials attempted to explain this to the public. Bank Indonesia laid emphasis on the healthiness of Lippo Bank. Finally, there was virtually no run at Lippo Bank branches and the group was able to resume its normal operations.

Due to the earlier-mentioned problem, Lippo Group management were forced to learn the risks regarding debt financing. Although other Indonesian business groups benefited from aggressive investments based on heavy offshore debt finance, the Lippo Group experienced the fragility of a debt-financed balance sheet and downside risks of the value of its investments due to the pressure of payment commitments.[9] In other words, the group was facing a potential crash, which, according to Fisher and Minsky, was the most important risk of debt. In addition to the offshore debt market, the group could not access the equity market during 1995. However, after this problem had settled the Lippo Group further accelerated equity finance, which does not imply any payment commitment, and simultaneously liquidated its investments in Indonesia.

The Lippo Group has been the most active user of equity markets among Indonesian business groups. At the onset of the East Asian crisis, the group owned 14 listed companies in Indonesia, five in Hong Kong, one in Singapore and one in the Philippines.[10] The group listed the majority of them, but some were acquired.[11] These listed companies have been most important funding vehicles. Between 1994 and 1997, the Lippo Group obtained Rp.6.0 trillion (US$2.3 billion) through the Jakarta Stock Exchange. This accounted for around 11.6 per cent of total cash calls through the exchange.

In addition to access to third party money through the equity markets as discussed previously, the Lippo Group directly introduced overseas strategic investors' capitals into its established businesses in both Indonesia and Hong Kong. In particular, the group built close relationships with leading business groups in Hong Kong and China, such as the Cheung Kong Group, the China Resources Group and the China Travel Group. For example, in 1992, shortly after beginning its business expansion in Hong Kong, the Lippo Group introduced the Cheung Kong Group into Lippo Limited, the group's flagship company in Hong Kong, by issuing a HK$100 million note, which was subsequently converted into 74.1 million shares of the company.[12] In July 1993, the group formed a partnership with the China Resources Group by selling a stake in The Hongkong Chinese Bank Limited to the group. In Indonesia, China Resources acquired 4.2 per cent share of Lippo Land and 5.2 per cent of Lippo Karawaci in 1996.

In this way, the critical difference between the Lippo Group's and other leading Indonesian business groups is that:

1   It is heavily exposed to financial and real estate sectors with very small non-core manufacturing businesses;
2   It experienced a crisis in 1995, during the financial boom, when other groups rapidly and aggressively expanded their debt;
3   It aggressively used the equity rather than the debt market;
4   It actively introduced strategic partners' money into its established core businesses.

The first two characteristics (1) and (2), influenced the group to adopt the last two financial strategies, (3) and (4).

These financial strategies led the Lippo Group into a different position from other leading business groups at the onset of the Indonesian crisis.[13] Most business groups that aggressively utilized debt finance faced totally collapsed financial positions and were put under massive repayment pressure by offshore bankers. Management had to run from one banker meeting to another to obtain the offshore bankers' understanding and support. The Lippo Group was also requested to repay its offshore debt. However, the volume was far less than the others and the exposure of the group was also not so substantial for offshore bankers. The Lippo Group's financial structure was already enhanced by equity finance and supported by domestic funding from its financial institutions and other domestic banks. In addition, the Lippo Group had already liquidated a large part of its investments by corporate restructuring by that time.

This chapter argues: (i) in contrast to other leading business groups, the Lippo Group had limited access to offshore debt markets, and thereafter aggressively utilized equity markets to finance new investments and to liquidate its existing investments; and as a result (ii) the Lippo Group managed to avoid collapse at the onset of the crisis due to sudden repayment requests by offshore bankers and also (iii) the Lippo Group was an example of a conglomerate that did not change its financial position from robust to fragile as defined by Minsky, despite aggressive expansion during the finance boom.

The Lippo Group's financial activities and results during the finance boom of the 1990s

As discussed earlier, three factors influenced the Lippo Group's ability to raise funds through the offshore bank market, namely:

1   The nature of the group's core businesses, that is, financial services and real estate development;
2   Speculative rumours and incidents surrounding the groups, for example, Lippo Bank's clearing imbalance issue in 1995, and the Riady family's US campaign donation to the Clinton campaign in 1996;
3   The group's high-profile operation in Indonesia.

Even during the finance boom from 1994 to the first half of 1997, the Lippo Group obtained only US$430 million through 11 offshore syndicated debts. Moreover, some of these were refinancing transactions (Table 7.1).

As Table 7.1 illustrates, the group was unable to improve on its borrowing terms. Tenors were almost constant throughout the period and longer-term finance was unobtainable. Margins were also higher than those dispensed to other leading business groups.[14] Moreover, the facility amount was relatively small. Only Lippo Bank, regarded as a major borrower by offshore bankers, was able to improve margins from 185.0 basis points in 1994 to 101.0 basis points in 1997, and to enlarge the facility amount from US$20 million to US$60 million. Other group borrowers had to accept a higher margin, pledging security and/or providing guarantees/letters of comfort issued by leading group companies, such as Lippo Bank.

Among the participants of these facilities were 'relationship banks' and non-Japanese Asian banks and non-banks, in particular, Korean financial institutions. These institutions were burdened with higher funding costs and thus sought

Table 7.1 The Lippo Group's syndicated debts during the 1990s boom (US$ million, years, basis points per annum)

Date	Issuer/ borrower	Facility	Amount	Average tenor	All-in margin	Repayment	Security
June-93	Matahari Putra Prima	RC	20	2.0	245.0	Bullet	Fix + floating
Oct.-93	Lippo Pacific Finance	RC	11	1.0	190.0	Bullet	LG (Lippo Bank)
Feb.-94	Lippo Bank	FRCD	30	2.1	185.0	Bullet	NA
Sep.-94	Lippo Pacific Finance	RC	30	1.0	190.0	Bullet	LCft (Lippo Bank)
Jan.-95	Lippo Bank	FRCD	30	2.0	100.0	Bullet	NA
Apr.-95	Matahari Putra Prima	TL	55	2.9	263.0	Balloon	Fix + LG
Oct.-95	Lippo Bank	FRCD	20	2.1	92.0	Bullet	NA
Nov.-95	Hotel Prapatan	TL/RC	51	3.0	250.0	Bullet	NA
June-96	Matahari Jaya Putra Perkasa	NA	65	NA	NA	NA	NA
July-96	Bangunmustika Intipersada	TL	10	3.0	333.0	Amortized	NA
Nov.-96	Lippo Merchant Finance	RC	19	2.0	197.5	Bullet	LG (Lippo Pacific) LCft (Lippo Bank)
Nov.-96	Lippo Land Development	FRN	60	2.0	323.0	Bullet	LG (Lippo Land)
Feb.-97	Lippo Bank	FRCD	60	2.0	101.0	Bullet	NA
Dec.-97	Siloam Gleneagles Health Care	TLF/ FRN	28	2.0	206.3	Bullet	Fix+LG (Lippo Land + Gleneagle)

Source: Privately collected data (checked with IFR).

Notes

TL: term loan; RC: revolver; PF: project finance; Bdg: bridge finance;

Float: floating asset; Fix: fixed asset; LG: guaranttee; LCft: letter of comfort.

high-return investments.[15] This meant that the Lippo Group was considered to be a relatively high-risk and high-return borrower by offshore financial institutions. Furthermore, the Lippo Group set up a US$300 million Asian currency note programme for Lippo Land in November 1996, and at the same time issued US$60 million FRN through this.[16] This programme is a typical capital market product designed for targeting high-risk-high-return-oriented investors rather than ordinary offshore bank investors. Therefore, due to constraints in the offshore market, the group's funding activities were different from other leading Indonesian borrowers, and funding capacity was limited. Consequently, the Lippo Group had to rely on the domestic bank market for its debt finance.

The Asian equity markets, where investors generally expected large returns backed by high growth rather than stable return, were the most important funding sources for the Lippo Group. In Indonesia, it took full advantage of the stock market boom between 1994 and 1997 and was the most active stock market player of all business groups. As Tables 7.2 and 7.3 indicate, the group raised

Table 7.2 The Lippo Group's fund raising through the Jakarta stock exchange during the 1990s finance boom (summary)

	New issue (Rp. billion)	*Rights issue (Rp. billion)*	*Total*	
			(Rp. billion)	*(US$ million)*
1994	110	450	560	258
1995	0	105	105	47
1996	100	1,104	1,204	515
1997	553	3,539	4,091	1,462
Total	763	5,197	5,960	2,282

Sources: ING and MSDW.

Table 7.3 The Lippo Group's fund raising through the Jakarta stock exchange during the 1990s finance boom (breakdown)

Listing	*Issuer*	*Type*	*No. of share (million)*	*Offer price (Rp./share)*	*Amount raised (Rp. billion)*
Mar.-94	Lippo Securities	New issue	14	8,150	110
Jun.-94	Lippo Life	3-for-1 rights issue	36	2,800	101
Oct.-94	Lippo Land	1-for-1 rights issue	124	2,800	348
June-95	Matahari	1-for-2 rights issue	75	1,400	105
June-96	Lippo Karawaci	New issue	31	3,250	100
June-96	Lippo Bank	1-for-2 rights issue	143	2,100	300
July-96	Multipolar	3-for-1 rights issue	103	1,000	103
July-96	Lippo Life	1-for-1 rights issue	1,450	193	280
July-96	Lippo Securities	3-for-2 rights issue	1,000	196	196
Oct.-96	Matahari	1-for-1 rights issue	1,000	226	226
Mar.-97	Siloam Gleaneagles	New issue	2,950	47	139
July-97	Mutipolar	55-for-10 rights issue	1,509	500	754
July-97	Lippo Securities	12-for-5 rights issue	1,566	500	783
July-97	Lippo Life	29-for-10 rights issue	1,119	850	951
July-97	Lippo Cikarang	New issue	109	925	100
July-97	Royal Sentul	New issue	400	500	200
July-97	Lippo General Insurance	New issue	51	2,225	113
Nov.-97	Matahari	2-for-1 rights issue	1,804	500	902
Nov.-97	Hotel Prapatan	3-for-1 rights issue	149	1,000	149

Sources: ING and MSDW.

Rp.5,960 billion (US$2,282 million) on the Jakarta Stock Exchange, and this corresponds to approximately 11.6 per cent of the total funds raised through this market (i.e. cash calls) during the period. In particular, it reorganized the group holding structure and diluted a significant amount of group holdings via aggressive equity transactions in 1996 and 1997 (discussed in the section that follows), considering the fact that the group's equity fund raising accounted for 9.2 per cent and 31.2 per cent respectively of the total funds raised through the stock exchange.

In this way, due to its limited access to the offshore syndicated loan market and a financial strategy based on shifting from debt to equity, the Lippo Group aggressively raised a huge volume of equity money. As equities do not entail any payment commitments, the Lippo Group de-leveraged its financial position for both its financial and non-financial sectors during the economic and finance boom in the 1990s. Moreover, its leverage level was very moderate when compared to other business groups throughout the period (Table 7.4).

The group's de-leveraging is also confirmed at the level of individual companies. First, looking at the financial services division in Indonesia, three core companies, Lippo Securities, Lippo Life and Lippo Bank, controlled their financial positions at a sound level. In particular, Lippo Life and Lippo Bank were substantially de-leveraged.[17] Second, on examining three urban development companies and one retailer, Lippo Land, Lippo Cikarang, Lippo Karawaci and Matahari, it can be seen that these companies also managed their leverages within a sound level.[18] Lippo Land was slightly leveraged but substantially de-leveraged from its peak year. The leverage ratio of 2.27 and the net debt to equity ratio of 1.19 in 1995 declined respectively to 0.81 and 0.70 in 1997. Other companies were dramatically de-leveraged during the period. Third, a study of the group's Hong Kong operation reveals that the group was active in funding through both the equity and debt capital markets and introduced third party equity money. Furthermore, the group financed its investments in China by disposing of its real estate portfolio in Hong Kong. As a result, the group also maintained a sound financial position in its Hong Kong operation.[19]

In sum, constraints on the use of offshore bank debt led the Lippo Group to de-leverage its financial position and build a relatively robust financial structure by aggressive use of equity markets during the economic and finance boom of the 1990s. This financial structure enabled it to avoid the total financial collapse as was experienced by other groups after the East Asian crisis.

Table 7.4 The Lippo Group's financial position in the 1990s (times)

Ratios	Divisions	1990	1991	1992	1993	1994	1995	1996	1997
Leverage	Financial services	11.62	11.18	12.04	8.16	8.15	7.98	6.04	5.00
	Non-financial services	0.27	0.80	1.23	0.90	1.19	1.35	1.35	1.38
Equity	Financial services	0.08	0.08	0.08	0.11	0.11	0.11	0.07	0.17
	Non-financial services	0.78	0.55	0.45	0.53	0.46	0.40	0.43	0.42

Source: Annual reports.

The Lippo Group's corporate restructuring and liquidation of its investments in the 1990s

The restructuring of the Lippo Group's financial service division in Indonesia

In September 1996, the Lippo Group proposed a restructuring of its Indonesian financial services division, which mainly involved three listed companies, Lippo Securities, Lippo Life (Asuransi Lippo Life) and Lippo Bank. This restructuring altered the division's corporate holding structure from horizontal to vertical (in other words, pyramid type) and enabled the Lippo Group to save capital investment.[20] The group stressed synergy effects from the integration of all financial service businesses in the division, such as access to a large customer base for a variety of financial products. However, minority investors, non-Lippo broker analysts, and the media claimed that the Riady family was cashing out through restructuring at the expense of minority shareholders' interests.[21]

BAPEPAM, the Indonesian capital market supervisory agency, discouraged the Lippo Group from carrying out the restructuring plan by pointing out the series of cross holdings in the new structure.[22] The agency sent a letter to the Lippo Group asking them to cancel the plan and questioning its benefits to minority shareholders. However, BAPEPAM had no legal authority to halt the plan and could only request a clarification in order to make minority investors aware of the risk.[23] Finally, after reviewing the purchase price levels and other terms and conditions, minority shareholders of both Lippo Securities and Lippo Life approved these restructuring transactions at the extraordinary general meeting held in September 1996.[24]

Before this restructuring, the Lippo Group had a horizontal corporate holding structure, that is, the group's holding companies, such as Lippo Asia (Jakarta) and Lippo Asia Limited (Hong Kong), directly or semi-directly owned Lippo Securities, Lippo Life and Lippo Bank. After this restructuring the group's corporate holding structure became vertical. The Lippo Group's holding companies owned Lippo Securities, Lippo Securities owned Lippo Life and Lippo Life owned Lippo Bank. As shown in Figure 7.1, this restructuring was carried out by selling the group companies' holding shares of Lippo Life and Lippo Bank to Lippo Securities and Lippo Life respectively.

The Lippo Group sold all its shares in Lippo Life (26.99 per cent equivalent) to Lippo Securities for Rp.236.36 billion (US$102 million). At the same time, it sold all its shares in Lippo Bank (40.15 per cent equivalent) to Lippo Life for Rp.638 billion (US$274 million).[25] As of the end of 1996, Lippo Securities became the single largest shareholder of Lippo Life with a 36.30 per cent share. Lippo Securities bought further shares from the market and other sources and increased its investment to a 44.21 per cent holding by April 1997. Finally the company became a majority shareholder with a 59.82 per cent share by the end of 1997. Lippo Life also became the single largest shareholder with a 41.09 per cent share by the end of 1996. In this way, Lippo Bank was consolidated into Lippo Life and these two companies were consolidated into Lippo Securities.

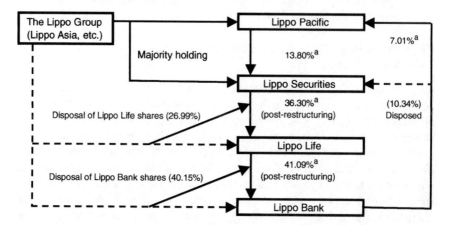

Figure 7.1 The restructuring of the Lippo Group financial service division in Indonesia.
Sources: Annual reports, Asian Wall Street Journal and Bloomberg.

Note
a As of the end of 1996.

The Lippo Group obtained approximately Rp.875 billion (US$376 million) in cash through these transactions. As Lippo Securities and Lippo Life paid the proceeds to the Lippo Group by Rp.100 billion upfront payments and 15-month promissory notes payable in January 1998 respectively, the Lippo Group were able to collect them by the beginning of 1998. The issue was how these two companies managed to settle the payments by the maturity date of the promissory notes.

Lippo Securities and Lippo Life had already obtained additional capital by Rp.195.8 billion (US$82.9 million) and Rp.279.6 billion (US$118.3 million) through 1-for-1 rights issues and 3-for-2 rights issues respectively in July 1996, just before the earlier-mentioned acquisition transactions.[26] Both companies were in relatively good positions with respect to cash and used their internal cash flow and bank borrowings from local banks for upfront payments in the transactions. However, they carried out further rights issues. In July 1997, Lippo Life raised Rp.950.8 billion (US$329 million) through 29-for-10 rights issues for funding its payments for the promissory notes. Due to the change of holding structure in 1996, in which Lippo Life became a subsidiary of Lippo Securities, Lippo Securities paid in money for Lippo Life's rights issue and funded its own payment of promissory notes. In July 1997, Lippo Securities also raised Rp.783.0 billion (US$271 million) through a 12-for-5 rights issue.[27]

Furthermore, Lippo Pacific (Lippo Pacific Finance), another listed company of the group's financial service division and the single largest shareholder (13.8 per cent) of Lippo Securities, paid in money for Lippo Securities' right issues by bank debt.[28] As a result, the investment and gross debt accounts of Lippo Pacific jumped from Rp.100.4 billion and Rp.227.5 billion in 1996 to Rp.82.9 billion and Rp.242.5 billion in 1997 respectively. Lippo Pacific had not required any equity finance since 1994, so there was no financial burden on the company's shareholders, the majority of which were Lippo Group's holding companies, such as Lippo Asia Limited (44.98 per cent) and Lippo Asia (19.54 per cent).

As the Lippo Group held its interests in Lippo Pacific and Lippo Securities through other group offshore finance vehicles besides the structure described earlier, the group had to inject some part of obtained cash through the earlier-explained restructuring back into its financial service division in Indonesia. Nevertheless, it was able to liquidate its investments in Indonesia, retain a substantial part of the obtained cash, increase the efficiency of its capital structure and keep control of the financial services division. The combination of the change of corporate holding from horizontal to vertical structure and the aggressive use of equity markets contributed greatly towards these results.

As this example shows, the Lippo Group's finance strategy was in striking contrast to the Salim Group's. Both groups changed their corporate holding structures, aggressively liquidated owners' investments through restructuring and used their listed companies strategically for financing it. However, the Salim Group adopted an aggressive leveraging strategy with foreign currency debt through offshore syndicated debts, while the Lippo Group used equity money and rupiah borrowings from domestic banks.[29] As a result, the Lippo Group experienced less payment pressure during the East Asian crisis and were able to avoid fire sales of their assets.

The restructuring of the Lippo Group's corporate holding structure in Hong Kong

The Lippo Group has four listed companies in Hong Kong: Lippo Limited, Lippo China Resources Limited (formerly Hongkong China Limited), The HKCB Bank Holding Company Limited and The Hong Kong Building and Loan Agency Limited. In September 1997, the Lippo Group restructured its core corporate holdings, which involved these listed companies. The aims of this restructuring were:

1 To strengthen the relation between the Lippo Group and the China Resources Group owned by Chinese government by introducing its capital into the group's core operations in Hong Kong;
2 To create liquidity for the group by altering its corporate holding structure into a more vertically integrated one and reducing its shareholding to the minimum level for corporate control;
3 To change the groups operational weight in Hong Kong and China from real estate development to financial services, and in particular, by using the political power of the China Resources Group in China.[30]

Prior to this restructuring, the Lippo Group had already established a strong strategic alliance with the China Resources Group through a 50:50 investment in

The Hong Kong Chinese Bank Limited, minority investments in real estate projects in Indonesia and minority investments in Hongkong China Limited (Figure 7.2). Nevertheless, the Lippo Group further strengthened this alliance.[31] In June 1997, Lippo Limited sold an 8 per cent stake of Hongkong China Limited to the China Resources Group for HK$589 million (US$76 million) and changed the company's name to Lippo China Resources, and the China Resources Group's share in the company increased from 2 to 10 per cent.

Furthermore, the Lippo Group used the China Resources Group's financial power for other financial services businesses by transferring the latter's investment from The Hong Kong Chinese Bank Limited to The HKCB Bank Holding Company Limited, the holding company (through Lippo CRE (Financial Services) Limited).[32] Besides commercial banking businesses through the former, the latter had merchant banking, securities and futures brokerage and insurance services.

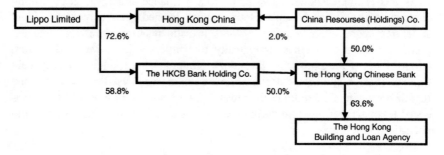

Figure 7.2 The Lippo Group's investment structure in Hong Kong (pre-1997 restructuring).
Source: Annual reports.

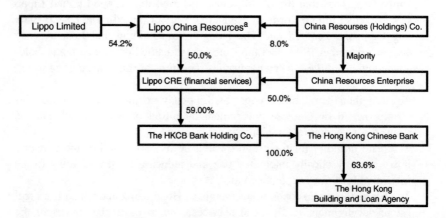

Figure 7.3 The Lippo Group's investment structure in Hong Kong (post-1997 restructuring).
Source: Annual reports.

Note
a The name was changed from Hong Kong China.

In particular, the China Resources Group was an indispensable partner for expanding the group's banking businesses in China, a politically difficult market.

After the completion of this restructuring, the Lippo Group sold its stake in Lippo China Resources Limited by 8.7 per cent (126 million shares) to Beijing Enterprise Holdings, an investment company controlled by the Beijing city government and the market, and collected HK$897 million from the transactions.[33] Summing up the shares held by the China Resources Group (10 per cent), Bank of China (5 per cent) and Beijing Enterprise Holdings (2.3 per cent, 30 million shares), China's strategic investors held around a 20 per cent share of Lippo China Resources Limited. Through a series of share sales, the Lippo Group's position moved from majority shareholder to single largest shareholder. However, the Lippo Group was able to collect at least HK$1.5 billion (US$200 million) from the market.

Second, before the 1997 restructuring, as Figure 7.2 illustrates, the Lippo Group directly held shares of Hong Kong China Limited and The HKCB Bank Holding Company Limited of 72.6 per cent and 58.8 per cent respectively. That is to say, the group had a horizontal corporate holding structure to control these two companies. As Figure 7.3 indicates, the 1997 restructuring changed this horizontal structure to a vertical one. The group applied the same concept of the 1996 restructuring of its Indonesia financial services division to its corporate holding structure in Hong Kong. It attained capital-efficient control of its Hong Kong operations and furthermore liquidated its investments.

In this way, the Lippo Group introduced the China Resources Group's substantial shares into its core operations in Hong Kong and strengthened the relationship between the parties. This made a contribution towards

1   Enhancing the financial stability of the Lippo Group's Hong Kong operations;
2   Hedging the group's political positions in both China and Indonesia;
3   Expanding its financial service business in China, a closed market for foreign investors.

The change in corporate holding structure into a more vertically integrated form enabled the Lippo Group to liquidate its investments and shift the money to other high-yield investment opportunities, such as in China's financial services.

The not-realized restructuring of the Lippo Group's urban development division in Indonesia

The Lippo Group had three flagship companies in its urban development division in Indonesia: Lippo Land (Lippo Land Development), Lippo Karawaci (formerly Lippo Village) and Lippo Cikarang (formerly Lippo City). Lippo Karawaci was a huge town development, consisting of houses, offices, a shopping mall, a college, a golf course, hospital and so forth. Lippo Cikarang was an industrial town development, consisting of an industrial estate, offices, a hotel, a shopping mall

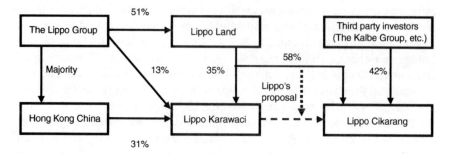

Figure 7.4 The not-realized restructuring of the Lippo Group's urban development division.
Sources: Annual reports, prospectuses, circulars and various news.

and so forth. Lippo Land owned Lippo Karawaci and Lippo Cikarang as a holding company. That is to say, the Lippo Group had a horizontal corporate holding structure for this division (Figure 7.4).

As is shown in Figure 7.4, as of June 1996, the Lippo Group totally controlled the real estate businesses in Indonesia through direct and indirect majority share-holdings of the three core companies: Lippo Land, Lippo Karawaci and Lippo Cikarang. Lippo Land and Lippo Karawaci were already listed on the Jakarta Stock Exchange. However, Lippo Cikarang was unlisted and was held by the Lippo Group and other third party investors.[34]

In 1997, the Lippo Group unofficially proposed a restructuring of its urban development division holdings similar to that which the group had undergone in its Indonesia's financial service division in 1996.[35] It planned for Lippo Karawaci to purchase around 50 per cent of Lippo Cikarang from Lippo Land and other shares from the Lippo Group and to merge the operations of both companies.[36] The group tried to liquidate its investments in Lippo Cikarang while retaining the control of the company by introducing a vertical holding structure into the urban development division. However, third party shareholders opposed this proposal because they preferred an IPO of Lippo Cikarang rather than merging its operations with Lippo Karawaci through the share sales.[37] Finally, the Lippo Group withdrew the proposal and listed the Lippo Cikarang shares on Jakarta Stock Exchange in July 1997. This is a good example of how the Lippo Group attempted to liquidate its interests through corporate restructuring and equity transactions.

Conclusions

In the same way as the Salim Group, the Lippo Group also restructured its corporate holdings by strategically using listed companies. The basic method of this restructuring was to change from horizontal shareholdings to vertical ones for efficient and effective capital utilization. Under the vertical shareholding structure, the Lippo Group were able to control the whole group by holding the ultimate holding company of the structure, for example, Lippo Securities in the financial service division. Furthermore, this effective holding was attained by a single largest shareholder's position in the ultimate holding company, that is, control with minimum ownership. Therefore, the Lippo Group was able to reduce its shareholdings and liquidate its investments by the vertical shareholding structure with an effective shareholding.

However, this restructuring required third party investments into the companies to enable the Lippo Group to cash out. The difference between the Salim Group and the Lippo Group was that the former aggressively used offshore syndicated loans but that the latter aggressively used equity finance. Under the economic and finance boom in the 1990s, the Salim Group rapidly improved its bargaining power vis-à-vis offshore bankers and accumulated offshore debt with almost yearly improvements in borrowing terms. As discussed above, the Lippo Group had constraints on obtaining sizable funds through the offshore bank market. It adopted a strategy of exploiting equity markets for funding. The 1995 crisis due to speculative rumours concerning Lippo Bank and Lippo Land made the Lippo Group acknowledged the fragility of debt-financed investments and accelerated the use of equity markets and the dilution of the Riady family's investments.

As a result, the Salim Group leveraged its financial positions during the period, while the Lippo Group de-leveraged its financial positions and had a relatively low-leveraged financial profile when the Indonesian crisis occurred. In particular, the minimal use of offshore loans helped the Lippo Group to avoid total collapse after the crisis. Its aggressive equity finance coupled with corporate restructuring was heavily criticized as sacrificing minority shareholders' interests. However, one of the important characteristics of equity, that is, no repayment/prepayment commitments saved the Lippo Group during the crisis. In other words, the financial activities of both groups indicate that the two group owners' liquidity preference with different approaches led to totally opposite financial positions in terms of stability.

Furthermore, from a political economy viewpoint, the Salim Group was able to use offshore international bankers to hedge its political fragility in the post-Suharto period. On the other hand, the Lippo Group used its offshore shareholders, in particular, its strategic investors, such as China Resources and Cheung Kong, to hedge its political weakness since the end of the Suharto era. The third party investments were an important political protection as well as a provider of liquidity for the group.

Looking at the Lippo Group from the viewpoint of Minsky's financial instability hypothesis, the group maintained a relatively robust financial profile and was less susceptible to financial turmoil because it shifted its core funding to equity finance. However, considering the Lippo Group's aggressive profit-seeking behaviour and strong liquidity preference, if the offshore debt market had been opened to the group, it would have been heavily leveraged with the debt and one of endogenously destabilizing forces, as noted by Minsky, in the Indonesian economy. The Lippo Group contrasts well with the Salim Group but was one of the exceptions in the Indonesian corporate sector during the 1990s.

8   Case study 3

The Sinar Mas Group's financial activities in the 1990s

General views on the Sinar Mas Group

The Sinar Mas Group, which was owned by the Widjaja family, was the second largest Indonesian business group in the 1990s.[1] It was a diversified conglomerate arranged into the following four divisions: (i) pulp and paper; (ii) agribusiness, foods and consumer products; (iii) financial services and (iv) real estate and property. The group was the top Indonesian paper producer with more than 70 per cent of the domestic market and actively exported its products to other Asian countries. During the latter half of 1990s, it aggressively expanded its production and sales activities into other Asian countries, in particular, China.[2] In the agribusiness, foods and consumer products division the group was one of the top three Indonesian private palm oil plantation owners producing palm oil for domestic consumption and for export to other Asian markets.[3] These two business fields generated not only abundant cash flow but also foreign exchange income into the group and for this reason it was able to attract investors' interest. In Minsky's terms, the margin of safety, supported by the capacity to generate abundant foreign exchange cash flows, enabled the group to accumulate a huge external fund.

In addition, the group was also very active in commercial banking through BII (Bank International Indonesia), the second largest private bank in Indonesia, and had good capacity to access stable rupiah cash flows. Although BII was also subject to legal lending limits to the group companies, BII's rupiah cash flows supported the group's real estate development projects, such as commercial complexes, hotels, offices and golf courses, in which it sought quick growth. Furthermore, it attempted to diversify its geographical investment risk through aggressive overseas investments in the same way as Salim and Lippo.

With regards to financial activities, the Sinar Mas Group was the most aggressive fund raiser in Indonesia. In terms of the number of listed companies, it was the third most active user of equity markets and had ten listed companies in both domestic and overseas stock exchanges.[4] It was also the most aggressive user of offshore debt finance markets among Indonesian business groups. In particular, it was the most frequent and large-scale borrower of offshore syndicated debts and an Indonesian pioneer user of international fixed income bond markets. During the finance boom in the 1990s, the Sinar Mas Group aggressively raised funds in any types of financial market that it was able to. It placed top priority on the size of funding, rather than optimum capital structure and funding costs. When the East Asian crisis erupted in 1997, the Sinar Mas Group was the most heavily indebted business group in Indonesia with more than US$15 billion outstanding debt.[5]

This chapter analyses the Sinar Mas Group by focusing on its financial activities during the finance boom of the 1990s, that is, the period from 1994 to the first half of 1997. Furthermore, the analysis focuses on the group's financial apparatus that enabled it to obtain huge amounts of mobile capital on global financial markets. The analysis also clarifies how large volumes of several forms of mobile capital were absorbed into the group's financial structure through a variety of financial products. Finally, this chapter demonstrates how complex, fragile and unstable financial structures, which exceeded even those that Minsky envisaged in his financial instability hypothesis, emerged at the corporate level.

The Sinar Mas Group's shareholding structure in the 1990s

In order to efficiently push forward with the earlier-mentioned financial activities, the Sinar Mas Group formed a pyramid-type and cross-border group holding structure in the 1990s (Figure 8.1).[6] Before 1993, it had a family business type of group holding structure, which most Indonesian–Chinese business groups had adopted at that time. The Widjaja family and/or its holding vehicles directly owned operating companies and projects, and the group did not have a clear strategy for shareholding structure. Moreover, although it completed IPOs of four flagship companies before the finance boom, they were not directly related to the building of a group holding structure.[7] The IPOs simply created liquidity for the family's investments and enabled the family to control the companies by virtue of their position as single largest shareholders. However, during the boom in the 1990s it rapidly built up a dynamic group holding structure.

As is seen in Figure 8.1, the group holding structure had the following two characteristics, (i) pyramid shape of corporate holdings by industry segments and (ii) cross-border shareholdings by offshore and onshore holding companies.[8] In particular, other leading business groups, such as Salim and Lippo, attempted to build cross-border group holding structures but were unable to build structures as dynamic as the Sinar Mas Group. The dynamic holding structures provided the following three opportunities: (i) large-scale offshore funding; (ii) political protection through shareholdings in overseas legal domiciles and listings in overseas stock exchanges and (iii) orderly transfer of wealth from the first to the second generation.[9] As is argued in the following sections, the group aggressively exploited the opportunity of (i) during the finance boom. The opportunities of (ii) and (iii) were critical issues for not only the Sinar Mas Group but also for other Indonesian–Chinese business groups, which were historically weak vis-à-vis the state and had not experienced the handover of the businesses from the first to the second generations at that time.[10]

In terms of accounting and financial reporting, cross-border pyramid structures enabled the group to use its flagship operating companies' financial statements on at least a few occasions in order to obtain third party's funds. The financial

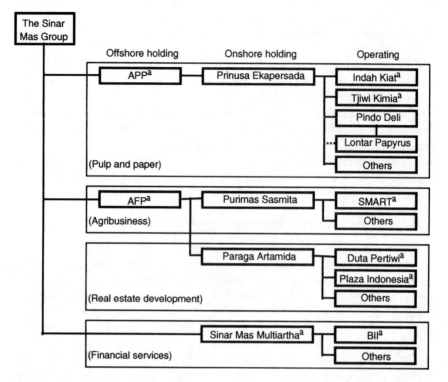

Figure 8.1 The Sinar Mas Group's shareholding structure for Indonesian operations (1997).

Source: Annual reports.

Note
a Listed companies.

statements were first used to obtain offshore funds for the operating companies themselves (e.g. Indah Kiat and Tjiwi Kimia). Next the financial statements were consolidated into onshore holding companies and used to obtain funds for the companies (e.g. Prinusa Ekapersada). Third, the financial statements of onshore holding companies (consolidating the financial statements of operating companies) were also consolidated into offshore holding companies and used to obtain offshore funds for the companies (e.g. Asia Pulp and Paper Co. Ltd. (APP)).[11] Furthermore, the formation of large holding companies through the merger of scattered group and family companies put it in a stronger position vis-à-vis banks. For example, APP was presented as the largest and most integrated pulp and paper company in non-Japan Asia. The strong appeal of such credit stories attracted exuberant offshore lenders during the finance boom. In addition, through the merger processes, the Widjaja family liquidated a number of its small- and medium-size investments using third party capital. In other words, the holding companies were used for the encashment of family businesses. This strategy was almost identical to those used by other leading Indonesian business groups, such as Salim and Lippo.

In the group's cross-border pyramid structure, the offshore holding and onshore core operating companies played the main role in offshore funding. The offshore holding companies, which consolidated a number of their subsidiaries, appealed to offshore investors and lenders. In 1997, APP had US$1,997 million sales and US$13,831 million assets and Asia Food and Properties Ltd. (AFP) had US$964 million sales and US$4,107 million assets. They were comparable in size to the leading companies in developed countries. During the finance boom, APP, in particular, was able to absorb huge amounts of global funds not only through equity but also debt finance although the funds were placed in subordinated positions against funds in their operating companies. The onshore operating companies, on the other hand, were able to directly access actual cash flows, which also appealed to offshore investors and lenders. In particular, core companies in the group's pulp and paper and agribusiness divisions, which had top positions in the industries and abundant export income, attracted offshore capital and made a major contribution towards the group's offshore funding. Indah Kiat and Tjiwi Kimia in the pulp and paper division and SMART Corporation in the agribusiness division represented this category.

Although the Sinar Mas Group aggressively took advantage of the cross-border pyramid structure in order to obtain large amounts of offshore funds, the group was unable to fully exploit the structure before the East Asian crisis emerged in 1997. First, AFP, the offshore holding company of agribusiness, foods and consumer products and real estate and property divisions listed its shares in Singapore just after the East Asian crisis began in July 1997.[12] AFP could have also been an aggressive offshore funding machine for the group with its huge financial resources, but the crisis prevented the company from doing so. Furthermore, onshore holding companies were not actively used for dynamic offshore funding but mainly functioned as binding onshore operating units, arranging inner-group funding and fulfilling occasional funding needs. Only Sinar Mas Multiartha, the onshore holding company of the financial services division, listed shares on the Jakarta Stock Exchange in 1995, and thereafter actively accessed offshore syndicated debt. The three onshore holding companies, Prinusa Ekapersada (pulp and paper), Purimas Sasmita (agribusiness) and Paraga Artamida (real estate development), were not as active in offshore markets. From time to time, they took bilateral and/or club loans, acted as corporate guarantors for subsidiaries' debts in their divisions, and coordinated inter-company debts inside the group.[13] If the East Asian crisis had not occurred and the group had had enough time to activate the entire group holding structure, it could have accessed financial markets on a truly gigantic scale.

The Sinar Mas Group's financial positions in the 1990s

First, as Table 8.1 shows, the Sinar Mas Group had a relatively sound financial position in 1992. The leverage ratio was almost one and the gross debt to equity ratio was also less than one. This was mainly because it raised Rp.814 billion (US$425 million) through the three IPOs, between 1990 and 1992 (Tjiwi Kimia, Indah Kiat and SMART Corporation) and thereby reinforced its capital structure.[14] Looking at the groups individual companies, the leverage ratios of Indah Kiat and SMART Corporation were respectively 1.14 and 0.45 times and the gross debt to equity ratio was respectively 0.92 and 0.23. These unleveraged financial positions indicate that it did not need to concern itself with debt management at that time. On the contrary, it could use its sound financial position to direct offshore financiers' lending to its fund raising.

The group's leverage ratio increased constantly from 1992 to 1996 and accelerated during the finance boom. In the end the Sinar Mas Group was one of the most highly leveraged Indonesian business groups in 1996, the peak year of the finance boom. The leverage ratio reached 1.85, the gross debt to equity ratio hit 1.44 and the gross debt to CS + APIC ratio achieved 3.15 times. These ratios were lower than the Salim Group but higher than the Gajah Tunggal Group. However, throughout the period, the group's ratios of gross debt to EBITDA and liability to EBITDA were much higher than those of other business groups.[15] This means that the Sinar Mas Group's borrowing relative to its capacity to generate cash flow was much higher than the other business groups.

The core operating companies of the group sharply increased their leveraging until 1996, the peak year of the finance boom. This was simply because the growth of debt was much higher than the growth of their equity. In other words, it relied heavily on debt finances during the period. First, Indah Kiat, the flagship operating company of its pulp and paper business in Indonesia increased its leverage ratio by 31.2 per cent, from 1.38 at the beginning of 1994 to 1.81 at the end of 1996. The gross debt to equity ratio rose by 29.5 per cent from 1.22 to 1.58, and the gross debt to CS + APIC ratio increased by 9.6 per cent from 1.77 to 1.94. The average annual growth of the company's liability and gross debts were respectively 34.8 per cent and 34.6 per cent. The average annual growth of the

Table 8.1 The Sinar Mas Group's financial position (listed non-financial companies) (times)

	1992	1993	1994	1995	1996	1997
Leverage ratio	1.04	1.42	1.64	1.77	1.85	1.39
Equity ratio	0.49	0.41	0.38	0.36	0.35	0.42
Gross debt to equity	0.82	1.22	1.40	1.62	1.44	1.23
Net debt to equity	0.81	1.18	1.38	1.35	1.02	1.00
Gross debt to CS + APIC	1.08	1.88	1.78	2.64	3.15	2.38
Net debt to CS + APIC	1.07	1.83	1.76	2.20	2.22	1.95
Gross debt to EBITDA	6.75	6.83	4.86	5.03	8.90	16.89
Net debt to EBITDA	6.66	6.62	4.80	4.18	6.29	13.82
Liability to EBITDA	8.57	7.95	5.68	5.52	11.44	19.18
Current ratio	1.25	1.09	1.50	1.61	1.93	2.07
Long-term to short-term ratio	2.52	3.06	3.85	2.74	9.24	3.43

Source: Annual reports.

company's equity was 23.6 per cent. Indah Kiat increased its liabilities by around 1.5 times more than its equity.

Tjiwi Kimia, the second flagship operating company of the group's pulp and paper business in Indonesia, also increased leveraging during the same period, by 42.5 per cent from 1.67 to 2.38. The average annual growth of the company's liabilities and gross debts were respectively 31.5 per cent and 32.9 per cent. Yet, the average annual growth of the company's equity was only 16.4 per cent. The company did not raise funds through equity finance during the period, thus the increase in equity was basically accumulated internal cash flow. Tjiwi Kimia also increased its liability and debts twice as fast as its equity.

SMART Corporation, the flagship operating company of the group's agribusiness division in Indonesia, sharply increased the leverage during the period. The leverage ratio sharply rose from 0.42 to 1.70 times, the gross debt to equity ratio went up from 0.22 to 1.50 times and the gross debt to CS + APIC ratio also jumped from 0.29 to 2.67 times. The average annual growth of the company's liability and gross debts were respectively 94.6 per cent and 149.5 per cent. On the other hand, the average annual growth of the company's equity was 11.1 per cent. The company raised funds through equity finance just before the beginning of the finance boom but did not do further equity finances. The Sinar Mas Group re-leveraged SMART Corporation during the period.

Fourth, Duta Pertiwi, the flagship operating company of the group's real estate development division in Indonesia, enhanced its equity through the IPO finance in 1994. At the end of 1994, although the company aggressively became involved in large-scale real estate development projects, its financial position was relatively sound. The leverage ratio, the gross debt to equity ratio and the gross debt to CS + APIC ratio were respectively 1.35, 0.89 and 1.28. However, this sound financial position quickly changed to a leveraged financial position in 1995 and 1996. These three ratios sharply increased to 2.49, 2.12 and 3.58 at the end of 1996. More amazingly, the gross debt to EBITDA ratio jumped sharply from 2.75 in 1994 to 18.90 times in 1996. The average annual growth of the company's liability and gross debts were respectively 68.6 per cent and 96.5 per cent. On the other hand, the average annual growth of the company's equity, which was affected by the decreased EBITDA level, was 23.5 per cent. Duta Pertiwi also re-leveraged its financial positions in 1995 and 1996 through aggressive debt finances.

However, the Sinar Mas Group suddenly pushed forward aggressive equity finances in 1997. The group obtained US$1.5 billion just within 1 year and thereby improved the leverage. The leverage ratio, the gross debt to equity ratio and the gross debt to CS + APIC ratio respectively decreased to 1.75, 1.52, and 2.00 times. The groups' financial position appeared to recover to the level that existed between 1994 and 1995. However, the gross debt to EBITDA ratio jumped to an extremely high level, 16.89 times. The group could not generate adequate cash flow to compensate for increased debt service, and moreover, the East Asian crisis deteriorated its cash flows. Following Minsky, the margin of safety of the group deteriorated.

The most important thing was that the group did not use the cash inflow through equity finance to reduce its debt, but instead allocated these funds for new investments even under fragile business conditions. It continued to borrow and financiers also continued to provide funds. Surveying individual companies within the group, we can clearly see that the group did not reduce its debt in 1997.[16] Indah Kiat and Tjiwi Kimia, which increased their equity by 69.3 per cent and 72.1 per cent through huge equity finances in 1997, increased their debts 29.1 per cent and 34.3 per cent in the same year. In sum, the group simply stretched its balance sheet through equity financing in 1997.

In this way, the Sinar Mas Group quickly leveraged its financial positions during the finance boom just as other Indonesian business groups. Considering its aggressive fund raising through offshore debt markets, its leverage could have been much higher. However, its aggressive equity financing mitigated the increase in the leverage. If cash inflow through equity finance had been used to reduce its debt, leveraging would have decreased steeply and the group would have been able to achieve financial stability. However, it used the cash inflows for new investments and increased its debts by accepting offshore investors' and lenders' aggressive and enthusiastic financial offers. Injections of equity and off-shore debts inflated the Sinar Mas Group's balance sheet and it grew to become the largest debtor in Indonesia. As argued so far, in order to understand the process accurately, it is necessary to analyse the group's financial transactions during the period.

The Sinar Mas Group's financial activities during the finance boom

With regards to financial activities, the Sinar Mas Group was the most aggressive Indonesian business group. It used third party funds on a massive scale through a variety of means, including equity, syndicated loans, FRNs and fixed income bonds. This was supported by its cross-border pyramid structures, which were designed to attract offshore mobile capital and to enable the Widjaja family to control the entire group on the basis of minimum capital contributions. During the finance boom in the 1990s, the Sinar Mas Group aggressively raised funds as if the group was seeking to absorb all of the money that the financial market could offer. Offshore investors and lenders also appeared to be intoxicated with financing the group.

First, looking at equity finance, the Sinar Mas Group was the second largest fund raiser on the Jakarta Stock Exchange, following the Lippo Group, and its activities had a significant impact on the market.[17] The group obtained Rp.5.8 trillion (US$2.1 billion) in the stock exchange and held an 11.3 per cent share of total cash calls during the finance boom (Table 8.2). The majority of this equity finance was obtained in 1997, the final year of the finance boom. In this year, the Sinar Mas Group was the largest user of the stock exchange with Rp.4.4 trillion (US$1.5 billion) in cash calls and a 23.1 per cent share. As is argued in the previous section, this huge scale of equity finance sharply improved the group's financial position in 1997.

Table 8.2 The Sinar Mas Group's equity finance in the 1990s boom (summary)

	New issue (Rp. billion)	Rights issue (Rp. billion)	Total (Rp. billion)	(US$ million)
1994	79	211	290	134
1995	108	0	108	48
1996	0	1,010	1,010	434
1997	0	4,425	4,425	1,531
Total	187	5,645	5,832	2,147

Sources: ING and MSDW.

The Sinar Mas Group started to access equity finance at the end of the 1980s. The group's core operating companies had already listed their shares before the finance boom began in 1994. Bank International Indonesia was listed in November 1989, Tjiwi Kimia in April 1990, Indah Kiat in July 1990 and SMART Corporation in November 1992. Equity finance during the finance boom was mainly rights issues through these core operating companies (Tables 8.2 and 8.3). In the group's operation, pulp and paper was clearly the most popular business segment for overseas portfolio investors. In the US market, APP, the offshore holding company of the business segment, successfully raised funds in 1995 and 1997.[18] However, during the boom, they aggressively sought upside returns on their investments in Indonesia and provided large funds to relatively risky business segments of the group, that is, real estate development and financial services. This situation was exactly the same as that of the Lippo Group.

As is argued in Chapter 5, the Sinar Mas Group was the most aggressive user of offshore syndicated debt among the leading Indonesian business groups.[19] From 1994 to 1997, it raised US$5.0 billion through 62 offshore syndicated debts, including refinancing. In particular, it obtained US$3.6 billion through 42 syndicated debts within the two years 1995 and 1996. Given that the syndication process requires at least 1 or 2 months, it is easy to imagine how busily, enthusiastically and mechanically the group and the offshore lenders digested these syndicated loans during the finance boom. The rapid accumulation of external debt through offshore syndicated debts was central to the group's debt-restructuring problem in the post-crisis period.

As is shown in Table 8.4, the group's pulp and paper division played the most important role in obtaining offshore syndicated debts. These for the division accounted for 62.4 per cent of those for the entire group from 1994 to 1997. Focusing on 1996, the peak year, offshore syndicated debts for the division accounted for 71.4 per cent of those for the entire group. The core borrowers in the division were three flagship listed companies, APP, Indah Kiat and Tjiwi Kimia. As is argued in the first section of this chapter, the Sinar Mas Group appealed to offshore lenders because of its strong business positions in the industry, large income flows and abundant foreign exchange income. Combining funding through offshore syndicated debts with that of equity finance and fixed income

Table 8.3 The Sinar Mas Group's equity finance in the 1990s boom (breakdown)

Listing	Issuer	Type	No. of shares (million)	Offer price (Rp./share)	Amount raised (Rp. billion)
Feb.-94	BII	1-for-5 rights issue	4,000	53	211
Nov.-94	Duta Pertiwi	New issue	3,150	25	79
July-95	Sinar Mas Multi Artha	New issue	1,800	60	108
Apr.-96	Indah Kiat	5-for-20 rights issue	1,250	410	513
Nov.-96	Sinar Mas Multi Artha	20-for-20 rights issue	750	663	497
Jan.-97	BII	2-for-3 rights issue	750	1,290	967
Apr.-97	Duta Pertiwi	1-for-1 rights issue	500	694	347
July-97	Indah Kiat	45-for-50	1,000	2,523	2,523
July-97	Tjiwi Kimia	16-for-20 rights issue	1,000	587	587

Sources: ING and MSDW.

Table 8.4 Offshore syndicated debts for the Sinar Mas Group (transactions, US$ million)

Year	Pulp and paper		Agribusiness		Real estate		Finance		Others		Total	
	No.	Amount	No.	Amount	No.	Amount	No.	Amount	No.	Amount	No.	Amount
1993	2	187	0	0	0	0	2	88	1	25	5	300
1994	6	481	1	60	0	0	3	105	1	25	11	671
1995	8	805	1	150	4	376	7	245	0	0	20	1,576
1996	9	1,434	3	85	0	0	9	318	1	40	22	1,878
1997	1	400	0	0	1	22	7	450	0	0	9	872
Total	26	3,307	5	295	5	398	28	1,206	3	90	67	5,296

Source: Privately collected data (checked with IFR).

bonds, these three companies functioned as cash generators for the Sinar Mas Group during the finance boom.

Considering the fact that the credibility of these three companies was at its highest, coupled with offshore lenders' enthusiasm for these companies, they could have improved their borrowing terms as did other leading Indonesian companies, such as Indocement and Indofood of the Salim Group.[20] First, as Table 8.5 indicates, their margins are not consistent. In particular, three FRNs issued by APP in 1996 paid much higher margins than previous syndicated debts. Second, their syndicated debts were overpriced. They paid higher than 150 basis points for 1-year borrowings and 250–300 basis points for 3-year borrowings. They clearly paid higher margins for their offshore debts than other leading

Table 8.5 Offshore syndicated debts for the Sinar Mas Group (pulp and paper) (million, years, basis points)

Year	Borrower/ issuer	Facility	Amount	Average tenor	All-in margin	Repayment	Security
1993	Indah Kiat	NA	US$37	NA	NA	NA	NA
1993	Tjiwi Kimia	TL(1)	US$30	6.3	NA	Amortized	Fixed assets
		TL(2)	US$60	3.5	279	Amortized	
		TL(3)	US$30	5.5	300	Amortized	
1994	Indah Kiat	CP	US$30	1.0	NA	Bullet	No
1994	Indah Kiat	TL	US$149	3.0	238	Bullet	Fixed and floating assets
1994	Wirakarya Sakti	TL	US$100	3.0	300	Bullet	LG (holding co)
1994	Tjiwi Kimia	TL(1)	US$40	5.0	180	Amortized	Fixed and floating assets
		TL(2)	US$12	5.0	180	NA	
1994	Tjiwi Kimia	TL	US$30	5.0	NA	NA	NA
1994	Tjiwi Kimia	TL	US$120	2.9	270	Amortized	No
1995	Lontar Papyrus	CP	US$96	5.0	189	Bullet	No
1995	Indah Kiat	TL	US$200	3.0	267	Bullet	No
1995	Lontar Papyrus	LC	US$50	1.0	180	Bullet	No
1995	Lontar Papyrus	RC	US$110	1.0	185	Bullet	No
1995	Tjiwi Kimia	TL(1)	US$73	3.0	300	Amortized	LG (holding co)
		TL(2)	US$50	3.5	293	Amortized	
1995	Indah Kiat	NA	US$76	NA	NA	NA	NA
1995	Univenus	TL(1)	US$35	3.2	200	Amortized	Fixed and floating assets, LG (holding co)
		RC(2)	US$15	1.0	200	Bullet	
1995	Indah Kiat	TL	US$100	1.0	175	Bullet	No
1996	Linden Trading	RC	US$50	1.0	165	Bullet	Floating assets, LG (Indah Kiat)
1996	APP	TL(1)	US$200	3.0	175	Bullet	NA
		TL(2)	US$100	5.0	190	Bullet	
1996	Indah Kiat	NA	DEM 9	8.0	NA	NA	NA
1996	Tjiwi Kimia	NA	DEM 9	8.0	NA	NA	NA
1996	APP	FRN	US$200	3.0	288	Bullet	No
1996	Indah Kiat	Discount	US$72	0.3	150	Bullet	P. Notes
1996	APP	FRN	US$600	5.0	400	Bullet	No
1996	Tjiwi Kimia	TL	US$100	3.0	245	Bullet	No
1996	APP	FRN	JPY 11,000	1.0	170	Bullet	LG
1997	Indah Kiat	TL	US$400	3.0	260	Bullet	NA

Source: Privately collected data (checked with IFR).

Notes
TL: term loan, RC: revolver; CP: commercial paper; LC: letter of credit; Discount: discount note; LG: letter of guarantee; FRN: floating rate note; P. Notes: promissory note; NA: not available.

companies that had the same level of credit risk. These high margins attracted not only leading international lenders but also emerging Asian lenders, such as Korean and Taiwanese financial institutions. In sum, the group's pulp and paper division strategically sacrificed margins in order to attract offshore lenders and increase funding volume. As a result, the division accumulated more than US$14 billion debts at its restructuring stage.[21]

The group's agribusiness division also appealed to lenders owing to its strong business position in Indonesia (e.g. one of the top three private palm oil producers and leading cooking oil brand 'Filma') and its foreign exchange income through palm oil exportation. SMART Corporation was the flagship listed company and the main offshore funding vehicle in the division (Table 8.6). However, the nature of the business, that is, agriculture, prevented a number of offshore banks from aggressively increasing exposures and improving lending terms to the division. As Table 8.6 shows, the division was unable to improve borrowing terms either.

The funding situation of the Sinar Mas Group's real restate development division was almost identical to the Lippo Group and relied heavily on domestic funding sources, including inner-group funding, and third party equity.[22] This was simply because offshore debt providers, that is, commercial banks and bond investors, were generally reluctant to finance the Indonesian real estate sector, fearing over investment (Table 8.7). In particular, the group aggressively pushed forward major development projects, mainly in greater Jakarta.[23] This created a negative image of the group's real estate businesses. Nevertheless, Japanese trading companies and other Asian business organizations aggressively injected capital into the group's projects through joint ventures.[24]

Table 8.6 Offshore syndicated debts for the Sinar Mas Group (agribusiness) (million, years, basis points)

Year	Borrower/ issuer	Facility	Amount (US$)	Average tenor	All-in margin	Repayment	Security
1994	SMART Corp.	RC	60	2.0	263	Bullet	Fixed assets
1995	SMART Corp.	TL(1)	100	3.0	233	Bullet	Fixed and floating assets
		TL(2)	50	5.0	220	Bullet	
1996	Forestalestari Dwikarya	TL	40	3.0	290	Bullet	LG (SMART, holding co)
1996	Nacika Beverage	RC	15	3.0	207	Amortized	NA
1996	Bumi Permai Lestari/ Lembu Jaya	TL	30	3.0	258	Bullet	Offtake + LG

Source: Privately collected data (checked with IFR).

Notes
TL: term loan; RC: revolver; LG: letter of guarantee; NA: not available.

Table 8.7 Offshore syndicated debts for the Sinar Mas Group (real estate development) (million, years, basis points)

Year	Borrower/ issuer	Facility	Amount (US$)	Average tenor	All-in margin	Repayment	Security
1995	Shanghai Golden Beach Real Estate	TL	175	5.0	216	Bullet	LG (holding co)
1995	Duta Pertiwi	TL	21	1.5	243	Amortized	LG (holding co)
1995	Duta Pertiwi	TL	50	3.0	300	Bullet	LG (holding co)
1995	Plaza Indonesia	TL(1)	94	3.0	270	Amortized	Fix and floating assets
		TL(2)	37	4.4	288	Amortized	
1997	Ningbo Jinye Land	TL	22	3.0	300	Amortized	LG (holding co)

Source: Privately collected data (checked with IFR).

Notes
TL: term loan; LG: letter of guarantee.

In 1997, AFP, offshore holding companies for agribusiness and real estate development, acquired Amcol Holdings Ltd., a troubled Singapore listed company, and absorbed its agribusiness, food and real estate businesses. AFP's balance sheets suddenly jumped from S$412 million (US$294 million) in 1996 to S$6,893 million (US$4,107 million) in 1997. Furthermore, in the acquisition process, the company strategically introduced Japanese trading company capital and listed the shares on the Singapore Stock Exchange in July 1997.[25] In this way, AFP generated a good credit story to appeal to offshore lenders. However, the outbreak of the East Asian crisis prevented the group from fully utilizing AFP's potential financial capacity for active offshore funding.

As Table 8.8 illustrates, the Sinar Mas Group's financial services division was extremely active in offshore borrowing through BII, Sinar Mas Multiartha and BII's subsidiaries. BII, the second largest private commercial bank in Indonesia and the flagship company of the division, was a long-standing participant in off-shore syndicated debt markets. As Table 8.8 indicates, BII consistently improved its borrowing terms throughout the period. In 1993, BII paid 175 basis points for 2-year funding. In 1996, the bank successfully pushed down its funding margin to 97–100 basis points for three-year funding and to 93 basis points for two-year funding in 1997. However, BII was placed under the control of BI for its offshore borrowings through the Pinjaman Komersian Luar Negeri (PKLN) regulation. It was therefore difficult for BII just as other commercial banks to dramatically increase offshore funding volumes.

In 1995 the group established Sinar Mas Multiartha by merging BII and scattered group finance companies. In addition, the group avoided the PKLN regulation by using BII's subsidiaries with BII's letter of comfort and thereby increased offshore borrowing. Offshore lenders were generally cautious about lending to Indonesian finance companies even when they belonged to leading

Table 8.8 Offshore syndicated debts for the Sinar Mas Group (financial services) (million, years, basis points)

Year	Borrower/ issuer	Facility	Amount	Average tenor	All-in margin	Repayment	Security
1993	BII	NA	US$38	1.0	NA	Bullet	No
1993	BII	RC	US$50	2.0	175	Bullet	No
1994	BII	TL	US$30	2.5	200	Bullet	No
1994	Internas Arta Finance	TL	US$40	1.0	175	Bullet	LG (holding co)
1994	Internas Arta Finance	TL	US$35	1.0	208	Bullet	LG (holding co)
1995	BII Finance Center	TL	US$30	1.0	172	Bullet	LCom (BII)
1995	Sinar Mas Multiartha	TL	US$40	1.0	155	Bullet	No
1995	Sinar Mas Multiartha	NA	US$25	NA	NA	NA	NA
1995	BII	NA	US$NA	0.5	NA	Bullet	NA
1995	Sinar Mas Multiartha	NA	US$25	NA	NA	NA	NA
1995	BII	TL	US$25	5.0	141	Bullet	No
1995	BII	Discount	US$100	1.0	100	Bullet	Bill
1996	Sinar Mas Multiartha	NA	US$12	NA	NA	NA	NA
1996	BII	NA	US$13	NA	NA	NA	NA
1996	Sinar Mas Multiartha	Note	US$60	2.0	238	Bullet	No
1996	Sinar Mas Multiartha	FRN	US$60	NA	NA	NA	NA
1996	BII	FRCD	US$50	3.0	97	Bullet	No
1996	Sinar Mas Multiartha	FRN	US$50	1.0	163	Bullet	No
1996	BII Finance Center	TL	US$15	2.0	215	Bullet	No
1996	Sinar Mas Multiartha	NA	JPY 1,500	2.0	NA	Bullet	No
1996	BII	FRCD(1)	US$22	5.0	113	Bullet	No
		FRCD(2)	US$22	3.0	100	Bullet	No
1997	SMM Finance	FRN	US$190	2.0	265	Bullet	Shares (Sinar Mas Multiarhta), LG
1997	BII	FRCD	US$35	5.0	109	Bullet	No
1997	BII	FRCD	US$35	NA	NA	NA	NA
1997	Sinar Mas Multiartha	NA	US$20	NA	NA	NA	NA
1997	BII Finance Center	TL	US$35	2.0	225	Bullet	LCom (BII)
1997	BII Finance Co Ltd.	TL	US$35	2.0	175	Bullet	LCom (BII)
1997	BII	TL	US$100	2.0	93	Bullet	No

Source: Privately collected data (checked with IFR).

Notes
TL: term loan; RC: revolver; Discount: discount note; FRN: floating rate note; FRCD: floating rate certified deposit; LG: letter of guarantee; L Com: letter of comfort.

business groups and/or major commercial banks. The group's finance companies offered attractive margins to offshore lenders to justify the added risk. As can be seen in Table 8.8, the margins on offshore syndicated debts for Sinar Mas Multiartha, BII Finance Center and BII Finance Co. Ltd. were higher than those for BII and other non-financial group borrowers. Furthermore, the group attempted to place their debt with new types of offshore lenders, which aggressively sought higher returns on their loans, for example, Korean leasing companies and merchant banks.

The Sinar Mas Group had accessed overseas institutional investor markets even before the finance boom in the 1990s (Table 8.10). The group continued and accelerated its use of these markets during the finance boom by issuing fixed income bonds. Bond issuance during the boom period reached US$5.4 billion, and the group's pulp and paper companies accounted for 98.9 per cent of the volume.[26] APP, Indah Kiat and Tjiwi Kimia were the top three issuers and accounted for 41.5 per cent, 28.6 per cent and 14.9 per cent respectively.[27] The group approached the market on the basis of the strong credit quality and superior positions of its pulp and paper businesses. Overseas institutional investors, which were cautious regarding the Indonesian private sector as compared to offshore banks, started aggressive investments in the sector in the later stages of this finance boom. Reflecting the situation, 67.5 per cent of the group's issuance during the period occurred in 1997.

Fixed income bonds were useful instruments for the group because these enabled it to raise funds efficiently and to obtain larger-scale and longer tenors than was the case for offshore syndicated loans. In single transactions, APP raised US$550 million in 1995 and US$1,438 million in 1997. Indah Kiat raised US$500 million in 1994 and US$600 million in 1997. Tjiwi Kimia raised US$600 million in 1997. The group was unable to raise these amounts through single offshore syndicated loan transactions. On the other hand, the average tenor of the fixed income bonds issued by the group during the period was around 9.6 years. Even during the finance boom, offshore syndicated loans could only offer a maximum of 5 years to the leading Indonesian private borrowers,

Table 8.9 Offshore syndicated debts for the Sinar Mas Group (others) (million, years, basis points)

Year	Borrower/ issuer	Facility	Amount (US$)	Average tenor	All-in margin	Repayment	Security
1993	Dwimas Intiwisesa	USD	25	NA	NA	Amortized	LG (holding co)
1994	Dwimas Intiwisesa	SBLC	5	3.3	288	Amortized	Project
1996	Dwimas Intiwisesa	TL	40	1.5	225	Amortized	Project

Source: Privately collected data (checked with IFR).

Notes
SBCL: stand-by letter of credit; TL: term loan; LG: letter of guarantee.

Table 8.10 Fixed income bonds issued by the Sinar Mas Group (1993–7) (million, years, %)

Date	Issuer	Amount	Tenor	Coupon
Oct.-93	Indah Kiat	US$175	7	8.875
June-94	Indah Kiat	US$150	5	11.375
	Indah Kiat	US$200	8	11.875
	Indah Kiat	US$150	12	12.5
Aug.-94	Tjiwi Kimia	US$200	7	13.25
Sep.-95	APP	US$100	5	10.25
	APP	US$450	10	11.75
Feb.-96	Indah Kiat	US$100	2	0
	Indah Kiat	Yen 37,000	4	6.15
Apr.-96	Sinar Mas Multiartha	US$60	2	8
June-97	Indah Kiat	US$600	5	10
July-97	APP	US$245	3	2
July-97	Tjiwi Kimia	US$600	7	10
Sep.-97	Pindo Deli	US$100	5	10.25
	Pindo Deli	US$450	10	10.75
	Pindo Deli	US$100	20	11.75
	Pindo Deli	US$100	30	10.875
Nov.-97	APP	US$1,438	15	0

Sources: MSDW, Barclays Capital, Bloomberg.

including the Sinar Mas Group. Therefore, bonds made a major contribution towards improving the maturity profile of debt by stretching tenors.

However, the group had to pay a premium in order to attract overseas institutional investors, which were more returns oriented and less protected than offshore commercial banks.[28] The issuing costs of fixed income bonds were clearly expensive for the group. However, it was willing to pay such premiums in order to diversify its funding sources, to obtain huge funds efficiently, and to stretch its debt maturities. Overseas institutional investors also responded to its funding needs aggressively. Even after the onset of the East Asian crisis, the institutional investors market absorbed the group's large issuances. APP raised US$1.4 billion in November 1997, US$500 million in April 1998 and US$403 million in March 2000 (through APP China). In this way, the Sinar Mas Group's fund raising through fixed income bonds, which were placed to overseas institutional investors, contrasted with other leading business groups' financial activities, such as Salim and Astra, who also tapped into the same market, but their issuances were *ad hoc*. The group might have been a pioneer of offshore fixed income bonds in the Indonesian private sector, but the bonds exacerbated problems in the debt-restructuring processes.

Conclusions

During the finance boom in the 1990s, the Sinar Mas Group bullishly accessed global financial markets, which were suddenly and widely open to the Indonesian private sector. It introduced a variety of international mobile capital into its financial structures through a variety of financial means. Equity investors, offshore commercial banks, offshore investment banks, trading companies, ECAs (export credit agencies) and international public financiers also approached the group enthusiastically. Its balance sheet absorbed their equity, syndicated loans, FRNs, FRCDs, fixed income bonds, trade finances, project finances, ECA finances, IFC loans and other financial products. At both holding and operating companies levels, the group successfully caught the mood of offshore financiers' investment imperatives and absorbed a huge amount of mobile capital over a very short period. It raised funds as if it were willing to accept any financial opportunity.

This was achieved by the group's (i) advanced cross-boarder and pyramid shareholding structures; (ii) export-oriented and strongly positioned businesses and (iii) non-pricing(cost)-sensitive financial strategies. With regards to financial strategy, the group gave top priority to the volume of funding. It made a sacrifice of funding margins in return for increasing funding. Other leading business groups aggressively improved borrowing terms, while the Sinar Mas Group maintained its payment of high margins. This gave it a number of opportunities to access a variety of financial sources. Some non-Japan Asian financial institutions as well as leading international financial institutions provided sizable funds to the group. Its balance sheets sharply expanded by bullishly absorbing the funds during the finance boom.

In 1997, the year of the East Asian crisis, the group introduced a large scale of equity finance and mitigated the increasing pressures of leveraging that came from its aggressive debt financing during the finance boom. However, it did not improve its balance sheet by reducing debt with cash obtained through equity finance. It continued to increase its balance sheet and tried to obtain more debt. Behind these financial activities, there were the group's aggressive profit-seeking attitude towards mushrooming investment opportunities, the encashment of owner's investments in Indonesia, the preservation of the owner's liquidity and the geographical diversification of the group's investments. During the finance boom, its voracious funding appetite was timely combined with enthusiastic offshore financiers' investment imperatives.

The most important problem was that the dramatically stretched group financial structure, as a result, accumulated a huge volume of external debt that led to Kindleberger's 'crashes and panics' in financial crises. In addition to that, the financial structure became very complex, fragile and unstable due to the increased share of mobile capital within it. As the group actually experienced after 1998, mobile capital generated a variety of actions against the group and the situation was totally uncontrollable.[29] In sum, its fragility and instability originated from the volume of external debt and the dominance of mobile capital in its financial structure. The Sinar Mas case illustrates speculative financing units' behaviour that created the financial complexity of modern capitalist economy, which exceeded that of Minsky's argument in his financial instability hypothesis.

9   Case study 4

The Gajah Tunggal Group's financial activities in the 1990s

General views on the Gajah Tunggal Group

The Gajah Tunggal Group, which was controlled by the Nursalim family, was one of the rapidly growing Indonesian business conglomerates in the 1990s, holding powerful positions in a few industrial concerns, and which attempted to aggressively diversify its business lines.[1] The Gajah Tunggal Group is divided into the following six business segments: (i) financial services (commercial banking, non-bank finance, insurance, securities and so forth); (ii) manufacturing (tyre and related materials production, cable production and so forth); (iii) natural resources (shrimp farming and so forth); (iv) property; (v) retail and trading and (vi) international trading and investments. Among these, tyre production and commercial banking were the flagship businesses for the group.[2]

With regards to finance activities, the group was the third most active user of the Jakarta Stock Exchange (in terms of cash call) during the 1990s boom and at present has seven listed companies.[3] In the same way as other leading Indonesian business groups, such as Salim and Lippo, strategically used the listed companies as finance vehicles, the Gajah Tunggal Group also took advantage of its listed companies as tools for financing the group's and the family's funding requirements. During the finance boom, an access to equity investors' and offshore banks' funds, that is, mobile capital, suddenly and widely opened up to these growing business groups. Their aggressive profit-seeking attitudes towards mushrooming investment opportunities, voracious funding appetites and, simultaneously, their owner families' liquidity preferences were timely combined with enthusiastic equity investors' and offshore bankers' investment imperatives. These groups absorbed a huge size of mobile capitals over a very short period, and thereby their financial structures became very fragile in the face of unpredictable changes of business circumstances and the retreats of mobile capital from Indonesia, in particular, offshore banks' repayment requests as contracted.

This chapter analyses the Gajah Tunggal Group, as a representative of the Indonesian business groups that were rapidly growing in the 1990s but were heavily damaged by the Indonesian crisis, by focusing on its financial activities during the 1990s boom. Moreover, an attempt is made to clarify how mobile capital was built in the group's financial structure by scrutinizing their activities.

Finally, it is argued as to how an unstable and fragile financial structure, which Minsky defines at macroeconomy level in his financial instability hypothesis, was able to emerge at corporate level.

The Gajah Tunggal Group's financial position during the finance boom

During the finance boom of the 1990s, the group's financial activities can be divided into two phases: the first in 1994, and the second from 1995 to the first half of 1997. In the first phase, the group began active fund raising but this was still moderate. It used more equity than offshore debt finance. As a result, although its balance sheet was slightly stretched the leverage was maintained at a relatively low level. On the other hand, in the second phase, the group aggressively collected mobile capital through both equity and offshore debt markets. However, it accumulated more offshore debt than equity. As a result, the group's financial position was leveraged and the mobile capital occupied a dominant position in its financial structure.

In 1993, just prior to the onset of the boom, the Gajah Tunggal Group possessed a robust financial structure, as all leverage indicators for both non-financial and financial service divisions in Table 9.1 illustrate. In 1994, the leverage indicators were improved or remained at sound level except for the gross debt to EBITDA ratio in the non-financial service divisions, which jumped from 3.98 to 7.28 times. This is due to the fact that the group's equity finance went ahead of its offshore debt finance in 1994. It collected Rp.1,650 billion (US$764 million) through equity finance as opposed to US$288 million through offshore syndicated finances (including refinance). Both non-financial and financial service divisions raised more funds through equity finance than through offshore syndicated finances. In sum, the group's equity-weighted fund raising maintained its financial structure at a sound level.

Since 1995, the leverage indicators in Table 9.1 clearly indicate the deterioration of the Gajah Tunggal Group's financial position. Among all indicators, the gross debt to EBITDA ratio sharply increased in the non-financial service divisions. This meant that the growth of cash flow, which is substituted by EBITDA, was unable to catch up with the expansion of the debt in the non-financial service divisions. The EBITDA interest coverage and the EBITDA cost (interest + foreign exchange loss) coverage ratios severely deteriorated from 6.81 and 4.43 in 1994 to 3.14 and 2.39 in 1995 respectively. The growth of income from new investments could not compensate for the increased funding costs. It is clear that the margin of safety, which Minsky defined as the excess of cash available over cash outflow for debt service and/or the excess of asset value over debt-obligation amount, deteriorated from 1995.

The another critical problem concerning the Gajah Tunggal Group's financial structure was the currency position between the group's income cash flow (Indonesian rupiah) and debt-service cash outflow for offshore borrowing (mainly US dollars). The sharp depreciation of the Indonesian rupiah, triggered

Table 9.1 The Gajah Tunggal Group's financial position in the 1990s (times)

	1990	1991	1992	1993	1994	1995	1996	1997
Non-financial services								
Leverage ratio	0.57	1.07	1.22	0.92	0.82	0.97	1.00	3.98
Equity ratio	0.64	0.48	0.45	0.52	0.55	0.51	0.50	0.20
Gross debt to equity	0.45	0.72	1.03	0.74	0.68	0.87	0.90	3.31
Gross debt to CS + APIC	0.52	1.05	1.42	1.05	0.98	1.39	1.49	3.63
Gross debt to EBITDA	2.91	3.84	4.38	3.98	7.28	7.68	8.95	19.56
Financial services								
Leverage ratio	7.31	9.73	12.30	6.93	7.55	8.23	9.68	12.11
Equity ratio	0.12	0.09	0.08	0.13	0.12	0.11	0.09	0.08
Debt[a] to equity	2.79	2.45	2.84	1.53	1.42	2.37	2.37	4.80
Deposit + debt[a] to equity	7.07	9.44	12.05	6.80	7.39	7.85	9.31	NA
Debt[a] to CS + APIC	3.25	3.09	3.60	2.20	1.76	3.20	4.04	7.85
Deposit + debt[a] to CS + APIC	8.24	11.89	15.30	9.76	9.18	10.59	15.88	NA
Debt[a] to EBITDA	14.31	11.31	9.63	10.84	6.68	11.22	8.27	19.04
Depost + debt[a] to EBITDA	36.24	43.55	40.85	48.04	34.87	37.11	32.53	NA

Source: Annual reports.

Note
a The debt includes offshore loans/FRCDs, bonds and interbank borrowing.

by the East Asian crisis, and the not-hedged currency position dramatically stretched the group's foreign currency denominated debt in terms of the Indonesian rupiah and totally eroded its financial position. As the all leverage indicators in Table 9.1 show, the group's financial structure was extremely leveraged in 1997 and reached such a level that the soundness of the financial position was unrecoverable without additional cash injection.[4]

Within only two and half years of the second phase, the Gajah Tunggal Group drove its collection of mobile capitals by taking advantage of financiers' enthusiasm. It obtained Rp.6,908 billion (US$1,443 million) through equity finance and US$1,607 million through offshore syndicated finance during this phase. In comparison with the first phase, the group relatively accented offshore syndicated finance for its funding sources. However, in contrast with equity finance, this offshore syndicated finance exposed the group to the following double risks: foreign currency depreciation risk and the sudden withdrawal of the finance. In a similar way to other leading business groups, the Gajah Tunggal Group's financial structure became extremely unstable and fragile in such a short period due to the aggressive use of offshore debt.

The Gajah Tunggal Group's fund raising during the finance boom

During the finance boom of the 1990s, the Gajah Tunggal Group collected Rp.5.2 trillion (US$2.2 billion) through equity finance (Table 9.2). It was the third most active users of the Jakarta Stock Exchange and held a 10.1 per cent share of total cash calls during the period, following the Lippo Group (11.6 per cent) and the Sinar Mas Group (11.3 per cent). This huge funding through equity finance was related to two restructurings of the group corporate holdings of financial services and manufacturing divisions in 1996. In that year, the Gajah Tunggal Group took over as the leading user of the stock exchange with Rp.2.3 trillion (US$997 million) cash calls and a 17.8 per cent share.

The most active vehicles used for the group's financial strategy were BDNI and Gajah Surya Multifinance (later changed to BDNI Capital Corp., followed by GT Investama Kapital) of the financial services division and Gajah Tunggal and Andayani Megah (later changed to GT Petrochem Industries) of the manufacturing division. These were key companies for the earlier-mentioned dramatic corporate restructuring in 1996, and vehicles to accumulate mobile capital for the Gajah Tunggal Group (Table 9.3).

On the other hand, with regard to other mobile capital, that is, offshore banks' funds, the Gajah Tunggal Group borrowed US$2.0 billion through 23 offshore syndicated loans during the 1990s finance boom. Its non-financial services divisions borrowed US$1.1 billion through six syndicated loans, and the financial services division borrowed US$923 million through 17 syndicated loans/FRCDs. However, it should be noted that the latter figure might be overstated due to the fact that the deals include refinances and waivers of put options of existing loans.[5] In addition to this, the group actively borrowed bilateral loans from Singapore-based offshore banks; therefore the total debts it accumulated during the period must have been much larger than the funds it collected from the equity market (Table 9.4).

The Gajah Tunggal Group launched almost the same number of syndicated debts every year throughout the period. Until 1995, the facility amount per deal

Table 9.2 The Gajah Tunggal Group's equity finance during the finance boom (summary)

	New issue (Rp. billion)	Rights issue (Rp. billion)	Total (Rp. billion)	(US$ million)
1994[a]	0	1,650	1,650	764
1995	200	0	200	89
1996	0	2,321	2,321	997
1997	0	1,033	1,033	357
Total	200	5,004	5,204	2,208

Sources: ING and MSDW.

Note
a Including BDNI's rights issue in December 1993.

Table 9.3 The Gajah Tunggal Group's equity finance during the finance boom (breakdown)

Listing	Issuer	Type	No. of shares (million)	Offer price (Rp./share)	Amount raised (Rp. billion)
Dec.-93	BDNI	1-for-1 rights issue	235	2,500	587
Feb.-94	Gajah Tunggal	1-for-1 rights issue	198	3,250	644
May-94	Gajah Surya Multifinance	3-for-1 rights issue	120	1,500	180
Nov.-94	Andayani Megah	1-for-1 rights issue	80	3,000	240
Oct.-95	BDNI Reksadana	New issue	400	500	200
Oct.-96	Gajah Surya Multifinance	7-for-2 rights issue	561	1,300	729
Oct.-96	Gajah Tunggal	1-for-1 rights issue	792	1,000	792
Oct.-96	Andayani Megah	5-for-2 rights issue	800	1,000	800
Jan.-97	Kabel Metal	1-for-1 rights issue	140	1,000	140
Feb.-97	BDNI	3-for-4 rights issue	616	1,450	893

Sources: ING and MSDW.

Table 9.4 The Gajah Tunggal Group's offshore syndicated debts (summary) (US$ million)

	Non-financial services			Financial services			Total		
	No. of deals	Amount raised	Amount per deal	No. of deals	Amount raised	Amount per deal	No. of deals	Amount raised	Amount per deal
1992	1	35	35	3	106	35	4	141	35
1993	0	0	NA	4	117	29	4	117	29
1994	1	117	117	4	171	43	5	288	58
1995	0	0	NA	6	243	41	6	243	41
1996	4	685	171	3	266	89	7	951	136
1997	1	300	300	4	243	61	5	543	109
Total	7	1,137	162	24	1,146	48	31	2,283	74

Source: Privately collected date (checked with IFR).

was constantly less than US$50 million. However, this suddenly jumped to US$136 million in 1996 and to US$109 million in 1997. This was due to the fact that the group managed to obtain several jumbo deals, such as a US$180 million syndicated loan for Grand Paradise, a US$150 million Euro-FRN for BDNI, and syndicated loans of US$360 million for Gajah Tunggal, US$105 million for Kabel Metal Indonesia, US$100 million for Gajah Surya Multifinance and US$300 million for Andayani Megah (Table 9.5).

Looking at the size per deal from business segments during the period, the average size of deal for the non-financial service division was US$184 million, while that for the financial service division was US$54 million. This is consistent with the then offshore banks' industrial preference for Indonesian borrowers.

Table 9.5 The Gajah Tunggal Group's offshore syndicated debts (breakdown) (US$ million, basis points)

Date	Borrower	Amount	Type	Average tenor	All-in margin	Repayment	Security
Apr.-92	BDNI	50.0	TL/ FRCD	NA	150.0	Bullet	NA
May-92	BDNI	21.0	RC	1.0	175.0	Bullet	NA
July-92	Gajah Tunggal	35.0	RC	2.0	215.0	Bullet	NA
Sep.-92	BDNI	38.0	RC	1.0	60.0	Bullet	NA
May-93	BDNI	21.0	RC	1.0	175.0	Bullet	NA
July-93	BDNI	20.0	NA	NA	NA	NA	NA
Sep.-93	BDNI	38.0	RC	1.0	NA	Bullet	NA
Dec.-93	BDNI	38.0	RC	1.0	187.5	Bullet	NA
Mar.-94	BDNI	33.0	FRCD	1.0	140.0	Bullet	NA
June-94	BDNI	50.0	TL/FRCD	1.0	NA	Bullet	NA
Aug.-94	BDNI	50.0	TL	1.9/3.0	116.7/ 126.0	Bullet	NA
Sep.-94	BDNI	38.0	TL	1.0	NA	Bullet	NA
Nov.-94	Gajah Tunggal	117.0	RC	2.0	165.0	Bullet	Cash equiv. (dischargable)
Jan.-95	Gajah Surya Multifinance	20.0	RC	2.0	197.5	Bullet	Float
Apr.-95	BDNI	33.0	FRCD	1.0	112.5	Bullet	NA
June-95	BDNI	50.0	RC	1.0	150.0	Bullet	NA
Sep.-95	BDNI	100.0	FRCD	3.0	100.0	Bullet	NA
Nov.-95	BDNI	20.0	NA	NA	NA	NA	NA
Dec.-95	Gajah Surya Multifinance	20.0	TL	1.0	157.0	Bullet	Float
Apr.-96	Grand Paradise (JV)	180.0	TL	5.5	216.4	Amortized	Fix, LCom
Apr.-96	BDNI Megacity	150.0	FRCD	3.0	106.7	Bullet	NA
June-96	Development Corp. (JV)	40.0	TL	3.0	337.5	Bullet	LG
July-96	Gajah Tunggal	360.0	TL	3.0	110.5	Bullet	NA
Sep.-96	Gajah Surya Multifinance	45.0	NA	1.0	245.0	Bullet	Float
Nov.-96	BDNI	71.0	TL	3.0	92.5	Bullet	NA
Nov.-96	Kabel Metal	105.0	TL	3.0	155.0	Bullet	NA
Mar.-97	BDNI Capital Corp (Gajah Surya Multifinance)	100.0	TL	2.0	105.0	Bullet	BDNI shares
Mar.-97	BDNI	25.0	PP	3.0	NA	NA	NA
Mar.-97	BDNI	78.0	FRCD	3.0	85.0	Bullet	NA
May-97	Gajah Surya Finance	40.0	TL	2.0	225.0	Bullet	Float
July-97	GT Petrochem Industries (Andayani Megah)	300.0	TL	4.4	115.0	Amotized	NA

Source: Privately collected date (checked with IFR).

Notes
TL: term loan; RC: revolver, FRCD: floating rate certified deposit; PP: private placement; Float: floating charge; Fix: fixed assets; LCom: letter of comfort; LG: letter of guarantee; NA: not available.

The banks generally preferred lending to manufacturing and service company borrower, which held dominant positions in the Indonesian economy, rather than financial service companies, the portfolios of which were exposures to weak medium and small corporate and/or household sectors.[6] In the financial sector, only leading commercial banks and finance companies owned by elite business groups were able to access the offshore market.

With regards to borrowing terms, it is clear that the Gajah Tunggal Group were able to improve them during the finance boom. Until mid-1995, BDNI could obtain only 1-year facilities, and the size of those was less than US$50 million.[7] The all-in margins were also in the range of 150.0 to 180.0 basis points. These borrowing terms were equivalent to the other leading private banks, such as Lippo Bank and Bank Panin. From mid-1995, BDNI was able to stretch its borrowing tenor to 3 years and reduce the funding costs to less than 100.0 basis points. This drastic improvement in the bank's borrowing terms was mainly due to its position in the private banking sector, in business circles, and the offshore banks' enthusiasm. Furthermore, in examining the borrowing terms of Gajah Tunggal, a flagship company of the group, this improvement is also obvious. In 1992, Gajah Tunggal borrowed a US$35 million 2-year syndicated loan with the all-in margin of 215.0 basis points. In 1994, it borrowed a US$117 million 2-year syndicated loan with the all-in margin 165.0 basis points. It was able to successfully increase the facility amount and decrease the funding costs. Instead, the company was required to pledge its holding marketable securities and deposits as a security on the loan (but dischargeable). In 1996, Gajah Tunggal managed to obtain a US$360 million 3-year syndicated loan with an all-in margin of 110.5 basis points. The company almost tripled the facility amount, stretched the tenor, cut the funding cost and did not pledge any security. During the finance boom in the 1990s, Gajah Tunggal dramatically improved its borrowing terms.

In 1996 and 1997, offshore banks adopted a more aggressive approach to the Gajah Tunggal Group. They arranged and participated in much riskier finances with bullish lending terms. The group obtained two jumbo syndicated loans with competitive borrowing terms, that is, US$360 million for Gajah Tunggal and US$300 million for Andayani Megah. It also obtained real estate finance for funding Gajah Tunggal Center, which was developed by Grand Paradise. Furthermore, Gajah Surya Multifinance obtained acquisition finance for funding of its intra-group purchase of BDNI shares from the Nursalim family, that is, the encashment of the family interests in BDNI. In addition, Gajah Surya Finance, a subsidiary of Gajah Surya Multifinance, obtained a US$40 million 2-year syndicated loan unsupported by its parent company.

Although offshore banks challenged risky finances during the period, as is discussed in the case study on the Lippo Group, financial services (excluding leading commercial banks) and real estate companies still found it relatively difficult to obtain offshore bankers' money. In order to break through this barrier the Gajah Tunggal Group approached non-Japan Asian financial institutions, in particular NIES financial institutions and Indonesian banks' offshore lending units which aggressively sought for high-return investment opportunities. For example, the substantial share (both the number of participants and the funds of commitment) of (i) the US$20 million facility signed in December 1995 for Gajah Surya Multifinance; (ii) the US$180 million in April 1996 for Grand Paradise and (iii) the US$40 million in May 1997 for Gajah Surya Finance was taken by non-Japan Asian financial institutions.[8]

In this way, the Gajah Tunggal Group accelerated its financial activities and enjoyed improving issuance and borrowing terms during the booms in the 1990s. Moreover, these seemed to be sustainable, and because of that, offshore mobile capitalists' enthusiastic approach to the Indonesian corporate sector was continuously strengthened during the period.

The Gajah Tunggal Group's corporate restructuring and the encashment of the Nursalim family's investments in the 1990s

The restructuring of the Gajah Tunggal Group's manufacturing division

In 1996, the Gajah Tunggal Group drastically restructured the corporate holdings of its manufacturing division, which focused on tyre and related businesses. Until this was completed, the division possessed a partial holding structure. Two flagship listed companies in the division, that is, Gajah Tunggal, a tyre manufacturer, and Andayani Megah, a tyre code manufacturer, had a holding and sub-holding relationship. However, many member companies were still placed under the Nursalim family's direct ownership. As a whole, the division comprised a relatively horizontal corporate holding structure under the family. The aim of this restructuring was to alter this corporate holding into a vertically integrated structure by consolidating several family-owned member companies in its listed companies and simultaneously to liquidate the family's investments (Figure 9.1).

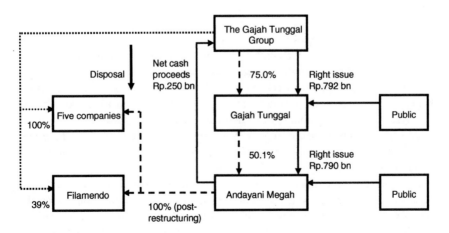

Figure 9.1 The restructuring of the Gajah Tunggal Group's manufacturing division.
Sources: Annual reports and various news.

As a first step of the restructuring, Andayani Megah acquired five closely held companies, which became involved in producing tyre-related raw materials, from the Nursalim family.[9] The company spent around Rp.668 billion (US$283 million) in the acquisition of three core companies manufacturing polyester products and ethyl glycol; Prima Ethycolindo, Gemapersada Polimer and Berinda Mitra Stafindo. In the second step of the restructuring, Andayani Megah purchased 39 per cent of the shares of Filamendo Sakti (Filamendo), the company's subsidiary and a polyester filament producer, from Gajah Tunggal Mulia, one of the Gajah Tunggal Group's holding companies.[10]

In order to finance these intra-group share transactions, Andayani Megah raised Rp.790 billion (US$334 million) through its rights issue. At the same time, Gajah Tunggal raised Rp.792 billion (US$335 million) in order to buy in the Andayani Megah's rights issues and maintain its shareholding in the company. Both companies collected around Rp.884 billion (US$380 million) through rights issues in 1994. Thus, new rights issues were additional burdens for third party investors. These third party investors and stock analysts heavily criticized the new equity finances as damaging to minority shareholders' interests and a cashing out by the Nursalim family while maintaining its control of the companies.[11]

However, the Gajah Tunggal Group successfully obtained the minority shareholders' approvals and completed the vertical (pyramid-type) corporate holding structure of the manufacturing division.[12] After buying in the Gajah Tunggal Group's rights issue for maintaining its control, the family obtained net around Rp.250 billion (US$106 million) cash proceeds through these transactions. Furthermore, the new corporate holding structure enabled the Nursalim family to minimize its capital use for the division's future business expansion.

On the other hand, as an accounting effect of these transactions, Andayani Megah's total assets jumped from Rp.941 billion in 1995 to Rp.2,079 billion in 1996, and Gajah Tunggal's total assets, which consolidated the Andayani Magah's asset, also leaped from Rp.2,737 billion in 1995 to Rp.4,918 billion in 1996. In terms of asset size, Gajah Tunggal became one of the largest among Indonesian companies, such as Indocement (the total asset of Rp.4,607 billion) and Indofood (the total asset of Rp.5,574 billion). This accounting illusion that was created by mergers, acquisition and consolidation became an important appeal for obtaining new equity investors' and offshore bankers' money.

In July 1997, despite the occurrence of the Thai baht crisis, Andayani Megah, whose name had been changed to GT Petrochem Industries, successfully arranged a US$300 million syndicated loan. This huge offshore loan was the largest that the group had ever borrowed from both domestic and offshore markets. Even BDNI, the group's frequent offshore borrower, was not able to borrow at this volume.

However, the huge offshore debt and the widespread effects of the East Asian crisis caused the financial position of the Gajah Tunggal Group's manufacturing division to crash. The leverage ratio and the gross debt to EBITDA ratio of Gajah Tunggal jumped from 0.85 and 8.75 in 1996 to 4.05 and 15.45 in 1997 respectively. The ratios of Andayani Megah also leaped from 0.54 and 8.86 in

1996 to 4.80 and 19.68 in 1997. These increases were caused by not-hedged offshore foreign debt and account payable to offshore suppliers. Gajah Tunggal, which consolidated a Rp.427 billion foreign exchange loss of Andayani Megah, booked a Rp.947 billion foreign exchange loss in 1996. This loss was almost three times as large as the company's operating profit in 1996 and 45 times as large as its foreign exchange loss in the previous year.

The case of the Gajah Tunggal Group's manufacturing division is a typical example that illustrates (i) the encashment of owner shareholder's investments through corporate restructuring and equity finance; (ii) the leveraging of financial position by offshore borrowing and (iii) the process leading to an unstable and fragile financial position.

The restructuring of the Gajah Tunggal Group's financial services division

In 1996, at almost the same time as the manufacturing division's corporate restructuring explained earlier, the Gajah Tunggal Group's financial services division also altered its corporate holding structure from a horizontal to vertical style. In addition, the Nursalim family liquidated its investment in the division while maintaining its control as it did in the manufacturing division.

Prior to this restructuring, the Gajah Tunggal Group directly owned Gajah Surya Multifinance, a non-bank finance company, and BDNI, a flagship commercial bank. That is to say, the group had a horizontal corporate holding structure. However, it sold its controlling share (51.8 per cent) in BDNI to Gajah Surya Multifinance, and thereafter indirectly owned and controlled the bank by means of a vertical corporate holding structure. Furthermore, the Nursalim family were able to obtain cash proceeds through the disposal of BDNI shares to Gajah Surya Multifinance (Figure 9.2).

The sales price of the BDNI shares was Rp.1,725 per share, and the gross cash proceeds from Gajah Surya Multifinance to the Nursalim family were Rp.734 billion (US$315 million).[13] Gajah Surya Multifinance funded this share purchase through a 7-for-2 rights issue (Rp.729 billion). The Nursalim family bought in this rights issue by paying around Rp.480 billion in order to maintain its control of Gajah Surya Multifinance, and the third party investors contributed Rp.249 billion. As a result, the restructuring of the group financial services division's corporate holdings by funding through rights issue provided Rp.254 billion (US$109 million) to the Nursalim family.[14]

On the other hand, BDNI needed to strengthen its own equity structure. A newly introduced regulation required all banks to increase their CAR (capital adequacy ratio) to 10 per cent by September 1999 and to 12 per cent by 2001. This regulation was a heavy financial burden for bank owners in Indonesia. In February 1997, BDNI collected Rp.893 billion through a 3-for-4 rights issue for improving its CAR. In January 1997, Gajah Surya Multifinance, the controlling shareholder, borrowed US$100 million through offshore syndicated loans for buying into this BDNI's rights issues (Figure 9.2). The Gajah Tunggal Group was

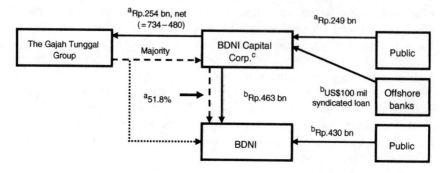

Figure 9.2 The restructuring of the Gajah Tunggal Group's financial services division.

Sources: Annual reports and various news.

Notes
a Transaction in 1996.
b Transaction in 1997.
c Gajah Surya Multifinance.

able to improve the BDNI's CAR by using funds of the BDNI's third party investors and offshore banks. That is to say, the restructuring of corporate holdings in 1996 enabled the group to achieve this without the Nursalim family's financial burden placed upon it.

In particular, offshore banks' enthusiasm helped the Gajah Tunggal Group to raise funds in the debt markets. In comparison with the syndicated loans previously borrowed by the group, the syndicated loan that Gajah Surya Multifinance obtained for buying in the BDNI's rights issue was aggressively arranged by offshore banks. The syndicated loan for Gajah Surya Multifinance (under the name of BDNI Capital Corp) was a US$100 million secured term loan facility.[15] This had a 2-year tenor with bullet payment and was secured by the BDNI shares held by Gajah Surya Multifinance. The all-in margin for top-tier participant level was 105 basis points, and this margin was less than half of the previous syndicated loan's margin.[16]

Conclusions

This case study illustrates the fact that the Gajah Tunggal Group aggressively introduced mobile capital into its financial structure through equity and offshore syndicated finances during the economic and finance boom in the 1990s. In addition, this case study has clarified the following financial strategies that the group adopted in the process of building up the mobile capital in its financial structure:

1   The restructuring of the group's corporate holdings from horizontal to vertical;
2   The acquisition of the Nursalim family's privately held assets by the group public companies;

3   The maximum use of the minority shareholders' money while maintaining the family's controls of the group companies;
4   The leveraging of the group financial position by foreign currency debts via offshore syndicated loans.

Furthermore, this case study has discussed how the group's public companies, which were tightly controlled by the family, for example, Gajah Tunggal, Andayani Megah, BDNI and Gajah Surya Multifinance, played critical roles throughout the process.

These financial strategies enabled the Nursalim family not only to liquidate its investments and realize the gain on them while maintaining corporate control, but also to expand the existing group businesses and take in mushrooming new investment opportunities with the family's minimum capital contributions. The Gajah Tunggal Group had strong incentives to push forward the financial strategies, that is, by using third party investors' equity money and offshore debt finance as growth drivers for the group and liquidity sources for the family. As a result of this financial process which lasted a mere three and a half years, the Gajah Tunggal Group's financial structure became highly unstable and fragile with a leveraged financial position and mobile capitals.

On the other hand, the emergence of an unstable and fragile financial structure over such a short period generally requires financial enthusiasm, which is caused by both fund users' and providers' strong investment/lending imperatives. In this context, during the 1990s boom, the Gajah Tunggal Group's aggressive profit-seeking attitude towards mushrooming investment opportunities, voracious funding appetites and the family's liquidity preferences were combined in a timely manner with equity investors' and offshore bankers' enthusiastic financing attitudes. This combination accelerated huge capital flows into the group over a very short period, and thereby the group's financial position became extremely unstable and fragile when faced with the unpredictable changes of business circumstances, such as retreats of equity investors and offshore bankers, that is, mobile capitals, from Indonesia.

The Gajah Tunggal Group's transformation process from a robust to an unstable and fragile financial structure is one of the micro-level examples of evidence with regard to how an unstable and fragile financial structure of the Indonesian economy, which can be defined by Minsky's financial instability hypothesis, emerged during the finance boom of the 1990s. Furthermore, the aggregates of the financial activities that the Gajah Tunggal Group and other business groups developed at micro-level became a large disequilibrating force affecting the Indonesian economy during the period.

10 The collapse of cash-flow chains

The Indonesian crisis and the institutional arrangements carried out by the government

The period from 1997 to 1998 in Indonesia was filled with a great number of realized economic, political and social risks, which together amounted to the Indonesian crisis. Complex and fierce conflicts among ethnic, religious and political groups broke out as the financial system collapsed and the economy contracted. The period saw the end of the 32-year Suharto regime and the degeneration of its political foundations. Numerous disturbances, including nationwide political protests in May 1998 against the Suharto regime and in November 1998 against the new internal security law, provoked social unrest throughout the country. Independence movements in East Timor and Aceh threatened the disintegration of the nation, and military action taken against these separatists heightened domestic and international criticism of the government and the military. In short, the Indonesian crisis was far wider and deeper than the East Asian crisis.

The arrival of the Indonesian crisis in 1997 forced Indonesian corporates to the wall. Their highly leveraged financial positions and unhedged foreign currency debts combined with the collapse in value of the Indonesian rupiah, sharply rising domestic interest rates and offshore lenders' sudden aversion to Indonesian debt closed off all avenues to escape. Corporate balance sheets were stretched by foreign currency borrowings and trade credits, the value of which increased sharply in rupiah terms thereby increasing the leverage. Cash outflows (in rupiah terms) for debt service of and the settlement of trade accounts also skyrocketed. The corporate sector could not produce enough cash inflows to set off against the increased outflows through ordinary business activities and therefore suffered negative cash flows. Business conditions also disintegrated as political problems began to weigh heavily on the Suharto regime. Overseas trade and investment counter parties became extremely cautious and attempted to withdraw rapidly from Indonesia. The worsening business environment lowered expectations of future cash inflows, and therefore asset values collapsed. In Minsky's terms, the margin of safety in the corporate sector was totally eliminated and the sector slipped from speculative to Ponzi financing.[1] This problem was naturally transferred to the banking sector and offshore creditors (i.e. lenders, investors and trade counter parties) in the form of distressed financial and commercial assets. The complex chains of cash flows between the corporate sector, the banking sector and offshore creditors finally broke down. Fisher's debt deflation decimated the Indonesian financial system.

In all of the severely affected East Asian countries, including Indonesia, debt-rescheduling negotiations took place between domestic debtors and offshore creditors. The enormous and one-sided pressures on repayment and asset disposal pushed both the corporate and banking sectors into insolvency. In order to deal with this, governments adopted similar institutional arrangements for corporate and bank restructuring, such as corporate workout programmes, asset management and resolution agencies and bank recapitalization programmes.[2] In early 1998, the Indonesian government established the Government Guarantee Program as a deposit insurance scheme. In the same year, with the advice and support of international financial authorities and institutions, the Indonesian government introduced the Jakarta Initiative Task Force (JITF) and the Indonesian Debt Restructuring Agency (INDRA) to work out the corporate sector's debt problems. The government also established the Indonesian Bank Restructuring Agency (IBRA) to manage and recover the bank assets, which were handed over to the agency. IBRA was also made responsible for restructuring the banking sector. In addition, between 1998 and 1999 the related legal infrastructure, such as bankruptcy and banking laws and foreign ownership regulations for domestic banks, were revised in order to ensure that these agencies carried out their respective missions.[3] However, due to a lack of execution capacity, creditors' and debtors' weak incentives and chaotic political conditions the restructuring did not proceed as the government had originally planned. In December 1999, the Financial Sector Policy Committee (FSPC) was established in order to accelerate the pace of corporate debt restructuring and bank rehabilitation through improved coordinating of JITF, INDRA, IBRA, BI and the Ministry of Finance. Furthermore, an Oversight Committee (OSC) was established within IBRA to strengthen corporate governance, such as monitoring rent-seeking activities related to asset disposal. The IMF, The World Bank and Asian Development Bank (ADB) also monitored the situation through the Independent Review Committee (IRC).

JITF and INDRA were established in response to the Frankfurt Agreement, which was concluded between the Indonesian government and 13 international private banks (as the Steering Committee Banks) in June 1998. The aim of the agreement was to stabilize chaotic negotiations between Indonesian debtors and offshore creditors through a restructuring framework for the corporate sector's external debt, a repayment programme for Interbank debts (called the 'Exchange Program') and a maintenance scheme for trade finance facilities. JITF was assigned the task of facilitating the restructuring of corporate debt through out-of-court settlements. JITF, moreover, provided one-stop services for all regulator filings necessary to implement restructuring plans and recommendations on any legal, regulatory and/or administrative matters needed to facilitate corporate restructuring. INDRA was modelled on 'FICORCA', which had been set up following the crisis in Mexico. INDRA was designed to provide foreign exchange rate risk protection in order to facilitate the restructuring of private corporate debt outside the banking system. The agency also guaranteed the availability of foreign exchange to both debtors and creditors. In concrete terms, debtors made rupiah payments to the agency at predetermined exchange rates, while the agency made foreign exchange payments to creditors. The agency required both parties to restructure foreign currency debts with a minimum maturity of 8 years, inclusive of a minimum 3 years grace period. In addition, INDRA did not assume commercial risk. INDRA targeted around 2,000 indebted local companies which together owed US$64.5 billion to foreign creditors (Kyodo 3 August 1998).

IBRA was established in January 1998 in order to carry out the restructuring of the banking sector. Bank Indonesia handed over to IBRA the management of assets and liabilities of closed banks (BDL, or Bank Dalam Likuidas), frozen banks (BBO, or Bank Beku Operasi and BBKU, or Bank Beku Kegiatan Usaha), taken over banks (BTO, or Bank Taken Over), recapitalized banks (Bank Rekapitalisasi) and state banks. IBRA was given the task of the restructuring banks, effective mergers and/or the sale of taken over banks, and the recapitalization of surviving banks. This mission also included the recovery of the Bank Indonesia Liquidity Assistance (BILA) or in Indonesian Bantuan Likuiditas Bank Indonesia (BLBI) loans from banks and their owners. BLBI loans were provided as bridging loans to banks experiencing liquidity problems.[4] As the Indonesian crisis deepened with the collapse of the Suharto regime, a number of leading private banks were suspected to bank runs as panicked depositors withdrew their savings. Therefore, BI, as lender of last resort, injected around Rp.145 trillion in BLBI into the private banks in order to avoid systemwide collapse.[5] The agency played a critical role in restructuring of corporate debt as the largest domestic non-bank creditor.

In December 1998, on the basis of the bank audits to determine Capital Adequacy Ratios (CAR), or the ratio of equity capital to risk-weighted assets, all banks were sorted into three groups: Category A (with a CAR of 4 per cent or higher), Category B (with a CAR of lower than 4 per cent but higher than minus 25 per cent) and Category C (with a CAR of lower than minus 25 per cent) (Cameron 1999, p.20).[6] In March 1999, based on this categorization and on further audits, the government took the decisive step of reviving the private banks (128 banks with around 40 per cent of the banking sector's assets) (ADB 2000, pp.17–21; Bank Indonesia 2000, p.8; Enoch *et al.* 2003, pp.81–2). Category A banks were considered strong enough to manage their affairs without government financial assistance.[7] The Category B banks were deemed to be solvent and salvageable. Among this group, nine banks were judged to be eligible for joint recapitalization financed by themselves, the government and the bank owners (Bank Indonesia 2000, p.8).[8] In May 1999, seven of these banks were recapitalized to bring their CARs up to 4 per cent.[9] The other seven banks in the category were unable to qualify for joint recapitalization but were deemed to have a significant impact on the payment system through their extensive branch networks (Bank Indonesia 2000, p.8). Therefore, these banks were taken over by

IBRA. The bank owners were excluded from management in the taken-over banks and were required to settle excess connected lending. Seventeen Category C and 21 other Category B banks were judged to be non-salvageable and did not qualify for recapitalization. Their assets were taken over by IBRA, and their deposits were transferred to designated banks (Bank Indonesia 2000, p.8). By the end of 1999, IBRA held Rp.234 trillion (US$33 billion) in private loans (IBRA 1999, p.24).[10]

To facilitate the recovery of transferred assets and the repayment of BLBI loans to the government, IBRA introduced the Shareholders Settlement Program or Penyelesaian Kewajiban Pemegang Saham (PKPS). IBRA claimed that bank owners or controlling shareholders must be held responsible for the recovery pro-gramme because most BDL, BBO/BBKU and BTO banks breached Legal Lending Limits. Bank owners concluded either the Master Settlement and Acquisition Agreement (MSAA) or the Master Refinancing and Notes Issuance Agreement (MRNIA) with IBRA and pledged their financial and/or commercial assets against net liabilities incurred by their respective insolvent banks.[11] In most cases, bank owners established holding companies to pledge their assets and/or companies to IBRA, and the pledged companies continued to operate under their management. However, the Asset Management Investment Unit of IBRA super-vised the operations. By the end of 1999, 228 commercial assets (mostly owners' shares in group companies) were pledged and Rp.112 trillion (US$15.8 billion) in promissory notes for repayment were issued by nine bank owners through PKPS (IBRA 1999, p.27).[12]

The restructuring of corporate debt and the disposal of assets transferred to IBRA assets did not progress as the government had expected. As of July 1999, 2 years after the outbreak of the East Asian financial crisis, a total of 234 cases were registered under the JITF (US$21.0 billion of external debts and Rp.13.4 trillion of domestic debts) (World Bank 1999). Cases resolved through restructuring and/or standstill agreements, totalled a mere 16 (US$2.9 billion of external debts and Rp.2.1 trillion of domestic debts). These accounted for only 4.1 per cent of total external debt and 1.0 per cent of total domestic debt, respectively.[13] Only 1.9 per cent of external debt and 0.6 per cent of domestic debt were restructured. Although the government attempted to accelerate corporate restructuring, progress was extremely slow, and Indonesia was the worst per-formed among the heavily damaged East Asian countries (Indonesia, Thailand, Korea and Malaysia) (Pomerleano 2000). The utilization of the INDRA scheme was also similar to that of JITF. At the initial stage, the lack of capacity of these agencies was to some extent responsible for delays in the restructuring process. In addition, a number of creditors were reluctant to sign restructuring plans. Creditors were unhappy with the tenor of the plan proposed by INDRA (i.e. a minimum of 8 years), and sought more rapid recovery through asset sales and/or claims to the personal assets of controlling shareholders. Debtors for their part were still attempting to negotiate bilateral write-offs with their creditors.

The reorganization and recapitalization of the banking sector progressed slowly in 1998 and 1999. By the middle of 2000, a nominal value of around

Rp.546 trillion (US$64 billion, or around 57 per cent of GDP) was transferred to the control of IBRA (World Bank 2000, p.13).[14] Domestic private banks were consolidated through closures and mergers, and their number was reduced from 164 in 1996 to 81 in 2000 (Sato 2001, pp.325–46). However, divestment of taken-over assets by IBRA was delayed for the first IBRA's 2 years. Criticism was levelled against IBRA both inside and outside Indonesia.[15] This was in part due to IBRA's limited staff capacity (in both quantity and quality) and also to perverse court decisions in favour of debtors. Moreover, debtors and the government were also directly responsible for the delays. A number of debtors remained reluctant to move beyond the step of MOU (Memorandum of Understanding) (indicative term sheet for the restructuring proposal) (World Bank 2001, p.2.4). That is to say, they did not implement the restructuring proposals, such as the disposal of assets, equity dilution and the repayment of creditors.[16] The government was also reluctant to formalize the loss of value that occurred through disposals of assets (World Bank 2000, p.13).[17] After 2000, the government intention moved forward more decisively by shifting assets back to the private sector and by recovering the value of assets (World Bank 2001, pp.2.1–2.6). IBRA began to dispose financial claims against corporates and outsource payment collections of small and medium claims (IBRA 1999 pp.51–5).[18] The disposal processes began to gather pace 3 years after the onset of the crisis.

With time offshore creditors became increasingly frustrated and exhausted as restructuring negotiations dragged on mainly due to the repetition of unattractive restructuring plans, uncooperative behaviours among debtor companies' owners (controlling shareholders) and continuously deteriorating business conditions in Indonesia. A number of offshore creditors abandoned their claims and sold them to distressed asset investors and traders at extremely large discounts.[19] Western investment banks and funds, which had expertise and known track records in Latin American distressed asset investments, aggressively bought up Indonesian claims. Indonesian investment banks also became involved in these transactions, often as intermediaries between Western investment banks and onshore buyers. Surprisingly, some debtor companies' owners also bought back their own debts at large discounts through these trades.[20] These transactions effectively allowed the debt 'haircuts' that the government had explicitly ruled out. Distressed asset transactions created not only new capital flows but also different types of cash-flow chains under the chaotic financial situations in Indonesia.

Most importantly, the restructuring of both the corporate and banking sectors imposed huge costs on the Indonesian economy. The cost of recapitalizing and rehabilitating the banking sector was initially estimated at Rp.643 trillion (US$91 billion) or about 60 per cent of GDP (ADB 2000, p.18). The government issued a total of Rp.510 trillion (US$72 billion) in domestic bonds for the purpose by the end of 1999. Bond issuance reached Rp.660 trillion (US$93 billion) and easily exceeded the original estimated cost by the end of 2000 (Sato 2001, p.356).[21] In addition, restructuring was associated with large operational expenses incurred by government institutions such as JITF, INDRA and IBRA and also costs to the private sector. For example, in 1999 IBRA recovered operational expenses of

Rp.900 billion (US$115 million) including salaries and consultant fees (IBRA 1999). Furthermore, shifting assets back from the state to the private sector was also costly, including expenses related to asset disposal, IPOs and privatization. The government needed to maximize income from the recovery of assets and minimize costs. IBRA in particular was charged with the responsibility for raising fresh capital from the divestment of assets to finance the state budget and recover expenses incurred in the process of the bailing out of the banking sector. However, IBRA's assets were heavily impaired.[22] Around Rp.149 trillion (US$21 billion), 64 per cent of IBRA's loan assets in custody, were relegated to in the lowest classification for non-performing assets by BI (IBRA 1999, p.23).[23] In this way, the collapse of cash-flow chains imposed huge and unnecessary costs on the economy.

Business groups' struggles during and after the crisis

Overall situation

By March 1998, the external debt of the Indonesian corporate sector had reached US$64.5 billion (around 46.7 per cent of Indonesia's external debt) and US$26.3 billion (around 64.5 per cent of total short-term external debt) was scheduled to mature by March 1999 (INDRA 1998a, p.3).[24] The situation was much worse and more complex than the Mexican crises of 1983 and 1993 (Kenward 1999; World Bank 1998). These facts show that the financial crisis in Indonesia was essentially an external debt problem in the corporate sector although most analysts have directed their attention to the banking sector. The problem in the banking sector naturally emerged as a domino effect from the corporate sector crisis, and the deepening of the problems in the banking sector stemmed from the significance and complexity of the corporate sector collapse. The size and complexity of the crisis were due to the pre-crisis financial activities of the business groups. With regards to the utilization of external debt, the data in Chapter 3 illustrate that the leading business groups accounted for most offshore debt. IBRA's asset portfolio also reflected the concentration of debts within the business groups. For example, at the end of 1999 the top 20 business group debtors accounted for around 34 per cent of the IBRA's debt exposure (IBRA 1999, p.50).[25] The case studies in Chapters 6 to 9 provide examples of the complexity of the financial transactions undertaken by the business groups. In short, the Indonesian crisis was a crisis of big capital.

The rupiah exchange rate collapsed in October 1997 and reached its historically lowest rate of Rp.16,650 per dollar in June 1998. The average annual rupiah exchange rate dropped sharply from Rp.2,327 in 1996 to Rp.2,890 in 1997 and then to Rp.10,224 in 1998. The rate thereafter remained at an extremely high level and has never recovered to below Rp.6,500. Foreign currency liabilities in rupiah terms skyrocketed to an unmanageable amount. Even the leading business groups, which had occupied monopolistic business positions and earned huge rupiah cash flows, were unable to fulfil their foreign currency obligations.[26]

A number of borrowers intentionally stopped servicing their debts in order to avoid selling assets at distressed prices. Most business groups defaulted on both external and domestic debts and owners attempted to protect their businesses from mounting repayment pressure. The financial crisis interrupted the ordinary operations of the business groups as the owners and the managers were forced to spend most of their time in debt negotiations with creditors. Many borrowers abused the chaotic situation and intentionally halted repayments in order to seek *haircuts* regardless of whether or not they could make repayments.[27]

The following sections survey the ways in which the four business groups included in the case studies negotiated and resolved their debt problems. The Salim Group, the Sinar Mas Group and the Gajah Tunggal Group, which held massive foreign currency debts, struggled to restructure their obligations. In particular, the Sinar Mas Group and the Gajah Tunggal Group lost control of their core assets. The Salim Group was able to maintain its flagship non-financial companies but lost a substantial part of its businesses. On the other hand, the Lippo Group, which was less leveraged and had limited foreign currency debts, managed to survive the crisis in fact. The results are consistent with the case studies in Chapters 6–9.

The Salim Group

The Salim Group entered the Indonesian crisis as one of the most indebted conglomerates. The non-financial listed companies in the group had accumulated debts of Rp.16.0 trillion (US$3.0 billion) in 1997 and Rp.22.2 trillion (US$2.8 billion) by 1998. Including the debts of the non-listed companies, the Salim Group accounted for a substantial portion of Indonesian corporate debt. The case study in Chapter 6 shows that the group aggressively introduced external funds to finance changes in its financial structure during the finance boom, and as a result, foreign currency loans occupied a large part of the group's debt structure. In addition, the Salim Group had for many years secured financing through political channels, such as directed finance from state banks with the support of former President Suharto. Therefore, the status of the Salim Group emerged as a vital matter for Indonesian economies, international relations and politics.

The main objective of the Salim Group in the restructuring process was how to protect the family's business interests and wealth from creditors. Management concentrated on negotiations with international lenders and IBRA.[28] The counter parties (creditors) in debt negotiations for the groups' non-bank companies, such as Indofood, Indocement and UIC, were mainly international lenders, while BCA negotiated mostly with IBRA.[29] The IBRA negotiations had heavy political overtones and were extremely difficult for the group. The government's budgetary needs and the political pressure led the agency to attempt to accelerate the disposal of Salim Group pledged assets related to the bailing out of BCA.[30] The assets (shares in companies) were purchased mainly by the joint-venture partners and through IBRA's auctions.[31] The Salim Group also attempted to buy back assets via offshore funds in order to maintain its empire. The attempts sparked political criticism of the group's lack of business ethics. In November 1999, FSPC banned IBRA from selling assets to the Salim Group (*Bloomberg News* 23 November 2000) until it had repaid the government for bailing out BCA. Furthermore, IBRA attempted to take the most profitable assets away from the Salim Group. The agency repeatedly requested that the group pledge its remaining stakes in Indocement and Indofood to cover the shortfall in the value of pledged assets and repayment obligations to the government in relation to BCA (*Bloomberg News* 4 October 2000, 4 December 2000). Repayment obligations emerged as the core issue in the Salim Group's debt work-out.

During the political chaos in May 1998, BCA, the flagship bank of the Salim Group, experienced a severe run on deposits. Panicked depositors reacted to rumours that banks with links to former President Suharto would be forced to close. Mobs also attacked BCA branches during the riots.[32] BCA received BLBI of more than Rp.20 trillion (US$2 billion) to cover the drain of deposits.[33] On 28 May 1998, BCA was placed under IBRA supervision and the agency appointed a team of proxy directors to manage BCA's daily operations. Violations of the Legal Lending Limit were immediately revealed. The majority of loan assets in BCA were debts of the Salim Group itself (BCA 2000, p.2).[34] The government required the Salim family to take responsibility for repaying government support, including BLBI.

In September 1998, the Salim Group concluded a Master of Settlement and Acquisition Agreement (MSAA) with IBRA on Rp.53 trillion (US$6.6 billion) in payment obligations following the Shareholders' Settlement Programme.[35] In December 1998, the Salim Group established Holdiko Perkasa (Holdiko), a special company for holding the group's pledged assets to IBRA, and transferred 108 companies to Holdiko as collateral against the group's repayment obligations. BCA's exposure of Rp.53 trillion to the Salim Group was also transferred to IBRA.[36] IBRA was tasked with recovering capital directly from the group and through the disposal of pledged assets under Holdiko. IBRA's recovery activities were the most critical issue facing the Salim Group. In May 1999, BCA was recapitalized by the government with Rp.60.9 trillion in government bonds, and IBRA then controlled 92.8 per cent of BCA share.[37] In April 2000, the bank was released from the status of BTO and IBRA supervision. In May 2000, BCA shares were offered to the public, and the bank exited from the Salim Group. Salim Group's repayment obligations to the government remained and the group's struggles to meet its obligations continued.

When the Indonesian crisis erupted, Indofood was massively in debt to overseas creditors. At the end of 1997, the company booked Rp.6.2 trillion (US$1.2 billion) in gross debt, including around US$1 billion in foreign debt.[38] However, Indofood was able to meet payments using the company's abundant cash flow through its monopolistic business position in instant noodles and flour milling. The company, therefore, was of central importance to the restructuring and revival of the Salim empire, and the Salim Group could not surrender majority ownership of Indofood to third parties, including IBRA. In June 1999, the Salim family sold its substantial shareholdings (around 40 per cent) in Indofood to First Pacific, one of the Salim Group's offshore investment companies in Hong Kong.[39] Furthermore, in July 1999, the group sold 12.56 per cent of its stake in Indofood in order to repay debts (*Bloomberg News* 16 July 1999). However, the group kept a 10.1 per cent direct holding of Indofood shares and therefore maintained its control of the company together with the 40 per cent of shares held by First Pacific.

At the same time, the Salim Group faced pressure from the government to relinquish Indofood's monopoly position in flour milling and also to pledge more shares of Indofood and/or repay debt to IBRA. In January and April 1999, IBRA sold all pledged shares of Indofood (5.5 and 4.75 per cent stakes respectively) to pay off the Salim Group's debt to IBRA. Nevertheless, IBRA requested that the group pledge its remaining stakes in Indofood as the agency attempted to obtain the most profitable group assets in order to accelerate debt collection. The group strongly resisted this pressure. However, in September 1999, the Salim Group announced the decision to separate Indofood's flour milling business (Bogasari) into four subsidiaries and to divest a maximum 60 per cent of each subsidiary to strategic and/or financial investors.[40] Bogasari was perhaps the most notorious as a symbol of crony capitalism under the Suharto regime. The Salim Group attempted to obtain a compromise from IBRA by opening and disposing Bogasari.

Indofood's capacity to generate cash flow for the group was the key to the rehabilitation of the Salim Group. In July 2000, Indofood successfully issued Rp.1 trillion (US$103 million) in 5-year domestic bonds. In 2001, Indofood retired US$200 million in debt, thus halving the total debt level of 1997.[41] In 2002, Indofood obtained a US$100 million term loan facility from offshore banks and issued US$280 million in 5-year Eurobonds to refinance its existing debt.[42] By 2003, Indofood had nearly returned to normal operational levels. In Minsky's terms, the high capacity of Indofood to produce cash flows maintained a positive margin of safety even under the pressure of the Indonesian crisis, and therefore the Salim Group was able to shelter Indofood from the debt burden of the group.

Indocement by way of contrast declared a standstill for all debt service in July 1998. Immediately after this, creditors formed a Steering Committee for restructuring negotiations.[43] In August 1999, Indocement and Indo Kodeco Cement (Indo Kodeco), a subsidiary of Indocement, presented a restructuring plan (named 'A Terms' or 'Stand-alone Restructuring Plan') to the creditors.[44] In October 1999, the Salim Group and Heidelberger Zement (Heidelberger), a German-based international cement company, entered into an agreement to jointly control Indocement and Indo Kodeco. In April 2000, Indocement, the Steering Committee and Heidelberger agreed to the term sheet (named 'B Terms' or 'Indocement/Heidelberger Restructuring Plan'). In September 2000, Indocement merged with Indo Kodeco as part of the debt-restructuring process. Finally, all parties agreed to the restructuring of Indocement's outstanding debt of Rp.7.8 trillion.[45]

The debt-restructuring proposal promised the satisfaction of principal and accrued interest claims, the installation of a cash-sweep mechanism and the upfront issuance of warrants to all creditors. The restructured debt had a repayment period of 8 years from the restructuring date and included an amortization schedule. As explained above, the programme had two optional terms depending on the participation of Heidelberger (A and B Terms). The A Terms were to be applied before Heidelberger began joint operations with Indocement, and thereafter the B Terms were to come into force. A Terms had warrants for 8 per cent of Indocement shares (4 per cent upfront and an additional 4 per cent if Heidelberger did not participate), interest rates of LIBOR plus 200 basis points with step up margins for a US dollar tranche, Long-Term Prime Rate plus 100 basis points with step up margins for a Japanese yen tranche, 15 per cent for a rupiah tranche and budget control by the Monitoring Committee. If Indocement and Heidelberger chose to move to B Terms, it had to reduce the debt by US$150 million (through debt buy-back by Heidelberger and the conversion into Indocement's equity).[46] The interest rate would stay at LIBOR plus 200 basis points subject to the target debt level. No budget control was required, and an additional 4 per cent warrants to the creditors could be waived.

In April 2001, Heidelberger placed Indocement under its control by holding its 61.7 per cent shares through purchasing a part of the government's stake in Indocement, the previously explained US$150 million debt to equity conversion and subscription of right issues (UBS March 2003, p.114).[47] Finally, the Salim Group was released from Indocement debt but lost control of the company. This meant a substantial shrinkage of the Salim Empire, which had been built during the Suharto regime.

In this way, the Salim Group was able to resolve the debt problems of its major group companies, although the group had to expend a large amount of management time and costs for debt negotiations. The group lost control of some core businesses, such as BCA and Indocement, but was able to defend ownerships in other core businesses, such as Indofood. In addition, the Salim Group's overseas assets were also untouched by creditors.[48] This outcome differed from the debt restructuring of the Sinar Mas Group and the Gajah Tunggal Group as described later. The Salim Group's payment obligations to IBRA in relation to BCA were a setback for the Salim empire in Indonesia as the disposal of pledged assets and repayment of obligation led to the dissolution of the group as constituted during the Suharto year.

The Lippo Group

As is explained in Chapter 7, the Lippo Group was unable to gain access to external debt on a large scale due to the nature of its businesses (i.e. real estate and finance), and the rumour-driven liquidity crisis in 1995. The Lippo Group had therefore pursued an equity-driven funding strategy. In addition, prior to the Indonesian crisis, the Riady family liquidated its investments in Indonesia through changes in the holding structures, IPOs and the introduction of third party partners. As a result, the damage to the group and the family was limited in comparison to the major conglomerates. The family was able to manage the group on a relatively healthy financial basis even during the crisis.[49] Furthermore, as the Riady family had maintained a reasonable distance from Suharto, the group succeeded in avoiding severe political attacks such as those directed at the Salim Group and the other business groups after the regime collapsed.[50] However, once Suharto ended his 32-year reign in 1998, the Riady family developed close tie to his successor President Habibie and his team. The Habibie government frequently asked Mochtar Riady for advice and support on the repatriation of Chinese Indonesian capital to Indonesia and the restructuring of the banking sector.[51] It is obvious that the relatively sound financial structure of the group had enabled the family to step into the political arena.

At the end of 1998, the gross debt of the Lippo Group's Indonesian listed non-bank companies was Rp.4,346 billion (US$612 million) gross debts. Including the setting off of cash and cash equivalents against debt, the net debts totalled Rp.3,043 billion (US$429 million).[52] Excluding joint-venture listed companies (Bukit Sentul, Aryaduta Hotels and Siloam Gleneagles), the gross and net debt were Rp.3,071 billion (US$432 million) and Rp.1,842 billion (US$259 million) respectively. The external debt of the group's Indonesian companies was around US$150 million.[53] The Lippo Group debt was therefore much smaller than that of other leading business groups in Indonesia. The group restructured US$100 million in debt through JITF in 1999 and around 60 per cent of the group's debt by the middle of 1999 (*Bloomberg News* 16 June 1999; World Bank 1999, p.2.4).[54] The speed of restructuring was much faster than that of other leading business groups. The Lippo Group's low-leveraged financial positions and less reliance on external debt facilitated and accelerated debt restructuring.

The Lippo Group also pushed forward the restructuring of Lippo Bank, its flag-ship company. In late 1998, Lippo Bask wrote off more than one trillion in bad loans (*Jakarta Post* 1 December 1998). In December 1998, Lippo Bank raised Rp.1,008 billion through a twenty-for-one rights issue. The bank maintained positive net worth, but the CAR did not reach 4 per cent. In May 1999, Lippo Bank was recapitalized by the government.[55] However, the recapitalization required the banks' owners to contribute 20 per cent in cash. The Lippo Group sold around 40 per cent of its shares in Lippo General Insurance (Lippo Life Utama), Lippo Life's subsidiary insurance company, to AIG (United States) and raised around Rp.3 trillion for this contribution. On the basis of their recapitalization operation the group achieved financial stability in its Indonesian subsidiaries.

Lippo Group's overseas activities began to recover. In the middle of 2000, the Lippo Group formed AcrossAsia Multimedia by consolidating its multimedia businesses, such as broadband, e-commerce and internet solutions, and listed shares on the Hong Kong stock exchange. AcrossAsia Multimedia held a major-ity stake in Multipolar, a group company in listed Jakarta, which in turn held 39 per cent of the Matahari, a department store also listed in Jakarta. The group created another vertical holding structure between three group companies, AcrossAsia Multimedia, Multipolar and Matahari, and obtained liquidity in the equity market. At the same time, the group expanded cross-border shareholding structures between Indonesia and Hong King to increase its presence in overseas market and hedge political risks against its ownerships in Indonesian operations.[56] Thus the Lippo Group continued with its pre-crisis financial strategy in the post-crisis period.

The Sinar Mas Group

As in the case of the collapse of Enron Corp. in the United States, large-scale debt problems in Indonesia were often coupled with fraudulent financial reporting, concealed debts, complex financial structures and a long restructuring process. The case of the Sinar Mas Group was emblematic of the trusts and turns of debt work-outs in the aftermath of the collapse of complex cash-flow chains. In addition, the group's debt-restructuring process illustrates the costs of crisis at the corporate level.

The Sinar Mas Group's debt problems began with BII, the flagship company of its financial service division and one of the top private banks in Indonesia. BII did not have outstanding BLBI at the end of 1999, but its lending assets were heavily damaged like other leading banks in Indonesia. Furthermore, the bank had breached the Legal Lending Limit regulations, and around 60 per cent of its loans (around US$1.25 billion) were directed to companies within the Sinar Mas Group (*Bloomberg News* 10 February 2001). In May 1999, BII was recapitalized by the government, and as a result, the government obtained a majority stake in the bank.[57] In August 1999, the management of BII was changed from the Widjaja family to IBRA appointees. The family also surrendered BII shares to complete the restructuring of the Asia Pulp and Paper Co. Ltd (APP) Group. At the end of 2003, the government sold these shares to the public, and Sorak, an investment consortium jointly owned by four overseas investors, obtained a majority stake in BII.[58] Kookmin Bank, one of Sorak's owners, sent its management team to BII. The government bailout of BII resulted in BII's exit from the Sinar Mas Group.

The vital issue for the Sinar Mas Group was the debt problems of the APP Group (the paper and pulp division). The APP Group held the largest offshore debt in Indonesia, and the issue became highly politicized as overseas courts and governments became involved. The APP Group was one of the most indebted companies in East Asia during the finance boom.[59] It had evolved a complex financial structure as it had increased leverage. The group's debt was held at both the holding and operating company levels and accumulated to around US$12 to 13 billion by 2000. The group had to make annual interest payments of between US$800 million and US$1 billion, the payments that were larger than the group's EBITDA (*Bloomberg News* 2 February 2001). Lenders and investors included not only onshore and offshore banks but also trading companies, leasing companies, institutional and retail investors and ECAs in a variety of countries.[60] The group had aggressively deployed various financial products, such as syndicated loans, notes and bonds, asset-backed securities (ABS) and export credits. Complex cash-flow chains were created between the group and global financial markets. Nevertheless, at the early stages of the Indonesian crisis, the APP Group had still been considered one of the few Indonesian companies that were unlikely to default.[61] The group had access to a relatively large foreign currency income through its export activities. Nevertheless, the pressure of debt service and an extended and complex process of restructuring finally pushed the group into solvency.

In the middle of 2000, the APP Group began to reveal the extent of its distress. In July 2000, APP arranged a US$100 million loan at a 25 per cent interest rate in order to avoid immediate default. Concerns regarding the group's repayment capacity had heightened, and a number of stockbrokers began reporting on the group's liquidity problems. The share price of APP also sharply dropped.[62] At the time, the Sinar Mas Group payment disputes erupted between the group and its suppliers. Furthermore, in order to create cash to meet debt-service obligations, the group attempted to dispose of non-core assets, such as power plants, packaging units and tissue production plants. APP, the offshore holding company, collected dividends from its operating subsidiaries. In September 2000, the APP Group submitted an exchange offer to the investors of a US$2.0 million bond maturing in 2001 and sent a signal to the market that the group was close to default.

In the early part of 2001, the APP Group announced its intention to reschedule and restructure its debt (*UBS* February 2003, pp.63–78). At the same time, the group had asked some of its main suppliers to agree to a payments extension of 180 days (*AWSJ* 30 January 2001). In February 2001, Tjiwi Kimia, one of the group's operating companies, failed to pay US$43.3 million in interest payments on two bonds.[63] Finally, on 12 March 2001, the APP Group announced a debt standstill and suspended all payments.[64] When APP Group defaulted, the total debt of the group was around US$14 billion.[65] The situation worsened as the group declared that financial accounts from 1997 to 1999 could not be relied on due to false statements.[66] The group also missed the filing deadline for its audited financial statements for the financial year 2000 in related jurisdictions. In November 2001, Arthur Andersen, the group's auditor, resigned. A large number of legal actions, including a US class action suit, were entered against the APP Group in relation to false disclosure.

In January 2002, the APP Group and investors in Rp.2.4 trillion in domestic bond agreed to a change in payment terms.[67] In February 2002, the APP Group proposed a debt-restructuring plan to its other creditors. However, the plan was immediately rejected by creditors as it was obviously too favourable to the APP Group.[68] Creditors also cited unequal treatment of domestic bondholders and creditors in China versus other creditors.[69] In April 2002, the chief financial officer of the APP Group was forced to resign in response to the creditors' criticisms. In the middle of 2002, creditors became impatient with the APP Group's failure and/or refusal to put forward a feasible restructuring plan. In June 2002, Deutsche Bank and BNP Paribas launched a lawsuit against the group in Singapore in order to ask the court to appoint an administrator for debt restructuring.[70] The banks' legal actions were supported by a majority of creditors but support was not unanimous.[71] IBRA initially announced its support for the legal action but later dropped its support. In August, Grant Thornton, the new auditor of the

APP Group, issued its disclaimers opinion in the 2001 accounts. The situation grew increasingly more chaotic.[72]

In the latter half of 2002 IBRA, which held around US$1 billion in APP Group debt, became more actively involved in formulating the group's restructuring plan. In September 2002, IBRA dispatched Burhanuddin Abdullah, the former economics minister and deputy governor of BI, and five other officials in order to monitor the group's finances. In December 2002, the APP Group produced a new restructuring proposal, which was agreed and signed by IBRA and domestic bondholders (*Bloomberg News* 18 December 2002).[73] A steering committee representing offshore bondholders rejected the proposal once again, as protection of bondholders was still insufficient. Instead, the committee submitted a counter proposal to the APP Group, which asserted the claims of creditors' legal rights and structures and included the wealth of the Widjaja family (UBS December 2002, p.50). Four key export agencies of Japan, Sweden, the United States and Germany, also rejected the proposal. Finally, other creditors threw out the proposal (*Bloomberg News* 18 December 2002). In March 2003, domestic bondholders objected to the restructuring proposal and appealed to maintain the originally agreed terms for them. Since then, the restructuring negotiation has not moved forward as creditors had expected. The attitude of the Widjaja family has produced frustration among creditors.[74] A number of creditors were extremely disappointed with the situation and sold their exposure on the secondary market.[75] On 10 March 2003, 11 ambassadors of the countries whose Export Credit Agencies (ECAs) were exposure to the APP Group sent a letter to the then President Megawati to bring pressure to bear on the Indonesian government.[76] The APP Group's debt problem had finally emerged in the international political arena.

In June 2003, the APP Group, IBRA, nine ECAs, two Japanese trading companies and domestic bondholders reached non-binding agreements on a revised restructuring plan and proposed the plan to the other creditors.[77] In September 2003, the APP Group also presented a debt to equity swap proposal of APP China to creditors.[78] The proposal requested the creditors to convert existing all APP China debt into equity, in order to release APP's guarantee.[79] In October 2003, the creditors of APP China voted in favour of the proposed debt to equity swap.[80] In the same month, the APP Group, IBRA and most ECAs signed the Master Restructuring Agreement (MRA) (approximately 40 per cent of creditors). However, the group was unable to obtain a majority approval for the agreement and the approval of more than 90 per cent of creditors was required to make the restructuring plan effective.[81] The expiration date of the negotiations was stretched until March 2004.

Around the same period, IBRA, which played a central role in the APP Group's debt-restructuring negotiations, was forced to sell its exposure to the group due to strong pressure from the government to raise funds for the state budget. IBRA finally decided to auction its APP assets but required bidders to support the restructuring proposal as a prior condition. In December 2003, Orleans Offshore Investment (Singapore) won the bid for IBRA's US$880 million exposure to the APP Group for Rp.1.8 trillion (*Bloomberg News* 19 December 2003).[82]

Some creditors voiced strong objections to the restructuring proposal. In particular, the secured creditors claimed that they should be treated differently from unsecured creditors. In late 2002, Gramercy Advisors, Oaktree Capital Management and GE Capital filed litigation against APP in New York seeking priority in payments.[83] Even among ECAs, US EXIM, which had US$104 million exposure to the APP Group, took a different view and separate course of action against the APP Group. The agency judged that the debt-restructuring proposal, which was supported by IBRA and other ECAs, was not fair and equitable to creditors and that the repayment conditions did not adequately reflect the debtors' debt-service capacity. The agency filed a lawsuit against APP in October 2003. The APP Group also launched counter legal actions against some of the secured creditors.[84] These legal battles delayed progress towards agreement and implementation of the restructuring plan.

In December 2004, the APP Group obtained approval on a restructuring proposal covering 90 per cent of creditors to the group's operating companies. The creditors, including Goldman Sachs, JP Morgan, Deutsche Bank and UBS, issued letters supporting the restructuring proposal and stating that the approach taken by Gramercy Advisors and Oaktree Capital Management was not acceptable to them (*Bloomberg News* 6 December 2004). Gramercy Advisors and Oaktree Capital Management attempted to block the restructuring plan.[85] Nevertheless, in April 2005, the APP Group resumed the payments to creditors who had signed onto the restructuring agreement. The APP Group had spent 5 years, incurred huge costs and sustained perhaps irreparable damage to its reputation in order to achieve the final restructuring. The APP Group, the centrepiece of the Sinar Mas Group, was placed under the control of creditors. Nevertheless, the APP Group still faces an uphill struggle to remain a solvent corporate entity.

The AFP Group, the food and property division of the Sinar Mas Group, was no exception. In 2000, the AFP Group's net worth was less than nil. Since October 2001, the group has rescheduled payments on more than US$1 billion in debt in a series of deals.[86] It was revealed that AFP and Golden Agri-Resources, the core offshore listed companies of the AFP Group, held S$625 million (US$338 million) in deposits and S$88 million (US$47 million) in swap transactions with BII Bank Limited (Cook Islands) controlled by the Widjaja family. The companies also held S$85 million (US$46 million) in deposits with BII under the control of IBRA. In addition, it was disclosed that some of the deposits in BII Bank had been lent to other companies in the Sinar Mas Group.[87] In short, the Sinar Mas Group had used the AFP Group to finance struggling Widjaja family businesses. Naturally, the bank had lost the capacity to repay these funds to the AFP Group. Investors and creditors were sharply critical of the family's management and, like the APP Group, the AFP Group had to carry out debt-restructuring negotiations under extremely heavy pressures from creditors.

The Gajah Tunggal Group

Although the Gajah Tunggal Group was a medium-sized business group in Indonesia, it had accumulated a volume of debt comparable to the top business groups. As the case study in Chapter 9 illustrates, the group fully exploited the booming financial markets. At the end of 1998, the group's listed non-bank companies held Rp.16.5 trillion (US$2.1 billion) in gross debt, and net debt was Rp.15.7 trillion (US$2.0 billion). In addition, BDNI, the group's flagship bank, had sizable borrowings through syndicated loans, bonds and FRCDs (excluding interbank borrowings and deposits).[88] Total group debt was estimated at more than US$3.0 billion (Sato 2001, p.388). In addition, the Gajah Tunggal Group was one of the top five Indonesian private borrowers in the offshore debt market and had accumulated huge foreign currency debts.[89] Although the group was able to produce some foreign currency income through its export activities, this income could not meet such huge foreign currency debt-service requirement.[90] The sharp depreciation of the rupiah pushed the group quickly into insolvency.

The first problems emerged at BDNI. During the Indonesian crisis, BDNI faced a severe liquidity shortage and was heavily reliant on BLBI (Rp.28.4 trillion).[91] The bank was placed under government control in April 1998 and finally ordered to cease operations as a BBO bank (frozen bank) in August 1998. BDNI's loan assets were virtually worthless, as a large proportion of loans had been directed to group companies.[92] The bank did not qualify for recapitalization. It was liquidated and its assets transferred to IBRA.[93] Sjamsul Nursalim, the bank's owner, signed a MSAA with IBRA under the Shareholder Settlement Program in September 1998, established Tunas Sepadan Investama (Nursalim's special holding company for the programme) in December 1998, and pledged 12 companies, including Gajah Tunggal and GT Petrochem Industries, Dipasena Citra Darmaja, a part of the BDNI's BLBI repayment obligations. The promissory note issued by Nursalim under the programme (Rp.27.5 trillion) was the second largest, following that of Soedono Salim for BCA (Rp.52.6 trillion) (IBRA 1999, p.27). Through this transaction, the Nursalim family lost control of the pledged companies.

At the same time, other group companies revealed debt-service problems in turn. In April 1998, Gajah Tunggal, the group flagship company, sought lenders' support to stretch the terms of US$916 million in foreign currency debt maturing in 1999 and 2000. Other group companies also attempted to reschedule payments. However, the group's huge debts and the worsening political and economic situation made restructuring negotiations extremely difficult. In 1998, the group's shrimp farms in Lampung, South Sumatra, were looted by mobs and processing factories were severely damaged. The sales value of Dipasena Citra Darmaja (shrimp farming) dropped significantly to a sixth of the appraised value (that is, Rp.4.0 trillion) (*Bloomberg News* 6 May 2000). Finally, negotiations on the group's core debt restructuring took almost 4 years to achieve any real progress.

In 2002, GT Kabel Indonesia, the group's cable manufacturer, obtained creditors' approval to reschedule around 81 per cent of US$131.2 million in debt. In 2002, Gajah Tunggal also concluded a restructuring of around US$300 million 'non-IBRA debts' with international lenders (UBS 2005, pp.107–9). Under the agreed restructuring programme, Gajah Tunggal bought back US$245 million in debt at a discount and restructured the remaining amount into a new

US$296 million FRN with principal amortization until 2008 and a step-up coupon. In 2004, IBRA sold its 78 per cent stake in Gajah Tunggal and 20 per cent stake in GT Petrochem Industries to Garibaldi Venture Fund (Singapore) for Rp.1.89 trillion (US$213 million).[94] Garibaldi Venture Fund also absorbed the loans payable to BDNI, which were largely on-lent to Gajah Tunggal's subsidiaries. A part of the payments due in 2004 were retired by Gajah Tunggal through the issuance of a US$53 million FRN. GT Petrochem Industries also concluded debt restructuring through debt to equity swap, and creditors, including HSBC, took a 34.9 per cent stake in the company. On all, the completion of the Gajah Tunggal Group's debt restructuring took around 8 years to complete.[95]

11 Conclusions

This study has applied Hyman P. Minsky's financial instability hypothesis to an open and developing economy. We have seen how fragile and unstable financial structures, which ultimately led to the financial crisis, emerged during the finance boom. Indonesia rapidly opened its domestic financial markets to global financiers and experienced an extreme boom-bust cycle within 10 years of liberalization. The evolution of financial structures during the finance boom from 1994 to 1997 enabled Indonesia's corporate capitalists to pursue a range of economic and political objectives. Taken together, these actions increased systemic risk and ultimately led to a historic economic depression, the impact of which has included human suffering on a massive scale and political instability for at least a generation.

Minsky identifies the following characteristics of capitalist economies:

1 Investment in long-life capital assets by debt finance;
2 Chains of payment commitments, that is, indebtedness;
3 The existence of profit-seeking and forward-looking capitalists.

He argues that speculative financing units, which need finance to fund the shortfall between cash inflows and payment commitments, endogenously expand due to capitalists' profit-seeking and forward-looking behaviour. Finally, he concludes that financial structures evolve endogenously and fragility and instability emerge in capitalist economies. In order to explain the process of evolving financial structures, Minsky uses the following dichotomy in his model:

1 The real (or non-financial/non-intermediary) sector that invests in capital assets by cash-flow-matched finances (hedging financing units); and
2 The financial (or intermediary) sector that maximizes margin revenues through cash-flow-mismatched finances (speculative or Ponzi financing units).

Based on this dichotomous model, he assumes that the positive margin of safety in the real sector encourages the financial sector to evolve towards speculative financing, that is, cash-flow-mismatched financing. The financial structure of the economy thereby becomes fragile and unstable.

Indebtedness, capitalists and the financial sector play the key roles in the financial instability hypothesis. In particular, as Irving Fisher argues in his debt-deflation theory, indebtedness plays the most important role in the creation of financial fragility and instability. Indebtedness tends to increase dramatically when combined with euphoric forecasts. It has devastating power to break down the economy and discount asset values when combined with forecasts of economic slowdown. Then, in the words of John M. Keynes, volatility in the behaviour of indebted agents and the value of capital assets becomes a 'beauty contest' among financiers.

In the 1990s, intensifying liberalization pressures forced developing economies to open their financial markets to internationally mobile capital. Their financial markets were rapidly integrated into global markets. Internationally mobile capital enthusiastically financed not only the financial but also corporate sectors. Capitalists in developing economies, which had generally both financial and non-financial businesses, also aggressively absorbed finance for investment. Offshore commercial banks enthusiastically lent to these capitalists with the result that they were integrated into chains of international payment commitments. Developing country capitalists rapidly leveraged their financial positions. As a result, speculative financing units expanded rapidly and fragility and instability emerged in developing economies. In sum, the situation of the developing economies in the 1990s boom was almost identical to the endogenous processes of financial fragility and instability in the financial instability hypothesis.

However, Minsky was primarily concerned with closed and advanced economies. The present study proposes the following adjustments, corrections and clarifications to Minsky's theory in order to apply it to an open and developing economy:

1   A focus on the 'leverage of financial positions' as the measurement of speculation at the same level as the mismatch of cash flows in the model;
2   The introduction of foreign exchange risk into the model as a measurement of speculation, considering the fact that borrowers in developing economies must hedge foreign currency positions against their home currencies;
3   The introduction of 'liberalization' (which allowed complex, advanced and massive financial transactions to enter developing economies) into the model as a disequilibrating force;
4   A focus on the 'corporate (non-financial/non-intermediary) sector' in the model as speculative financing units in the evolution of financial structures, considering the fact that capitalists in developing economies generally form business groups and often use non-financial group companies as vehicles to obtain funds for other group members;
5   The introduction of 'offshore financial institutions' into the model as a disequilibrating force that has a major impact on the financial structures of developing economies;
6   The introduction of the domestic capitalists' 'complex motivations' into the model as a disequilibrating force that has a major impact on the financial structures.

Based on this modified financial instability hypothesis, this book has analysed Indonesia's finance boom in the 1990s and the growing fragility and instability of the Indonesian economy during the period. We have focused on the corporate sector, the financial activities of which were outside of government control.

On the liability side of the economy, Indonesia in the 1990s experienced an age of private capital mobilization. In the 1980s, due to the decline in oil and gas prices and related state revenues, the state was no longer able to act as the main agent of economic development as it had done in the 1970s. The government expected the private sector to restructure the Indonesian economy through the expansion of non-oil and gas and export-oriented businesses. Simultaneously, the government also expected the private sector to mobilize private capital to finance this restructuring. The basic financial architecture to achieve this purpose had been already installed before the 1990s through the adoption of a series of financial liberalization measures. In addition, with regards to external debt, although Indonesia needed to control its growth, the government pursued a policy of creating room for private sector external borrowing by reducing public external debt. The government basically expected the private sector to raise the necessary funds through its direct access to offshore financial markets.

In the 1990s, the private corporate sector, which dominated Indonesia's real economy, was offered three choices for fund-raising: equity finance, domestic debt finance and offshore debt finance. The combination of these three forms of finance determined the leverage and characteristics of the sector's financial structure and ultimately the fragility and instability of Indonesia's financial system. From this viewpoint, this study has argued that the shift in the sector's financial structure in the 1990s occurred during the period from 1994 to the outbreak of the East Asian crisis. This was the 'finance boom'. During this period, both finance providers and recipients became extremely enthusiastic and all of the three options above were fully utilized. In particular, offshore capitalists maintained a euphoric view of the sector's potential and financial position and enthusiastically pumped funds into it.

At the beginning of the 1990s, the private corporate sector faced two dynamic funding opportunities in the context of the liberalized financial architecture: an equity finance boom and a domestic banking boom. During the period 1990–2, tight monetary policies, epitomized by the 'Sumarlin Shock' in February 1992, were adopted to control inflation. This policy weighed heavily on the stock market and slowed down the growth of the domestic banks, which, nevertheless, continued to increase their exposure to the private corporate sector. The sector thereby increased its leverage and reduced after-funding-cost profitability and debt-service capacity. At the time, offshore bankers were still sceptical about financing the sector and did not contribute to the increase in the sector's leverage. In sum, the increase in leverage was driven by domestic bank money during this period.

The period 1993–4 was a turning point in the 1990s. Global mobile capital began moving into emerging markets on a large scale, in particular, non-Japan Asian markets. The Indonesian stock market entered its second equity finance boom of the 1990s by actively absorbing global capital. The private corporate sector significantly improved its after-funding-cost profitability and debt-service capacity. In addition, offshore strategic investors increased foreign direct investment in the private corporate sector, mainly in manufacturing. In particular, Japanese manufacturing companies started shifting new investments from China to South-East Asia, mainly into Thailand and Indonesia. This led to a foreign direct investment boom in the corporate sector. Furthermore, offshore bankers also started taking risks in the private corporate sector. Euphoria emerged in the minds of investors, lenders and borrowers at the onset of the finance boom.

The finance boom lasted from 1994 to the onset of the East Asian crisis. Contagion effects from the Mexican peso crisis in 1995 temporarily depressed the equity market in Indonesia. Nevertheless, supported by positive factors such as the privatization of state companies and the Asian investment boom, equity financing recovered until the end of the finance boom. Debt finance expanded on a significantly larger scale than equity finance. With regards to the domestic banking sector, the government faced several critical problems, such as bad debt (particularly in the state banks), rapidly increasing exposure to the property sector and the endemic violation of new bank regulations for market-based controls. The government was forced to introduce non-market interventions in the banking sector, such as limitations on the banks' exposure to the property sector and lending and borrowing by non-bank finance companies. However, other activities of the financial sector were not restricted. Thus domestic debt in the corporate sector increased steeply and steadily. The most important source of finance for private corporate sector during the period was offshore debt. The government did not impose any restrictions on the sector's fund raising through offshore debt finance but rather welcomed the sector's access to offshore loans. Under the finance boom, offshore lenders provided enormous amounts of capital to the sector and the external debt of Indonesian corporates grew much faster than domestic debt.

As a result, the private corporate sector rapidly expanded its balance sheet and steeply leveraged its financial structures. Moreover, in the middle of the finance boom, its after-funding-cost profitability and debt-service capacity started to decline. Nevertheless, offshore lenders were caught up in a 'mania' as described by Kindleberger and further accelerated lending to the sector (Kindleberger 1978). The sector dramatically increased its reliance on external and foreign currency debt. This increase in external debt meant that mobile capital was built into the financial structure and that market-based foreign currency debt accounted for a substantial share of the liability structure. In sum, the rapid increase in leverage led by offshore debt finance created fragility and instability in private non-financial firms. The realization of fragility and instability, that is, the shift from *mania* to 'panic' and/or 'crash' depended on the outcome of Keynes' *beauty contests* among offshore lenders.

As external debt accumulated in the private corporate sector, bargaining power clearly shifted from offshore lenders to Indonesian borrowers. As the empirical studies in Chapter 5 demonstrate, Indonesian borrowers significantly improved their borrowing terms during the finance boom. They increased borrowing volumes, decreased costs and stretched tenors. In addition, offshore lenders' enthusiasm led not only to improved terms but also to an expansion in the range of borrowers enjoying access to foreign debt. Prior to the finance boom, only flagship companies of the leading business groups were able to raise funds through offshore syndicated debt. However, once the finance boom got underway, offshore lenders actively provided offshore syndicated debt to second-class borrowers, such as elite business groups' second-tier subsidiaries and medium-size business groups. Offshore lenders also accepted even *pribumi* companies, Suharto-related companies, and other politically connected firms, which they had avoided in the past. During the latter half of the finance boom, offshore lenders started accepting riskier finance for Indonesian private borrowers, such as real estate, share collateral, acquisition and large-scale projects. Offshore bond investors seeking high-risk, high-return investment opportunities invested in fixed income bonds issued by Indonesian companies. Even offshore individuals purchased these bonds without adequate knowledge of the firms involved. Furthermore, non-traditional Asian lenders, such as Korean and Taiwanese financial institutions, moved aggressively into the Indonesian market. This situation was particularly true in the private corporate sector, which was preferred by offshore investors and lenders. Offshore parties entered Kindleberger's *mania* phase.

Meanwhile, domestic banks were prevented from increasing or even maintaining their exposure to favoured clients. Domestic banks were forced to extend funds to higher-risk borrowers and more speculative projects, such as medium and small traders and real estate development. Competition from overseas and other domestic lenders sharply increased funding costs also pushed domestic banks to expand into riskier fields. In other words, rapidly mobilized onshore and offshore private capital forced domestic banks to expand their balance sheets, simultaneously driving down portfolio quality. As a result, while internationally mobilized private funds went to favoured borrowers, domestically mobilized private funds largely went to high-risk clients. This was another aspect of Indonesia's financial structure during the finance boom.

During the finance boom contact points between the private corporate sector and offshore markets multiplied and diversified. The relationship between the Indonesian economy and global financial markets became more complex. In addition, as argued earlier, the increase in leverage, the spread and deepening of mobile capital, the increased reliance on external debt, the introduction of riskier and more complicated financial transactions and the double mismatch of maturity profiles and currencies were all characteristic of the boom, and caused the financial structure to become fragile and unstable. Minsky identifies 'evolving financial structures' on the basis of the mismatch between cash inflows and outflows, that is, the mismatch of tenor. However, as argued earlier, in applying Minsky's theory to open and developing economies such as Indonesia it is necessary to consider a variety of alternative factors as the driving force in the introduction of fragility and instability into financial structures.

Indonesian business groups, the main recipients of private offshore funds, initiated complex financial activities during the finance boom. Behind the financial activities were complex motivations reflecting political, social and economic factors specific to the 1990s. During this period, Indonesian business groups operated under the following concurrent yet contradictory assumptions about the near future: (i) the approaching denouement of Suharto's New Order regime raised concerns about political uncertainty in the post-Suharto era and (ii) mushrooming domestic investment opportunities, rapidly expanding domestic markets and increasing foreign direct investment meant that in the short period investment prospects in Indonesia were favourable. It was in this context that business group owners had to decide whether to cash out of or cash into Indonesia.

Suharto brazenly used political power to grant new and ever more profitable business opportunities to his children and other cronies. This ultimately gave rise to the anti-KKN (corruption, collusion and nepotism) movement against the Suharto regime. Political attacks were also directed against the business groups allied to Suharto. Protests often included elements of anti-Chinese sentiment as most business groups belonged to Chinese Indonesians. Yet Chinese capital had reason to feel threatened by Suharto. Their pre-eminent position was being challenged by Suharto and his children, as in the case of the MOBNAS, national car project. At the same time, three decades of political quiescence that had provided the basis of rapid capital accumulation came to an end. Labour disputes became more frequent and militant and put pressure on business groups' operating costs. There were no guarantees that the political situation in post-Suharto Indonesia would be more conducive to big business. Populist politicians were gaining influence and popularity, and some of these political entrepreneurs saw the conglomerates as easy targets.

However, on the positive side, the Indonesian economy was in the midst of an economic and investment boom. Foreign direct investment, which aimed at cost-efficient production using low-cost labour, rushed into the country. In addition, the so-called Asian boom brought a variety of investments into Indonesia. These created new business opportunities for Indonesian business groups through joint ventures and better job prospects for Indonesian people. Increased domestic demand created further investment opportunities for business groups. Even under the earlier-mentioned unfavourable political and social business conditions, business group owners could not resist such lucrative business opportunities.

The finance boom in many ways resolved the dilemma, because it enabled business group owners to make new investments without additional contributions of their own capital. Moreover, it enabled them to liquidate their Indonesian investments. In other words, the finance boom enabled them to preserve and even increase liquidity in private hands. To achieve this purpose, the business group owners fundamentally changed their ownership and corporate control methods. They abandoned 100 per cent ownership and adopted majority or single largest shareholding structures. While business group owners reduced their capital contributions to their businesses through the introduction of third party capital, they continued to control the businesses. This has often been discussed as a minority shareholder problem. In addition, cheap offshore debt finance also helped them to liquidate their investments without losing control of their businesses.

Active leveraging was often used not only to raise returns to shareholders' equity, but also to create liquidity for business group owners.

Based on this financial strategy, business group owners aggressively absorbed third party capital through equity and debt finance during the finance boom. These funds were not only used for new investments but also for the encashment of their private investments. Complex and opaque capital transactions, such as the restructuring of group shareholdings and the sale of group owners' private assets to the group's public companies, were often used to create liquidity for group owners. However, during the finance boom, enthusiastic minority investors and offshore lenders actively supported such transactions. Indonesian business groups transformed themselves from 'industrial capital' to huge 'private equity funds' and the group owners acted as fund managers. The business groups traded their industrial assets as if they were financial assets. They attached great importance not to 'recognized profits' in the income statements but to 'realized profits' in cash-flow statements. The primary purpose of their activities accordingly shifted to the maximization of their personal cash flow. During the finance boom, conglomerate-type structures and non-financial businesses, whose financial activities were not bound by strict regulations, played an important role in the funding mechanisms of the groups.

This book has provided case studies of the Salim Group, the Lippo Group, the Sinar Mas Group and the Gajah Tunggal Group to provide details of the leading business groups' financial activities in the 1990s. The activities of these groups shed light on the microeconomic dynamics of financial fragility and instability in Indonesia. In the 1990s, the Salim Group carried out several huge capital transactions using its two flagship listed companies, Indocement and Indofood. In this way the group generated massive liquidity for the Liem family and other investors. The group aggressively restructured shareholdings, undertook intra-group asset transfers and the disposal of Liem family private assets to the group's listed companies. It strategically combined equity finance, domestic bank loans and offshore syndicated loans to finance these transactions. However, as these capital transactions required finance on a huge scale, the group relied heavily on offshore syndicated loans. Offshore lenders enthusiastically supported these transactions by offering competitive lending terms. As a result, the group heavily leveraged its financial positions with offshore mobile capital and created great fragility and instability in its financial structure.

The precise activities of the Lippo Group differed from the Salim Group, although the methods were similar. Due to the nature of Lippo's core businesses, that is, financial services and property development, many offshore banks were not willing to provide finance. Therefore, Lippo had to rely on the capital markets, mainly equity. It listed its companies on overseas as well as on Indonesian stock markets. Furthermore, it built a pyramid type of group holding structure by reorganizing horizontal into vertical shareholding, thereby generating a huge amount of liquidity for the Riady family. The group also introduced strategic partners, such as business groups in Hong Kong and China, into its ownership structure. It did not persist in traditional ownership concepts and actively disposed of investments in order to maximize realized profits and liquidity positions. Its strong preference for liquidity and heavy reliance on equity finance enabled it to survive the East Asian crisis. In Minsky's words, the Lippo Group was not as deeply built into chains of payment commitments and thus maintained a relatively robust financial structure.

During the finance boom, the Sinar Mas Group was the most aggressive fund raiser among Indonesian business groups and collected as much mobile capital as it could through a variety of financial transactions. It built up a cross-border and pyramid-type shareholding structure and thereby tried to obtain third party funds at all levels of its offshore holdings, onshore holdings and operating companies. In addition, it appealed to offshore financiers by stressing the performance and business position of its core business, pulp and paper. Offshore financiers generated extremely positive forecasts of the group's performance. Offshore mobile capital, such as equity investors, banks, bond investors, export credit agencies, trade counter parties and international public financial institutions, actively provided finance on a huge scale to the group. By accumulating third party funds, it not only generated abundant liquidity for the Widjaja family but undertook gigantic overseas investments, such as pulp and paper and real estate projects in China. As a result, it built up a huge balance sheet with as much offshore funds as it could obtain and created the most complex, fragile and unstable financial structure among Indonesian business groups. Both the group and its many creditors have since struggled with the maze of debts created by Sinar Mas once the group failed during the Indonesian crisis.

The Gajah Tunggal Group also built pyramid-type shareholding structures for its core business lines of tyres and related chemical products and financial services. Third party capital financed restructuring through equity and offshore syndicated debt. As in the case of the other business groups, the Gajah Tunggal Group also restructured to create liquidity for the Nursalim family. During the finance boom, the group further leveraged its financial structures by acquiring offshore syndicated loans. Prior to the finance boom, offshore lenders had categorized Gajah Tunggal as a second-tier borrower and therefore limited their exposure. However, once the finance boom had started, offshore lenders enthusiastically approached the group. Gajah Tunggal was able to obtain nearly the same amount in offshore syndicated loans as the leading business groups and its borrowing terms improved over time. The group's financial structure was also leveraged with offshore mobile capital and became increasingly fragile and unstable.

These four case studies shed light on the underlying motivations driving changes in financial structures and the emergence of fragility and instability at the microeconomic level. The primary motivation of business group owners as capitalists is the maximization of current and future profit streams (or cash flows), or in Minsky's terms, 'profit-seeking and forward-looking behaviour'. However, the financial revolution was also motivated by business group owners' liquidity preference reflecting unstable political and social conditions in Indonesia. In the capital structure of business groups, there are conflicts of interest between inside shareholders (business group owners), outside shareholders (third party or minority shareholders), and debt holders with regards to the maximization of cash flows. During the finance boom, bargaining power rapidly shifted from outside shareholders and debt holders to inside shareholders and the capital structure of Indonesian business groups was shaped by the motivations of these inside shareholders, most notably the generation of liquidity. Reflecting this situation, the business groups leveraged their financial structures with offshore mobile capital. The increase in payment commitments relative to equity, the introduction of volatile capital and the complexity of these financial transactions led to fragility and instability. Fragility and instability at the micro-level created fragility and instability at the macro-level.

In 1997 and 1998, the fragile and unstable financial structures of the finance boom degenerated into crisis. The sudden and large-scale retreat of offshore mobile capital precipitated the collapse of cash-flow chains across the economy. The corporate sector, which had absorbed huge amounts of offshore mobile capital, quickly became insolvent and took the banking sector with it. At the micro-level, a number of Indonesian business groups, which had highly leveraged financial positions through aggressive debt financing, experienced serious financial difficulty. Chapter 10 has described the post-crisis situation of the four business groups chosen for the case. The heavily leveraged business groups, that is, Salim, Sinar Mas and Gajah Tunggal, struggled to manage their debt loads and lost control of a substantial part of their business assets after debt restructuring.

Throughout the 1990s, corporate sector firms evolved into heavily leveraged speculative financing units under financial liberalization. In particular, during the finance boom, the sector drove up leverage through the use of offshore syndicated debt. Indonesian corporates rapidly increased their reliance on foreign currency debt and at the same time offshore mobile capital assumed a dominant position in the financial structure. Fragile and unstable financial structures, driven by the corporate sector, emerged endogenously in the Indonesian economy. The disequilibrating forces in the process were the leading business groups' aggressive financial activities and offshore financiers' enthusiasm for them. The empirical studies in this work clearly support the applicability and usefulness of the modified financial instability hypothesis.

In order to temper the tendency towards fragility and instability in capitalist economies, Minsky proposes a 'lender of last resort' and the strategic deployment of 'big government'. The aim of the former policy is to stabilize asset values under debt deflation, while the aim of the latter is to maintain profitability and cash flows. These policies were designed for closed and advanced economies. Therefore, in the context of the modified financial instability hypothesis, it is necessary to formulate policy proposals for open and developing economies. These small economies are embedded in liberalized and seamless global financial markets characterized by volatile mobile capital and complex financial chains. In particular, the management of the capital account is one of the most important subjects for developing economies such as Indonesia.

Since the East Asian crisis, a number of criticisms have been levelled against financial liberalization in developing economies. Nevertheless, post-crisis arguments have evolved based on a consensus that financial liberalization and growing cross-border capital flows are largely inevitable and irreversible (Eatwell and Taylor 2000; Eichengreen 1999, 2000). In addition, it is an undeniable fact that financial factors have played an increasingly critical role in recent crises. Highly liquid and innovative financing mechanism rapidly developed through financial liberalization and the IT revolution have dramatically increased the volatility of capital flows at the border and altered risk factors in the capitalist economy.

Based on this consensus, arguments regarding financial liberalization in developing economies have focused on the problem of premature capital account liberalization. In particular, the sudden and huge reversal of foreign mobile capital, which was the immediate cause of the East Asian crisis, focused attention on capital account liberalization. The essence of the argument is that the opening of the capital account should not precede financial market deregulation, and that liberalization of offshore bank borrowing should be last (Eichengreen 2000b). In addition, the opening of the capital account should not precede until the domestic banking system is strengthened through effective supervision, regulation and monitoring systems of cross-border capital flows (Eatwell and Taylor 2000, 2002; Eichengreen 2000; Furman and Stiglitz 1998; Stiglitz 2002).

Support for the proposition that capital controls are needed in countries in which financial systems are still developing has grown in recent years. Proponents of this view consider controls as part of the regulatory framework needed to manage systemic risks and contagion at both the macroeconomic and microeconomic levels (Eatwell and Taylor 2000).[1] Policies regarding capital controls are grouped into: (i) price-based capital controls on entry; (ii) quantitative capital controls on entry and (iii) capital controls at exit.[2] Price-level controls on entry are market based and discourage the rapid turnover of capital by imposing costs on incoming capital through Tobin-type taxes, special reserves and minimum-stay requirements. The Chilean capital controls, which were introduced in 1991 and required capital inflows to be subject to a flat-rate foreign exchange deposit with minimum stay at the central bank, are typical of these controls.[3] Quantitative capital controls on entry are direct controls on capital inflows. India's complex controls on short-term capital in the 1990s and Malaysia's controls on banks' and large corporations' foreign currency exposure in 1994 are examples of this type.[4] Capital controls at exit are direct controls on capital outflows and function as a circuit breaker on rapid and large-scale reversals of capital. The Malaysian capital controls introduced in 1998, which imposed limits on capital transfers by Malaysian residents and froze repatriation of foreign portfolio investments, are a recent example.[5]

The analysis of this book provides support for the argument that capital controls are needed in developing economies, including Indonesia. The empirical studies in this work illustrate the dynamism of capital flows during the finance boom. Offshore financiers pumped capital into Indonesia, while Indonesian business group owners liquidated their investments and cashed out through overseas investments. Liberalized and enthusiastic markets created high-speed and large-scale capital flows at the border. In particular, offshore debt finance created volatile capital flows and brought fragility and instability into the financial structure. Without capital controls, sudden and large-scale reversal of capital flows drove the financial structure into crisis and both the corporate and banking sectors totally collapsed.

As analysed in Chapter 10, the Indonesian crisis imposed a cost of more than US$100 billion (more than 65 per cent of GDP) on the government just to rehabilitate the banking sector. A substantial part of the cost was unrecoverable and was finally socialized. Furthermore, as explained in Chapter 1, the crisis caused a serious setback to economic growth and a huge contraction of national wealth. The social costs of the crisis were immense. Tens of millions of Indonesians were thrown into poverty. Huge operational costs for debt restructuring also occurred inside and outside Indonesia. Although many researchers still view capital controls as a source of inefficiency, these costs are negligible in comparison to the massive losses sustained by the Indonesian people during and after the crisis.

This work proposes comprehensive capital controls for open and developing economies such as Indonesia until they establish appropriate financial institutions to monitor and manage indebtedness and the volatility of capitalists' behaviour. As this work has argued, capital controls must control access to offshore debt capital. Controls should be directed at both the financial and non-financial sectors and cover not only short-term but also long-term debt. Both capital controls on entry and price-based capital controls are effective means in managing the aggregate leverage of the economy. However, depending on the development of financial institutions, price-based capital controls can substitute for capital controls on entry. At least at the early stages, capital controls on entry are needed to manage the leverage of the economy. On the other hand, developing economies need some form of capital controls at exit as a circuit breaker when unpredictable emergencies occur in order to minimize the costs of crises.

Comprehensive capital controls require transparent administration. Although the authorities in developing economies struggle to achieve autonomy from domestic political pressures, controls must be fair and universal. Furthermore, capital controls at exit need an alarm system to create predictability in order to avoid overuse and instability in the volume of capital flows. The authorities therefore should explicitly provide benchmarks and publish relevant indicators, such as the level of external debt, reserves, leverage and debt service.

Since the capital account was liberalized in the early 1970s, the Indonesian government has stressed the maintenance of an open capital account in order to release both overseas and domestic mobile capital from concerns about sudden capital controls at exit and thereby motivate them to make long-term investments in the country. In the 1990s, the government simplified the 'negative list' that had excluded foreign capital from specific sectors and eliminated ceilings on foreign ownership. As a result, capital controls on entry were reduced. These policies were in line with the liberalization policies promoted by international financial institutions and were warmly welcomed by them.

However, in the wake of the East Asian financial crisis enthusiasm has diminished (even among the international financial institutions), for open capital accounts at the early stages of the development of the financial system.[6] Capital controls are increasingly viewed as a practical tool that developing countries can use to maintain economic stability in the context of liberalized and globalized financial markets. The international financial community's benign response to the imposition of selected capital controls in Malaysia in 1998 reflects the growing awareness that under certain conditions capital controls facilitates international integration rather than hinder it.[7] In part, the willingness of international agencies to reconsider previous opposition to all capital controls stems from the recognition of the political dimensions of financial integration. Adjustment that requires prolonged deflationary measures simply to assuage foreign creditors can undermine political stability and hence economic growth. To the extent that capital controls allow some relaxation of monetary and fiscal policy, as in the Malaysian case, they can reduce the economic and political costs of adjustment (Athukorala 2000). Such an approach would have been feasible in Indonesia if the country's donors had come to this realization earlier and the political system had not become so brittle in the waning days of the Suharto regime.

In Minsky's terms, during the finance boom, sharply decreased funding costs and stabilized rupiah exchange rates dramatically improved the margin of safety on investments in Indonesia. By taking advantage of offshore capitalists' enthusiasm, Indonesian business groups aggressively absorbed offshore mobile capitals and steeply leveraged their balance sheets. Indonesian financial structures became increasingly fragile, unstable and crisis prone. Minsky's margin of safety collapsed (Kregel 1998). If Indonesia had adopted capital controls on entry, the rapid financial evolution, which was driven by offshore mobile capital, could have been avoided.[8] Although some economists object that controls inhibit capital inflows to developing economies, long-term industrial investments would not be affected by well-developed capital controls. Developing economies should prioritize stable growth rather than fragile and unstable rapid growth associated with free capital movement (Cole and Slade 1998b). Furthermore, if Indonesia had rapidly introduced capital controls at exit at the inception of the 1997–8 financial crisis the slide into a full-blown crisis could have been avoided and the government would not have had to rely on austerity to remedy the situation. For example, when the government provided BLBI to banks facing cash shortages during the crisis, this liquidity injection was quickly transferred overseas through repayment of external deposits and debts due to the absence of capital controls (Enoch *et al.* 2003, p.24). This resulted in further depreciation of the rupiah and damage to the economy. In sum, developing open economies need capital controls at exit to make Keynes' and Minsky's lender-of-last-resort policy effective under crisis situations. The development of open economies requires comprehensive capital controls in order to moderate endogenous financial evolution and stabilize the fragile and unstable nature of the economies.

Finally, capitalist economies cannot avoid endogenous fragility and instability by their very nature. Minsky's financial instability hypothesis shows that crises are endemic to capitalism. The modified financial instability hypothesis presented in this book would lead us to expect repeated crises in developing economies that are tightly connected to global cash-flow chains. The burden of financial fragility and instability falls more heavily on poor people in these developing economies through the loss in real output and employment and declining living standards than on the capitalists involved in these financial transactions. The challenge of stabilizing an unstable economy must be met if the mass of the population is to be protected from the risks imposed on them by the actions of a small number of capitalists.

Notes

Introduction

1 See Chapter 3 for selection criteria for the four business groups chosen for the case studies.

1 Indonesia's external debt problem in the 1990s

1 In this work, the 'Indonesian crisis' is also used. It is defined as a series of political and economic deteriorations caused by financial crisis and the fall of the Suharto regime from 1997 to 1998.

2 The exchange rates used for these figures are Rp.2,890 per dollar in 1997 and Rp.10,224 per dollar in 1998.

3 As a matter of fact, the companies that booked a net loss accounted for merely 4.3 per cent in 1995 and 8.1 per cent in 1996, and the average net profit per company was Rp.45.0 billion (US$20.9 million) and Rp.50.5 billion (US$21.7 million) in 1996. The data is based on author's study. The leading non-financial companies include listed companies on the Jakarta Stock Exchange and Indonesian-owned listed companies on overseas stock exchanges.

4 These data are based on Bank Indonesia, *Indonesian Financial Statistics* (various issues).

5 CGI is an aid group for Indonesia, established in July 1992 by disbanding IGGI (Inter-Governmental Group on Indonesia), the previous Dutch-led aid group.

6 The following description regarding investors is simple but true: 'Just as exuberant investors were careless of risks during the speculative boom period, they became overly conscious of risks during the speculative burst period' (Yoshitomi and Staff of ADB Institute 2003, p.72).

7 Widely known as the 'KEPPRES 39', this regulation was used for the purpose of controlling not only external debt but also budgetary expenditure, such as infrastructure projects. The team was responsible for setting an annual ceiling on external commercial debt, monitoring the borrowing situation and coordinating access to the markets. Offshore borrowings by the private sector were exempt from the annual ceiling and advance approval requirements. However, borrowers for such projects were required to notify the team of any new offshore commercial borrowings. In addition, a Presidential Instruction issued in 1984 stipulated that export credits in foreign currencies should only be utilized to finance approved priority development projects, as set forth in an annual list prepared by the government. However, after 1995, the control by the KEPPRES 39 became weaker due to political pressure from Suharto's family and other politically connected groups (Komatsu 2000).

8 The Soeryadjaya family attempted to sell the shares of Astra International (the holding company of the Astra Group) to its joint venture partners, such as Toyota (Japan), at

prices over market and retain the group ownership as much as possible. Finally, the family could not maintain ownership of the group. The family disposed substantial shares of Astra International and compensated for the loss of the Summa Group.

9 In this scandal, Eddy Tansil, a Chinese businessman, and Bapindo's officials were accused of misusing a loan from Bapindo.

10 In 1996 Indonesia received the world's third largest share of private foreign capital inflows (US$17.9 billion) (Grabel 1999).

11 In May 1989, quantitative ceilings on foreign borrowing by banks were replaced by a net open position limit for all authorized foreign exchange banks, aiming to discourage banks from taking excessive foreign exchange positions. This opened up opportunities for banks to access long-term offshore funding and banks attempted to obtain funds mainly through FRCDs (Floating Rate Certificate of Deposit) or syndicated loans. However, annual offshore borrowing of banks was placed under the controls of Bank Indonesia again.

12 The technocrats were Suharto's economic policy team. They were drawn mostly from the University of Indonesia and were trained in Western universities. Suharto actively used this group to establish the credibility of his regime with international financial institutions. Winters explains the technocrats' structural power in the context of state financial conditions (Winters 1996).

13 The most important deregulation policies in the 1980s were the liberalization of interest rates in 1983 and the deregulation package (PAKTO) in 1988. In particular, the latter removed tight controls on establishing new banks, opening branches and opening foreign bank operations (branches, joint ventures and representation offices). As a result, the number of banks (state banks, private banks, foreign and joint-venture banks and regional development banks, excluding people's credit banks) increased sharply from 109 in 1987 to 240 in 1994, and the number of offices also increased from 1,588 to 4,888. These increases mostly derived from the mushrooming of new private banks (increased by 102 banks) and the aggressive expansion of their branch networks (by 2,699 offices).

14 SBI is a short-term liability of Bank Indonesia, and SBPU is a standardized banker's acceptance and can be purchased at discount by Bank Indonesia. See Chapter 4 for detailed explanations.

15 The concept of 'increased risk potential' was originally used for the Latin America's financial crisis caused by sudden capital reversal of rapidly increased portfolio and short-term investments (Grabel 1999).

16 Corporate loans usually include financial covenants in agreements, such as leverage ratio and interest coverage ratio. When currency crises occur, deeply depreciated local currencies suddenly enlarge foreign exchange liabilities in terms of local currency, borrowers easily breach the covenants and trigger default and lenders can then accelerate the loan repayment.

17 Keynes explains investors' behaviour as devoting their intelligence to 'discovering what average opinion believes average opinion to be' (Eatwell and Taylor 2000, p.12; Keynes 1936 p.159). Eatwell and Taylor support this view (Eatwell and Taylor 2000, pp.12–14, 208–9).

18 Lazard Freres, Lehman Brothers and UBS (then SBC Warburg) (financial advisors) *Memorandum* (various issues).

19 Even such top business groups could not regularly issue bonds in the offshore markets due to the limited number of investors. The leading companies tried to place their bonds in European and US markets, but they tended to be sold back to Asian investors within a short period after issuance.

20 Most loans were secured by intangible assets, such as accounts receivables and inventories. Moreover, owners of debtor companies provided their personal guarantees to offshore banks. However, offshore banks considered such guarantees merely as tools to put pressure on debtors in case of distress.

21 In the Hong Kong market, state banks (e.g. BNI, Bank Dagang Negara (BDN), Bank Bumi Daya (BBD) and Bank Rakyat Indonesia (BRI) and top private banks (e.g. Bank Central Asia (BCA), Lippo Bank and Bank Bali) were popular names as FRCD issuers.

22 Chinese proprietors of small and medium firms, such as textile company owners in Bandung, actively used this 'back-to-back finance'. The most popular scheme was as follows: A company owner pledges his/her personal offshore cash deposit to an offshore bank and receives interest on it. The offshore bank gives a secured loan to his/her company, and the company pays interest on the loan to the bank. If the company becomes insolvent, the bank sets off the loan against the pledged deposit. The spread between the interest on the loan and interest on the pledged deposit is the offshore bank's profit. This finance appears to be an irrational transaction as the company owner simply pays the spread to the offshore bank that does not take any risk at all. However, this finance is driven by three purposes: (i) to transfer the company's profit offshore; (ii) to avoid his/her equity investment and (iii) to save corporate tax in Indonesia. The offshore bank's concern is only the spread between two interest rates above (e.g. the then standard spread was 50 to 100 basis points per annum). Therefore, the company owner usually demands a much higher interest rate on deposit than the market rate but is happy to make his/her company pay much higher interest on the loan to the bank. This is the same as a company owner transferring profits from his/her company in Indonesia to offshore in the form of interest. In addition, the company owner considers that paying back the loan to the offshore bank will be politically much easier than disposing and sending back his/her invested equity offshore. Furthermore, interest on the loan is deductible from the company's taxable income, so the company owner expects a tax saving effect by using this finance. This *back-to-back finance* had also been used for speculative purposes, such as investment in listed equities. In this case, these equities were pledged for the finance. Private bankers are located in Singapore, Hong Kong and Taiwan, and cover Indonesian clients from there.

2 Minsky's financial instability hypothesis: interpretation and critical adjustments for the Asian context

1 In contrast to the Latin American model, the Asian high-debt economy model assumes that high savings and heavy bank lending created highly leveraged financial structures, with a high risk of default, and that these structures were sustained by coordination among banks, corporates and government. The model argues that the 1980–90s IMF-endorsed liberalization in East Asia removed underpinnings of highly leveraged financial structures, that is, the earlier-mentioned coordination, and thus destabilized the economy (Wade and Veneroso 1998).

2 However, Indonesia had already liberalized its capital accounts in 1971 and has maintained the policy ever since. In the late 1960s and the early 1970s, offshore capital, including Indonesian–Chinese capital, kept funds outside the country. In 1971, Indonesia opened its capital account to encourage capital inflows, including the return of Indonesian–Chinese capital. Since then, the technocrats have kept freedom of capital movement as a core economic policy despite capital flight. Therefore, the abandonment of free capital movement would mean the abandonment of a core principal of the technocrats (Komatsu 2000; Pincus and Ramli 1998).

3 From 1971 to 1997 there were crises. However, because of the large weight of state enterprise deposits in the banking system, there was no run on banks. This changed in 1990s. See Pincus and Ramli (1998).

4 Minsky formed the following general macroeconomic assumptions characterizing crises: (i) the total wealth in capitalist economy is macroeconomically determined, dependent on confidence and the state of the cycle and (ii) separated portfolio decisions by firms and households can interact to create crises.

5 Others argue that Minsky's unpopularity is due to his concern for microeconomic and institutional detail (Taylor and O'Connell 1985).

6 With regards to this point, Fisher severely criticized the classical economists' assumptions as follows: 'But the exact equilibrium thus sought is seldom reached and never long maintained. ... It is as absurd to assume that, for any long period of time, the variables in the economic organisation, or any part of them, will "stay put," in perfect equilibrium, as to assume that the Atlantic Ocean can ever be without a wave' (Fisher 1933, p.339).

7 Besides these two primary variables, that is, over-indebtedness and deflation, Fisher considered the following seven factors as the secondary variables: (i) circulating media; (ii) velocity of circulation; (iii) net worth; (iv) profits; (v) trade; (vi) business confidence and (vii) interest rates.

8 At the inception of panics, interest rates rise, investments are cut back and profit rates fall. As a consequence, the valuation of firms' capital assets declines, and so does the net worth. The stage is set for the debt-deflation process.

9 Following Keynes's theory, Minsky considered investment as a time-consuming process based upon profit expectations. Decisions to invest are always made under conditions of uncertainty (Minsky 1986, p.119).

10 With regards to asset prices, Minsky stated, 'Thus 1) the capitalist technique of valuing outputs and valuing capital assets, 2) the market determination of liability structures and 3) the possibility of sharp increases and decreases in the market price of capital assets and financial instruments lead to systematic increases and decreases in the price of assets relative to the price level of current output' (Minsky 1993, p.14). Interpreting this statement in financial terms, Minsky argues that the multiple of asset price against current cash-flow is determined by (i) valuation of the asset by the discounted cash-flow method, (ii) debt structure financing the asset and (iii) prevailing market prices of assets and this multiple fluctuates.

11 Minsky focused on balance sheet crises based on expectation and uncertainty. On the other hand, in a similar way to Minsky, Marxists attempted to analyse the effects of the deterioration in real economy (e.g. slowing down of productivity) on crises (Ito and Lapavitsas 1999).

12 Minsky explained the value of capital and financial assets as follows: 'The price of capital assets and financial instruments are present prices for future streams of incomes' (Minsky 1993, p.9). Furthermore, Minsky stressed the role of interest rates in determining asset values in the present. Minsky clearly kept in his mind the formula of discounted cash flows.

13 The institutional framework means experiences, customs, habits and performances of capitalists.

14 This work defines fragility as a crisis-prone financial structure that contains a potential break in the chain of debts and the instability of the economy as a continuing situation of fragility.

15 Since the early 1900s, both economists and accounting professionals have argued for the linkage between economics and accounting and the interpretation of terminology, such as 'income' and 'depreciation'. Among economists, Fisher and Canning were deeply involved in this argument (Fisher 1930).

16 These three types of corporate cash flows are based on Generally Accepted Accounting Principles (GAAP) in the United States. The stipulated order of these cash flows is: (i) cash flows from operating activities; (ii) cash flows from investment activities and (iii) cash flows from financing activities.

17 Following the Kalecki-Levy equation, gross profit equals the sum of investment, consumption out of profit, governmental deficit/surplus and net exports minus savings out of wages. Based on this formula, Minsky stressed the importance of big government under deep depression to increase the gross profits of the economy. Minsky also

stressed the control of governmental spending under inflation (Minsky 1992c, p.5; Papadimitriou and Wray 1999).

18 In standard corporate accounting, cash flows from operating activities are roughly defined by the following formula: net profit (after tax) + depreciation and amortization + working capital movement + capital gain/loss adjustment + minority interest adjustment + others. The net profit (not gross profit, after interest and tax) is the most important component of the cash flows from operating activities. Therefore, Minsky's arguments by using *income* and/or *gross income* may be appropriate for his arguments regarding cash flows.

19 The following sentence indicates that Minsky put new debt finance in the portfolio cash flows: '[U]nder robust financial structure, at the inception of investment, negative balance sheet cash flow is financed by portfolio cash flow, and thereafter negative cash flow is financed by income cash flow throughout the time.'

20 See Minsky (1986), p.202 (footnote), regarding the origin of the term 'Ponzi'. Also see Eatwell and Taylor (2000), p.53 (footnote).

21 Minsky states, '[W]hen hedge financing is the dominant posture the interest rate structure offers inducement to increase indebtedness and increase the proportion of short-term financing that requires the rolling over of outstanding debts' (Minsky 1992a, p.16).

22 Minsky states, 'An equity liability has only a contingent commitment to make payments, dividends need to be paid only if earned and declared, and there is no contractual need to repay principle. For any given cash flows, from operations or from the fulfilment of owned contracts, the greater the share of equity financing in a balance sheet the greater the margin of safety that protects the owners of the non-equity liabilities' (Minsky 1991, p.12).

23 However, he indicated the possibility of expanding his model to an open market model (Minsky 1992c, p.5).

24 Minsky states, 'As economic theory, the financial instability hypothesis is an interpretation of the substance of Keynes's "General Theory"' (Minsky 1992c, p.1).

25 Focusing on the financial indebtedness, the leverage can be tested by the following two ratios used for corporate finance: (i) the ratio of debt to equity and (ii) the ratio of debt to EBITDA (earning before income and tax plus depreciation and amortization).

26 In the open and developing country model, as is argued in the following section, if the payment commitments are denominated in foreign currencies, the depreciation of local currencies, which may be caused by the crises, actually increases the payment commitments in terms of local currencies.

27 The 'controllable' level differs from economy to economy, and depends on the financial structure of the economy, including interest rate levels and the relative dependency on offshore markets.

28 The short-term debt to reserves ratios of the troubled Asian countries reached levels higher than 1.0 in 1996, for example in Indonesia (1.9), Thailand (1.2) and Korea (2.0) (Furman and Stiglitz 1998, pp.51–2). The ratios of short-term to total debt of these countries in 1996 were as follows: Indonesia (25 per cent), Thailand (58 per cent) and Korea (41 per cent) (based on the data from World Bank and BIS). Note: the short-term to total debt ratio of Indonesia was lower than that of Malaysia (28 per cent).

29 See Chapters 4 and 5.

30 The sharp increase in total debt in local currency terms suddenly pushed up leverage-related ratios, the maximum of which were generally stipulated in loan agreements. Breaches of these ratios triggered default, and therefore offshore banks required Indonesian borrowers to repay loans immediately.

31 The excess profit, that is, saving of funding cost, can be estimated by the following calculations: domestic banks' lending rate − (US$ lending rate + US$–rupiah foreign exchange loss). Using state banks average lending rate for domestic banks' lending

rate, six-month US$ BBA LIBOR for US$ lending rate, and annual average depreciation of rupiah against US$ for US$–rupiah foreign exchange loss, the excess profit of offshore debt borrowers averaged 6.44 per cent between 1994 and 1996. This excess profit for the period was lower than that between 1991 and 1993 (average 12.60 per cent).

32 Eichengreen also has the same type of question (Eichengreen 1999, p.157).

33 However, there were some loopholes in the controls. For example, guarantees to the banks' subsidiary and/or affiliate non-bank companies for offshore borrowings were out of quota. Therefore, if the banks guaranteed subsidiary and/or affiliate non-bank finance companies' offshore borrowings and received them as deposits, it is the same as if the banks borrowed offshore loans outside quota. However, as far as the external debt level by non-bank financial sector (Chapter 1) and the detailed analysis of off-shore debt transaction (Chapter 5) show, the method was not heavily used.

34 Seven target state banks for offshore lenders were Bank Negara Indonesia (BNI), Bank Ekspor-Impor Indonesia (Bank EXIM), Bank Rakyat Indonesia (BRI), Bank Bumi Daya (BBD), Bank Dagang Negara (BDN), Bank Pembagunan Indonesia (Bapindo) and Bank Tabungan Negara (BTN). The top six private banks as of June 1997 and regular offshore finance users were Bank Central Asia (BCA), Bank International Indonesia (BII), Bank Danamon Indonesia, Lippo Bank, Bank Bali, Bank Niaga and Panin Bank.

3 Methods and databases for empirical studies

1 For example, Minsky studied the transactions of certificates of deposit (CD), which were introduced into the US financial markets in the early 1960s (Minsky 1986). Based in part on Minsky's theory, Kindleberger analysed a number of underlying financial transactions that had caused 'manias, panics, and crashes' in economic history (Kindleberger 1978).

2 The aggregate financial statement has been generated by the author by combining individual companies' financial data with appropriate technical adjustments. As discussed later, the data were obtained from companies listed in the Jakarta and other stock exchanges. Reflecting the rapid increase of the stock listing of Indonesian companies during the 1990s, this number increased from year to year. Thus, the time-series analysis of currency value of aggregated data is irrelevant, and ratio analysis is used for solving this problem.

3 See Claessens, Djankov and Lang (1998) and Wade and Veneroso (1998).

4 Operating cash flows should be calculated by adjusting EBITDA with working capitals and other non-cash items. For the empirical studies in this work, EBITDA is used as a proxy for operating cash flows because EBITDA is a core part of the cash flows and because the adjustment items are not so significant.

5 In terms of operating volume, five state banks (BNI, BBD, BDN, Bank EXIM and BTN) held more than a 40 per cent market share in 1995. Private banks positioned among the top 15 were Bank Central Asia (Salim), Bank Danamon, Bank International Indonesia (Sinar Mas), Bank Dagang Nasional Indonesia (Gajah Tunggal), Lippo Bank, Bank Bali, Bank Umum Nasional (Ongko), Bank Niaga and Panin Bank.

6 Since 1995, the government began pushing forward the privatization of state companies. It identified 166 state enterprises for privatization, such as BNI (state commercial bank), Perusahaan Listrik Negara (PLN) (state electricity company), Aneka Tambang (mining company), Krakatau Steel (steel maker) and Jasa Marga (toll-road operator).

7 The financial authorities strictly controlled all Indonesian banks' offshore borrowings through annual quota. In particular, they held a tight rein on state banks' offshore borrowings, such as the terms and conditions and the timing of their entry into the market. See Chapters 1 and 5.

8 Examples of this problem are domestic debt data presented in Chapter 1 and offshore syndicated debts data in Chapter 5.

9 At the latter stage of the finance boom, the Indonesian financial authority ceased issuing new licenses for non-bank finance companies and introduced offshore debt controls on them. This is because affiliated non-bank finance companies were used by their parent commercial banks in order to obtain offshore debts outside Pinjaman Komersian Luar Negeri (PKLN).

10 The other Indonesian–Chinese business groups with at least two listed companies consist of: (i) four listed companies: Ciptra, PSP, Tiga Raksa, Ongko, Napan; (ii) three listed companies: Modern, CP, Maspion, Soeryadjaya (iii) two listed companies: Mulia, Sucaco, Sampoerna, Barito, Raja Garuda Mas, Sekar, Gunawan, Panggung, Hero, Roda Mas, Sungai Budi, Sierad, Panasia (Hadtex), Bakik Keris, Sulistyo, Mayapada, Pudjiadi, Bahkti, Steady Safe, Jakarta Steel, Apec, Sudarma (Lion), Dynaplast, Kita, Artha Graha.

11 The status of borrowers, such as 'listed companies', 'members of leading business groups' and 'business partners of international capitals', are important qualifications for offshore borrowing. In particular, information disclosures by listed companies were much better than those by non-listed companies even in Indonesia. Thus, listed companies had much better accesses to offshore debt markets. In this context, there are arguments regarding a positive correlation between the development of the stock market and the leverage of corporate balance sheet at the early stage of the development in developing countries (Kunt and Maksimovic 1995a,b, 1996).

12 Four listed companies were directly owned and fully controlled by the Suharto family. The Bakrie Group had four listed companies.

13 Eight Indonesian–Indian companies were listed in Jakarta Stock Exchange. Six of them belonged to the Texmaco Group.

14 For example, the average tenor of a 5-year term loan facility with a 1-year grace period and five equal annual instalments is 3 years ($=1 + (5 - 1)/2$).

15 Indonesian issuers (borrowers) of offshore fixed income bonds were limited to the central government, top state commercial banks and a small group of top private companies (e.g. Astra International, Indah Kiat (Sinar Mas), Tjiwi Kimia (Sinar Mas), Pindo Deli (Sinar Mas) and Asia Pulp and Paper (Sinar Mas)). Only the Sinar Mas Group was a regular Indonesian issuer of offshore fixed income bonds during the period but had to pay high premiums on their standard offshore funding costs.

16 Term sheets are summaries of terms and conditions that are stipulated in final loan agreements. They are used for offering syndicated debt transactions to borrowers and inviting participating banks to the transactions. *IFR* is a professional magazine for international bankers and the most reliable and reputable information source regarding international financial transactions. Its information is collected through professionally trained writers' direct interviews with banks and borrowers. The nature of the information is very simple and focuses mainly on the basic borrowing/issuing terms, such as borrower/issuer, arranger, participants, facility type, structure, amount, tenor, spread, fee, security and guarantee. The arranger banks also make an offer to inform *IFR* accurately concerning syndicated loans arranged by them. This is because the magazine is used for the purpose of book running (placing syndicated debts) and advertising arrangers' performance. Potential participating banks also try to find investment opportunities (syndicated loans) that match their targets. During the period between 1993 and 1997, backed by both arrangers' and participants' strong demand for Indonesian syndicated loans, *IFR* expanded its coverage of Indonesian debt. A typical case is the data following the East Asian crisis. As a matter of course all banks attempted to withdraw their exposure to Indonesia; thus there was no demand for information regarding new syndicated loans.

17 The transaction date is the signing (execution) date in principle. If the date is not available, launching or closing date is used. If the loan is subject to put option (lenders' cancellation right), the tenor is the duration until the put option date. For example, the tenor for a 5-year loan with a put option at the end of the third year is not 5 but 3 years. This is simply because lenders retain legal termination rights of loans at the put option dates and borrowers need waivers of lenders' put option rights in order to use the loans for the remaining tenor. The waivers usually require borrowers to pay fees to lenders. This is a standard practice. Average tenor is also calculated in consideration of put options. If the repayment method is unknown or the amortization schedule is not clear, the average tenor cannot be calculated. In this case, the loan is deemed to have a bullet repayment at the maturity or put option date. Syndicated loans often have several facilities (multi-tranche facility), for example, loans with both term loan and revolver tranches. These loans are deemed to be one transaction for counting the number of transactions.

18 Examples of state non-bank borrowers are Pertamina (state oil company), and PLN (state electricity company). Examples of state independent projects are natural gas exploration and power stations.

19 See Chapter 5.

20 This data set includes syndicated loans guaranteed by the companies in Table 3.7.

21 One of the exceptions was the Astra Group which had a modern structure. Astra International functioned as the head office of group subsidiary companies and provided a variety management functions, such as financial arrangements and assignments of management members (Sato 1996).

22 The function of capital markets includes venture capital or private equity providers, debt providers (through internal funds and group banks) and auditors or appraisers of investment performances. The functions of labour markets include management and staff training (by group management institute, business school, and/or polytechnic) and relocation of management and staff. The functions of product markets can enable the group companies to save costs for communications concerning products, collecting information on trade counter parties and building credible brands. In addition to these three functions, business groups can provide themselves with lobbying powers against authorities, bargaining powers against international trade counter parties and internal contract enforcement.

23 Perspectives on corporate governance generally fall into two groups: namely, the shareholder-value view; and, the stakeholder view (Aoki 2001, pp.303–4). The former, now a standard component of neoclassical theory, is built on the framework of the principal (shareholder) versus the agent (management), and seeks to model governance systems that will ensure profit maximization for shareholders. The latter view concerns control over the distribution of quasi-rents and profits generated by corporate activities.

24 CalPERS in the United States is a typical example of activists.

25 For example, the directors and commissioners of the Salim Group's core companies, such as Indocement and Indofood, were occupied by the members of the Salim family and investors. See Chapter 6, Sato (1992).

26 The problem of independent auditor was not only in Indonesian but also in other East and South-East Asian countries. See Backman (1999).

27 See Chapter 4.

28 See Chapters 6–9 and Backman (1999).

29 The Japanese main bank system can be defined by the following three characteristics: (i) multidimensional relationships between banks and borrowers with regards to finance, information and management; (ii) mutual relationships among (city) banks and (iii) relationship between (city) banks and regulatory board (Ministry of Finance and Bank of Japan) (Aoki 1996, pp.221–45). State banks in Indonesia were different from main banks in Japan. State banks were directly controlled by the government but

more distant from corporate borrowers. State banks' equity investments in private companies and the dispatch of management members from the banks were not so frequently observed in Indonesia compared with the main bank system in Japan.

30 State banks' finance to Timor Putra Nasional (Tommy Suharto's car company) in MOBNAS (national car project) was one of the best examples of directed finance by politico-bureaucrats (Backman 1999, pp.269–72). Private banks were also involved in directed finance in order to keep relationships with powerful bureaucrats.

4 The financial positions of the Indonesian corporate sector in the 1990s

1 As defined in Chapter 1, the corporate sector means the private non-financial sector.

2 See Chapter 3.

3 However, non-bank finance companies were also placed under the control of BI in 1995. The controls attempted to slow down non-bank finance companies' lending to speculative investments, such as property (World Bank 1996, p.20). Finally, in 1997, the government introduced restrictions on offshore borrowing of non-bank finance companies. This was because commercial banks used their non-bank finance companies in order to borrow offshore outside their offshore borrowing limits (*IFR* 1177 (5 April 1997), *IFR* 1178 (12 April 1997), *IFR* 1181 (3 May 1997)).

4 See Claessens, Djankov and Lang (1998) and Pomerleano (1998).

5 The figures for 1997 include foreign exchange effects due to the devaluation of the rupiah.

6 The cross-country study by Claessens, Djankov and Lang indicates that the gross profit margin of the Indonesian corporate sector (average around 33 per cent) was the highest among nine major East and South-East Asian countries during the period (Claessens *et al.* 1998, pp.6–7). They term the gross-profit margin 'operating margin' in their paper. However, their calculation of the margin is the difference between sales and costs of goods sold as a share of sales. Therefore, the margin is gross-profit margin. Estimating from their cross-country study, the operating margins of Indonesian corporates could also be the highest among those countries.

7 In the study by Claessens, Djankov and Lang, the Indonesian corporate sector did not improve the ratio of long-term to total debt in the 1990s. Only during the finance boom, the ratio improved from 39.6 per cent (1993) to 43.3 per cent (1996). At least, the study can say that the sector did not build up massive short-term debts (Claessens *et al.* 1998, pp.11–13). In the study by Pomerleano, the ratio of current to total liabilities for the sector improved from 56 per cent in 1993 to 45 per cent in 1996 (Pomerleano 1998, pp.12–13).

8 Stiglitz technically sought the stability (or instability) of the financial structure in foreign exchange reserves against offshore short-term debts, and Minsky sought it in cash inflows against cash outflows.

9 PAKDES I vaguely made a statement regarding the foreign ownership of listed companies, and foreign investors were allowed to buy shares of listed companies up to an amount allowed by the provisions of the Investment Coordination Board (Badan Koordinasi Penanman Modal/BKPM). Finally, the 49 per cent limit to foreigner's ownership was stipulated in the Minister of Finance's decree in September 1989 (Cole and Slade 1996, pp.160–5). Furthermore, in September 1997, this limit was eliminated except for bank shares.

10 In terms of number of listed shares, the foreign ownership jumped from 10.0 per cent in 1989 to 24.2 per cent in 1990, and furthermore increased to 30.4 per cent in 1993 (Cole and Slade 1996, p.177).

11 This data is taken from Cole and Slade (1996). According to Bloomberg's screen, the highest Jakarta Composite Index Price was 681.94 on 4 April 1990. However, the price appeared to be irregular.

12 Sato (2001), p.379.

13 The then-existing situation was described as follows: 'In the optimistic climate of the time, investors taking a position in primary market issues could expect to make a significant capital gain within a short time interval. This optimism fed on itself, encouraging more and more investors to try their luck in the capital market. The prevalence of quick gains created a strong demand for new issues, which in turn encouraged more and more firms to seize the opportunity to raise capital cheaply. For many months, demand continued to outstrip supply, and share prices rose accordingly' (Noerhadi 1994, p.210). Also see Taubert (1991), p.129.

14 The number of private banks sharply increased as follows: 63 in 1988, 88 in 1989 and 109 in 1990, finally reaching 164 in 1996. The number of private banks' offices also rapidly increased as follows: 559 in 1988, 1,238 in 1989 and 2,052 in 1990. This further increased to 3,964 in 1996 (Table 4.9).

15 See Nasution (1994). p.133.

16 The examples of the top private companies were Astra International and Indocement (Salim).

17 The acceptable inflation rate as stated in the REPELITA V document was up to 5 per cent, but the actual inflation rate was 9–10 per cent.

18 Leading business groups were criticized over their overseas investments by transferring a considerable part of the capital they raised through equity finance (Taubert 1991, p.129).

19 Bank Indonesia had the following three tools for controlling liquidity: SBI, SBPU and liquidity credit. SBI is a short-term liability of BI that can be used to absorb liquidity and was introduced in 1984. SBPU is a standardized banker's acceptance and can be purchased at discount by BI in order to supply reserve. It was introduced in 1985. Liquidity credit is BI's special finance provided at low rate to specific business fields and activities.

20 See Pangestu (1992), pp.143–6.

21 The First Sumarlin Shock was in June 1987. The Minister of Finance required private banks to buy back SBPUs from BI, and state enterprises to transfer time deposits from state banks to BI. The policy also targeted foreign exchange speculation.

22 In March 1989, limitations on net open positions, 25 per cent of the banks' capital, were introduced. In May 1989, the ceiling on foreign currency borrowing by banks was abolished. However, BI revived the control within the annual offshore borrowing quota system. The capital adequacy ratios requirement was introduced in February 1991 and phased in as follows: 5 per cent by March 1992, 7 per cent by March 1993 and 8 per cent by December 1993. At the same time, the loan to deposit ratio requirement was introduced. The ratio was initially 110 per cent. In 1993, banks' capitals were allowed to be included into the ratio's denominator. The legal lending limit requirement was introduced in 1989 and 1990, modified in 1991 and further modified in 1993. This restricted the aggregate amount of loans and other exposure to single borrowers or groups of related borrowers as well as to insiders (for example, shareholders, directors, commissioners, senior managers and their related entities and persons). The aim of the requirement was to prevent business groups from using their banks to finance their group and family businesses.

23 Typical examples are Bank Duta's violation of net open position and Bank Summa's violation of legal lending limit.

24 Actually, debt accumulated by the private non-bank sector continued from US$29.9 billion in 1990, US$35.0 billion in 1991 and US$38.0 billion in 1992 (Tables 1.4 and 1.5 in Chapter 1). The data of the corporate sector is unavailable.

25 The return on assets ratios in their study are as follows: 9.4 per cent in 1990, 9.1 per cent in 1991 and 8.6 per cent in 1992 (Claessens *et al.* 1998, pp.4–6).

26 In theory, the following formula represents the investor's rationalization of leverage: return on equity = {return on assets + (return on assets − funding yield − foreign exchange loss or hedging costs)*debt/equity}*(1 − tax). Therefore, if the return on

assets is higher than the funding cost yield (= funding yield + foreign exchange loss or hedging costs) the company prefers to leverage, and vice versa.

27 The government increased its concerns about offshore borrowings when it discovered 120 projects worth US$80 billion in the pipeline (Pangestu 1992, p.152).

28 See Chapter 1.

29 World Bank (1996), pp.10–11.

30 See Chapter 1.

31 In the first quarter of 1993, steep inflation emerged. The government revived the tight monetary policy. In the second quarter of 1993 inflation fell sharply; therefore BI redeemed around 17 per cent of its high interest rate SBI. Huge liquidity was provided to banks. After August 1993, inflation re-emerged.

32 The ratios of debt to equity in the study by Claessens, Djankov and Lang are as follows: 2.097 times in 1992, 2.054 times in 1993 and 1.661 times in 1994 (Claessens *et al.* 1998, pp.8–10). On the other hand, the ratios of debt to equity in the study by Pomerleano are as follows: 0.59 times in 1992, 0.54 times in 1993 and 0.58 times in 1994 (Pomerleano 1998, pp.6–8). The two studies show different movement of the ratio in 1994. Note: their definitions of debts are different.

33 The Jakarta Stock Price Index is a modified capitalization-weighted index of all stocks listed on the regular board of the Jakarta Stock Exchange. The index was developed with a base index value of 100 as of 10 August 1982.

34 The increase of listed companies in 1989 and 1990 was a total of 99 companies.

35 The source of the data is Morgan Stanley Dean Witter (March 2000).

36 The state banks' working capital and investment lending rates respectively decreased from 22.17 and 18.83 per cent in 1992 to 19.36 and 16.48 per cent in 1993. These rates further dropped to 16.77 and 14.25 per cent in 1994. In 1993, US dollar 3-month LIBOR also reached 3.31 per cent, the lowest in the 1990s. However, the rate increased to 4.75 per cent in 1994. The depreciation of the rupiah against the US dollars (year-end base) was 1.7 per cent in 1993 and 4.6 per cent in 1994 (Table 4.9).

37 The shares of long term in total debts in the study carried out by Claessens, Djankov and Lang are as follows: 40.8 per cent in 1992, 39.6 per cent in 1993 and 41.6 per cent in 1994 (Claessens *et al.* 1998, pp.11–12). On the other hand, the shares of current to total liabilities in the study by Pomerleano are as follows: 52 per cent in 1992, 56 per cent in 1993 and 56 per cent in 1994 (Pomerleano 1998, pp.12–13).

38 Historically, politically directed lending in state banks portfolios was not repaid. World Bank reports repeatedly appealed that 'better collections (of bad debts) are likely to require support from the highest political level' (The World Bank 1996, p.xxviii).

39 The debt to equity ratios in the study carried out by Claessens, Djankov and Lang are as follows: 1.661 times in 1994, 2.115 times in 1995 and 1.878 times in 1996 (Claessens *et al.* 1998, pp.8–10). On the other hand, the ratios in the study by Pomerleano are as follows: 0.58 times in 1994, 0.81 times in 1995 and 0.92 times in 1996 (Pomerleano 1998, pp.6–8).

40 The state banks' working capital and investment lending rates during the period were as follows: 16.77 and 14.25 per cent in 1994, 16.86 and 14.51 per cent in 1995 and 17.02 and 15.08 per cent in 1996. US dollar 3-month LIBOR rates during the period were as follows: 4.75 per cent in 1994, 6.04 per cent in 1995 and 5.51 per cent in 1996 (Table 4.9). Therefore, the benchmark rates were relatively stable. With regards to borrowing margins, see Chapter 5.

41 The depreciation of the rupiah against the US dollars (year-end base) was as follows: 4.6 per cent in 1994, 4.0 per cent in 1995 and 3.3 per cent in 1996 (Table 4.9). The government had repeatedly stated that the rate of depreciation of the rupiah against the US dollars would be maintained at around 5 per cent.

42 Exceptionally, the return on equity in the data sets of 50 private non-financial companies sharply increased in 1996.

43 The ratios of long-term to total debts in the study by Claessens, Djankov and Lang are as follows: 41.6 per cent in 1994, 41.8 per cent in 1995 and 43.3 per cent in 1996 (Claessens *et al.* 1998, pp.11–13). In addition, the ratios of current to total liabilities in the study by Pomerleano are as follows: 56 per cent in 1994, 50 per cent in 1995 and 45 per cent in 1996 (Pomerleano 1998, pp.12–13).

44 The annual average of the Jakarta Stock Price Index moved as follows: 502 in 1994, 474 in 1995 and 585 in 1996 (Table 4.9).

45 Morgan Stanley Dean Witter (March 2000), p.1.

46 Morgan Stanley Dean Witter (March 2000), p.1.

47 Due to the limited availability of data, the number of the private non-bank sector is used.

48 The figures of the private non-bank sector are used.

49 New entry into finance companies was halted. Also, finance companies' total borrowing relative to net worth was limited to 15 times and to 5 times for offshore loans.

5 The analysis of offshore syndicated debt for Indonesian borrowers during the finance boom in the 1990s

1 This work defines the finance boom in Indonesia in the 1990s as the period from 1994 to the first half of 1997. See Chapter 1.

2 It is difficult to separate out syndicated debt transactions for the corporate sector (i.e. private non-financial companies) from those for the non-bank sector. Empirical studies in this chapter use data on syndicated debt transactions for the private non-bank sector. As explained in Chapters 1 and 3, non-financial companies had a dominant position in the sector's external debt.

3 Offshore syndicated debt includes: (i) debt originated by offshore banks and placed for offshore lenders and (ii) debt originated by onshore banks and placed for offshore lenders. Therefore, the definition of offshore syndicated debt in this work is equivalent to foreign currency syndicated debt.

4 At that time, offshore lenders considered BNI, Bank EXIM and BRI as the best borrowers among the seven state banks. The leading private banks, which were accepted by offshore lenders, included BCA, BII, Lippo Bank, Bank Bali, Bank Panin, and Bank Niaga.

5 An article in the *IFR* describes the onset of the Indonesian finance boom and offshore lenders' enthusiasm towards Indonesian transactions in the 1990s: as 'A borrower's market – In the second half of the year (1994), the trend for cheaper and longer offshore syndicated loans and bond issues has continued, despite higher official interest rates and generally unpredictable market conditions. The tone among bankers remains surprisingly bullish as international banks maintain their aggressive strategies in the market. Bankers say the Thai market is still favoured because of its greater stability, but banks have nevertheless boosted their internal limits for Indonesian credits and more foreign banks are setting up branches in Jakarta. The high demand for Indonesian paper has combined with a dearth of quality issuers and assets to cause over-subscriptions and overwhelming responses to both bank and corporate syndicated loans' (*IFR* 1049, 24 September 1994).

6 The data in Tables 5.1 and 5.2 cannot indicate the entries of new borrowers directly. However, assuming that offshore lenders had exposure limits to even high-quality borrowers, it can be estimated that the dramatic increase of offshore syndicated debt for Indonesian borrowers was at least in part based on the diversification of borrowers and lenders.

7 *IFR* 1021 (12 March 1994), *IFR* 1024 (2 April 1994), *IFR* 1037 (2 July 1994).

8 Industries in brackets indicate the business groups' major businesses that had alliances with foreign capital through joint ventures and technical assistances.

9 Other family members of the Dharmala Group owned the PSP Group, thus the two groups were combined for this study. In addition, the owner of the Ciputra Group held significant shares and played a significant managerial role in the Jaya Group (joint venture with the City of Jakarta) and the Metropolitan Group (joint venture with other Indonesian business groups); therefore the three groups were combined for this study.

10 *IFR* 997 (18 September 1993); The World Bank (1996), pp.xxii–xxv.

11 In 1996, the peak year of the finance boom, Bank Indonesia became concerned about the external debt of the corporate sector and studied new methods of monitoring debt (*IFR* 1129, 20 April 1996).

12 Examples of state non-bank borrowers are Pertamina (the state oil company) and PLN (the state electricity company). Examples of state independent projects are natural gas exploration and power stations.

13 Even if new participants are good credit risks, they generally require premiums on standard margins. Therefore, even if diversification is not downwards directed, diversification may increase the average all-in margins of the market.

14 In this chapter, 'state banks' refers to seven state commercial banks (BNI, Bank EXIM, BRI, BBD, BDN, Bapindo, and BTN) and the central bank (BI).

15 Banks Indonesia's borrowing terms were as follows: the 70.00 basis points all-in margin for the 7-year average life in 1995, the 60.09 basis points all-in margin for the 8-year average life in 1996 and the 70.14 basis points all-in margin for the 7-year average life in 1997.

16 In 1993, leading state commercial banks, such as BNI and Bank EXIM, insisted on a 5-year tenor to offshore lenders. However, offshore banks hesitated in providing 5-year finance, as *IFR* reported as follows: 'One source said Japanese banks were reluctant to commit to five years.' (*IFR* 965, 6 February 1993), 'Bankers are still reluctant to opt for a deal with over four years.' (*IFR* 970, 13 March 1993), '[A] 5-year maturity, a tenor which is impossible to syndicate for an Indonesian credit,...' (*IFR* 974, 10 April 1993). In 1994, leading state commercial banks requested a 7-year tenor to offshore lenders, again. Although the finance boom had begun, offshore lenders strongly hesitated to agree to such a long tenor. *IFR* reported as follows: 'However, the borrower's insistence that the offering – in whatever form – will include a seven-year tenor has most interested banks a bit concerned,...Most market players – including some who admitted to being quite keen to win the mandate – feel a seven-year Indonesian deal would be incredibly difficult to pull off at this juncture. In many cases, the majority of lenders who might step up for transaction are restricted to lending past five years. BNI's adamant request for a straight seven-year deal which these banks feel will be difficult to place' (*IFR* 1027, 23 April 1994), 'Several banks have categorically said that they are unable to get credit committee clearance for state bank deals in excess of five years' (*IFR* 1029, 7 May 1994).

17 Bapindo obtained US$125 million 5-year FRN (all-in margin 135 basis point) in 1995, US$150 million 5-year FRN (all-in margin 110 basis point) in 1996. BTN obtained US$30 million 5-year FRN (all-in 87 basis point) in 1995.

18 In a few cases, the banks paid a premium for obtaining large facilities.

19 During the period, the benchmark rates, such as LIBOR and SIBOR, were also stable.

20 Compared to other Asian countries, such as Thailand and Korea, offshore lenders were relatively conservative in taking risks in the Indonesian banking sector.

21 Private non-bank borrowers were required to report their offshore borrowings to BI. This liberal policy was basically maintained during the period. However, in 1996, at the peak of the finance boom, the government expressed concern about the quickly accumulating external debt in the private non-bank sector and began seriously monitoring its activities (*IFR* 1129, 20 April 1996).

22 *IFR* 997 (18 September 1993).

23 See Chapter 3, regarding the firms included in these data.

24 The revelation by the press was that 26 major business groups had accumulated more than 100 billion rupiah (US$48 million) in doubtful and bad debt to six state commercial banks (*IFR* 986, 3 July 1993). Moreover, the Asian press estimated that non-performing loans at state commercial banks were around 20–25 per cent of total loans (*IFR* 997, 18 September 1993). On the other hand, in June 1993, the governor of BI, Soedradjat Djiwandono, reported to parliament that bad state bank debt totalled Rp.2.4 trillion (US$1.15 billion) as of 31 March 1993, or 1.89 per cent of total domestic exposures (*IFR* 986, 3 July 1993). In 1993 and 1994, *IFR* frequently reported these problems (*IFR* 986, 990, 991, 997, 998, 999, 1027).

25 The following articles illustrate the market's scepticism: 'Nobody outside the Bank Indonesia, they said, knew the classification of the debt; whether complete write-offs or doubtful debts, those overdue from three months to just under two years. ... There is political pressure on Bank Indonesia to reveal more details; and the foreign banks themselves are approaching the state banks to give them the data on their provisions for doubtful and bad debts' (*IFR* 986, 3 July 1993).

26 See Schwarz (1999), pp.66–70.

27 *IFR* reported as follows: '[A]nd foreign financiers are cautious, conservative and selective. "There are plenty of borrowers in Indonesia," said one banker, "but finding banks confident of taking on Indonesian risks, especially on and over a medium term of three to five years – that is a tough task." ... They are more selective in terms of the quality of the borrower and the maturity period' (*IFR* 976, 24 April 1993).

28 The tightness of offshore lenders' views on Indonesian credit risks can be understood from the following articles in *IFR*: 'Foreign bank limits for Indonesian state banks are in many cases quite full and arranging banks will use the recent negative publicity regarding the banks' balance sheets as an excuse to squeeze a few extra basis points.' (*IFR* 997, 18 September 1993), 'Interestingly, in spite of concerns that banks' country limits have hit the roof, there still appears to be a healthy appetite for good Indonesian risks' (*IFR* 1005, 13 November 1993).

29 *IFR* 1020 (5 March 1994), 1024 (2 April 1994), 1072 (11 March 1995), 1073 (18 March 1995), and 1077 (15 April 1995).

30 Just prior to the signing of the FRCD, D. E. Setiyoso, Managing Director of BRI, announced that the bank's audited profit and loss figures differed by 5 per cent from the in-house figures used in the information memorandum for the transaction. The misrepresentation of financial figures is the worst problem from the normal viewpoints of credit judgments. However, offshore lenders easily forgave the bank's misrepresentations without imposing any penalties. *IFR* reported as follows: 'Although slightly shocked by the announcement, most bankers involved in the issue were pleased that BRI officials chose to disclose the discrepancy. "You expect that there would be a slight discrepancy between in-house and audited figures. In our opinion, the figures still improved from 1993 to 1994, making the five per cent difference of little consequence," said one participant on the FRCD' (*IFR* 1111, 9 December 1995). Offshore lenders' optimism on Indonesian risks can be sensed from this report.

31 Among Japanese banks, mainly Sanwa Bank, Dai-ichi Kangyo Bank, The Long-Term Credit Bank of Japan and Sumitomo Bank competed for arrangers' position fiercely.

32 Generally, their merchant banking arms in Singapore arranged syndicated loans and their investment banking arms in Hong Kong arranged FRCD and FRN.

33 *IFR* 1021 (12 March 1994), *IFR* 1024 (2 April 1994), *IFR* 1037 (2 July 1994).

34 *IFR* 1037 (2 July 1994). Leading Middle East banks, such as Arab Banking Corporation, took active roles in arranging offshore syndicated loans.

35 Since 1994, a number of offshore syndicated loans were arranged for absorbing Korean and Taiwanese moneys. For example, a US$40 million syndicated loan for Internas

Arta Finance (Sinar Mas) was strategically designed for Korean lenders and successfully closed as 'all Korean deals' (*IFR* 1040, 23 July 1994). A US$25 million syndicated loan for Sinar Mas Multiartha (Sinar Mas) was arranged for mainly Taiwanese banks (*IFR* 1985, 10 June 1995). An US$30 million syndicated loan for Bunas Finance Indonesia (Ongko) was targeted to Korean lenders (*IFR* 1139, 11 May 1996).

36 See Schwarz (1999), pp.321–3.

37 See Schwarz (1999), pp.331–2.

38 *IFR* 1145 (10 August 1996), *IFR* 1151 (21 September 1996).

39 Among Suharto's six sons and daughters, Siti Haridijanti Hastuti or Tutut (first daughter / the Citra Lamtro Gung Persada Group), Bambang Trihatmojo or Bambang (second son / the Bimantara Group), and Hutomo Mandara Putra or Tommy (third son / the Humpuss Group) were most active in business. During the period, large business opportunities tended to be presented to these three children. Among other family members, Probosutedjo (half-brother), Sudwikatmono (cousin of Suharto's wife, Siti Hartina or Ibu Tien), Sukamdani (brother-in-law), and Hashim Djojohadikusumo (brother of Prabowo Djojohadikusumo, husband of Suharto's second daughter), were active in business, but Hashim, the owner of the Tirtamas Group, aggressively obtained large business opportunities.

40 *IFR* 1151 (21 September 1996).

41 *IFR* 1151 (21 September 1996), reported as follows: 'Spreads trimmed – And as more Indonesian corporates tap the capital markets, the larger number of foreign banks vying for business has trimmed spreads. Top-tier corporates, in particular, have benefited from this. "They (Indofood Sukses Makmur) are achieving pricing which is very close or even slightly lower than what other BBB rated corporates in other parts of the world can get," said one banker. ..., he said. "That goes to show the market's appetite for good corporate names in Indonesia, as well as the banks' confidence in the economy. Because for such a long tenor – five years – banks were willing to come in." "There is a lot of competition out there. If you insist that spreads will have to go up, then you won't have any business," said a vice-president, syndications for a Japanese bank.'

42 The most active Indonesian private banks were Bank Bira, Bank PDFCI (joint venture), Bank Niaga and Bank International Indonesia. State commercial banks also actively participated in arranging and underwriting syndicated debt.

43 The government carefully controlled the external debt of state and private banks by squeezing PKLN, the quota of offshore borrowing, in the 1990s. In addition, the government attempted to reduce the external debt of the state sector through the privatization of state companies. It was seriously concerned about the sharp increase in domestic credit and external debt since 1995. In particular, the government carefully observed real estate finance by offshore debt. Bank Indonesia initially requested the banking sector limit their finance to property businesses and finally restricted finance. Reserve requirements were also increased from 2 to 3 per cent. The issuance of new licenses for non-bank financial services (leasing, factoring and consumer finance) was halted. Furthermore, Bank Indonesia attempted to improve its monitoring of the inflows of foreign commercial loans to non-bank borrowers, offshore fund-raising of which were unregulated (*IFR* 1129, 20 April 1996). Although BI introduced an 18 per cent target for the growth of domestic credit, growth reached 25 per cent in 1996 (*IFR* 1200, 13 September 1997). Finally, the government strengthened offshore borrowing regulations and introduced restrictions on offshore borrowing by non-bank finance companies in 1997 (*IFR* 1177, 5 April 1997; *IFR* 1178, 12 April 1997; *IFR* 1181, 3 May 1997). This is because the government thought that non-bank finance companies were used as a conduit for commercial banks in order to avoid PKLN.

44 Moral hazard problem on foreign exchange risk are popular arguments with regards to the East-Asian crisis and considered as one of main reasons for over-borrowing and over-lending during the pre-crisis period (Aoki 2001; Krugman 1998a).

45 Indonesian sovereign risk can be measured by lending margins to state banks. The simple average of all-in margins for eight state banks is used for the calculation in Table 5.14 as done in the previous sections.

46 The improvement in excess all-in margin for all Indonesian non-bank borrowers ((b) in Table 5.14) includes the factor that offshore lenders took more credit risks by downwards diversification of borrowers.

47 Due to the lack of data about historical default and recovery rates for the Indonesian corporate sector, it is impossible to calculate accurate risk-adjusted returns on lending to the sector.

6 Case study 1: the Salim Group's financial activities in the 1990s

1 Indofood is a typical example of the Salim Group's acquisition strategy. Among Indofood's three major noodle makers, Sarimi Asli Jaya, Sanmaru Food Manufacturing and Lambang Insan Makmur, the Salim Group established only Sarimi Asli Jaya by itself in the 1980s. Circa 1990, the group acquired Lambang Insan Makmur (Supermie Indonesia), which began as a family operation in 1969. Sanmaru Food Manufacturing was established by the Jangkar Jati Group in the early 1970s and became a part of the Salim Group in 1984 (Far Eastern Economic Review, 30 December 1993, 6 January 1994).

2 These companies are: Indofood (Indofood Sukses Makmur), Indocement (Indocement Tunggal Prakarsa), Indomibil (Indomobil Sukses), UIC (Unggul Indah Cahaya, previously Unggul Indah Corporation), Fastfood Indonesia (Fastfood Indonesia), IKI Indah (Sumi Indo Kabel, previously IKI Indah Kabel), Darya Varia (Darya Varia Laboratoria), Indosiar (Indosiar Visual Mandiri), BCA, First Pacific (First Pacific Corporation) in Hong Kong, and QAF (QAF Ltd) in Singapore.

3 The data of 'cash calls' is based on 'Indonesian stock market review: September 1999' by ING Barings. It should be noted that the *cash calls* amount is much smaller than the increase of CS + APIC accounts. This is because CS + APIC accounts include equity injection at the pre-IPO stage and other equity transaction and/or treatment. The aggregate gross debts by Indonesia-domiciled Salim Group companies, excluding Indofood (consolidated into Indocement) at the year end of 1993 and 1996 were only Rp.2,927 billion and Rp.4,294 billion respectively.

4 As First Pacific Bank is consolidated into First Pacific, the leverage of First Pacific is overstated compared with pure non-bank companies.

5 Holdiko was established for the purpose of the settlement between Salim Group and IBRA (Indonesian Bank Restructuring Agency) with regard to liquidity credits provided to BCA and affiliated loans, which exceeded the Legal Lending Limit given by BCA to Salim Group affiliate companies. As a part of the Settlement Agreement with IBRA, the Salim Group transferred shares and assets in 107 companies to Holdiko. Holdiko is legally owned by the Salim Group through Gemahripah Pertiwi (50 per cent) and Carakasubur Nirmala (50 per cent) but under the effective control of IBRA. (The transferred shares and assets were pledged to IBRA, and IBRA holds voting rights over pledged shares.) The ratio calculation used 83 non-listed companies' financial data. Some companies were consolidated subsidiaries of listed companies. However, the calculation includes those companies for the purpose of understanding non-listing companies' financial condition.

6 The Asian participating banks were: Boram Bank, DBS Bank, DCB Bank Labuan, Korea Long Term Credit Bank, Malayan Banking Bhd, Daehan Investment Banking Corp, Overseas-Chinese Banking Corp, Kexim Intl Singapore, Wing Hang Bank, Bangkok Bank, Daegu Bank, Dah Sing Bank, Dongnam Bank, E-Sun Commercial Bank, First Commercial Bank, First Merchant Banking Corp, Korea Merchant Banking Corp, Korean French Banking Corp, Pacific Bank Bhd, Tat Lee Bank, Chung Chong Bank, Daedong Bank, Far Eastern Intl Bank, Hyundai Finance Asia, KEB Leasing & Finance, Korea Leasing Singapore, Taishin Intl Bank, Bank of Ayudhya plc,

Bumi Daya Intl Finance, KDLC Leasing Singapore, Kexim Asia, Siam Commercial Bank and Ta Chong Bank.

7 The gross purchase consideration for Bogasari was Rp.1,179 billion, including Rp.350 billion liability assumption. The cash consideration for a 51 per cent interest in food companies of Indofood was Rp.777 billion. The remainder was for a central Jakarta office building.

8 This acquisition angered the Indocement minority shareholders as they had minimal opportunities to claim on it. BAPEPAM, an Indonesia's stock market supervisory board, altered the rule which required listed companies to obtain the minority share-holders' approval on any material actions, such as substantial acquisition (Far Eastern Economic Review, 22 June 1995, p.92).

9 Furthermore, Indomulti tried to expand its businesses into the field of department stores by establishing joint ventures with the Great River Group. The Salim Group (Indomulti Inti Industri), and the Great River Group (Inti Fasindo International), established two joint ventures: a department store and a sports shoes and fashion goods production company. The former was 40 per cent owned by the Salim Group and 60 per cent by the Great River, and on the other hand, the latter was 60 per cent owned by the Salim Group and 40 per cent owned by the Great River. The former, Indo Hanshin International, had a technical assistance arrangement with Hanshin Department Store (Japan) and planned to begin operations in 1998.

10 This purchase price consisted of (i) Rp.1,625 billion Bogasari's fixed assets, (ii) Rp.85 billion current and other assets and (iii) Rp.150 billion for construction in progress.

11 Interview with the Salim Group.

12 The six companies are Salim Ivomas Pratma, Intiboga Sejahtera, Salim Oil Grains, Bitung Menado Oil Ltd., Argha Giri Perkasa and Indomarco Adi Prima.

13 In terms of minority shareholders' interest, Backman criticizes stock-listings with controlling shareholders in Asia from the following three aspects: (i) stock-listings are used for maximizing controlling shareholders' interests at the expense of minority shareholders, (ii) controlling shareholders use their listed companies for selling their private investments at inflated prices and (iii) controlling parties enjoy extra profits by forcing their listed companies to purchase operational materials from their private companies at inflated prices. Then, he states that two important methods for exercising these three issues are: (i) 'right issue' to maintain the control of shareholders' control-lability of listed companies and force minority shareholders to inject additional capital into the companies and (ii) non-arm's-length 'related party transactions' to transfer the profit at the expense of minority shareholders. Backman strongly criticized the Salim Group's transaction of six palm oil-related companies from the view point of non-arm's-length related party transaction (Backman 1999, pp.106–17).

14 The purchase price in an information memorandum for syndicate banks was Rp.5,100 per share. However, this was later reduced. The figures in Figure 6.3 are based on those in the memorandum.

15 Marga Lestari Abadi was 95 per cent owned by New co and 5 per cent directly held by the Salim Group.

16 The Salim Group owned Qualif Pte Limited through KMP, which was Salim Group's strategic offshore investment company in Singapore.

17 The Sampoerna Group planned to sell a part of its Indofood share (5.63 per cent equivalent) and retain the remaining share (10.54 per cent equivalent) directly. Furthermore, the group planned to hold around 11 per cent of QAF share by proceeds from the share sale.

18 This finance prepared for the Salim Group's acquisition included the Sampoerna Group's portion.

19 In September 1999, the Salim family and partners and First Pacific concluded a sales and purchase agreement of Indofood shares through CAB Holdings Limited

(Mauritius), the latter's investment vehicle. Thereby, First Pacific became a 40 per cent shareholder of Indofood. In December 2000, First Pacific further acquired an additional 8 per cent of Indofood shares from the Salim family and partners, and became a 48 per cent shareholder.

7 Case study 2: the Lippo Group's financial activities in the 1990s

1 Since 1975, the Riady and the Salim families have jointly developed finance businesses in Indonesia via two investment lines: BCA and the Lippo Group. The Riady family held 17.5 per cent of BCA and Mochtar Riady himself led the restructuring of the bank, fostered it into the largest Indonesian private bank, and furthermore expanded into other finance businesses by forming joint ventures with foreign partners (for example, a non-bank financial institution with The Long-Term Credit Bank of Japan, Jardine Fleming and Royal Bank of Scotland and a leasing company with Japan Leasing). On the other hand, the Riady family (through Lippo Holding, the family's holding company) and the Salim family held equal shares of the Lippo Group and developed it into another large finance business unit in Indonesia. Therefore, until the early 1990s, the families had two conflicting finance business units in Indonesia.
2 Mochtar Riady restructured and developed the businesses of Bank Kemakmuran from 1960 to 1963, Bank Buana from 1963 to 1971, Panin Bank from 1971 to 1975 and thereafter BCA. The Riady family earned and accumulated its capitals by obtaining some shares of those banks as rewards for Mochtar's management. Most Indonesian Chinese capitalists accumulated their capitals through merchant activities during the early stages, while Mochtar mainly accumulated his capitals by selling his finance know-how as a professional.
3 Since around 1992, the Lippo Group was active in their investments in China through Lippo China Resources Limited (formerly Hongkong China Limited), the group's property investment arm in Hong Kong. The group diversified its investment risks by participating in joint ventures with local partners. The majority of investments were placed in real estate projects, such as industrial estate and town development such as its urban development business in Indonesia, for example, infrastructure projects in Fuzhou City, Fujian Tati Meizhou Industrial Park Development and Meishou Resort Island (Fujian Province), Beijing Tati Turbo Dragon Real Estate Development and Beijing Tati Enfort Estate (Beijing) and Shanghai Lippo Fuxing Real Estate and Shanghai Singkong Industrial Park Development (Shanghai). Since around 1994, the Lippo Group diversified into industrial and infrastructure activities in China by investing in three cement manufacturing joint ventures in Shandong (a 60 per cent stake), a float glass plant in Jiangsu Province (a 20 per cent stake) and a joint venture to construct and operate a highway in Guangdong (a 70 per cent stake), a joint-venture of ceramic tile production in Guangdong (Guangdong Kabo Ceramic Industry) (a 31.5 per cent stake), a cable production joint venture (Chongqing TSK Cable) (a 20 per cent stake) and so forth.
4 Interview with Mochtar Riady.
5 Even joint venture partners, such as Tokai Bank (Japan) and BNP (France), were very conservative regarding loans to the Lippo Group (Interview with the Lippo Group).
6 According to Jakarta Post (13 November 1995), the total amount of Lippo Bank's accounts with BI and other banks was Rp.117 billion, while over Rp.696 billion promissory notes were placed for settlement.
7 This issue was widely reported in Asia. In Hong Kong, The South China Morning Post (6 November 1995) reported this issue as 'Bank run fear over clearing problem', and Lippo Bank strongly denied the report and claimed it against the publisher (Interview with M. Permadi, President Director of Lippo Bank). Asian Week (November 1995), also reported on the Lippo Group's businesses by severely criticizing its urban development projects in Indonesia, as in 'Is Lippo in trouble?' In Singapore, The Business

Times (13 November 1995) reported this problem in a relatively unbiased manner. In Japan, Nikkei (15 November 2003) reported it by investigating the group's outstanding business acumen and interpreting this problem as being removed from the usual 'business style'.

8　Jakarta Post on 13 November 1995.

9　The Lippo Group's announcement that Lippo Land's debt had increased to Rp.999.1 billion as of June 1995, from Rp.46.4 billion in the previous June shocked investors and knocked the group's share prices, even though many of the group's subsidiaries holding debts simply consolidated to Lippo Land. Investors speculated that Lippo Bank held much of the debt and the solvency of the group was threatened. After this problem was dealt with, Mochtar explained that the group was fragile vis-à-vis rumour due to debt finance (Interview with Mochtar Riady). 1995 was the keystone year that heralded the turning point of the group's financial strategy.

10　The 14 Jakarta listed companies are: Lippo Bank, Lippo Securities, Lippo E-Net (both name and business were changed from Asuransi Lippo Life), Lippo General Insurance, Lippo Pacific, Lippo Land Development, Lippo Kawaraci (formerly Lippo Village), Lippo Cikarang (formerly Lippo City), Multipolar Corporation, Matahari Putra Prima, Siloam Gleneagles Health Care, Lippo Enterprises (formerly Lippo Industries), Royal Sentur (35–40 per cent owned by the Lippo Group) and Hotel Prapatan (45 per cent owned by the Lippo Group). The seven overseas listed companies are: Lippo Limited, Lippo China Resources (formerly Hongkong China Limited), The HKCB Bank Holding Company, Hongkong Building and Loan Agency, AcrossAsia Multimedia Limited (Hong Kong), Auric Pacific Group Limited (Singapore) and Medco Holdings (Philippines).

11　The Lippo Group and Sumitro Djojohadikusumo's family jointly acquired Hotel Prapatan. The group gained the majority control of Auric Pacific Group Limited from Endang Mokodompit, a daughter of Ibnu Sutowo (a former head of Pertamina). Royal Sentur was a joint venture between the Lippo Group and the Bimantara Group owned by Bambang, a son of Suharto.

12　The Lippo Group began to heavily invest in Hong Kong from the beginning of the 1990s. In 1991, Lippo International Consortium Limited acquired the controlling stake of Lippo Limited. In the same year, the Lippo Group began to purchase a number of prime properties in Hong Kong. In 1992, the Lippo Group acquired The Hongkong Chinese Bank Limited. In 1992, the Lippo Group acquired 63.6 per cent of Hongkong China Limited.

13　The political status of the Lippo Group among leading Indonesian Chinese business groups also became stronger than before. Lippo Bank became one of the first to obtain support through the government's recapitalization plan and was able to successfully retain the control with approximately 20 per cent share (post-capital injection by the government). In addition, B. J. Habibie, the then President, appointed James Riady, a special envoy to other Asian countries and Australia for retrieving fled Indonesian Chinese capital and encouraging fresh foreign investments (Asian Wall Street Journal, 8 March 1999).

14　Generally, the offshore banks were not eager to lend to Indonesian non-bank finance companies; thus the non-bank finance companies were mainly targets for offshore financial institutions seeking high returns or domestic banks. In October–November 1996, four Indonesian finance companies tapped the Singapore market for 1- to 2-year transactions: Lippo Merchant Finance (the Lippo Group), Internas Arta Finance, Panin Overseas Finance (the Panin Group) and Bunas Finance (the Ongko Group). All-in yield varied rather widely from 197.5 basis points for Lippo Merchant Finance to 220 basis points for Panin Overseas Finance; 245 basis points for Bunas Finance. The Lippo Group was in a relatively good position among these non-banks.

15　The Lippo Group's *relationship banks* were The Long-Term Credit Bank of Japan and Daiwa Bank. The following Asian banks and non-banks were discovered as participants: Singapore Leasing, Korea Japan Finance, UOB, Indover Bank, KKBC International, Hanil International Finance, First Commercial Bank, Hyundai Finance Asia, KDB Intl Singapore, Chinatrust Commercial Bank, Kookmin Bank, Bank Negara Indonesia, Taiwan Co-operative Bank Offshore and so forth.

16 Bear Stearns Asia arranged the programme for Lippo Land Development International Finance Co BV, guaranteed by Lippo Land Development and Lippo Cikarang jointly and severally, and by Lippo Land Karawaci severally. Issuances through this programme were at maturities of between 2 and 10 years.

17 The leverage ratios of Lippo Securities, Lippo Life and Lippo Bank respectively changed from 0.04, 2.10 and 14.80 in 1994 to 1.50, 1.40 and 11.9 in 1997. The equity ratios of the companies also changed from 0.45, 0.32 and 0.06 in 1994 to 0.40, 0.42 and 0.08 in 1997.

18 The leverage ratios of Lippo Land, Lippo Cikarang, Lippo Karawaci and Matahari respectively changed from 0.54, 8.78, 2.47 and 2.49 in 1994 to 0.81, 1.16, 1.29 and 1.19 in 1997. The net debt to equity ratios of them also changed from 0.14, 4.12, 1.25 and 1.24 in 1994 to 0.70, 0.97, 0.91 and −0.15 (net cash) in 1997. Furthermore, it should be noted that the figures in 1997 were not heavily affected by the depreciation of the rupiah.

19 The leverage ratios of Lippo Limited, Lippo China Resources, HKCB Bank Holding Co. and Hong Kong Building and Loan respectively changed from 1.88, 0.29, 7.78 and 2.04 in 1994 to 2.59, 0.27, 5.97 and 3.05 in 1997.

20 This is because the Riady family could only control those three companies by investing in Lippo Securities. The family managed to liquidate their investments in Lippo Life and Lippo Bank by using non-family shareholders' funds in Lippo Securities and Lippo Life. See Figure 7.1.

21 The Asian Wall Street Journal (28 August 1996) reported this news as did the Far Eastern Economic Review (12 September 1996). The Lippo restructuring plan draws scepticism. See also Backman (1999).

22 BAPEPAM pointed out the division's cross-holding structure by focusing on the fact that Lippo Bank owned 10.34 per cent share of Lippo Securities (as of 1995) (Bloomberg News, 6 September 1996). The share was increased to 14.18 per cent by August 1996 but finally disposed to a third party (The 1997 annual report of Lippo Bank).

23 Finally, the Lippo Group promised to reinvest Rp.650 billion of the cash obtained through these transactions by taking up its right when Lippo Life and Lippo Securities were to sell their shares in 1997 (Bloomberg News, 27 September 1996). (However, this was not a legal commitment.)

24 See later regarding the change of purchase prices and elimination of fee payment.

25 Initially, the Lippo Group planned to sell the Lippo Life share for Rp.243.67 billion (US$105 million) and the Lippo Bank share for Rp.684.14 billion (US$294 million). In addition, the group intended to obtain a management fee for this transaction from Lippo Bank. However, due to the strong complaints from their investors and the necessity to obtain the minority shareholders' approval, the Lippo Group could not help but cut the sales prices for both transactions by 3 per cent and gave up the fee.

26 Lippo Bank also obtained Rp.299.9 billion (US$126.9 million) cash through a rights issue in June 1996. Therefore, the Lippo Group's financial service division obtained around Rp.775 billion (US$333 million) in a single month through rights issues. N.B., the Lippo Group paid in a large part of the funds as a controlling shareholder. However, the payments burden was large for other shareholders.

27 Before this equity transaction, Lippo Securities obtained an additional short-term facility from Lippo Bank amounting to Rp.108.5 billion for the bridging purpose. A sum of Rp.48.5 billion was used from the facility as of June 12 1997.

28 Exceptionally, Lippo Pacific used an offshore syndicated loan arranged by two Japanese banks, The Long-Term Credit Bank of Japan and Daiwa Bank. However, around half of the debt was domestic rupiah borrowings.

29 For example, as of the end of 1996, Lippo Securities had Rp.22 billion term loan and Rp.13.5 billion outstanding overdrafts from Lippo Bank, Rp.85 billion term loan and Rp.10 billion outstanding overdrafts from Bank Danamon Indonesia and Rp.20 billion from Jayabank International. The companies paid an 18.25 per cent to 20.8 per cent interest on them.

30 Lippo China Resources actively sold its real estate projects and shifted its business focus to financial services (Stephen Riady's explanation, Bloomberg News, 29 September 1997).

31 Mochtar Riady stressed this strong alliance with the China Resources Group in his chairman's statements in all the 1997 annual reports of Lippo Limited, Lippo China Resources and The HKBC Bank Holding Company Limited. On the other hand, the China Resources Group intended to become a conglomerate and participate in financial services, as Zhu Youlan, the chairman of the group, stated (Bloomberg News, 19 June 1997).

32 Before this transaction, the China Resources Group completed its internal transaction, that is, China Resources Enterprise Limited purchased a 50 per cent share of The Hong Kong Chinese Bank Limited from China Resources (Holding) Co., its parent company, for HK$2 billion.

33 Bloomberg News, 29 September 1997.

34 Other third party investors included the Kalbe Group and a group of investors associated with a businessman, Ferry Sonneville (Bloomberg News, 16 April 1997).

35 Bloomberg News, 7 May 1997.

36 In 1997, the Lippo Land share in Lippo Cikarang was reduced from 58 per cent to approximately 50 per cent.

37 Bloomberg News, 16 April 1997.

8 Case study 3: the Sinar Mas Group's financial activities in the 1990s

1 Eka Tjipta Widjaja, the founder of the Sinar Mas Group, had a number of children. The other active family members who became involved in the group management were Teguh Ganda Wijaja (pulp and paper division), Indra Widjaja (financial services division), Franky Oesman Widjaja (agribusiness, foods and consumer products), Muktar Widjaja (real estate and property), Sukmawati Widjaya (new business) and Frankle Djafar Widjaja. Oi Hooi Leong, the first son of Eka Tjipta Widjaja, managed China Resources in Hong Kong.

2 The group expanded its paper business into China, Malaysia and India. In particular, it invested large-scale capital in China by establishing APP China. APP China was then the largest paper company in China and consisted of the following business lines: (i) printing and writing paper (Gold East Paper (Jiangsu) and Gols Huasheng Paper (Suzhou Industrial Park)); (ii) packaging (Ningbo Zhonghua Paper, Ningbo Asia Paper Tube and Carton Box, Ningbo Asia Paper Converting, Cold Hai Paper (Kunshan) and Asia Paper (Shanghai)); (iii) tissue (Gold Hongye Paper (Suzhou Industrial Park) and Jin Yu (Qingyuan) Tissue Paper Industry and (iv) forestry (Jin-Shaoguan First Quality Timberland (Paper Mill), Guangxi Jinqinzhou High-Yield Forest and Hainan Jinhua Forestry). From 1997 to 1999, the group invested approximately US$2.2 billion in Chinese paper operations and finally accumulated US$3.8 billion in debt. Furthermore, the group attempted to enter the Japanese paper market. The Sinar Mas Group actively invested in China through other businesses. For example, in Ningbo, the group established a palm oil refinery, a bank (Bank International Ningbo) and a real estate company (Ningbo Jinye Land).

3 The state held a dominant position in palm plantations. The top three private palm plantation owners were Salim, Sinar Mas and Astra.

4 These ten listed companies were Indah Kiat Pulp and Paper (pulp and paper), Pabrik Kertas Tjiwi Kimia (pulp and paper), BII (commercial bank), Sinar Mas Multiartha

(holding company for financial services), Duta Pertiwi (real estate development), Plaza Indonesia Realty (real estate development), Sinar Mas Agro Resources and Technology Corporation (SMART Corporation / agribusiness), Asia Pulp and Paper Co. Ltd. (APP / holding company for pulp and paper) and Asia Food and Properties Ltd. (AFP / holding company for agribusiness and real estate development) and Golden Agri-Resources Ltd. (sub-holding company for agribusiness). Among the ten listed companies, the following three were listed in overseas stock exchange markets: APP (New York), AFP (Singapore) and Golden Agri-Resources Ltd. (Singapore). Golden Agri-Resources Ltd. was formed in 1996 and was not active before the East Asian crisis. It started serving as the intermediary holding company in 1999. Plaza Indonesia Realty was a joint-venture listed company with the Ometraco Group and the Bimantara Group. The Sinar Mas Group presented the company as a group listed company in its official group report. This study therefore treats the company as a member of the group.

5 This figure was estimated by summing up the reported debt figures of the pulp and paper division, AFP and Sinar Mas Multiartha. See annual reports and Paribas Asia Equity (1998), p.1.

6 See Paribas Asia Equity (1998), pp.6–7.

7 The IPOs were BII (November 1989), Tjiwi Kimia (April 1990), Indah Kiat (July 1990), and SMART Corporation (November 1992).

8 The actual group holding structures were more complicated and had lots of irregular shareholdings. This is because technical problems, such as taxes and licenses, were sometimes barriers against transferring shares. Figure 8.1 shows the essences of the group holding structures. However, the structures in Figure 8.1 were the most important parts of the Sinar Mas Group and made a great contribution towards the accumulation of offshore funds.

9 See Paribas Asia Equity (1998), p.6.

10 Eka Tjipta Widjaja had many more children than other first-generation owners of Indonesian Chinese business groups. Therefore, the handover was a critical issue for the group. See Backman (1999), pp.127–9.

11 Using the unconsolidated basis numbers at the restructuring stage, the pulp and paper division's operating companies accumulated around US$5.5 billion debts, the onshore holding companies accumulated around US$0.5 billion debts and offshore holding companies and their direct subsidiaries accumulated US$5.6 billion debts (UBS 2004).

12 The listing of AFP was carried out as a part of the processes used to acquire Amcol Holdings Ltd., which was a troubled Singapore-listed company and became involved in real estate development and electronic goods production.

13 For example, Prinusa Ekapersada had US$453 million debts in the forms of (i) US$361 million bank debts and (ii) US$92 million inter-company notes as restructuring debts (excluding consolidated debts) (UBS 2004). The company also guaranteed the syndicated loans for Tjiwi Kimia and Univenus in 1995. Supra Veritas and Sinar Mas Tunggal, the Sinar Mas Group's ultimate holding companies, were also active as corporate guarantors. On the other hand, Purimas Sasmita had approximately US$270 million short-term debts (Paribas Asia Equity 1998, p.23).

14 Paribas Asia Equity (1998), p.11.

15 For example, during the same period, the gross debt to EBITDA ratios of the Salim Group and the Gajah Tunggal Group were 2.59–5.27 and 3.98–8.95.

16 If the company's accounting currency was the rupiah, its US dollar debts were stretched in terms of rupiah due to the depreciation of the rupiah. On the contrary, if the company' accounting currency was US dollars, its rupiah denominated debts decreased in terms of US dollars under the same situation. Therefore, the increase of debts of the company that used US dollars for the accounting currency could exclude the increase of debts due to the currency effects. Among the Sinar Mas Group's listed

companies, APP, Indah Kiat and Tjiwi Kimia used US dollars for their accounting currency.

17 The Lippo Group had an 11.6 per cent share of total cash calls during the period.

18 APP raised US$311 million in April 1995 (IPO) and US$207 million in November 1997.

19 Fuji Bank (Japan), which had a joint venture bank with BII, aggressively arranged syndicated loans for the Sinar Mas Group.

20 However, at least, they improved the security conditions from the pledge of fixed and/or floating assets to the guarantees by the group holding companies and/or the family members. At the later stage of the finance boom, unsecured borrowings became common for the group.

21 At the restructuring stage, each member companies of the paper and pulp division accumulated debts (excluding consolidated debts) as follows: US$1.8 billion in APP, US$453 million in Purinusa Ekapersada, US$2.7 billion in Indah Kiat, US$1.1 billion in Tjiwi Kimia, US$1.1 billion in Pindo Deli, US$576 million in Lontar Papyrus, and US$3.8 billion in APP China (UBS 2004).

22 Duta Pertiwi obtained 'BBB' rating from Pefindo, the Indonesian government's debt rating agency, and issued rupiah bonds. For example, the company issued a Rp.500 billion 5-year bond in March 1997 (Bloomberg News, 19 March 1997).

23 The core projects were the mixed development of residential, office, commercial and leisure facilities (Bumi Serpong Damai) in Serpong, West Jakarta, the development of shopping facilities (Mega ITC Shopping Mall) and the redevelopment of a semi-slum area in Mangga Dua, North Jakarta, the development of industrial and residential estates and golf course in Karawang, West Java, the mixed development of shops, houses, shopping centres, office towers and condominiums (Cempaka Mas Superblock) in Jakarta, the joint-venture hotel development (Hotel Dusit) with the Dusit Thani Group (Thailand) and the equity investment in hotel and shopping mall (Plaza Indonesia) in Central Jakarta.

24 The Japanese trading companies were Itochu, Marubeni and Nissho-Iwai. The other Asian business groups were, for example, the Dusit Thani Group (Thailand) and the LG Group (Korea).

25 The initial shareholdings of the company were as follows: the Sinar Mas Group (76.4 per cent), the shareholders of Amcol Holdings Ltd. (16.4 per cent) and Japanese trading companies (Itochu and Nissho-Iwai) (7.0 per cent).

26 Including global floating rate notes, which are included in offshore syndicated debts in this study, the number reaches US$7.0 billion.

27 Including global floating rate notes, the share of the top three issuers became 50.6 per cent, 22.1 per cent and 11.5 per cent respectively. APP was clearly the most important among the group entities for raising funds in overseas bond markets.

28 Generally, bonds did not have complex protections, such as financial covenants, which were normally included in syndicate loans.

29 At the beginning of 2004, the debt restructuring of the Sinar Mas Group had not been concluded. On 31 October 2003, APP's operating companies, such as Indah Kiat and Tjiwi Kimia, signed the Master Restructuring Agreement with most ECAs (export credit agencies) and IBRA, which represented around 40 per cent of all creditors. However, the Master Restructuring Agreement required more than 75 per cent creditors' approvals in order to push forward with the restructuring.

9 Case study 4: the Gajah Tunggal Group's financial activities in the 1990s

1 The Gajah Tunggal Group was the seventh largest business group in Indonesia with sales of approximately Rp.4.2 trillion and total assets of approximately Rp.36.3 trillion (Warta Ekonomi, 25 November 1996).

2 Gajah Tunggal held the dominant market share in the secondary (replacement) tyre market. (The OEM (original equipment manufacturing) tyre market was occupied mainly by foreign joint ventures, such as Goodyear and Bridgestone.) Bank Dagang Nasional Indonesia was one of the top private banks and very active in arranging domestic syndicated loans for second-layer companies which could not access offshore markets.

3 The seven listed companies are as follows: Gajah Tunggal (tyre producer), GT Petrochem Industries (formerly Andayani Megah, producer of tyre-related chemical materials, such as tyre code and polyester filament), GT Kabel Indonesia (formerly Kabel Metal Indonesia, telecommunication and power cables producer), BDNI (commercial bank), Asuransi Dayin Mitra (insurance), GT Investama Kapital (formerly Gajah Surya Multifinance, and then BDNI Capital Corp., multifinance company) and Indonesia Prima Property (real estate company).

4 Following Minsky's argument, this is a typical case of a 'speculative finance' becoming a 'Ponzi finance', which needs additional finance to pay debt service (Minsky 1986).

5 The put option is the lender's right to request repayment. Thus, the waiver of the put option is the same as the refinance.

6 BDNI was under the control of BI for its offshore borrowing (quota system). The annual regular borrowing/issuance and the relatively small amount per deal can be explained by this quota system.

7 Most facilities were 3-year loans or FRCDs with annual put options. As these options were the participating banks' termination rights, BDNI had to request the participating banks to waive the options every year. In addition, BDNI had to pay 'waiver fees' for the acceptances of the requests. The participating banks also had to perform internal credit processes for the acceptance of the waiver requests. Therefore, the 3-year facilities with annual put options were actually 1-year facilities. These were used for minimizing heavy documentation processes and costs.

8 Non-Japan Asian participants in the US$20 million facility were Kyongnam, Changhwa Commercial Bank, Hanil Leasing and Finance, Korean Exchange Bank and Tat Lee Bank. Those in the US$180 million facility were DBS, OCBC, Keppel Bank, Bank of China, Bank of Taiwan, Bank of Commerce Labuan, KDB Int'l and Tat Lee Bank, DBS Buana Tat Lee Bank. Those in the US$40 million facility were BNI (Singapore), Indover Bank, Kookmin Leasing, Korea Int'l Merchant Bank.

9 Some of them were still at the preparation stage of operation and unable to operate before 1998.

10 That is to say, Andayani Megah purchased the share that the company did not own from the group holding company.

11 Bloomberg news, 14 August 1996.

12 On 24 September 1996, the minority shareholders of Gajah Tunggal approved the fund raising and the purchase of a power plant controlled by the Nursalim family. On 1 October 1996, the minority shareholders of Andayani Megah approved the fund raising and acquisitions.

13 The family owned the BDNI shares through Daya Patria.

14 The Gajah Tunggal Group came under the same criticism as did the restructuring of its manufacturing division's shareholding. However, on 23 September 1996, the minority shareholders of Gajah Surya Multifinance approved the company's plan to acquire a 51.8 per cent share of BDNI and raise Rp.728 billion.

15 BNP, BHF, DKB Merchant Bank, Fuji Bank, JP Morgan Securities and Sakura Merchant Bank were the arrangers of the syndicated loan.

16 Prior to the syndicated loan, Gajah Surya Multifinance borrowed a US$40 million secured syndicated term loan facility. The tenor of the facility was 2 years (4 years with a put option at the end of second year), and the security was an assignment of accounts

receivables at 120 per cent of outstanding loan. The loan paid an all-in of 225 basis points (on a tax-absorbed basis) at the top-tier participant level. The arrangers were Arab Banking Corp., Indover Bank, Sakura Merchant Bank and BNI.

10 The collapse of cash-flow chains

1 At the end of 2000, non-performing corporate debt was estimated at Rp.37 trillion (US$3.8 billion) for onshore debt (out of Rp.62 trillion) and Rp.23 trillion (US$2.4 billion) for offshore debt (out of Rp.57 trillion) (Table 2.2 in The World Bank 2001, p.2.3). In other words, almost half of the value of Indonesian debt was estimated as non-performing. Moreover, these figures were an underestimate.

2 Korea had the Corporate Restructuring Coordination Committee (for restructuring corporate debt), Korea Asset Management Corporation (KAMCO), for purchasing and recovering the financial sector's non-performing debt) and the Korean Deposit Insurance Corporation (for recapitalizing banks). Malaysia had the Corporate Debt Restructuring Committee (CDRC) (for restructuring corporate debts), Danaharta Nasional (for recapitalizing banks) and Danamodal Nasional (for purchasing non-performing debts). Thailand had the Corporate Debt Restructuring Advisory Committee (CDRAC) (for facilitating corporate restructuring), Financial Sector Restructuring Authority (FRA) (for recovering closed financial institutions' loans), Asset Management Company (AMC) (for bidding as the last resort) and the CDRAC (for restructuring corporate debts). See IBRA (1999) and Pomerleano (2000).

3 Since 1999, foreign capital has been permitted to hold 99 per cent ownership of domestic banks.

4 By the middle of December 1997, 154 banks representing around half of the total assets of the banking system faced erosion of their deposit bases (Enoch *et al.* 2003, p.24).

5 The banks used BLBI in part to cover withdrawals of foreign exchange deposits. Therefore, some observers argue that BLBI only served to fuel the continuing depreciation of the rupiah (Enoch *et al.* 2003, p.24). IBRA was tasked with recovering Rp.144.5 trillion in BLBI extended to 16 BDL banks, 34 BBO/BBKU banks and 4 BTO banks (Sato 2001, p.329). BDNI (The Gajah Tunggal Group) received Rp.37.1 trillion, BCA (The Salim Group) received Rp.26.6 trillion, Bank Danamon used Rp.23.0 trillion and BUN (The Ongko Group) received Rp.12.1 trillion (IBRA 1999). Bank Indonesia also provided BLBI to seven state banks of Rp.174.4 trillion (Rp.101.8 trillion to Bank EXIM, Rp.40.4 trillion to Bapindo, Rp.11.3 to BBD, Rp.8.7 trillion to BDN, Rp.8.2 trillion to BRI, Rp.2.6 trillion to BNI and Rp.1.4 trillion to BTN) (Sato 2001, p.329).

6 All of the seven large state banks (with nearly 50 per cent of the banking sector's assets) were in Category C. As part of the restructuring programme of state banks, in 1999, Bank Mandiri was formed by merging four of them (Bank EXIM, BBD, BDN and Bapindo) and was recapitalized by the government. The other three state banks (BNI, BRI and BTN) were recapitalized in 2000.

7 This category consisted of 74 banks with around 5 per cent of the banking sector's assets. The majority of them were small banks.

8 Bank owners were obliged to contribute at least 20 per cent in cash and the government supported up to 80 per cent in the form of bonds. The owners had the option to buy back the government's shares within 4 years, that is, by June 2002.

9 These banks were Bank Arta Media, BII (the Sinar Mas Group), Bank Bukopin, Lippo Bank (the Lippo Group), Bank Patriot, Bank Prima Express, Bank Universal (the Astra Group).

10 This consisted of Rp.118.7 trillion in rupiah loans (50.7 per cent) and Rp.115.5 trillion in foreign currency loans (49.3 per cent). Seven state banks transferred Rp.101.7 trillion in loans, seven recapitalized banks transferred Rp.13.2 trillion in loans, 12 taken over

banks transferred Rp.45.1 trillion in loans and 49 frozen banks transferred Rp.74.2 trillion in loans to IBRA (IBRA 1999, p.6).

11 The MSAA required only the corporate assets of the bank owners' pledged companies, while the MRNIA additionally required the bank owners' private assets.

12 The nine bank owners were Sjamsul Nursalim (The Gajah Tunggal Group/Bank Dagang National Indonesia/Rp.27.5 trillion/12 companies), Kaharuddin Ongko (The Ongko Group/Bank Umum Nasional/Rp.8.3 trillion/21 companies), Mohammad (Bob) Hasan (The Nusamba Group/Bank Umum Nasional/Rp.5.3 trillion/30 companies), Samadikun Hartono (The Modern Group/Bank Modern/Rp.2.7 trillion/ 10 companies), Sudwikatmono (The Golden Truly Group/Bank Surya/Rp.2.0 trillion/ 6 companies), Soedono Salim (The Salim Group/Bank Central Asia/Rp.52.6 trillion/ 108 companies), Usman Admadjaja (The Danamon Group/Bank Danamon/Rp.12.5 trillion/ 27 companies), Hokiano (The Hokiano Group/Bank Hokindo/Rp.0.3 trillion/10 companies) and Ibrahim Risyad (The Risjadson Group/Bank Risjad Salim International/Rp.0.3 trillion/4 companies) (IBRA 1999, p.27; Sato 2001, p.373). Note: the ( ) indicates (name of business group/name of bank/the face value of issued promissory note/number of pledged companies).

13 The figures are calculated by US$70.0 billion total external debts and Rp.215 trillion total domestic debts (INDRA 1998a, p.3; World Bank 2001, p.2.3).

14 IBRA's assets consisted of around Rp.289 trillion in non-performing loans and other assets, Rp.130 trillion in equity investments in BTO and recapitalized banks and Rp.127 trillion in claims on former bank owners' shareholder assets (through PKPS) (World Bank 2000, p.13).

15 Heavy criticism was also made of IBRA's disposal operations. The previous owners often bought back their assets under the control of IBRA. The previous owners frequently used their offshore entities and/or close business friends as dummy purchasing entities. For example, FSPC banned IBRA from selling assets to the Salim Group. See section titled The Salim Group.

16 IBRA classified debtors into four categories (Category A to D) by the likelihood of repayment. Category A included the debtors with good intentions to pay and good business prospects. Category B included the debtors with good intentions to pay but poor business prospects. Category C included the debtors with less good intentions to pay but good business prospects. Category D included the debtors with less good intentions to pay and poor business prospects. The agency intended to support the restructuring of the Category A debtors and take over loan collateral from the Category B debtors. The agency also intended to take legal action against the Category C and D debtors (Pardede 1999, pp.31–2). In particular, IBRA took strict legal actions against unsupportive debtors, such as the Dharmala/PSP Group.

17 The World Bank observed that: 'The pace of IBRA's asset disposition has been slow. ... The key reason for slow recovery has been the Government's reluctance to recognize the loss of value that will necessarily occur' (World Bank 2000, p.13).

18 In 2000, IBRA outsourced the commercial loan portfolio of Rp.12.9 trillion with 1,112 debtors to local banks, sold shares in Astra International to Cycle & Carriage Limited (Singapore) and its consortium by US$493 million and made the first tender of Rp.972 billion corporate loan portfolio (IBRA 1999, pp.51–4).

19 In the late 1990s and the early 2000s, all Japanese banks were under the forced restructurings in their business strategies and investment portfolios and therefore were the most active suppliers of not only Indonesian but also other East Asian distressed debts to the market.

20 Author's interviews with staff of Asian Debt Management Hong Kong Limited (in August 1998), Indonesian Recover Company Limited (in August and October 1999) and Samuel Sekuritas Indonesia (in October 1999).

21 The government issued three types of bonds: floating rate notes, fixed income bonds and inflation-indexed bonds. The floating rate notes were designed to recover banks'

negative equity to zero. The fixed income bonds were designed to increase the banks' CAR to 4 per cent. The inflation-indexed bonds were designed for Bank Indonesia's deposit guarantee program. The first bonds were issued in September 1998.

22 The World Bank also anticipated problems associated with IBRA assets: 'Estimating the returns on the pledged shareholder assets may well disappoint also, as many of the pledged assets have lost significant value' (World Bank 2000, p.13).

23 The worst category was 'Category Five (Loss)', the definition of which was late payments overdue more than 270 days.

24 Bank Indonesia, the World Bank and other financial authorities use these external debt figures for their post-crisis analyses. However, the figures are totally different from those in the historical data published by BI and used in Chapter 1.

25 The book value of their debts was Rp.87.4 trillion (US$12.3 billion). IBRA reports the aggregates as the 'top 21 business groups'. I have combined the Dharmala Group and the PSP Group into the Dharmala/PSP Group and therefore present the aggregates as 'top 20 business groups'. The top ten business group borrowers were the Texmaco Group (Rp.17.0 trillion), the Barito Pacific Group (Rp.7.3 trillion), the Dharmala/PSP Group (Rp.6.9 trillion), the Nusanba Group (Rp.6.3 trillion), the Humpuss Group (Rp.5.7 trillion), the Djajanti Group (Rp.3.8 trillion), the Napan Group (Rp.3.7 trillion), the Bimantara Group (Rp.3.4 trillion) and the Danamon Group (Rp.3.1 trillion). IBRA's exposure to Suharto-related business groups was Rp.17.7 trillion and 20.3 per cent of the top 20 obligors' debts and 9.1 per cent of the corporate claims. Including the exposure to the Texmaco Group (the largest debtor to IBRA), the figures increased to Rp.34.7 trillion and the shares also increased to 39.7 per cent and 17.9 per cent respectively (IBRA 1999).

26 At the early stage of the crisis, the business groups increased their borrowings from their group banks to settle group companies' debts and trade accounts payable regardless of violations of the Legal Lending Limit. Ten of the 14 banks taken over or closed in 1998 had violated prudential rules, generally breach of the Legal Lending Limit (Enoch *et al.* 2003, p.87). In addition, reciprocal lending between business group banks was a common mechanism used to avoid the Legal Lending Limit.

27 The absence of appropriate bankruptcy procedures worked in favour of debtors over creditors (World Bank 2001, p.2.5).

28 Soedono Salim (Liem Sioe Liong) remained outside of Indonesia in order to avoid criticism and received medical treatment. Andre Halim retired from the Managing Director's position of BCA, moved to Singapore and started the family businesses in China in KMP. Anthony Salim had taken over the Salim Group and devoted himself to tough negotiations with international lenders and IBRA (Author's interviews with Andre Halim in Singapore and Benny Santoso in Jakarta).

29 Indofood booked debts of Rp.6.2 trillion (US$1.2 billion) in 1997 and Rp.8.5 trillion (US$1.1 billion) in 1998. Indocement held debts of Rp.5.0 trillion (US$0.9 billion) in 1997 and Rp.7.8 trillion (US$1.0 billion) in 1998. UIC had debts of Rp.0.7 trillion (US$127 million) in 1997 and Rp.1.3 trillion (US$157 million) in 1998.

30 By the end of 2000, IBRA had sold around 15 trillion assets of the Salim Group (Sato 2001, p.389).

31 For example, Salim's stake in Standard Toyo Polymer (chemical) was purchased by Mitsui and Toso, its joint-venture partners. Salim's stakes in Pacific Indomas Plastic (chemical) and Indomiwon Citra Inti (MSG producer) were also sold to Dow Chemical and Daesang respectively.

32 Mobs also looted Soedono Salim's house.

33 BCA received BLBIs on 25 May, 28 May and 26 June 1998 and the outstanding total reached Rp.29,276 billion as of 31 December 1998. The amount was reduced to Rp.29,100 billion when the bank was recapitalized by the government and to Rp.26,596 billion by the end of 1999, IBRA 1999, p.114).

34 The total amount of BCA loans directed to the Salim Group and later transferred to IBRA was Rp.52.7 trillion (US$6.6 billion) (BCA 2000, p.28).

35 Soedono Salim, representing the Salim Group, issued a promissory note for the payment obligations, and the outstanding amount was Rp.52,627 billion as of the end of 1999 (IBRA 1999, p.27).

36 Rp.47,751 billion was transferred on 21 September 1998 and Rp.4,975 billion on 26 April 1999 (BCA 2000, p.28). On 27 April 1999, Rp.10,424 billion in loans categorized as 'Loss' were also transferred to IBRA after being written off by BCA (ibid. p.2).

37 On 28 May 1999, BCA received Rp.60,877 billion newly issued government bonds. The payment consisted of (i) Rp.52,726 billion payments for the BCA's loans to the Salim Group, which were transferred to IBRA; (ii) Rp.8,771 billion accrued interests, less (iii) the excess of Rp.29,100 billion BLBI over Rp.28,480 billion recapitalization payment (BCA 2000, p.28).

38 Indofood's Press Release (12 June 2002).

39 The Salim family and investors held approximately 53 per cent ownership of First Pacific. Prior to this transaction, the Salim Group had scrapped two opportunities to transfer its shareholdings in Indofood, that is, the acquisition by QAF and by First Pacific and Nisshin (Japan). In 2001, First Pacific wrote down US$286 million on its investment in Indofood. In short, the Salim family and investors maintained their ownerships of Indofood by abusing minority shareholders in First Pacific.

40 The four companies were Bogasari Sentra Flour Mills (flour milling in Jakarta), Intisari Flour Mills (flour milling in Surabaya), Inti Abadi Kemasindo (manufacturing of flour bags) and Indobahtera Era Sejahtera (shipping operation).

41 Indofood's Press Release (12 June 2002).

42 The Eurobond was launched with US$200 million but oversubscribed to US$280 million. Indofood had 'B' rating from S&P, 'B3' from Moody's and 'AA+' from Pefindo (Indonesia) and the rating was higher than Indonesia's sovereign rating ('selective default').

43 The committee members were Bank of America, The Chase Manhattan Bank, BNP Paribas, The Fuji Bank, The Bank of Tokyo Mitsubishi and Marubeni Corporation.

44 Indo Kodeco Cement was a joint venture of Indocement (72.09 per cent), Korean Development Co. Limited (24.91 per cent) and Marubeni Corporation (3.00 per cent) for cement production in South Kalimantan. In 2000, the plant had not yet started commercial production.

45 The breakdown of the restructured debts were US$720 million for US$ Tranche, JPY42.3 billion for Japanese Yen Tranche and Rp.211 billion for Rupiah Tranche (according to the figures of 31 December 1999).

46 Concurrent with the restructuring, Heidelberger proposed to acquire US$150 million debts, US$80 million of which were on a conditional basis with payments to be made upon its entry into Indocement and US$70 million of which were on an unconditional basis. The price for conditional purchase is 80% of US$80 million principal, while that for unconditional is 70% of US$70 million principal.

47 At that time, the government held around 44 per cent of Indocement shares. The government sold around 27 per cent of the shares to Heidelberger and retained the rest with a put option to sell a further around 4 per cent to Heidelberger.

48 The Salim Group diversified its assets overseas (mainly in Asia) through its offshore investment companies including First Pacific (Hong Kong), KMP (Singapore) and QAF (Singapore). In the early 1990s, the Salim Group aggressively invested in property and financial sectors in China (e.g. Yuan Hong Industrial Park (Fujian) and Fujian Asia Bank Limited). The group also expanded its instant noodle and edible oil businesses in China.

49 See 'Banking on recovery – Lippo Group rethinks its middle-class gambit' in *Far Eastern Economic Review* (18 June 1998), pp.55–6.

50 However, the Lippo Group was also involved in several joint ventures with the Suharto family, for example, Bukit Sentur (property development). The group's outstanding properties, such as shopping malls in Lippo Karawaci and Lippo Cikarang and Lippo Bank's branches and ATM machines, did not avoid heavy damage caused by mobs during the anti-Suharto riots in 1998.

51 In 1999, James Riady was appointed as a special envoy to encourage Chinese–Indonesian businessmen to repatriate their capital to Indonesia (The Asian Wall Street Journal, 8 March 1999). Several executives of the Lippo Group moved to the government to support state policies, such as the restructuring and privatization of state companies. On the other hand, nationalist groups attacked the Riady family's relationship with US President Clinton and its donation to his 1992 and 1996 presidential campaigns in the United States. The Federal Election Commission reported that the Riady family had donated around US$100,000 to the US Democratic Party since 1992, including the 1996 US political campaign. James Riady became acquainted with the then President Clinton when he was the governor of Arkansas in the early 1980s (Bloomberg News, 22 May 1999).

52 These debt figures are based on the author's research and the aggregate of the group's non-bank listed entities with the necessary consolidation adjustments.

53 This figure was taken from the Far Eastern Economic Review (18 June 1998, p.55).

54 In an interview in June 1999, James Riady said that the group debts were US$200 million (Bloomberg News, 16 June 1999). However, the definition of the group debts was unclear, so it is impossible to ascertain whether the number was understated or overstated.

55 Lippo Bank closed its overseas branches. The Riady family sold Lippo Bank California to the Commercial Bank of San Francisco) for US$15.9 million in cash (Bloomberg News, 9 November 1999).

56 See Chapter 5 regarding Lippo's overseas investments.

57 The Rp.6,171 trillion in non-performing assets with 586 debtors was also transferred from the bank to IBRA by 1999 (IBRA 1999, p.110).

58 The shareholders of Sorak were Temasek (Singapore, 50 per cent), Kookmin Bank (Korea, 25 per cent) and ICB Financial Holdings (controlled by Daim Zainuddin, the former Finance Minister of Malaysia, 20 per cent) and Barclays Capital (United Kingdom, five per cent). Kookmin Bank held a 50 per cent voting right under its investment agreement. Sorak's shareholdings reached 57 per cent in 2005.

59 APP (Asia Pulp and Paper Limited), the offshore holding of the APP Group, was incorporated in Singapore and its shares had been traded in New York.

60 The APP Group had more than US$3 billion in payment obligations to 11 overseas ECAs (Austria, Canada, Denmark, Finland, France, Germany, Italy, Japan, Spain, Sweden and the United States).

61 Therefore the APP Group had still obtained financing from offshore lenders and investors. For example, in August 1999, Indah Kiat arranged a US$100 million 1-year loan by pledging APP shares. APP Paper Trading Singapore obtained a US$75 million 2-year syndicated loan by pledging its trade receivables. In September 1999, the APP Group arranged a US$100 million 2-year secured loan, and Ninbo Paper Board Co. of APP China obtained a US$40 million 1-year loan. In March 2000, Indah Kiat refinanced the maturing loan to a US$270 syndicated loan with all-in margins of 450 basis points for a 1-year tranche and 475 basis points for a 2-year tranche. In March 2000, APP China issued a US$403 million high-yield bond. However, comparing the group's funding during the finance boom, the size became much smaller, the tenor became much shorter and the margins sharply increased.

62 The share price dropped from the level of US$5.0 per share to US$0.5 per share towards the end of 2000.

63 The non-payments were US$30 million interest payments on a US$600 million bond due in 2004 and US$13.3 million in interest payments on a US$200 million bond due in 2006. However, the company paid the US$30 million within the remedy period.

64 In April 2001, APP missed interest payments on a US$500 million convertible note and triggered an early payment clause of US$250 million asset bank securities. In June and July 2001, Indah Kiat and Tjiwi Kimia announced non-payment to their lenders and investors. APP China defaulted on a US$403 million bond and triggered cross default by other group companies.

65 The figures are from the APP Group's announcement. The group's operating companies in Indonesia had US$6.1 billion debt in total, US$476 million EBITDA and 12.8 times debt to EBITDA. Indah Kiat had US$2.9 billion – US$238 million EBITDA. So, Debt-EBITDA was 12.0 times. Tjiwi Kimia had US$1.2 billion debt, US$113 million EBITDA and 11.0 times Debt to EBITDA. Pindo Deli has US$1.3 billion debt and EBITDA of 63 million, debt to EBITDA was 21.4 times. Lontar had US$638 million debt, US$62 million EBITDA and 10.3 times Debt to EBITDA (UBS February 2003, p.76).

66 Two swap contracts and related losses were concealed. The group hired Deloitte Touche Tohmats to investigate the contracts.

67 The new payment terms were the principal amortization by 25 per cent in May 2004, May 2005, May 2006 and November 2006.

68 The plan requested creditors to exchange existing debt for a 13-year zero coupon bonds at a margin of 100 basis points, and waive accrued interest from standstill. It did not include a debt to equity swap. The proposal also treated secured and unsecured creditors equally except that secured creditors would continue to hold their original security. The restructuring considered that the six times debt to EBITDA would be a sustainable level.

69 Since July 2001, due to threats made by domestic bondholders, the APP Group resumed payments on domestic bonds. The group also continued to pay to creditors in China (Bloomberg News, 26 June 2002).

70 The Singapore Court initially reserved judgement with respect to the judicial management litigation filed by the two banks in order to monitor the progress of the restructuring. In August, the court rejected the banks' application citing the difficulty in taking effective control of the group's operation in Indonesia and China through judicial management.

71 The actions were supported by US$3.6 billion creditors but less supported by US$2.7 billion creditors (Bloomberg News, 31 July 2002).

72 The problems in the transactions between the APP Group and the family-controlled companies, such as Arara Abadi and BII Bank Limited (Cook Island), were revealed. The non-verification of US$1.2 billion in trade debt was also discovered (Bloomberg News, 20 February 2002; 14 March 2002).

73 The initial announcement was made on 2 October 2002.

74 The chief representative of Nippon Export and Investment Insurance criticized the Widjaja family's behaviour in the debt negotiations as 'a history of unprofessional and hostile conduct in these restructuring negotiations' (Bloomberg News, 28 April 2003).

75 The bondholders held the majority of the four Indonesian operating companies' debts. A substantial part of the original bondholders had exited in 2002 and 2003 through selling to hedge funds, distressed funds and investment banks. The members of 'Bondholders Steering Group' was also changed (UBS 2003).

76 The letter mentioned that the restructuring of the APP Group would be of high political importance and lead to repercussions in terms of Indonesia's international reputation (UBS March 2003, p.90). The letter was signed by the ambassadors from Austria, Canada, Denmark, Finland, France, Germany, Italy, Japan, Spain, Sweden and the United States. IBRA protested against the letter by halting restructuring negotiations on the APP Group's debts (Bloomberg News, 12 March 2003).

77 The US$6.7 billion debt of four Indonesian operating companies was to be divided into three tranches: Tranche A for US$1.2 billion 'sustainable debts', Tranche B for US$3.0 billion 'refinanceable debts' and Tranche C for US$2.5 billion 'unsustainable debts'. Tranches A and B had 10-year and 13-year maturity periods respectively with step-up margins starting from 100 basis points per annum up to 300 basis points.

Tranche B had a refinancing option. Tranche C had an 18- to 22-year maturity period and if not prepaid would be converted into shares. The margin would step up from 100 to 200 basis points. In particular, the creditors focused on the value of Tranche C. The restructuring of domestic bonds was also merged into the plan. Under the plan, the bondholders were treated favourably compared to other creditors. Their bonds were allocated to only Tranches A and B with SBI rate plus 200 basis points.

78 APP China's operating companies were Gold East Paper, Gold Huasheng Paper, Gold Hongye Paper and Ningbo Zhonghua.

79 The amount of the guarantee was around US$630 million. APP issued around US$3.9 billion in guarantees, including guarantees for the APP China Group (UBS November/December 2003, p.57).

80 However, the debt to equity swap resulted in awarding more than 20 per cent of shares to the Widjaja family as BII Bank (Cook Island), the family's private bank, had a sizable exposure (around US$140 million) to APP China.

81 The ECAs' primary concerns were default triggers and trading and cash management. The APP Group agreed with the ECA's requests, that is to say, delivering shares into a trust in front of the restructuring, an automatic default trigger into 75 per cent ownership stake in respective operating companies and the establishment of a separated trading function to control sales, procurement activities and cash flows. However, BAPEPAM, the Indonesia's capital market supervisory agency, objected to the structure because it might damage the minority shareholders' rights (Bloomberg News, 26 February 2003).

82 The APP Group had the right to buy back IBRA's APP assets subject to paying 1 per cent more than the highest bid. However, the creditors rejected the buy-back.

83 In October 2003, the secured creditors won a New York Court judgement against APP. In November 2003, they filed a foreclosure petition against Indah Kiat and the application was accepted by a district court in Bengkalis, Sumatra, Indonesia. However, in February 2004, the New York Supreme Court rejected a petition filed by the secured creditors seeking enforcement action over the collateral.

84 In September 2004, the APP Group won Indonesian court's judgement against a group of secured and structured bondholders.

85 In April 2005, Gramercy Advisors and Oaktree Capital Management won a judgement in Singapore.

86 AFP and Golden Agri-Resources of the AFP Group had rescheduled US$202 million (around 17 per cent of their total debts) (Bloomberg News, 20 December 2001).

87 Franky Oesman Widjaja, the CEO of the AFP Group, mentioned this fact to the investors (Bloomberg News, 31 July 2001).

88 Financial figures at the end of 1998 were not available because the bank was frozen in August 1998. Estimating long-term debt figures in 1996, the bank was assumed to hold more than Rp.3 trillion (US$1.4 billion by the exchange rate at the end of 1996) in borrowings.

89 See Chapter 5.

90 Gajah Tunggal had export income per month of around US$19 million in 1998 (Bloomberg News, 29 April 1998).

91 Outstanding BLBI to BDNI increased to Rp.37.0 trillion as of the end of 1999. This exposure was the largest among IBRA banks and accounted for 71.7 per cent of the total BLBI (IBRA 1999, pp.113–14).

92 For example, Gajah Tunggal borrowed US$365 million from BDNI.

93 As of the end of 1999, 16,663 transferred debtors with the Rp.24.9 trillion book value of exposures (from BDNI) were managed by IBRA (IBRA 1999, p.110–11).

94 There is no disclosed information regarding Garibaldi Venture Fund.

95 In 2005, Gajah Tunggal, GT Petrochem Industries and Filamendo Sakti still held US$336 million, US$115 million and US$71 million in debt respectively (UBS 2005, p.109).

11 Conclusions

1 Eatwell and Taylor, for example, propose capital controls as part of a World Financial Authority, which would manage systemic risk and prevents contagion during crises (Eatwell and Taylor 2000, pp.216–17).
2 See Edwards (1999).
3 The flat rate and minimum-stay period respectively reached 30 per cent and 12 months at their peak (Palma 2002). Eichengreen strongly supported the Chilean capital controls (Eichengreen 1999, 2000a).
4 China also uses this type of capital control. See Nayyar (2002) for India, Palma (2002) for Malaysia and Stiglitz (2002) for India and China.
5 Krugman strongly advised Malaysia to introduce capital controls at exit in his article in *Fortune* dated 7 September 1998. At the initial stage, overseas financial circles heavily criticized Malaysia's capital controls and were concerned about the recovery of market confidence. Finally, compared with other crisis-affected countries, in particular, Indonesia, academic as well as financial circles praised the Malaysian government for its management of the crisis situation (Stiglitz 2002). However, a number of scholars view their mechanism as inefficient (Edwatrds 1999)
6 Since the crisis, the IMF and World Bank have placed more emphasis on the sequencing of financial liberalization, including liberalization of the capital account, and the need for the prior establishment of prudential measures. See, for example, Ishii and Habermeier (2002).
7 See, for example, Meesook *et al.* (2001), Athukorala (1998, 2000)
8 Wade and Veneroso stress the necessity of capital controls for the Asian high-debt model, which was built by high savings and banking loans (Wade 1998).

Bibliography

Books and journals

Anderson, B. R. O. (1990) *Language and power: exploring political cultures in Indonesia*, Cornell University Press, Ithaca, NY.

Anderson, B. R. O. (1991) *Imagined communities: reflections on the origin and spread of nationalism* (revised edition), Verso, London and New York.

Aoki, M. (1995) *Keizai-shisutemu no shinka to tagensei: hikaku-seido-bunseki josetsu*, Toyo-Keizai-Shinpou-Sha, Tokyo.

Aoki, M. (2001) *Hikaku-seido-bunseki ni mukete (Towards a comparative institutional analysis)*, NTT Shuppan, Tokyo (English version: The MIT Press, Massachusetts).

Aoki, M. and Okuno, M. (ed.) (1996) *Keizai-shisutemu no hikaku-seido-bunseki (Comparative institutional analysis: a new approach to economic systems)*, University of Tokyo Press, Tokyo.

Arestis, P. and Demetriades, P. (1997) Financial development and economic growth: assessing the evidence, *The Economic Journal*, 107 (May 1997), pp.783–99.

Arestis, P. and Glickman, M. (2002) Financial crisis in Southeast Asia: dispelling illusion the Minskyan way, *Cambridge Journal of Economics*, 2002, 26, pp.237–60.

Asian Development Bank (2000) *Country economic review* (April 2000), Manila, The Philippines.

Athukorala, P. C. (1998) Swimming against the tide: crisis management in Malaysia, *ASEAN Economic Bulletin*, Vol.15, No.3, pp.281–9.

Athukorala, P. C. (2000) Capital account regimes, crisis, and adjustment in Malaysia, *Asian Development Review*, Vol.18, No.1, pp.17–48.

Aybar, S. and Lapavitsas, C. (2002) Financial system design and the post-Washington consensus, in Fine, B., Lapavitsas, C. and Pincus, J. (eds) *Development policy in the twenty-first century: beyond the post-Washington consensus*, Routledge, London, pp.28–51.

Azis, I. J. and Thorbecke, W. (2004) The effects of exchange rate and interest rate shock on bank lending in Indonesia, *Ekonomi dan Keuangan Indonesia (Economics and Finance in Indonesia)*, Vol.52, No.3, pp.279–95.

Backman, M. (1999) *Asian eclipse: exposing the dark side of business in Asia*, John Wiley & Sons (Asia), Singapore.

Ben-Ami, D. (2001) *Cowardly capitalism: the myth of the global financial casino*, John Wiley & Sons, London.

Bhattacharya, A. (2001) The Asian financial crisis and Malaysian capital controls, *Asia Pacific Business Review*, Vol.7, No.3, pp.181–93.

Booth, A. (ed.) (1992) *The oil boom and after: Indonesian economic policy and performance in the Soeharto era*, Oxford University Press, Singapore.

Bresnan, J. (1993) *Managing Indonesia: the modern political economy*, Columbia University Press, New York.

Cameron, L. (1999) Survey of recent developments, *Bulletin of Indonesian Economic Studies*, Vol.35, No.1 (April 1999), pp.3–40.

Canning, J. B. (1933) A certain erratic tendency in accountants' income procedure, *Econometrica*, Vol.1, No.1 (January 1933), pp.52–62.

Canova, F. (1994) Were financial crises predictable?, *Journal of Money, Credit and Banking*, Vol.26, No.1 (February 1994), pp.102–24.

Caporaso, J. A. and Levine, D. P. (1992) *Theories of political economy*, Cambridge University Press, Cambridge.

Chang, H. J. (2000) The hazard of moral hazard: untangling the Asian crisis, *World Development*, Vol.28, No.4, pp.775–88.

Chia, R., Usman, M., Gondokusumo, S. and Cheong, W. K. (1992) *Globalization of the Jakarta Stock Exchange*, Prentice Hall, Singapore.

Chowdhury, A. (1983) Mochtar Riady: the master builder of an Asian banking empire, *Asian Finance* (15 September 1983), pp.66–78.

Claessens, S., Djankov, S. and Lang, L. (1998) *East Asian corporates: growth, financing and risks over the last decade*, The World Bank, Policy Research Working Paper No.2017 (October 1998), Washington, DC.

Cole, D. C. and Slade, B. F. (1992) Financial development in Indonesia, in Booth, A. (ed.) *The oil boom and after: Indonesian economic policy and performance in the Soeharto era*, Oxford University Press, Singapore, pp.77–101.

Cole, D. C. and Slade, B. F. (1996) *Building a modern financial system: the Indonesian experience*, Cambridge University Press, Cambridge.

Cole, D. C. and Slade, B. F. (1998a) Why has Indonesia's financial crisis been so bad?, *Bulletin of Indonesian Economic Studies*, Vol.34, No.2 (August 1998), pp.61–6.

Cole, D. C. and Slade, B. F. (1998b) The crisis and financial sector reform, *ASEAN Economic Bulletin*, Vol.15, No.3, pp.338–46.

Corsetti, G. (1998) Interpreting the Asian financial crisis: open issues in theory and policy, *Asian Development Review*, Vol.16, No.2, pp.18–63.

Crouch, H. (1988) *The army and politics in Indonesia* (revised edition), Cornell University Press, Ithaca, NY.

Crouch, H. (1994) Indonesia: an uncertain outlook, in Institute of Southeast Asian Studies (ed.) *Southeast Asian Affairs 1994*, Singapore, pp.121–45.

Davis, P. E. (1995) *Debt financial fragility and systemic risk*, Clarendon Press, Oxford.

Delhaise, P. F. (1998) *Asia in crisis: the implosion of the banking and finance system*, John Wiley & Sons (Asia), Singapore.

Djiwandono, J. S. (2000) Bank Indonesia and the recent crisis, *Bulletin of Indonesian Economic Studies*, Vol.36, No.1 (April 2000), pp.47–72.

Eatwell, J. and Taylor, L. (2000) *Global finance at risk: the case for international regulation*, Polity Press, Cambridge.

Eatwell, J. and Taylor, L. (eds) (2002) *International capital markets: systems in transition*, Oxford University Press, Oxford.

Edwards, S. (1996) Exchange rates and the political economy of macroeconomic discipline, *The American Economic Review*, Vol.86, No.2 (May 1996), pp.159–63.

Edwards, S. (1999) How effective are capital controls?, *The Journal of Economic Perspectives*, Vol.13, No.4 (Autumn 1999), pp.65–84.

Eichengreen, B. (1999) *Toward a new international financial architecture: a practical post-Asian agenda*, Institute for International Economics, Washington.

Eichengreen, B. (2000a) *Taming capital flows, World Development*, Vol.28, No.6, pp.1105–16.

Eichengreen, B. (2000b) Strengthening the international financial architecture: where do we stand? in Woo, W. T. (ed.) *The Asian financial crisis: hindsight, insight and foresight, Asian Economic Bulletin*, Vol.17, No.2 (August 2000), Institute of Southeast Asian Studies, Singapore, pp.175–92.

Emmerson, D. K. (ed.) (1999) *Indonesia beyond Suharto: polity, economy, society transition*, M. E. Sharp, New York.

Enoch, C., Frecaut, O. and Kovanen, A. (2003) Indonesia's banking crisis: what happened and what did we learn?, *Bulletin of Indonesian Economic Studies*, Vol.39, No.1 (2003), pp.75–92.

Evans, K. (1998) Survey of recent developments, *Bulletin of Indonesian Economic Studies*, Vol. 34, No.3 (December 1998), pp.5–36.

Fane, G. (1994) The sequencing of economic deregulation in Indonesia, in McLeod, R. H. (ed.) *Indonesia assessment 1994: finance as a key sector in Indonesia's development*, Australian National University, Canberra, Australia and Institute of Southeast Asian Studies, Singapore, pp.101–17.

Fane, G. (2000a) Survey of recent developments, *Bulletin of Indonesian Economic Studies*, Vol.36, No.1 (April 2000), pp.13–44.

Fane, G. (2000b) Indonesian monetary policy during the 1997–98 crisis: a monetarist perspective, *Bulletin of Indonesian Economic Studies*, Vol.36, No.3 (December 2000), pp.49–64.

Fine, B., Lapavitsas, C. and Pincus, J. (eds) (2002) *Development policy in the twenty-first century: beyond the post-Washington consensus*, Routledge, London.

Fisher, I. (1896) What is capital?, *The Economic Journal*, Vol.6, No.24 (December 1896), pp.509–618.

Fisher, I. (1897a) Sense of 'capital', *The Economic Journal*, Vol.7, No.26 (June 1897), pp.199–213.

Fisher, I. (1897b) The role of capital in economic theory, *The Economic Journal*, Vol.7, No.28 (December 1897), pp.511–37.

Fisher, I. (1904) Precedent for defining capital, *The Quarterly Journal of Economics*, Vol.18, No.3 (May 1904), pp.386–408.

Fisher, I. (1930) The economics of accountancy, *The American Economic Review*, Vol.20, No.4 (December 1930), pp.603–18.

Fisher, I. (1933) The debt-deflation theory of great depressions, *Econometrica*, Vol.1, No.4 (October 1933), pp.337–57.

Freeman, N. J. and Bartels, F. L. (2000) *Portfolio investment in Southeast Asia's stock markets: a survey of institutional investors' current perceptions and practices*, ISEAS Working Paper, *Economics and Finance*, No.3 (2000), Institute of Southeast Asian Studies, Singapore.

Friedman, M. (1968) The role of monetary policy, *The American Economic Review*, Vol.58, No.1 (March 1968), pp.1–17.

Friedman, M. (1982) Monetary policy: theory and practice, *Journal of Money, Credit and Banking*, Vol.14, No.1 (February 1982), pp.98–118.

Friedman, M. and Schwartz, A. J. (1963) Money and business cycle, *The Review of Economics and Statistics*, Vol.45, No.1, Part 2, Supplement (February 1963), pp.32–64.

Friedman, M. and Schwartz, A. J. (1969) The definition of money: net wealth and neutrality as criteria, *Journal of Money, Credit and Banking*, Vol.1, No.1 (February 1969), pp.1–14.

Furman, J. and Stiglitz, J. E. (1998) Economic crises: evidence and insights from East Asia, *Brookings Papers on Economic Activity*, Vol. 1998, No.2, pp.1–114.

Gan Wee Beng and Soon Lee Ying (2001) Credit crunch during a currency crisis: the Malaysian experience, *ASEAN Economic Bulletin*, Vol.18, No.2, pp.174–92.

Garnaut, R. (1998) Exchange rate in the East Asian crisis, *ASEAN Economic Bulletin*, Vol.15, No.3, pp.328–37.

Gilpin, R. (2001) *Global political economy: understanding the international economic order*, Princeton University Press, Princeton, NJ.

Goeltom, M. S. (1995) *Indonesia's financial liberalization: an empirical analysis of 1981–88 panel data*, Institute of Southeast Asian Studies, Singapore.

Goldstein, M. (1998) *The Asian financial crisis*, Policy Brief 98–1, Institute for International Economics, Washington, DC.

Grabel, I. (1999) Rejecting exceptionalism: reinterpreting the Asian financial crises, in Michie, J. and Smith, J. G. (eds) *Global instability: the political economy of world economic governance*, Routledge, London.

Grenville, S. (2000a) Monetary policy and the exchange rate during the crisis, *Bulletin of Indonesian Economic Studies*, Vol.36, No.2 (August 2000), pp.43–60.

Grenville, S. (2000b) Capital flows and crises, in Noble, G. W. and Ravenhill, J. (eds) *The Asian financial crisis and the architecture of global finance*, Cambridge University Press, Cambridge, pp.36–56.

Grenville, S. (2004a) The IMF and the Indonesian crisis, *Bulletin of Indonesian Economic Studies*, Vol.40, No.1 (2004), pp.77–94.

Grenville, S. (2004b) What sort of financial sector should Indonesia have?, *Bulletin of Indonesian Economic Studies*, Vol.40, No.3 (2004), pp.307–27.

Habir, A. D. (1993) The emerging Indonesian managerial elite: professionals amid patriarchs, in Institute of Southeast Asian Studies (ed.) *Southeast Asian Affairs 1993*, Singapore, pp.161–82.

Habir, A. D. (1999) Conglomerates: all in the family?, in Emmerson, D. K. (ed.) *Indonesia beyond Suharto: polity, economy, society transition*, M. E. Sharp, New York, pp.168–202.

Haggard, S. (2000) *The political economy of the Asian financial crisis*, Institute for International Economics, Washington, DC.

Haggard, S. and Maxfield, S. (1996) The political economy of financial internationalization in the developing world, *International Organization*, Vol.50, No.1 (Winter 1996), pp.35–68.

Heryanto, A. (1997) Indonesia: towards the final countdown?, in Institute of Southeast Asian Studies (ed.) *Southeast Asian Affairs 1997*, Singapore, pp.107–26.

Hiizumi, K. (1994) *Kakyou no chousen (the challenge of overseas Chinese)*, The Japan Times, Tokyo.

Hill, H. (1988) *Foreign investment and industrialization in Indonesia*, Oxford University Press, Singapore.

Hill, H. (1996) *The Indonesian economy since 1966*, Cambridge University Press, Cambridge.

Hill, H. (1998) An overview of the issues, *ASEAN Economic Bulletin*, Vol.15, No.3, pp.261–71.

IBRA, The Indonesian Bank Restructuring Agency (1999) Annual Report.

Ishii, S. and Habermeier, K. (2002) *Capital account liberalization and financial sector stability*, IMF Occasional Paper 211, Washington, DC: IMF, April 12.

Ito, M. and Lapavitsas, C. (1999) *Political economy of money and finance*, Macmillan, Basingstoke, Hampshire.

Iwasaki, I. (ed.) (2003) *Ajia no kigyouka (Entrepreneurs in Asia)*, Toyo Keizai Shinpou, Tokyo.

Jackson, K. D. (ed.) (1999) *Asian contagion: the causes and consequences of a financial crisis*, Westview Press, Boulder, Colorado and Oxford.

Jomo, K. S. (ed.) (1998) *Tigers in trouble: financial governance, liberalisation and crises in East Asia*, Hong Kong University Press, Hong Kong.

Kahler, M. (ed.) (1998) *Capital flows and financial crises*, Manchester University Press, Manchester.

Kaminsky, G. L. and Reinhart, C. M. (1999) The twin crises: the causes of banking and balance-of-payments problems, *The American Economic Review*, Vol.89, No.3 (June 1999), pp.473–500.

Katzenstein, P. J. and Shiraishi, T. (eds) (1997) *Network power: Japan and Asia*, Cornell University Press, Ithaca, NY.

Kenward, L. R. (1999) Assessing vulnerability to financial crisis: evidence from Indonesia, *Bulletin of Indonesian Economic Studies*, Vol.35, No.3 (1999), pp.71–95.

Keynes, J. M. (1936) *The general theory of employment, interest and money*, Cambridge University Press, Cambridge.

Khan, M. and Jomo K. S. (2000) *Rents, rent-seeking and economic development: theory and evidence in Asia*, Cambridge University Press, Cambridge.

Khanna, T. (2000) Business groups and social welfare in emerging markets: existing evidence and unanswered questions, *European Economic Review*, Vol. 2000, No.44 (2000), pp.748–61.

Khanna, T. and Palepu, K. (1997) Why focused strategies may be wrong for emerging markets, *Harvard Business Review*, July–August 1997, pp.41–51.

Khanna, T. and Palepu, K. (1999) The right way to restructure conglomerates in emerging markets, *Harvard Business Review*, July–August 1999, pp.125–34.

Kindleberger, C. P. (1978) *Manias, panics, and crashes: a history of financial crises*, John Wiley & Sons, New York.

Komatsu, M. (2000) *Indoneshia niokeru keizai seisaku no kadai: keizai jiyuka seisaku saikou (The problems of economic policies in Indonesia: the reconsideration of economic liberalization policies)* (unpublished paper).

Kregel, J. A. (1998) *Yes, 'it' did happen again – a Minsky crisis happened in Asia*, Working Paper No.234 (April 1998), The Jerome Levy Economics Institute of Bard College, Annandale-on-Hudson, New York.

Kroszner, R. S. and Putterman, L. (eds) (1996) *The economic nature of the firm: a reader* (second edition), Cambridge University Press, Cambridge.

Krugman, P. (1979) A model of balance-of-payments crises, *Journal of Money, Credit and Banking*, Vol.11, No.3 (August 1979), pp.311–25.

Krugman, P. (1992) *Currency and crises*, The MIT Press, Massachusetts.

Krugman, P. (1994) *The myth of Asia's miracle, Foreign Affairs*, November/December, Vol.73, No.6, pp.62–78.

Krugman, P. (1998a) *What happened to Asia?* http://web.mit.edu/krugman/www/DISINTER.html.

Krugman, P. (1998b) *Will Asia bounce back?* http://web.mit.edu/krugman/www/suisse.html.

Krugman, P. (1999a) *Balance sheets, the transfer problem, and financial crises*, http://web.mit.edu/krugman.

Krugman, P. (1999b) *The return of depression economics*, Penguin Books, London.

Krugman, P. and Obstfeld, M. (2000) *International economics: theory and policy* (fifth edition), Addison-Wesley, Harlow.

Kunimune, K. (ed.) (2000) *Ajia tsuuka kiki: sono genin to taiou no mondaiten (Asian currency crisis: causes and problems in prescription)*, The Institute of Developing Economies, Chiba, Japan.

Kunt, A. D. and Maksimovic, V. (1995a) *Stock market development and firm financing choices*, The World Bank, Policy Research Working Paper No.1461 (May 1995), Washington, DC.

Kunt, A. D. and Maksimovic, V. (1995b) *Capital structure in developing countries: evidence from ten countries*, The World Bank, Policy Research Working Paper No.1320, Washington, DC.

Kunt, A. D. and Maksimovic, V. (1996) *Stock market development and corporate finance decisions*, The World Bank, Finance and Development (June 1996), Washington, DC.

Kuroiwa, I. (2002) *Ajia tsuuka kiki to enjo seisaku: indoneshia no kadai to tenbou (Asian currency crisis and aid policy: Indonesia's problems and prospects)*, The Institute of Developing Economies, Chiba, Japan.

Lawler, M. S. (1990) Minsky and Keynes on speculation and finance, *Social Science Journal*, Vol.27, No.4, pp.435–51.

Levine, R. (1997) Financial development and economic growth: views and agenda, *Journal of Economic Literature*, Vol.XXXV (June 1997), pp.688–726.

Levine, R. and Zervos, S. (1996) *Capital control liberalization and stock market development*, The World Bank, Policy Research Working Paper No.1622 (July 1996), Washington, DC.

Levine, R., Beck, T., Kunt, A. D. and Maksimovic, V. (2000) *Financial structure and economic development; firm, industry, and country evidence*, The World Bank, Policy Research Working Paper No.2423 (June 2000), Washington, DC.

Lim, L. Y. C. (1999) Free market fancies: Hong Kong, Singapore, and the Asian financial crisis, in Pempel, T. J. (ed.) *The politics of the Asian economic crisis*, Cornell University Press, Ithaca, NY, pp.101–15.

Linnan, D. K. (1999) Insolvency reform and the Indonesian financial crisis, *Bulletin of Indonesian Economic Studies*, Vol.35, No.2 (August 1999), pp.107–37.

Lynn Pan (1990) *Sons of the yellow emperor: the story of the overseas Chinese*, Martin Secker & Warburg, London.

Lynn Pan (ed.) (1998) *The encyclopedia of the Chinese overseas*, Archipelago Press, Singapore.

Macintyre, A. (ed.) (1990a) *Business and government in industrialising Asia*, Allen & Unwin, St Leonards, NSW, Australia.

Macintyre, A. (1990b) *Business and politics in Indonesia*, Allen & Unwin, St Leonards, NSW, Australia.

McKibbin, W. (1998) Modelling the crisis in Asia, *ASEAN Economic Bulletin*, Vol.15, No.3, pp.347–52.

Mackie, J. A. C. (1988) Changing economic roles and ethnic identities of the Southeast Asian Chinese: a comparison of Indonesia and Thailand, in Wang Gungwu (ed.) *Changing identities of the Southeast Asian Chinese since World War II*, Hong Kong University Press, Hong Kong, pp.217–60.

Mackie, J. A. C. (1991) Towkays and tycoons: the Chinese in Indonesian economic life in the 1920s and 1980s, in Kahin, A. (ed.) *Indonesia: the role of the Indonesian Chinese in shaping modern Indonesian life*, Cornell Southeast Asia Program, Ithaca, NY, pp.83–96.

Mackie, J. A. C. (1992) Changing patterns of Chinese big business in Southeast Asia, in McVey, R. (ed.) *Southeast Asian capitalists*, Cornell Southeast Asian Program, Ithaca, NY, pp.161–90.

Mackie, J. A. C. (2000) The economic roles of the Southeast Asian Chinese: information gaps and research needs, in Chan Kwok Bun (ed.) *Chinese business network: state, economy and culture*, Prentice Hall, Singapore, pp.234–60.

McKinnon, R. I. (1991) *The order of economic liberalization: financial control in the transition to a market economy*, The Johns Hopkins University Press, Baltimore and London.

McKinnon, R. I. and Pill, H. (1997) Credible economic liberalization and overborrowing, *The American Economic Review*, Vol.87, No.2 (May 1997), pp.189–93.

McLeod, R. H. (1994) Indonesia's foreign debt, in McLeod, R. H. (ed.) *Indonesia assessment 1994: finance as a key sector in Indonesia's development*, Australian National University, Canberra, Australia and Institute of Southeast Asian Studies, Singapore, pp.268–90.

McLeod, R. H. (2000) Survey of recent developments, *Bulletin of Indonesian Economic Studies*, Vol.36, No.2 (August 2000), pp.5–40.

McNelis, P. D. (1999) *The benefits of INDRA for stabilization and reactivation – an analysis of prototype contracts as options*, mimeo.

McVey, R. (ed.) (1992) *Southeast Asian capitalists*, Cornell Southeast Asian Program, Ithaca, NY.

Matsumoto, Y. (1992) *Japanese banks in Southeast Asia: the political economy of banking in Indonesia and Thailand*, Master Thesis at Cornell University, Ithaca, NY.

Maxfield, S. (1998) Effects of international portfolio flows on government policy choice, in Kahler, M. (ed.) *Capital flows and financial crises*, Manchester University Press, Manchester, pp.69–92.

Meesook, K., Lee, I. H., Liu, O., Khatri, Y., Tamirisa, N., Moore, M. and Krysl, M. H. (2001) *Malaysia from crisis to recovery*, IMF Occasional Paper 207, Washington, DC: IMF, August 27.

Michie, J. and Smith, J. G. (eds) (1999) *Global instability: the political economy of world economic governance*, Routledge, London.

Mihira, N. and Yasunaka, A. (eds) (1995) *Gendai Indoneshia no seiji to keizai: Suharuto seiken no 30-nen (30 years of Suharto government: its political and economic performance)*, The Institute of Developing Economies, Chiba, Japan.

Milgrom, P. and Roberts, J. (1992) *Soshiki no keizaigaku (Economics, organizations and management)*, NTT Shuppan, Tokyo (English version: Prentice Hall, New York).

Minsky, H. P. (1957a) Monetary systems and accelerator models, *The American Economic Review*, Vol.47, No.6 (December 1957), pp.859–83.

Minsky, H. P. (1957b) Central banking and money market changes, *The Quarterly Journal of Economics*, Vol.71, No.2 (May 1957), pp.171–87.

Minsky, H. P. (1964) Longer waves in financial relations: financial factors in the more severe depressions, *The American Economic Review*, Vol.54, No.3 (May 1964), pp.324–35.

Minsky, H. P. (1969) Private sector asset management and the effectiveness of monetary policy: theory and practice, *The Journal of Finance*, Vol.24, No.2 (May 1969), pp.223–38.

Minsky, H. P. (1975) *John Maynard Keynes*, Columbia University Press, New York.

Minsky, H. P. (1986) *Stabilizing an unstable economy*, Yale University Press, New Haven and London.

Minsky, H. P. (1989) Economic implications of extraordinary movements in stock prices: comments and discussion, *Brookings Papers on Economic Activity*, Vol.1989, No.2, pp.173–89.

Minsky, H. P. (1991) *Financial crises: system or idiosyncratic*, Working Paper No.51 (April 1991), The Jerome Levy Economics Institute of Bard College, Annandale-on-Hudson, New York.

Minsky, H. P. (1992a) *Reconstituting the United States' financial structure: some fundamental issues*, Working Paper No.69 (January 1992), The Jerome Levy Economics Institute of Bard College, Annandale-on-Hudson, New York.

Minsky, H. P. (1992b) *The capital development of the economy and the structure of financial institutions*, Working Paper No.72 (January 1992), The Jerome Levy Economics Institute of Bard College, Annandale-on-Hudson, New York.

Minsky, H. P. (1992c) *The financial instability hypothesis*, Working Paper No.74 (May 1992), The Jerome Levy Economics Institute of Bard College, Annandale-on-Hudson, New York.

Minsky, H. P. (1993) *Finance and stability: the limits of capitalism*, Working Paper No.93 (May 1993), The Jerome Levy Economics Institute of Bard College, Annandale-on-Hudson, New York.

Minsky, H. P. and Ferri, P. (1991) *Market processes and thwarting systems*, Working Paper No.64 (November 1991), The Jerome Levy Economics Institute of Bard College, Annandale-on-Hudson, New York.

Modigliani, F. and Miller, M. H. (1958) The cost of capital, corporation finance and the theory of investment, *The American Economic Review*, Vol.48, No.3 (June 1958), pp.261–97.

Modigliani, F. and Miller, M. H. (1959) The cost of capital, corporation finance and the theory of investment: reply, *The American Economic Review*, Vol.49, No.4 (September 1959), pp.655–69.

Modigliani, F. and Miller, M. H. (1963) Corporate income taxes and the cost of capital: a correction, *The American Economic Review*, Vol.53, No.3 (June 1963), pp.433–43.

Moreno, R. (2001) Pegging and macroeconomic performance in East Asia, *ASEAN Economic Bulletin*, Vol.18, No.1, pp.48–61.

Morgan Stanley Dean Witter (2000) memo (March 2000) unpublished.

Nasution, A. (1994) Banking sector reforms in Indonesia; 1983–93, in McLeod, R. H. (ed.) *Indonesia assessment 1994: finance as a key sector in Indonesia's development*, Australian National University, Canberra, Australia and Institute of Southeast Asian Studies, Singapore, pp.130–57.

Nasution, A. (2000) The meltdown of the Indonesian economy: causes, responses, and lessons, in Woo, W. T. (ed.) *The Asian financial crisis: hindsight, insight and foresight, Asian Economic Bulletin*, Vol.17, No.2 (August 2000), Institute of Southeast Asian Studies, Singapore, pp.148–62.

Nayyar, D. (2002) Capital controls and the World Financial Authority: what can we learn from the Indian experience?, in Eatwell, J. and Taylor, L. (eds) *International capital markets: system in transition*, Oxford University Press, Oxford, pp.99–125.

Nidhiprabha, B. (1998) Economic crisis and the debt-deflation episode in Thailand, *ASEAN Economic Bulletin*, Vol.15, No.3, pp.309–17.

Noble, G. W. and Ravenhill, J. (eds) (2000) *The Asian financial crisis and the architecture of global finance*, Cambridge University Press, Cambridge.

Noerhadi, D. C. (1994) The role of Indonesian capital market, in McLeod, R. H. (ed.) *Indonesia assessment 1994: finance as a key sector in Indonesia's development*, Australian National University, Canberra, Australia and Institute of Southeast Asian Studies, Singapore, pp.202–22.

North, D. (1990) *Institutions, institutional change and economic performance*, Cambridge University Press, Cambridge.

Obstfeld, M. (1984) Balance-of-payments crisis and devaluation, *Journal of Money, Credit and Banking*, Vol.16, No.2 (May 1984), pp.208–17.

Obstfeld, M. (1986a) Speculative attack and the external constraint in a maximizing model of the balance of payments, *The Canadian Journal of Economics*, Vol.19, No.1 (February 1986), pp.1–22.

Obstfeld, M. (1986b) Rational and self-fulfilling balance-of-payments crisis, *The American Economic Review*, Vol.76, No.1 (March 1986), pp.72–81.

Obstfeld, M. (1998) The global capital market: benefactor or menace?, *The Journal of Economic Perspectives*, Vol.12, No.4 (Autum1998), pp.9–30.

Obstfeld, M. and Taylor, A. M. (2001) *Globalization and capital markets*, Research paper presented at the NBER conference, Santa Barbara, 4–5 May 2001.

Osano, H. (2001) *Kouporeito-gabanansu no keizaigaku*, Nihon-Keizai-Shinbun-Sha, Tokyo.

Pagano, M. and Volpin, P. (2001) The political economy of finance, *Oxford Review of Economic Policy*, Vol.17, No.4, pp.502–19.

Palma, G. (2002) *The three routes to financial crises: the need for capital controls*, CEPA Working Paper No.18, Center for Economic Policy Analysis, New School for Social Research, New York.

Pangestu, M. (1992) The Indonesian economy: booms and macro-economic pressures, in Institute of Southeast Asian Studies (ed.) *Southeast Asian Affairs 1992*, Singapore, pp.140–59.

Pangestu, M. (1994) Recent economic developments, in McLeod, R. H. (ed.) *Indonesia assessment 1994: finance as a key sector in Indonesia's development*, Australian National University, Canberra, Australia and Institute of Southeast Asian Studies, Singapore, pp.21–48.

Pangestu, M. (1996) *Economic reform, deregulation and privatization: the Indonesian experience*, Center for Strategic and International Studies, Jakarta.

Pangestu, M. and Habir, M. (2002) *The boom, bust, and restructuring of Indonesian banks*, IMF Working Paper (WP/02/66), Washington, DC.

Papadimitriou, D. B. and Wray, L. R. (1997) *The economic contribution of Hyman Minsky: varieties of capitalism and institutional reform*, Working Paper No.217 (December 1997), The Jerome Levy Economics Institute of Bard College, Annandale-on-Hudson, New York.

Papadimitriou, D. B. and Wray, L. R. (1999) *Minsky's analysis of financial capitalism*, Working Paper No.275 (July 1999), The Jerome Levy Economics Institute of Bard College, Annandale-on-Hudson, New York.

Pardede, R. (1999) Survey of recent developments, *Bulletin of Indonesian Economic Studies*, Vol.35, No.2 (August 1999), pp.3–29.

Pempel, T. J. (ed.) (1999) *The politics of the Asian economic crisis*, Cornell University Press, Ithaca, NY.

Pincus, J. and Ramli, R. (1998) Indonesia: from showcase to basket case, *Cambridge Journal of Economics*, Vol.22, pp.723–34.

Pincus, J. and Ramli, R. (2003) *Deepening or hollowing out?: financial liberalization, accumulation and Indonesia's economic crisis* (unpublished manuscript).

Pomerleano, M. (1998) *The East Asia crisis and corporate finances: the untold micro story*, The World Bank, Working Paper No.1990 (October 1998), Washington, DC.

Pomerleano, M. (2000) *Managing corporate distress – lessons from Asia, Memorandum submitted for Seminar for Senior Bank Supervisors from Emerging Economies* (19 October 2000), Washington, DC.

Prawiro, R. (1998) *Indonesia's struggle for economic development: pragmatism in action*, Oxford University Press, New York.

Rajan, R. G. and Zingales, L. (2001) Financial systems, industrial structure, and growth, *Oxford Review of Economic Policy*, Vol.17, No.4, pp.467–82.

Rajan, R. G. and Zingales, L. (2003) *Saving capitalism from the capitalists: how open financial markets challenge the establishment and spread prosperity to rich and poor alike*, Random House Business Books, London.

Reid, A. (ed.) (1996) *Sojourners and settlers: the history of Southeast Asia and the Chinese*, Allen & Unwin, St Leonards, NSW, Australia.

Rizal, S. (1998) Indonesia: a year of politics and sadness, in Institute of Southeast Asian Studies (ed.) *Southeast Asian Affairs 1998*, Singapore, pp.105–23.

Robison, R. (1986) *Indonesia: the rise of capital*, Allen & Unwin, St Leonards, NSW, Australia.

Robison, R. (1990) Power and economy in Suharto's Indonesia, *Journal of Contemporary Asia Publishers*, Manila, The Philippines.

Robison, R. (1992) Industrialization and the economic and political development of capital: the case of Indonesia, in McVey, R. (ed.) *Southeast Asian capitalists*, Cornell Southeast Asian Program, Ithaca, NY, pp.65–88.

Robison, R. (1996) The middle class and the bourgeoisie in Indonesia, in Robison, R. and Goodman, D. S. G. (eds) *The new rich in Asia: mobile phone, McDonalds and middle-class revolution*, Routledge, London, pp.79–101.

Robison, R. (1997) Politics and markets in Indonesia's post-oil era, in Rodan, G., Hewison, K. and Robison, R. (eds) *The political economy of South-East Asia: an introduction*, Oxford University Press, Melbourne, pp.29–63.

Robison, R., Beeson, M., Jayasuriya, K. and Kim, H. R. (eds) (2000) *Politics and markets in the wake of the Asian crisis*, Routledge, London and New York.

Rodrik, D. (1997) *Has globalization gone too far?* Institute for International Economics, Washington, DC.

Rodrik, D. (1998a) Why do more open economies have bigger government?, *The Journal of Political Economy*, Vol.106, No.5 (October 1998), pp.997–1032.

Rodrik, D. (1998b) How far will international economic integration go?, *The Journal of Economic Perspectives*, Vol.14, No.1 (Winter 2000), pp.177–86.

Rosser, A. (2002) *The politics of economic liberalization in Indonesia: state, market and power*, Curzon Press, Richmond, Surrey.

Sachs, J. D. (1998) Alternative approaches to financial crises in emerging markets, in Kahler, M. (ed.) *Capital flows and financial crises*, Manchester University Press, Manchester, pp.247–62.

Sachs, J. D., Tornell, A. and Velasco, A. (1996) Financial crisis in emerging markets: the lessons from 1995, *Brookings Paper on Economic Activity*, Vol.1996, No.1, pp.147–98.

Sadli, M. (1998) The Indonesian crisis, *ASEAN Economic Bulletin*, Vol.15, No.3, pp.272–76.

Sato, Y. (1992) The Salim Group in Indonesia: the development and behavior of the largest conglomerate in Southeast Asia, *The Developing Economies*, Vol.XXXIII, No.3 (March 1992), pp.54–86.

Sato, Y. (1996) The Astra Group: a pioneer of management modernization in Indonesia, *The Developing Economies*, Vol.XXXIV, No.3 (September 1996), pp.247–80.

Sato, Y. (ed.) (2001) *Indoneshia shiryo deeta shuu (The collection of Indonesia's materials and data)*, The Institute of Developing Economies, Chiba, Japan.

Sato, Y. (2002) Keizai saihen to shoyuu saihen: keizai shoyuu kouzou eno kainyuu seisaku kara (Reforming economic structure: policies for intervening in economic ownership, in Sato, Y. (ed.) (2002) *Minshuka jidai no Indoneshia: seiji keizai hendou to seido kaikaku (Democratizing Indonesia: politics and economy in historical perspective)*, The Institute of Developing Economies, Chiba, Japan, pp.247–93.

Sato, Y. (2003) Indoneshia no Salim: seisho, konguromaritto, soshite kaitai-e (Salim in Indonesia: cukong, conglomerate, and then to dismantlement), in Iwasaki, I. (ed.) (2003) *Ajia no kigyouka (Entrepreneurs in Asia)*, Toyo Keizai Shinpou, Tokyo, pp.79–132.

Schwarz, A. (1999) *A nation in waiting: Indonesian's search for stability*, Allen & Unwin, St Leonards, NSW, Australia.

Sebastian, L. C. and Siregar, R. Y. (1996) Indonesia: setting the stage for Soeharto's re-election, in Institute of Southeast Asian Studies (ed.) *Southeast Asian Affairs 1996*, Singapore, pp.167–94.

Shiller, R. J. (1990) Market volatility and investor behavior, *The American Economic Review*, Vol.80, No.2 (May 1990), pp.58–62.

Shiller, R. J. (2000) *Irrational exuberance*, Princeton University Press, Princeton and Oxford.

Scholte, J. A. (2000) *Globalization: a critical introduction*, Palgrave, Basingstoke, Hampshire, and New York.

Shiraishi, T. (1996) *Indoneshia (Indonesia)* (new edition), NTT Shuppan, Tokyo.

Singh, A. (1997) Financial liberalization, stock markets and economic development, *The Economic Journal*, Vol.107, No.442 (May 1997), pp.771–82.

Singh, A. (1999) 'Asian capitalism' and the financial crisis, in Michie, J. and Smith, J. G. (eds) *Global instability: the political economy of world economic governance*, Routledge, London.

Sjahrir (1990) The Indonesian economy facing the 1990s: structural transformation and economic deregulation, in Institute of Southeast Asian Studies (ed.) *Southeast Asian Affairs 1990*, Singapore, pp.115–31.

Soesastro, H. (1998) Survey of recent developments, *Bulletin of Indonesian Economic Studies*, Vol.34, No.1 (April 1998), pp.3–54.

Soros, G. (1998) *The crisis of global capitalism: open society endangered*, Little, Brown and Company, London.

Steven, K. (1998) 1998: the 1930s revisited?, *Ecodate*, Vol.12, No.1 (March 1998), pp.1–4.

Stiglitz, J. E. (1963) *A re-examination of the Modigliani-Miller theorem*, The American Economic Review, Vol.59, No.5 (December 1969), pp.784–93.

Stiglitz, J. E. (2002) *Globalization and its discontents*, Allen Lane, London.

Strange, S. (1996) *The retreat of the state: the diffusion of power in the world economy*, Cambridge University Press, Cambridge.

Strange, S. (1997) *Casino capitalism*, Manchester University Press, Manchester.

Suryadinata, L. (1988) Chinese economic elite in Indonesia: preliminary study, in Cushman, J. and Wang Gungwu (eds) *Changing identities of the Southeast Asian Chinese since World War II*, Hong Kong University Press, Hong Kong, pp.261–88.

Suryadinata, L. (1992) *Pribumi, Indonesians, the Chinese minority and China* (third edition), Heinemann Asia, Singapore.

Suryadinata, L. (1997a) *The culture of the Chinese minority in Indonesia*, Times Books International, Singapore and Kuala Lumpur.

Suryadinata, L. (1997b) *Chinese and nation-building in Southeast Asia*, Singapore Society of Asian Studies, Singapore.

Tan, G. (1999) *The end of the Asian miracle?: tracing Asia's economic transformation*, Times Academic Press, Singapore.

Taubert, A. (1991) Liberalism under pressure in Indonesia, in Institute of Southeast Asian Studies (ed.) *Southeast Asian Affairs 1991*, Singapore, pp.122–37.

Taylor, L. and O'Connel, S. A. (1985) A Minsky crisis, *The Quarterly Journal of Economics*, Vol.100, Supplement (1985), pp.871–85.

Twang Peck Yang (1998) *The Chinese business elite in Indonesia and the transition to Independence 1940–1950*, Oxford University Press, New York.

Vives, X. (2001) Competition in the changing world of banking, *Oxford Review of Economic Policy*. Vol.17, No.4, pp.535–47.

Wade, R. (1990) *Governing the market: economic theory and the role of government in East Asian industrialization*, Princeton University Press, Princeton, NJ.

Wade, R. (1998) From 'miracle' to 'cronyism': explaining the Great Asian Slump, *Cambridge Journal of Economics* (1998), Vol.22, pp.693–706.

Wade, R. (2001) Showdown at the World Bank, *New Left Review*, January–February 2001, pp.124–137.

Wade, R. and Veneroso (1998) The Asian crisis: the high debt model versus the Wall Street-Treasury-IMF complex, *New Left Review*, March–April 1998, pp.3–23.

Waldron, S. (1995) *Indonesian Chinese investment in China: magnitude, motivations and meaning, Australia–Asia Paper*, No. 73, Griffith University, Queensland, Australia.

Wang, G. (1993) Greater China and Chinese overseas, *China Quarterly*, Vol.0, No.136, Special Issue: *Greater China* (December 1993), pp.926–48.

Wardana, Ali (1994) Financial reform: achievements, problems and prospects, in McLeod, R. H. (ed.) *Indonesia assessment 1994: finance as a key sector in Indonesia's development*, Australian National University, Canberra, Australia and Institute of Southeast Asian Studies, Singapore, pp.79–93.

Winters, J. A. (1996) *Power in motion: capital mobility and the Indonesian state*, Cornell University Press, Ithaca, NY.

Winters, J. A. (1999) The determinant of financial crisis in Asia, in Pempel, T. J. (ed.) *The politics of the Asian economic crisis*, Cornell University Press, Ithaca, NY, pp.79–97.

Winters, J. A. (2000) The financial crisis in Southeast Asia, in Robison, R., Beeson, M., Jayasuriya, K. and Kim, H. R. (eds) *Politics and markets in the wake of the Asian crisis*, Routledge, London and New York, pp.34–52.

The World Bank, *Financial flows and developing countries* (various issues), Washington, DC.

The World Bank (1994) *Indonesia: stability, growth and equity in Repelita VI*, Report No.12857-IND (July 1994), Washington, DC.

The World Bank (1995) *The emerging Asian bond market*, Washington, DC.

The World Bank (1996) *Indonesia: dimensions of growth*. Report No.15383-IND (May 1996), Washington, DC.

The World Bank (1997) *Indonesia: sustaining high growth with equity*, Report No.16433-IND (May 1997), Washington, DC.

The World Bank (1998) *Indonesia in crisis: a macroeconomic update* (July 1998), Washington, DC.

The World Bank (1999) *Indonesia: from crisis to opportunity* (July 1999), Washington, DC.

The World Bank (2000) *Indonesia: accelerating recovery in uncertain times* (October 2000), Washington, DC.

The World Bank (2001) *Indonesia: the imperative for reform* (November 2001), Washington, DC.

Wray, L. R. (1999) *The 1966 financial crisis: a case of Minskian instability?* Working Paper No.262 (January 1999), The Jerome Levy Economics Institute of Bard College, Annandale-on-Hudson, New York.

Wyplosz, C. (2001) *How risky is financial liberalization in the developing countries?* Research Papers No.14 for the Intergovernmental Group of Twenty-Four (G-24) on International Monetary Affairs, United Nations, New York and Geneva.

Yen Ching-Hwang (2002) *The ethnic Chinese in East and Southeast Asia: business culture and politics*, Times Academic Press, Singapore.

Yoshihara, K. (1988) *The rise of ersatz capitalism in South-East Asia*, Ateneo de Manila University Press, Manila, The Philippines.

Yoshihara, K. (ed.) (1989) *Oei Tiong Ham Concern: The First Business Empire of Southeast Asia*, The Center for Southeast Asian Studies, Kyoto University, Kyoto.

Yoshihara, K. (1999) *Building a prosperous Southeast Asia: from ersatz to echt capitalism*, Curzon Press, Richmond, Surrey.

Yoshitomi, M. and Staff of ADB Institute (2003) *Post-crises development paradigms in Asia*, ADB Institute, Tokyo.

Young, A. (1995) The tyranny of numbers: confronting the statistical realities of the East Asian growth experience, *Quarterly Journal of Economics*, Vol.110, No.3, pp.641–80.

Zarnowitz, V. (1985) Recent work on business cycles in historical perspective: a review of theories and evidence, *Journal of Economic Literature*, Vol.23, No.2 (June 1985), pp.523–80.

Zhu, Y. (ed.) (2000) *Ajia kajin kigyou-guruupu no jitsuryoku (The power of Asian Chinese business groups)*, Diamond, Tokyo.

Data

Annual reports, information memorandums, prospectuses and circulars of the Salim Group, the Lippo Group, the Sinar Mas Group, the Gajah Tunggal Group and other leading business groups.

Bank Indonesia, *Statistik Ekonomi Keuangan Indonesia (Indonesian Financial Statistics)*, Jakarta.

Bank Indonesia, *Report for the financial years* (various issues), Jakarta.

Bank of International Settlement, *Consolidated international banking statistics*, Basel.

Bank of Japan, *Kokusai yoshin tokei (International exposure statistics)*, Tokyo.

Barclays Capital, *Asia Pulp and Paper – one of the few "last men standing"*, Asian Rates and Credit Research, Credit Profile (9 March 2000).

IBRA (1999) – The Indonesian Bank Restructuring Agency (1999) *1999 annual report: race against time*.

INDRA – Indonesian Debt Restructuring Agency (1998a) *Trust and commitment*.

INDRA – Indonesian Debt Restructuring Agency (1998b) *Operating rule and forms of facility agreement*.

ING Barings, *Stock market review: waiting for the music to stop*, Indonesian Research (September 1999).

ING Barings, *Stock market review: glimmer of hope*, Indonesian Research (October 2000).

Lazard Freres, Lehman Brothers and UBS (then SBC Warburg) (financial advisors), *Memorandum: The Republic of Indonesia* (various issues) (not public paper).

Morgan Stanley Dean Witter (2000) *memo* (March 2000) (unpublished).

Paribas Asia Equity (1998) *The Sinar Mas Group – A financial study*, Paribas Asia Equity Report (27 April 1998).

Thomson Financial, *International Financing Review*: 1992–98.
UBS, *Asian/Asia-Pac Credit Analyser* (various issues).
UBS, *Asian High Yield/Asian/Asia-Pac Credit Compendium* (various issues).

Newspapers, magazines and other publications

Asian Finance
Asian Wall Street Journal (AWSJ)
Asia Week
Bloomberg News
The Business Times
Economist
Far Eastern Economic Review
Fortune
International Financing Review
Jakarta Post
Kompas
Newsweek
Nihon Keizai Shinbun (Nikkei)
South China Morning Post
Tempo
Warta Ekonomi

Index